# Umbria

*From the Italy Experts*

**Touring Club of Italy**

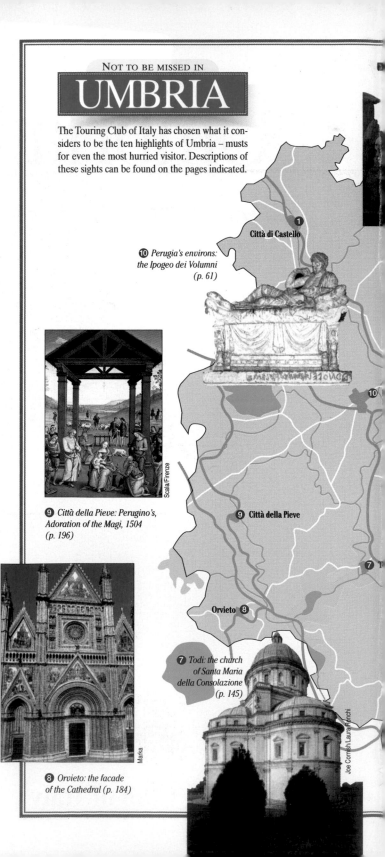

# NOT TO BE MISSED IN

# UMBRIA

The Touring Club of Italy has chosen what it considers to be the ten highlights of Umbria – musts for even the most hurried visitor. Descriptions of these sights can be found on the pages indicated.

Città di Castello ①

⑩ *Perugia's environs: the Ipogeo dei Volumni (p. 61)*

⑩

⑨ *Città della Pieve: Perugino's, Adoration of the Magi, 1504 (p. 196)*

⑨ Città della Pieve

⑦

Orvieto ⑧

⑦ *Todi: the church of Santa Maria della Consolazione (p. 145)*

⑧ *Orvieto: the facade of the Cathedral (p. 184)*

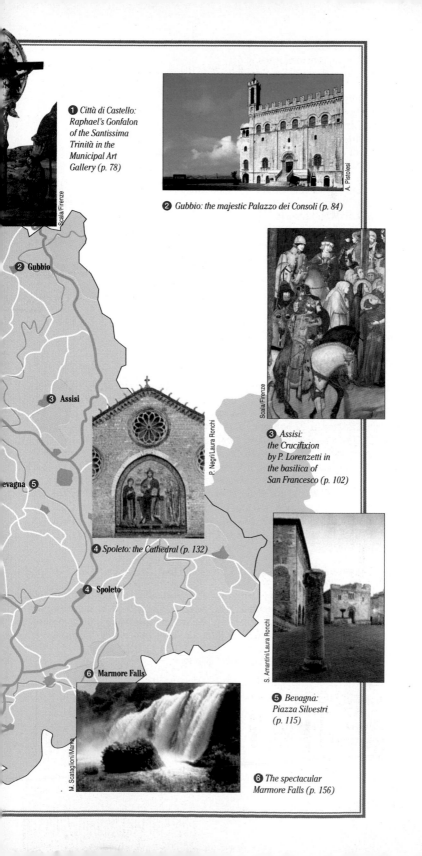

**1** *Città di Castello: Raphael's Gonfalon of the Santissima Trinità in the Municipal Art Gallery (p. 78)*

**2** *Gubbio: the majestic Palazzo dei Consoli (p. 84)*

**2** Gubbio

**3** Assisi

evagna **5**

**3** *Assisi: the Crucifixion by P. Lorenzetti in the basilica of San Francesco (p. 102)*

**4** *Spoleto: the Cathedral (p. 132)*

**4** Spoleto

**6** Marmore Falls

**5** *Bevagna: Piazza Silvestri (p. 115)*

**6** *The spectacular Marmore Falls (p. 156)*

**Touring Club of Italy**
President and Chairman: *Roberto Ruozi*
Chief Executive Officer: *Guido Venturini*

**Touring Editore**
Chief Executive Officer: *Guido Venturini*
Managing Director: *Alfieri Lorenzon*
Editorial Director: *Michele D'Innella*
Series Editor and Editorial Co-ordinator: *Anna Ferrari-Bravo*
International Department: *Fabio Pittella*

Authors: *Knickerbocker Iniziative Editoriali s.r.l./Paola Colombini, Barbara Preatoni* (routes and itineraries, boxes, "Information for Travelers" excluding hotels, restaurants, campsites and resorts); *Guglielmo Martinello* (hotels, restaurants, campsites and resorts); *Alberto Grohmann* ("The creation of a regional identity"); *Claudia Grisanti, Stefania Petrillo* ("Art and culture"); *Paola Colombini* ("Umbria: a visitor's guide").
Translation: *David Lowry* (pp. 1-39, 150-167); *Michael Leone* (pp. 40-149); *Andrew Ellis* (pp. 168-203); *Selida Grafica Editoriale* (pp. 204-228)
Editing: *Voltapagina Associati*
Layout: *Roberta Merlo*
Jacket layout: *Mara Rold*
Map design: *Cartographic Division - Touring Club of Italy*
Drawings: *Isabella Salmoirago*
Production: *Vittorio Sironi*

Picture credits: *Archivi Alinari*, pp. 49 bottom, 96; *G.Andreini*, pp. 64, 65, 66, 67, 69, 81, 100 top, 107, 108, 123, 141, 199, 200; *Archivio Perugina*, pp. 56-57 center; *Archivio TCI*, pp. 21, 22-23; *G.Belei/G. Carfagna & Associati*, pp. 53, 89, 115, 117, 160, 163, 175, 181, 183, 189; *G.Belfiore*, p. 22 bottom; *T. Carfagna & Associati*, pp. 72-73, 80; *G. Carfagna*, pp. 17, 25, 38 bottom, 40, 57 top, 62, 63, 79 top, 83, 85, 91, 109, 125, 131, 157, 165, 168, 176 bottom, 180; *K. Cattaneo*, pp. 16, 26, 30, 45 top, 119 top, 202; *Eikonos*, pp. 78-79 bottom; *M.Fraschetti*, pp. 13, 19, 33, 39, 50, 87, 92, 106, 111, 121, 127, 150, 151, 155, 159, 162, 167, 169, 173, 185, 194, 196; *S.Montanari/Eikonos*, pp. 119 bottom, 144, 153; *Archivio Museo di Corciano* pp. 32, 60; *P.Negri*, pp. 24, 38 top, 145 top, 174; *P.Orlandi*, pp. 20, 55, 70, 74, 78 top, 138, 140 top, 177, 190, 191, 192; *A. Pistolesi*, pp. 12, 27, 34, 36, 41, 45 bottom, 49 top, 58, 84, 97, 100-101 bottom, 113, 129, 134, 136, 140 bottom, 142, 145 bottom, 170-171, 179, 182, 184; *Scala/Firenze*, pp. 14, 15, 18, 23, 28, 29, 31, 59, 71, 77, 94, 103, 154, 187, 188, 197.

Cover photo: Flagwaver at the Feast of S. Benedict's Day *(D.Donadoni/Marka)*.

We have taken great care to ensure that the information provided in this guide is accurate. Some schedules, numbers, and addresses may have changed; we cannot accept responsibility for those changes, nor for any loss, injury, or inconvenience sustained by any traveler as a result of information or advice contained in the guide.

Colour separation: *EMMEGI MULTIMEDIA - Milano*
Printed by: *New Litho - Milano*

Touring Club of Italy
Corso Italia 10
20122 Milano
www.touringclub.it

© 2003 Touring Editore s.r.l. - Milano
Code L2AAD
ISBN 88-365-2837-6
Printed in February 2003

# Foreword

*When the Italians think of Umbria, a small region with a vast historical and cultural heritage, the first image that usually springs to mind is that of the "Green Heart of Italy", a definition coined years ago as a tourism promotion slogan. And when it comes to man's relationship with nature, it has been said that human life in Umbria has remained perfectly integrated with the natural environment in a way rarely seen elsewhere.*

*A good guidebook must above all else be a compendium of everything of interest to travelers, presenting information in the most organized, up-to-date way possible. But if it also succeeds in conveying a sense of the history of the area in question and of its inhabitants past and present, so much the better. This guide does indeed endeavor to present Umbria as much for what it is today as for what it used to be, and with this in mind has made a point of mentioning some of the less well remembered aspects of its past as well as recounting the major events that have gone down in history. This has meant weaving into the description of the "mainstream" historical happenings a whole range of minor (but no less intriguing) details about the traditions and cultural events that lie hidden away in this fascinating and extraordinarily vibrant region.*

*It is no exaggeration to describe the whole of Umbria as a rich storehouse of cultural treasures, as a glance through this guide will make clear. The introductory chapters present the region's historical and cultural background in all its variety; the main section systematically explores Umbria in nineteen routes through towns and countryside, and is followed by four itin-*

The sanctuary of the Madonna del Belvedere, near Città di Castello (*G. Reani*).

*eraries which explore various other aspects that make the region special: the luminous but complex figure of St. Francis of Assisi, Umbria's female saints, the importance of water in the region, and last but not least its mouth-watering local cuisine. There are of course plenty of maps, plans and photographs to provide all the visual information travelers need to make the most of their visit, and the various boxes featured throughout the book offer insights into some of the other less well-known aspects of life in Umbria. It may come as a surprise, for example, to learn of the region's extensive, advanced network of museums, which includes everything from the major art collections down to the region's sometimes quite tiny museums – statements of the enormous interest the Umbrian people take in their immediate surroundings. Other boxes describe the region's gastronomic delights, its colorful pageants, traditional events like the Corsa dei Ceri in Gubbio, the Christmas crèches of Città della Pieve, the Festival dei Due Mondi in Spoleto and the Umbria Jazz Festival in Perugia, the astounding natural phenomenon of the petrified forest of Dunarobba, whose huge tree trunks still stand in their original positions. The aim throughout has been to create a complete, reliable and informative guide to the Umbria region – a resource worthy of this "jewel in the heart of Italy".*

# Contents

## Introduction
*The region's historical
and cultural background*

*Maps: Nature parks
and protected areas, p. 37*

*Sunflowers in the Umbria countryside*

## A Guide to Umbria
*Detailed descriptions of the tourist sites*

### 1 Perugia and Lake Trasimeno

*Plans: Mechanically-assisted walkways in Perugia, pp. 46-47;
Perugia: Palazzo dei Priori, pp. 48-49*

### 2 The Val Tiberina

*Town maps: Città di Castello, p. 76*

### 3 The Eugubine valley and the Umbrian Apennine

### 4 The Valle Umbra

*Other town maps: Spello, p. 112; Montefalco, p. 121;
Trevi, p.123*
*Plans: Basilica of Santa Chiara, Assisi, p. 101; Basilica of
San Francesco, Assisi, pp. 104-105; Santa Maria degli Angeli,
Assisi, p. 109; Spoleto Cathedral, p. 133*

*Foligno Cathedral*

*Deruta:
artistic ceramicware*

## Information for Travelers
*Where to eat, where to stay, other tourist attractions*

*The Marmore Falls*

# Excursions through Umbria and index of maps and plans

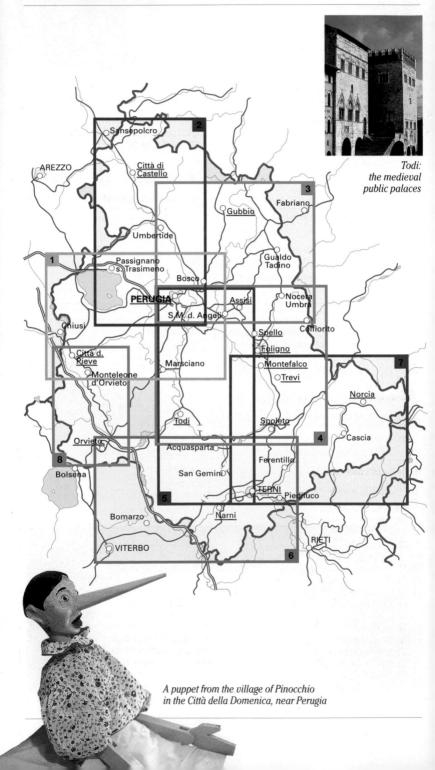

*Todi:
the medieval
public palaces*

*A puppet from the village of Pinocchio
in the Città della Domenica, near Perugia*

The regional map opposite brings together all the area tour maps used in the guide. The numbered list below gives the title and page reference of each tour.

*A view of the hill town of Amelia, dominated by its cathedral*

# How to use this guidebook

The guide opens with a series of introductory chapters outlining some of the main features of the region, followed by the guide proper, organized into itineraries. At the back of the book is an exhaustive list of addresses and useful information.

The color blue is used to indicate the most interesting monuments, museums, streets and squares in the city itineraries, and for the places worth stopping off at on the out-of-town excursions.

A single asterisk (*) denotes something of special interest; double asterisks (**) mean that the place described is of outstanding interest.

The abbreviation "elev." and figures in meters indicate the altitude above sea level of the towns and villages described; the most up-to-date population figures available at the time of going to press (pop.) are also given for municipal areas.

Other towns, monuments and artworks deserving attention are shown in *italics*.

Towns and monuments not shown in blue but nevertheless worth visiting are given in **bold type**.

### Ipogeo di San Manno*
*Ferro di Cavallo* (278 m), which developed in the early 20th century over a former nucleus resting on the church of San Manno, despite its 14th-century aspect is entirely decorated with fresco remains of the preceding century. Around the church, which was purchased by the Order of Malta, a rural fortified monastery was erected in the Middle Ages. Under this complex is hidden one of the major monuments of Etruscan funerary architecture, the **Ipogeo di San Manno**, which was utilized as a crypt and cellar. Steps, op-

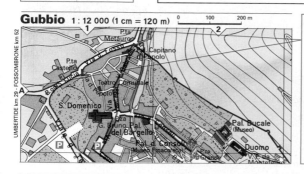

**Gubbio** 1 : 12 000 (1 cm = 120 m)

The street maps are divided up into grids with letters and numbers so that monuments, museums etc. can be located using the map references given in brackets in the descriptions.

E.g. *San Domenico* (A1), *Palazzo Ducale* (A2)

In the case of particularly complex walking tours, the suggested route is shown in blue on the **street maps**.

If the monument is off the map the closest map reference is given.

For extra visual clarity, monuments are **classified according to importance** as follows:

 monuments of outstanding artistic interest (3D drawing on the map)

 monuments of great interest (in black)

 monuments of interest (in dark brown)

other buildings (in light brown)

For a complete list of symbols used on the street maps see p. 10

## 6.1 Around Terni  6.2 Around Narni

The **maps** accompanying each excursion trace the suggested route in color, and show places worth stopping at along the way. The starting and finishing points are marked with a flag. For a complete list of symbols used on these maps see p. 10.

The **floor plans** of some of the more complex monuments are designed to facilitate the visit. Any reference numbers or letters are explained in the legend accompanying the plan or given in brackets in the description.

### Orvieto Cathedral

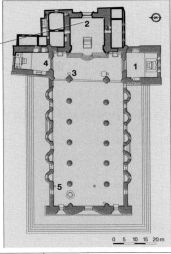

0  5  10  15  20 m

The descriptions are accompanied by **photographs**, taken by leading photographers, which illustrate some of the most beautiful sites, the most important monuments and other particularly interesting aspects of the region.

The **boxes** that appear here and there in the book shed more light on various things of interest by telling anecdotes or giving extra, more detailed information about the places and artworks described.

9

# How to use this guidebook

## Information for Travelers

**Hotels** are listed with their official star ratings. **Restaurants** are rated according to quality using the traditional silverware symbols (on a scale of one to five).

Visiting arrangements and opening times given for **museums** and **cultural institutions** are correct at the time of going to press. However, some subsequent changes may have been made to hours or schedules.

There are brief descriptions of **other places of interest**, including tourist amenities, places of entertainment and recreation, local festivals, and craft shops selling the typical products found throughout the region, with details of how to find them.

---

### Torgiano      ☒ 06089

*Page 227*

ℹ️   *Town Hall.* T. 075988601.

 **Hotels, restaurants, campsites and holiday camps**

★★★   **Le Tre Vaselle.** Via Garibaldi 48, t. 0759880447, fax 0759880214. 60 rooms. Facilities for disabled. Air conditioning, lift; parking, garage, garden, indoor and open-air pool.

🍴   **Le Tre Vaselle.** Via Garibaldi 48, t. 0759880447, fax 0759880214. Air conditioning, parking facilities. Classic and regional cuisine.

   **Museums and cultural insti-**

---

☐   Visitors should be aware that museums, monuments and archaeological sites are usually closed all day on 1 Jan, at Easter, on 25 Apr, 1 May, the first Sunday in June, 15 Aug and 25 Dec. Note also that visiting hours for churches are not given unless they differ from the normal opening times (traditionally 8am—noon and 4pm—7 pm).

## Key to symbols used in the maps and street plans

| | | | |
|---|---|---|---|
| Main throughfare | | Monument of outstanding interest |
| Main road | | Monument of particular interest |
| Other roads | | Other monuments to visit |
| Street with steps | | Church |
| Railway and station | | ℹ️ Tourist information office |
| Walking tour | | 🅿 Principal parking area |
| Contour map showing elevation and grave | | ✚ Garden, Hospital |

## Key to symbols used in sightseeing tours

| | | | |
|---|---|---|---|
| ➤ Sightseeing tour | | ═══ Motorway |
| ⊳ Start of itinerary | | ═══ Main road |
| ⊲ End of itinerary | | ═══ Other roads |
| **TERNI** Main town of the itinerary | | ♦ Church |
| ● Ponte Nearby place | | ✳ Natural curiosity |
| Urban area | | ⌒ Cave |
| Park and nature reserve | | ∴ Ruin, prehistoric remains |

# Introduction

## The region's historical and cultural background

# The creation of a regional identity

## The environment

The name Umbria conjures up an idea of peace and tranquillity, of beautiful landscapes dotted with austere medieval walled cities immortalized in Renaissance paintings. It is an image that has been perpetuated by promotional slogans such as "Umbria: the green heart of Italy," and by the "green and sacred land" definition invented during the years of Fascism. But it soon becomes clear to the visitor that today's single administrative unit, a small region of central Italy criss-crossed by roads running to and from its many towns and villages, is in fact a collection of historically and geographically quite distinct areas that modern regional organization may have brought together, but which the events of the past have so often torn apart. What, if anything, unites these areas is the fact that they have all suffered political marginalization at some time or other in their histories. Only in much more recent times have they broken free of their isolation, although it must be said that this has helped them to retain their original character, one based essentially on an ancient culture known for its refined simplicity, and revealed in its art and architecture, its countryside, its cuisine, its dialects and in the character and behavior of its people.

Central and southern Italy's only landlocked region is just 8,456 square kilometers in size, yet boasts an extremely varied landscape, whose appearance has been very much shaped by man. Much of the area is upland: a mere 6% is low-lying terrain, all of it situated between high ground, while hills cover 41% of the region and 53% is formed by mountains, though their peaks rarely rise above the 1,500 meters (on the eastern border). Elsewhere, altitudes vary between 800 and 1,300 meters, the land rising gradually towards the south and the east. The broad valley of the Tiber (between Città di Castello and Perugia) and Valle Umbra (through which the Chiascio, Topino and Clitunno rivers flow) cut the region into two distinct parts: to the west is a hilly area whose northern section ends at Lake Trasimene (Trasimeno); to the east the ground rises into parallel chains of mountains that describe a broad arc.

Umbria's present-day border, marked by the outer boundaries of the adjoining provinces of Perugia and Terni, shows clearly how the territory of this inland region is essentially the result of administrative map-making rather than any natural geographical divisions such as rivers or mountain ridges. The eastern border with the

*Sunflower crops, with the hill of Amelia in the background*

Marche region is largely defined by the Apennine watershed, but the border seldom runs along this geographical divide (at the Fossato pass and the Sibillini Mountains, for example). Some of the drainage basins that flow into the Adriatic Sea fall within Umbria's borders, while the source of the Nera river and the area of Visso belong to Marche. To the north and west the border cuts across the Tiber (the upper reaches of the Tiber valley flow through Tuscany), winds its way through the mountains that form the watershed between the Arno and Tiber rivers (though, again, not along the ridge itself) then just grazes Lake Trasimeno before turning south, down the Chiana valley and across the Paglia river, almost to Lake Bolsena. The border then follows the Tiber, but between Otricoli and Magliano Sabina veers east and continues its irregular course through mountains and valleys, dividing Umbria from the province of Rieti to the south.

## Administrative fiction and regional reality

Umbria has always been torn between two identities, a duality that historical events have only accentuated. On the one hand it is firmly anchored in the west, the land of the Etruscans, having natural links with Tuscany and the sea beyond; on the other it has felt the pull from the East, the more isolated, inward-looking land first of the Umbrians and then of the Romans. The demarcation line between these two cultural realities is the Tiber river, some 210 km of which flows through the region. The cities of Perugia and Orvieto, which grew up on the right bank of the river, traditionally had close links with the Tyrrhenian Sea and the Mediterranean in general. The towns on the left bank to the east were first Umbrian and then Roman – for example Spoleto, Todi, Assisi, Spello, and Tadinum – which were later joined by important centers such as Città di Castello (the ancient Tifernum), Foligno and Bevagna. When the Romans conquered the Etruscans and Umbrians in 295 BC and united their territories under a single dominion, some semblance of uniformity was created, but the rout at Trasimene by Hannibal's army, and the different ways in which the Umbrians and the Etruscans

*An olive tree in the vicinity of Stroncone*

reacted to the victors, only deepened the divisions that already existed.

Roman civilization, with its cities, its major land reclamation schemes in the plain, its network of roads (the *Via Flaminia* crosses the region), and its vast colonization and centuriation schemes, the results of which can still be seen in the way parts of the land is divided up, had a profound influence on the region.

The very name Umbria was a Roman invention, although it originally denoted not the present-day region but the area to either side of the Flaminian Way. Umbria was, in fact, the name given during the reign of Augustus to the "sexta regio," that is the land to the east of the Tiber between the Nera river and the Adriatic, extending to Otricoli, and excluding Norcia, which was part of the Sannio region, but including the Casentino area (now in Tuscany), and the "ager gallicus" between Rimini and Ancona; the Perugia area

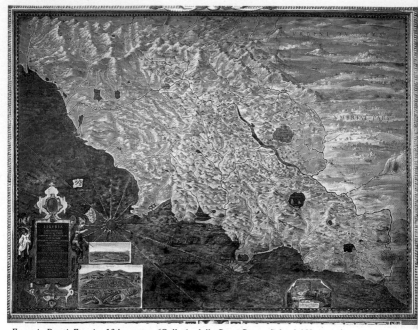

*Egnazio Danti, Etruria, 16th century (Galleria delle Carte Geografiche del Vaticano)*

was assigned to Etruria. Administrative reorganization by Diocletian, toward the end of the 3rd century AD divided the region still further, as well as abolishing the name: the areas to the east of the Tiber became known as *Flaminia* and *Picenum*, while the land to the west was referred to first as *Tuscia et Umbria* and later as *Tuscia* only.

The name Umbria did not reappear until the Renaissance, though this is less surprising in the light of the profound identity crisis that befell the region after the fall of the Roman Empire, the period of the Barbarian invasions and the wars between the Goths and the Byzantines, the Byzantines and the Longobards, and between the Longobards and the Popes for control of the roads leading from the Adriatic to Rome. This period also saw the spread of marshland, the collapse of the road network and the breakdown of urban organization. The good farmland in the plain was abandoned as the surviving local population fled in fear to the hills, settling in inaccessible woodland areas over which the new feudal lords vied for power. In the late Middle Ages, the only far-reaching authority was represented by the Byzantine axis between Rome and Rimini (based on a narrow corridor that took in Amelia, Narni, Todi, Bettona, Perugia and Gubbio and, to the west, Orte, Orvieto, Chiusi and Cortona), by the Duchy of Spoleto, founded by the Longobards in 571, and by the gradual spread of the temporal power of the popes. However, these three powers, which co-existed despite countless disputes between the various feudal lords, resulted in even greater fragmentation of Umbria. Because of its mountainous nature, the Longobard Duchy of Spoleto in particular was for a long period an extremely strong sub-regional unit that prevented the formation of any strong regional identity.

When the term Umbria reappeared in learned circles in the second half of the fifteenth century, it again did not coincide with the present-day region. In his well-known work "Italia Illustrata," Flavio Biondo divides Umbria into two regions: Etruria and Umbria. Biondo's definition corresponds largely to the Duchy of Spoleto, which did not include the land west of the Tiber. The great success of "Italia Illustrata" led to widespread acceptance of Biondo's ideas, and between the late fifteenth century and the seventeenth century geographers, mapmakers, historians and scholars continued to refer to Umbria as the area between the Tiber and Aniene rivers and the Apennine mountains. This was also the definition given by Leandro Alberti in his sixteenth-century "Descrittione di tutta Italia".

In the early seventeenth century G. A. Magini's "Italia" contains two plates of Umbria:

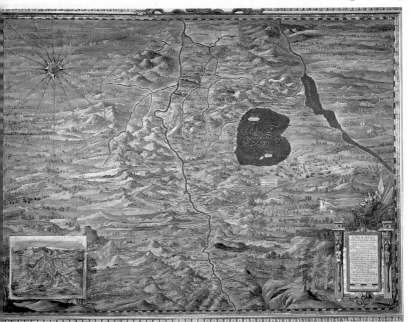

*Egnazio Danti, The Perugian farmlands, 16th century (Galleria delle Carte Geografiche del Vaticano)*

one entitled "Umbria or the Duchy of Spoleto" and the other "The Territory of Perugia," indicating the governments of Città di Castello and Orvieto as two other independent provinces.

Not until the eighteenth century did geographers and mapmakers begin to include the area to the west of the Tiber under Umbria. In the "General Map of the Province of Umbria," published in 1712 by Abbot Moroncelli of Fabriano, Umbria appears as a unified whole, but it did not include the Gubbio area (which came under Urbino), the Orvieto area (held by the Church), or the Città di Castello area. For Moroncelli, the province began in the north at Fratta (present-day Umbertide); to the west it included the areas of Castiglion del Lago and Città della Pieve and a wedge of the Orvieto area; to the south-east it included the Rieti area and the western slopes of the Sibillini mountains; while to the north-east Fossato, Sigillo, Sassoferrato and the mountain area all the way to the slopes of Mt. Catria were all part of Umbria.

Curiously, Valfabbrica to the east was considered as belonging to Gubbio, forming an Urbino-controlled enclave on Umbrian soil.

Formal unification of Umbria came in the Napoleonic years with the creation of the single department of Trasimeno, whose chief town was Spoleto. In 1816 Pope Pius VII created the two delegations of Perugia and Spoleto, which in 1853 were elevated to the rank of province on a par with Orvieto; the *contado* of Gubbio, on the other hand, was annexed to the province of Pesaro-Urbino. At this point Umbria was seen, both in administrative and in geographical terms as a region in its own right, despite the existence of certain border variations. Further recognition of its status came in 1860, when the Kingdom of Italy confirmed Umbria as a single province (chief town: Perugia) that re-incorporated the territories of Gubbio, Rieti and Sabina.

In 1923 Sabina became part of the neighboring region of Lazio, at which point Umbria had, with only slight variations, its current borders. Finally, in 1927, the second province of Terni was created, resulting in a two-province region that reflected its duality: a largely rural area centered around the cultural capital of Perugia, and another centering around the predominantly industrial city of Terni. Yet although Umbria was only considered as a geographical and administrative unit from the 19th century onward, the region was already the subject of study by historians, scholars and churchmen in the 18th century. And earlier still, in the mid-seventeenth century, works by Ferdinando Ughelli, Durante Dorio and Lodovico Iacobilli reveal the way in which an awareness of a distinctly Umbrian character was beginning to take shape, in terms of political, institutional, cultural and religious unity, despite any differences there might have been between its various towns. However, if such a collective Umbrian consciousness did already exist it was as yet very much in the minds of the writers mentioned and had no basis in reality.

## From international crossroads to isolated province

Although Umbria gradually became more isolated as it came geographically, politically and institutionally under papal rule, and became even more cut off when the new united Italy planned its road and rail networks (a situation more recent transport policies have only accentuated), insularity was not a typical historical trait of the region as a whole. Umbria can be divided into at least three areas that have seen quite distinct historical developments. The predominantly mountainous region (for centuries almost a "sub-region") was indeed closed and isolated, and in any case gravitated more toward the mountainous areas of Marche, Abruzzo and Rieti province than to the rest of the region. But the central area, with its lower-lying hills and plains washed by the Tiber and its tributaries, has at various times in history formed a major economical and cultural crossroads in Italy and internationally. And the largely hilly area to the west has always felt a greater pull from outside the region (from Rome, Viterbo, Arezzo and Siena) than from the region to which it belongs. It was already the hub of the central area of the Italian peninsula in the late Middle Ages, a phenomenon that was closely related to the increase in population that took place between the tenth and fourteenth centuries, with the rebirth of the cities, markets, trade and the increase in human contacts. Thanks to a well-structured system of roads, the region had been at the center of communications between Rome, the North and the Adriatic and between the Adriatic and Tyrrhenian seas as early as classical times. The road network, which had decided the fortunes of numerous towns, hinged mainly around the Flaminian Way, which connected Narni, Bevagna, Foligno, Forum Flaminii, Nocera Umbra, the Scheggia Pass, Furlo and the branch from Narni to Terni that touched Spoleto and rejoined the western section at Forum Flaminii. The other major highways were the section of the *Via Salaria* from Rieti to Terni; the *Via Amerina* (today's *Via Tiberina*), which branched off from the Via Cassia at Baccano, continued toward Amelia, Todi, Bettona, and Perugia, and rejoined the *Via Cassia* at Chiusi; the road that branched off from the Via Cassia at Todi, and followed the west bank of the Tiber to Perugia, joined the Valtiberina road and forked off toward Bocca Serriola and the Furlo valley and Gubbio and Scheggia; and the road connecting Foligno, Spello, Assisi, Bettona, and Perugia, with the Lake Trasimeno area and beyond into Tuscany.

After the calamitous events of the early Middle Ages, between the tenth and eleventh centuries, this network, which was still extremely important but much deteriorated and marshy in the valleys, expanded with a smaller network of dirt roads that were often little more than mule tracks, connecting the main roads to the new settlements growing up on the hills. Umbrian territory was gradually covered with a dense network of settle-

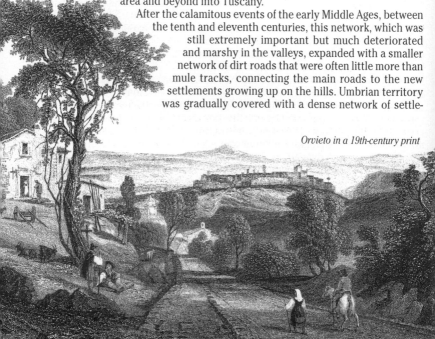

*Orvieto in a 19th-century print*

*An isolated farmhouse in the Terni countryside*

ments that divided it into a series of smaller areas each under the control of towns that came to challenge the old feudal power structure. This dense road network was dotted with towns, castles, villas, isolated houses, churches, monasteries, convents, hospitals and hospices. A hierarchy of large and small power centers around the cities, towns and villages developed. At the top were the busy commercial and industrial cities of Città di Castello, Gubbio, Perugia, Assisi, Foligno, Todi, Spoleto and Terni, which enjoyed positions of regional and even international prestige. It was thanks to the activities of these cities, especially Perugia and Foligno with their favorable geographical positions, that Umbria became a lively center of trade and culture. Until at least the fourteenth century valuable property, titled men, masses of skilled and unskilled workers and pilgrims were on the move, creating a vibrancy and uniformity of culture, and encouraging the development of a flourishing local craft industry that found an outlet on the international markets, and which in the main towns resulted in a profusion of merchants' and craftsmen's houses, corporation buildings, public edifices and churches. While most changes took place within or immediately outside the city walls, the whole region began to come to back to life as new settlers reclaimed and organized the land and waterways, grew vines and olives on the hills and crops in the plains, and built the farmhouses that became one of the region's most distinctive features. It was thanks to this renewed spirit of partnership among men who felt free, and to the growth of individual economic fortunes that townspeople were able to embark upon prestigious public works, such as the building of town walls (in the thirteenth and fourteenth centuries), the paving of streets and squares, the creation of well-engineered sewage systems and the construction of imposing public buildings, aqueducts, fountains, and cathedrals. From the thirteenth century onwards, especially after the death of St. Francis of Assisi, the movement that was growing up around the Franciscan and mendicant orders built beautiful works of architecture in which ideology, human genius and an eclectic approach to culture coalesced into a new style that blended the Umbro-Romanesque tradition with the International Gothic. This style, exemplified from both an architectural and an iconographical point of view first in the Basilica of St. Francis and later in the Basilica of Santa Chiara, was exported on a vast scale from the small town of Assisi – which for a century or so became an international melting-pot of style – to the far-flung corners of Europe, and from there to the other continents.

In the mid-fourteenth century the main Umbrian towns began to lose their status as international trading centers. The ravages of the Black Death together with the devastation caused by earthquakes and the ever more bitter fights between the municipal powers and papal authority and, within the towns themselves, between the haves (the rich middle classes of merchants and craftsmen) and the have-nots (the workers at the very bottom of the manufacturing system), marked the end of a sort of Umbri-

*One of Giotto's frescoes in the basilica of San Francesco at Assisi*

an golden age and ushered in a period of decline. Between 1348, the year the pestilence arrived, and the end of the fifteenth century, outbreaks of epidemic proportions were recorded in no fewer than forty separate years, killing off men of every social class, bringing social intercourse to a standstill and provoking a mass exodus from the towns (among other things it seriously held up work on the Assisi basilicas). And as if all this were not enough, no fewer than twelve major earthquakes between 1345 and 1604 razed towns to the ground, with tremendous loss of life. The region-wide city wall expansion work that was completed in the early decades of the fourteenth century on the assumption that populations would continue to grow, ended up enclosing areas that stood empty for a long time to come.

Between the 1350s and the 1370s, the strife between the individual municipalities and the Holy See worsened and resulted in bloody wars and subjugation. Papal delegate Cardinal Egidio Albornoz came to Assisi, Narni, Orvieto, Spello, Spoleto, Todi and many other smaller towns, decreeing major urban reorganization schemes, and building large, imposing strongholds at the towns' highest points, thereby sanctioning the end of municipal freedom and establishing the authority of the new power that replaced it. A revolt by the underclasses in Perugia in 1371 was quelled by the forces of the nobility, which had the backing of the pope, and the city came under the power of papal delegate Gerard du Puy, who had an imposing citadel erected on the Sole hill that was defined by chroniclers of the day as "the finest fortress in Italy".

It took three and a half years to build, but was freed by the townsfolk in 1376, after the last major uprising in the town. Between the second half of the fourteenth and the first half of the fifteenth century life in Umbria changed considerably: the old municipal system gave way to the new seigneuries, which brought lords and tyrants to the region: the Baglioni, Fortebracci, Vitelli, Trinci, and Malatesta families. This development was favored by the decline of the municipalities and the inability of the papal authorities to achieve cohesion, endeavoring instead to exploit the disputes between the big families and the rivalries between the nobility and the rich middle classes in an attempt to undermine the policies promoted by the popular classes and extend its own area of influence. Attempts first by Braccio Fortebracci and then by the Baglioni to ratify the supremacy of Perugia in the region, by the Trinci in Foligno, and by the Vitelli in Città di Castello came to naught, and instead of bringing the region together led to wars that only tore it further apart.

The gentleness, serenity and the pleasantness of the Umbrian countryside depicted in Giotto's frescoes for the upper basilica of St. Francis and a regular feature of artworks thereafter (paintings by Fra Angelico for the churches of Perugia; by Ottaviano di Martino di Nello in the church of *San Domenico* in Gubbio; by Nicolò di Liberatore "l'Alunno" in the church of *San Nicolò* in Foligno and in the cathedral of San Rufino di Assisi; by Benedetto Bonfigli and his school in the chapel of the Priori in Perugia and in that city's churches and those in Corciano, by Benozzo Gozzoli in the church of *San Francesco* in Montefalco; and most importantly of all by Pietro Vannucci and Bernardino di Betto) were now cultural rather than physical characteristics. Through these representations and through Franciscan ideology, Umbria acquired a sacral character, conveying a message of peace through its holy sites that was widely popularized by painters, poets, men of letters and men of the church, and yet the image was a highly intellectual one that had little basis in fact. The late fourteenth and fifteenth centuries were a period of great suffering for Umbria's people, who regularly fell victim to plague, pillage and plunder, their homes and harvests often ruined. As in all periods of economic recession and civil unrest, these hard times left an indelible mark on the towns and cities. The leading banking and merchants' groups gradually abandoned the region, leaving trade and industry to languish as the economy and society turned in on itself.

## The growth of the nobility and the farming economy

By the 16th century papal power had asserted itself in Umbria, crippling the merchant and craft economies and seriously undermining the role the region had previously played as an international crossroads. In 1540, the "salt war" and the construction of an imposing fortress by Paul III Farnese, put an end to the ambitions of autonomy in Perugia, the last outpost of independence on Umbrian soil. The history of the region became part of the wider history of a modern state, the Church State, whose influence now reached from Rome to Ferrara.

The crisis in the municipal structures and the behind-the-scenes machinations of the power-hungry lords enabled the nobility to win back considerable power, to gain a firm foothold in the towns, and to invest their capital in large property holdings. The new ruling classes founded their fortunes on their estates, on the clerical professions, and on financial investments in the state. In their efforts to hold onto power they did all they could to prevent their land from being parceled up as it passed from generation to generation, but this often forced noble families to live under one roof (large palaces began to appear in the cities), and obliged most

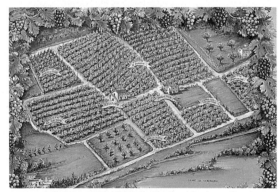

*A map of the grapes with which the Orvieto wine is produced*

of their offspring to take monastic vows, which resulted in a profusion of convents and monasteries, usually built on the edges of the towns on land left unbuilt after the demographic crisis of the late fourteenth century. The much smaller-scale medieval town buildings were dwarfed by these imposing convents, monasteries and noble palaces, whose bulky presence disrupted the previous architectural balance. In Umbria's towns and cities palaces built from scratch after large-scale demolition operations and excavation work are something of a rarity. It was much more common for the nobility to buy a "stack" of adjacent thirteenth- or fourteenth century buildings from merchants and craftsmen, who were forced out of the most prestigious parts of town, or indeed forced to move out into the country. The new owners would then gut a section of the interior to create a staircase to connect the various floors, add string courses to the facades, portals surmounted by the family crest, regular rows of windows decorated in stone or brick, and then whitewash or paint the fronts to create the effect of a single *palazzo* several stories high. These operations were only detected in much more recent times, thanks to the misguided policy introduced during Italy's Fascist period of stripping buildings of their plaster work to give Umbria's cities a more medieval feel. Architects, painters, cabinetmakers, famous and not-so-famous decorators were called in to furnish and decorate the interiors, and also the chapels the families had built in the region's various churches, convents, monasteries, confraternities and hospitals they had founded or supported. This created a vast collection of cultural treasures, although much of them disappeared from Umbria as a result of ill-advised decisions taken by families and looting subsequently made by invading forces, such as the wholesale confiscations made under Napoleon and following unification.

The ennoblement of society transformed the appearance of the towns in other ways too. The new architectural features often required the opening up of perspective views and the creation of theatrical backdrops for festivals and pageants. That the region was under the control of Rome could be seen in the styles and forms the urban spaces took on: the *Chiesa Nuova* in Perugia and the church of the same name in Assisi, the original basilica of *Santa Maria degli Angeli*, and the Bramantesque temple of *Santa Maria della Consolazione* in Todi are but a few examples.

The troubles that beset the merchant and craft economies in the towns and the huge investments made by the ruling classes in land and property turned Umbria into a much more rural society. Urban populations dwindled as inhabitants flocked to the countryside, which soon became dotted with farmhouses, since the widely-established tenant farming system required that families took up permanent residence on the land they worked. The growth of tenant farming from the sixteenth century onward also profoundly altered the appearance of the landscape: rows of trees and shrubs on which to train vine tendrils were planted, ditches were dug to divide fields and properties, dovecotes were built to provide a ready source of manure, and corn, oil, silk and paper mills appeared along the main waterways. Although in economic and cultural terms Umbria was very much in decline under church rule, the region nevertheless continued to be traversed by soldiers, pilgrims and other wayfarers who preferred Umbria's roads to the disastrous alternatives elsewhere as they traveled up and down the Italian peninsula. But during the Baroque period and the Age of Enlightenment, travelers generally overlooked the gentle countryside and its medieval sites, stopping only to admire briefly the Etruscan Arch in Perugia, the so-called Temple of Minerva in Assisi, the Roman bridge at Narni, the temple at Clitumnus, and the Marmore Falls. Travel and postal literature refers only to the main roads through the region, while hardly any mention is made of the by-ways, especially the roads through the mountainous Nursino area, with the exception of the excursion to the supposed Grotto of the Sibyl in the Sibillini mountains. This despite the fact that the region's mountainous areas were inhabited by farm hands and shepherds who periodically moved to the countryside around Rome and the Maremma area in Tuscany, and by the Norcini people who sold their cheese and meat products in Rome.

## The steady rise of the bourgeoisie

French rule did little to transform Umbria, its main legacy being the plundering of the region's art treasures. The farming economy fell into inexorable decline; there was a dearth of capital and innovative ideas, and most property was in the hands of the church. Craftsmanship, such as the rare ceramic manufacture in Deruta, Gualdo Tadino, and Gubbio, was at its lowest ebb.

By the time the region was annexed to the Kingdom of Italy, little if anything had changed. The Umbrian countryside was still inhabited by 87.86% of the total population and 62.8% of the working population was engaged in farming activities, while trade and the manufacturing and craft industries employed a mere 9% of the total population. Things were somewhat different in Terni, which in 1824 had a number of small firms, a thriving milling industry, and a relatively important woolen industry.

Historical sources all emphasize how the appearance of Umbria was influenced by tenant farming and man's influence immediately before and after unification, thereby helping to convey the image of a many-towered region of farms with an austere mystical aura. Not until the end of the nineteenth century, when large-scale industry came to Terni as part of an economic strategy quite extraneous to things Umbrian, did the region's traditional organization and image give way to a new Janus-like duality: Perugia in the north stood for the cultural heritage and continuity with the past, while Terni in the south looked to the future. Nevertheless,

*Handcrafted ceramics of local production, Deruta*

right up to the 1950s the region was characterized on the outside by its dense network of towns that were rich in medieval associations and by its agricultural activities, dominated by the tenant farming system. It should be remembered, however, that the late 19th and early 20th centuries saw a gradual but substantial rise in the bourgeoisie, which tended to take over land previously held by the clergy and the nobility and to make changes to farming life in the country and residential life in the towns.

### The rediscovery of the region

With the arrival of romanticism in the nineteenth century the Middle Ages came to be viewed in a new, more favorable light, and Umbria became a fashionable region where members of cultivated society began to take up residence. In 1818 and 1850, the region's sacred side came to the fore with the discovery of the bodies of St. Francis and St. Chiara of Assisi. Medieval culture and the Umbrian landscape as well as its towns came back into vogue and ancient monuments were restored. This focus of interest on medieval Umbria lasted well into the twentieth century and indeed in the Fascist years was taken to extremes, as some towns took on an ultra-Gothic appearance, of which Assisi provides the most glaring example. When the Foligno-Terontola rail line was built in 1866, It seemed that Umbria was about to break free from its isolation, and that an economic revival might be accompanied by profound changes to the urban areas as new centers

*Tilling the land at the start of the 20th century*

grew up near the railroad. It was not to be: the region's marginal role was clearly a deeply-rooted one and destined to stay that way.

Nonetheless, Umbria's towns and cities did undergo major urban reorganization in the late nineteenth and twentieth centuries. Ring roads were built outside the walls, which were often partly demolished, or even pulled down altogether, as in the case of Foligno. Parks, theaters and cafés – the typical features of bourgeois town life – appeared everywhere, and ancient streets were renamed after Italy's national heroes. The old religious buildings were taken over by the public authorities and turned into offices, law courts, army barracks, hospitals and schools, and middle-class villas and workers' houses were built outside the old towns. But despite the changes, the region's towns and their unassuming architectural styles retained that sense of spontaneity that had always been a distinguishing feature of their artists and craftsmen, the very people who had built them, happily combining functional purpose with popular culture. Thus Umbria's small settlements blended perfectly into their natural surroundings, conditioned by no external constraints. The layouts of the towns within their walls were a harmonious union between nature and geometry, resulting in some truly artistic masterpieces that make the region unique.

### From fascism to the present day

The first two decades of the twentieth century brought rapid changes to Umbria's urban organization and to the social and economic order in the Terni area, as small industries grew up around Città di Castello, Perugia and Foligno, industrial cultures spread to the upper Tiber valley and the Assisi plain, mining began in the Bastardo and Pietrafitta basins, and essential public services were modernized or created from scratch. But it was not until the Fascist period that the changes to the way services (bureaucracy, education, housing, leisure) were organized came into its own. Public gardens and memorial parks, playing fields, gymnasia, barracks, working men's clubs and Houses

of the People appeared in towns and cities, as the regime asserted its power throughout Umbria, with more success in the region's main cities and surrounding areas than in Apennine areas, which continued to be marginalized. The major urban development plans drawn up in the 1930s included Umbria's towns and cities: whole areas were to be cleared to make way for new spaces and rationalist architectural schemes. Mercifully, though, scarcity of funds prevented much of the demolition work from going ahead. The most prestigious works of architecture underwent period restorations and were stripped of everything that had been added on over the centuries so that they would tower above all else. The most substantial demolition work was carried out in Foligno, Spoleto and to an even greater extent in Terni, whose medieval fabric was greatly damaged by rationalist architecture.

Although the failure to actuate most of these redevelopment schemes saved Umbria from the kind of wholesale destruction that was seen elsewhere in Italy's main cities, it did perpetuate the regulatory body system, which led to frequent planning changes and ultimately encouraged the widespread speculative building projects that disrupted the architectural harmony of numerous cities. As local administrations came and went, the 1950s and 1960s – the years of agricultural crises and population explosions – did the most harm, destroying the ancient equilibrium that existed between town and country and within the towns and resulting in the growth of dormitory areas, industrial estates, and a poorly-planned road network that brought about the deterioration of life in the region as well as creating problems of overcrowding and traffic congestion. From the creation of the modern region to the present day, attempts have been made to halt the decline, but much remains to be done. While the skylines of most Umbrian towns retain their elegant medieval and Renaissance appearance when viewed from the countryside below, the views from the belvederes in the towns themselves reveal a quite different situation of disorderly growth in the postwar years of reconstruction,

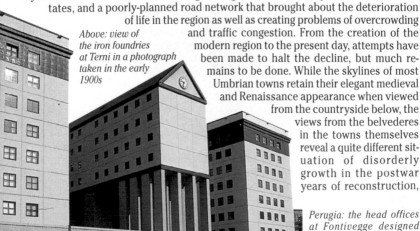

*Above: view of the iron foundries at Terni in a photograph taken in the early 1900s*

*Perugia: the head offices at Fontivegge designed by Aldo Rossi (1985)*

the crisis in tenant farming and the rapid growth of industry. And yet for all the ruinous actions by man down the ages and by the recent earthquake (which has done irreversible damage to the cultural heritage), Umbria's cities, towns and countryside still contain a wealth of artistic treasures and natural beauty that deserve to be carefully preserved for future generations to enjoy.

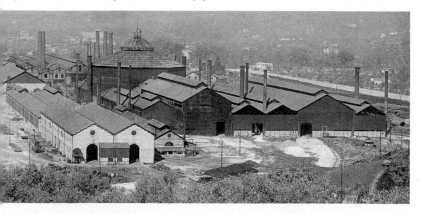

## Perugino and the invention of the modern landscape

In the *Adoration of the Magi* painted in Perugia in 1504 by Perugino, "Italy's greatest master," as his contemporaries described him, the procession of horses converging on the shed (the focal point of the composition) is set in one of the most elaborate landscapes the artist ever created. The countryside flattens out toward the center of the composition, perfectly framed by gently rolling hills, the horizon flattening out into a stretch of water, recalling the view from Città della Pieve toward Lake Trasimeno and Valdichiana, in one of Perugino's typical figurative schemes. Perugino's rendering of space and light creates landscapes that are a "perfect balance between the evocation of real life and the expression of a mental scheme" (B. Toscano), in which contemplation of the Umbrian countryside represents the modern yearning for balance and order. This "almost modern manner," as Vasari defined it, turned its back on the tormented visions of the Gothic landscape, and marked a decisive

*Perugino, Adoration of the Magi, 1504 (Città della Pieve)*

change in taste. The countryside itself had only recently changed: developments in farming involved land reclamation which, from the mid-15th century onward, had altered the appearance of the Valle Umbra and Valdichiana, whose marshes became orderly arable land, watered and farmed under man's control. The rural scene thus took on new, organic forms prompting a reappraisal of the ideal landscape, which was later captured so beautifully in Renaissance art.

# Art and culture

### Landscape and history

Today's regional divisions are fairly unhelpful when it comes to defining the identity of Umbria, a true understanding of which can only come from the often quite different historical "map" of its artistic and cultural past. This section will try not merely to list places, artists and their works and neatly pigeon-hole them into fixed periods, but rather to focus on some of the defining moments in the region's history and on some of the more enlightening examples that place Umbria in a much broader and less rigid temporal and physical context.

The landscape and its impact on the discerning visitor opens up a whole range of intriguing new angles from which to approach the region. Umbria certainly does live up to its reputation, however clichéd, as a region of green rolling hills dotted with picturesque medieval towns and cities. But by thinking more broadly in terms of an interwoven network of circuits, trading relations and other influences – from within and from outside the region – it becomes clear that this is indeed just one aspect among many (albeit the

*Ruins at the theater at the archaeological site of Carsulae (2nd century BC)*

most evident), a surface veneer beneath which lie so many other layers. Some of these stretch way back in time, most notably that of the region's ancient communications system along the Tiber river and the *Via Flaminia*.

The Tiber valley has been one of the main communication routes along the northeast–southwest axis since prehistoric times, the backbone from which a complex system of lesser routes branched off, establishing contact between the Tyrrhenian Sea and the Apennines. The Tiber also formed a natural border between the Etruscan and Umbrian civilizations to the west and east of the river respectively.

The *Via Flaminia*, built around 220 BC over previous, less well thought-out routes was the other essential means of communication from north to south, the road by which the Romans entered the region and along which the various ethnic groups (Etruscans, Sabines, and Umbrians) were eventually unified. This Roman road has over the centuries served as an element of geographical, cultural, and economic continuity for the towns along its route. Archaeological areas of considerable interest exist to either side of the Flaminian Way in Umbria, vestiges of a much more widespread cultural past. The most striking examples in the Etruscan area are Orvieto, with the extensive necropolises of Crocifisso del Tufo and Cannicella, and Perugia, where parts of the wall survive (containing the imposing Arch of Augustus), burial areas (the Volumni hypogeum) as well as extremely important finds – Etruscan or otherwise – in the National Archaeology Museum. Carsulae, built on the Flaminian Way in the 3rd century BC provides an excellent insight into the layout of a Roman town, its buildings and infrastructures still clearly identifiable.

In the Middle Ages the *Regio Castellorum* grew up over the ancient settlements, and changed the face of the towns in a way that is still visible today, a particularly well-preserved example being the Valnerina area. Less accessible because of its mountainous nature and for this reason not crossed by any of Umbria's main communications routes, the Nera Valley offers a clear insight into the checkered history of settlements in the area from protohistorical times to the Middle Ages. Because of its role as a link with the Adriatic, this area was anything but marginal. The Roman towns developed in the valley, whereas in the early Middle Ages the general uncertainty of life in the countryside, which was periodically overrun by Barbarians, pushed the population up onto safer ground, where fortifications were built that often incorporated earlier Longobard lookout towers, churches, and Benedictine monasteries.

St. Benedict himself was born in Norcia in around 480 AD and it was inevitable that the Valnerina area would soon become the "cradle of western monasticism," since it directly witnessed the rapid spread of monastic settlements that were so crucial to the politics, culture and economy of the region long after the end of the Middle Ages. The abbeys at San Pietro in Valle and Sant'Eutizio (dating back to somewhere between the 4th and 6th centuries) provide a key to an understanding of the fortunes of these power centers, under which culture and art of the highest quality flourished. As well as the celebrated marble slab by "Magester Ursus" at San Pietro in Valle, crafted in the period in which the abbey played a major role in the Longobard po-

*The abbey of San Pietro in Valle, Ferentillo (Terni)*

litical system, the frescoes depicting stories from the Old and New Testaments in the same church (among the oldest in the region) and the exquisite illuminated codices from Sant'Eutizio (now in the Vallicelliana Library in Rome and in Spoleto Art Gallery) give an idea of how much "cultural promotion" these workshops did. The theoretical assistance and practical teachings of the Sant'Eutizio abbey complex also explains the fame of the surgical school of Preci, whose members worked throughout Europe from the 13th to 18th centuries, specializing in the removal of kidney stones and cataracts.

The fortification of the Valnerina area, which did much to alter the appearance of the landscape, was the expression on a smaller scale of a phenomenon that was taking place regionwide, and which from a strategic point of view kept alive its importance for popes and emperors, who made sure they held onto power in such a vast area with a well-structured defense system, and close to Rome too. Well into the 14th century it was through fortresses (new ones or old ones enlarged) that the Church found an infallible means of asserting its power and control over a territory which was by then a state in all but name. The fortresses of Orvieto, Todi, Narni, Spoleto, and Assisi, decreed by Cardinal Albornoz, papal delegate from 1353 to 1367, were the hubs of a defense system that took in towns along the Tiber and the Flaminian Way, integrating them into a system that extended beyond the natural regional borders and which today retains a unique and visually unified appeal in the area between Narni, Spoleto, and Assisi.

But the system of fortifications through which the Church asserted its central power and strengthened its political presence in the region was not the first "Christian occupation" of Umbria. Centuries earlier the region had been shaped by a dense network of abbeys and churches as part of the organization of the region into dioceses. Religious building activity culminated in the blossoming of Romanesque architecture (11th–12th cent.), some of the most outstanding examples of which were seen in the dioceses of Spoleto, Todi, and Narni. The vitality of these towns is attested also by the production of other devotional items, including painted crosses and altarpieces, which had a long-lasting influence on the development of painted art in central and southern Umbria.

## Medieval spirituality and the arts

The intense religious sentiment of the Middle Ages came above all through the major figures of the period and the movements they inspired. Umbria's religious tradition in Umbria, and hence the region's art and culture must be seen in the light of events that left an indelible mark on the sensibility and spirituality of the day, the effects of which have lived on down the centuries and way beyond its regional borders. The Franciscan movement was indeed a global phenomenon that led to a profound renewal in quite distinct areas: in spirituality, in art history, in literary expression, and indeed even in the planning of towns that had had to be reorganized to accommodate the new Friars Minor communities.

In 1228, just two years after the death of the saint, work resumed on the Assisi basilica, whose architecture served as a model for other religious buildings in the area, and giving rise to a wider phenomenon that found expression in the spread of the mendicant orders. The Franciscan churches (*Santa Chiara d'Assisi* and *San Francesco al Prato* in Perugia), those belonging to the Dominican order (*San Domenico* in Perugia), and

to the Augustinians (*Sant'Agostino* in Perugia, *San Niccolò* in Spoleto) became the nodal points of a dense network that took in the entire the region. In many cases the sheer scale of these complexes influenced the way in which the towns themselves developed, frequently setting the for later expansion work that often meant the construction of new town walls. No less influential were the paintings with

*The convent of San Francesco at Assisi, in a print of the 1800s*

which the new basilicas were decorated: most notably Giotto's *Life of St. Francis* cycle, which became a reference point of no little importance for generations of artists, as well as exerting an enormous emotional pull on a popular sentiment that welcomed the precepts of the new order with open arms. Collective rituals involving processions, chanting and penitence were established, whose poetic and dramatic potential was expressed initially through the *lauda* and later expanded into more complex forms, such as miracle plays. The role of St. Francis played an important part in the *Canticle of the Sun*, a consummate example of vernacular poetry that was a defining moment in the development of Italian literature. This form of composition gave rise to increasingly complex liturgical chants – a rudimentary form of dramaturgy – consisting of solo voices alternating with choruses. The Flagellant Friars of Perugia, the brotherhood guided by Ranieri Fasani (1260), who led collective flagellation rites with choral chanting in dialog form, made an important contribution here. The subsequent inclusion of scenes with several different characters eventually resulted in an Umbrian version of the miracle play, a genre that established itself in particular through the work of religious poet Jacopone da Todi, author of the oldest surviving example of a dramatized *lauda* (*Donna de Paradiso*). In addition to these historically documented examples, most of the laudbooks by anonymous writers for collective convent use also originated in Umbria (Perugia, Assisi), though they soon spread to neighboring central Italian regions (Tuscany, the Marches, and Abruzzi).

Also of Umbrian origin was the transposition of religious themes to the stage through the use of scenically composed statue groups, rare examples of thirteenth-century wooden sculpture. Their use in passion plays is documented most notably by the group from the town of Montone (1260–70, now in the town's museum), from Roccatamburo (13th century, in the Castellina Museum, Norcia), and from Tivoli, by those now in the Louvre (undoubtedly Umbrian in origin), by some equally important fragments from Deruta (now in the National Gallery of Umbria) and from Gubbio (the church of *San Pietro*), and by others now in Milan's Sforza Castle and in the Stoclet collection in Brussels.

## Secular Medieval Art

As well as this profoundly religious development, the 13th and 14th centuries also saw the flowering of refined artistic expression in secular life in Umbria. Civic buildings (the city halls in Perugia, Todi and Gubbio) not only changed the appearance of the towns but also established a new rapport between political and religious power, a delicate balance often symbolized in the main square. In Perugia, for example, Palazzo dei Priori and the Cathedral face one another, with the Fontana Maggiore (1278) providing a central point of equilibrium. This fountain, designed by Nicola and Giovanni Pisano for the practical purposes of bringing water to the city center, blends civic culture with religious tradition, juxtaposing representations of the everyday life of man with Biblical and mythological scenes. This varied subject matter, for which the fountain has come to be seen as an "encyclopedia of medieval knowledge," continues inside Palazzo dei Priori in the cycle of frescoes in the Sala dei Notari, which was decorated with sacred and profane subjects between 1298 and 1300.

The same direct relationship between seat of city government and cathedral is seen equally clearly in the main square in Todi, although only fragments remain of its pictorial representation in the "chivalric"

*The Palazzo del Capitano in Todi (late 13th century)*

cycle in the Sala delle Pietre inside the Palazzo del Podestà. The careful harmonization of the doctrinal with the strictly secular was promoted on an institutional level by Perugia University, founded in 1308, which first taught theology and jurisprudence (the leading jurist of the day, Bartolo di Sassoferrato, taught there).

## The Quattrocento

The accentuation of secular philosophy founded on humanistic values in the 15th century came with the establishment of the seigniories. Above all the late Gothic fresco cycles placed Umbria in cultural circuits that involved the Adriatic regions (Marche and Emilia) in particular. The lost paintings in the Baglioni residence in Perugia, and the decorations in Palazzo Trinci in Foligno well express the level of patronage in early 15th-century Umbria and the refined culture that substantiated it. This complex iconographical program – extending from the loggia with its stories of the foundation of Rome, and the Rooms of the Stars, the Liberal Arts and the Planets, to the representation of the Seven Ages of Man, the Room of the Emperors and the palace chapel (which Ottaviano Nel-

*Perugino, Epiphany, 1521 (church of the Madonna delle Lacrime, near Trevi)*

li dates at 1424) – was a way of celebrating seigniorial government and of expressing its splendor and international culture.

This "enlightened court" climate is linked to the promotion of arts decreed by Braccio Fortebracci da Montone. He created a form of regional unification which in its short life stretched from Umbria and Marche to the Principality of Capua, attracting artists and artistic styles from such regions as Emilia, at whose court Bolognese architect Fioravante Fioravanti and Ferrari-born painter Antonio Alberti worked.

### The Renaissance and the influence of Perugino and Raphael

One of the periods that propelled Umbria to the forefront of Italy's national culture was undoubtedly that in which Pietro Perugino and his school were active. Working in the lively cultural context of the Perugia workshop and the court of the Baglioni, and influenced from an early stage by Florentine models (Fra Angelico, Piero della Francesca, Domenico Veneziano, and Agostino di Duccio), Pietro Perugino created a style whose popularity spread rapidly thanks to the skillful organization of the workshop, where the young Raphael also worked. Emblematic of the new pictorial style was the decoration of the Collegio del Cambio in Perugia (1498–1500), an Italian Renaissance masterpiece in "Perugia '500" style that become an endless source of inspiration for artists and craftsmen right up to the last century. Not only did the style and composition of the fresco cycle become an accepted model, but the lavish ornamentation that went with it provided a ready-made pattern book for engravers, inlayers, fabric designers and above all majolica manufacturers.

Stylistic features and decorative elements which Perugino and Pinturicchio had extensively codified soon found their way into majolica design. Ceramics manufactured in Deruta assimilated the rich vocabulary of figurines, grotesques and candelabra that became a trademark of the production of plates, vases and paving tiles, with a consistency of decoration that is exemplified particularly well in the Baglioni chapel in the church of *Santa Maria Maggiore* in Spello, frescoed by Pinturicchio around 1501 and embellished with a majolica floor (1566) decorated with similar ornamental devices.

During the Renaissance, the new artistic fervor spread to other Umbrian towns traditionally renowned for their ceramic production. One was Gubbio, where the manufacture of exquisite majolica was associated with the figure of Lombard-born Giorgio Andreoli, who moved to Umbria and established a thriving workshop renowned for its use of shiny glazes and highly receptive to influences from the neighboring Marche region, especially Urbino, under whose political influence Gubbio came.

The Renaissance and the Perugino school influenced art and culture right up to the nineteenth century when, during the programmatic retrieval of the "primitives" in devotional art, Umbrian tradition was the main source of material for purist painters and a host of copyists, who turned out endless works diligently based on those models. The Perugia Academy became something of a rallying point for the new artistic style, to which artists, from Italy and abroad, turned for inspiration in a context steeped in history and mystical atmosphere. Decidedly purist, neo-Renaissance variations on the theme came with a group of Nordic artists working in Perugia, who left their mark even on sites that were the very embodiment of Umbrian spirituality. This happened at the Porziuncola chapel in Assisi, where in 1829 German artist Overbeck painted his *Miracle of the Roses* to replace a 17th-century fresco.

Similarly neo-Quattrocento in style were the shrines of the *Madonna della Stella* (near Montefalco) and the *Madonna di Canoscio* (near Città di Castello), which, though based largely on the most widely adopted Renaissance revival trends, very evidently took their inspiration from local tradition.

## Umbria, the papacy and the politics of the arts

Just as the 19th-century sanctuaries constituted "outposts" through which the church manifested its political dominion during the years of Italian Unification over a region that had always been at the forefront of the temporal interest of the papacy, so certain episodes emblematic of Umbrian art history can be interpreted as part of the new political and religious impetus from Rome. The extensive reorganization and transformation of religious life carried out by the Church between the 16th and 17th centuries explains the twofold initiative that on the one hand focused attention on the main holy sites and on the other brought about a renewed interest in religious matters: a process of evangelization swept through the region, with new religious complexes appearing everywhere. The communities founded by the new Capuchin order, the rediscovery of places steeped in ancient Christian history (the abbey of Sant'Eutizio for example), the mystic fervor associated with the cult of new exemplary figures (such as the venerable Paola of Foligno) are just a few of the manifestations of the urge for reform that was everywhere in Umbria. One of the most evident outward signs of this change was the beginning of work on the basilica of *Santa Maria degli Angeli*, the grand scheme with which the ancient cult of St. Francis was brought back into favor and a site of prime importance in the circle of artists and ideas that linked Umbria to Rome.

In much the same way Orvieto had served as a way of furthering the cause of the more modern Roman culture, in what was gen-

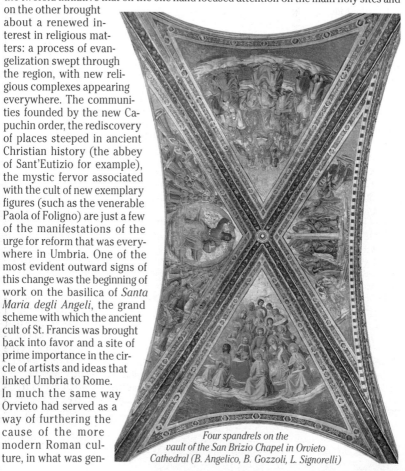

*Four spandrels on the vault of the San Brizio Chapel in Orvieto Cathedral (B. Angelico, B. Gozzoli, L. Signorelli)*

erally held to be a more unified artistic context: Orvieto Cathedral became a focus for painters and sculptors who had introduced the modern "manner" to Umbria between 1560 and 1580. Many of the fruits of this burst of activity fell victim to the purist ideals of 19th-century restoration (such as the removal of Francesco Mochi's colossal statues, now in the cathedral museum). A similar fate befell Todi Cathedral, the redesign of whose interior by a single artist (Ferraù Fenzoni) for Bishop Angelo Cesi in the late 16th century was almost completely obliterated in the 19th century.

The fundamental role played by leading church figures in the flourishing of the arts in Umbria in the 16th and 17th centuries cannot be over-emphasized, since they were the vital link between the region and Rome. One was the Bishop of Todi, mentioned earlier, another was Cardinal Fausto Poli, whose name was closely associated with the generous patronage of the Barberini family in Umbria. Maffeo Barberini, the Bishop of Spoleto and later Pope Urban VIII, did much to embellish his city and diocese, the greatest sign of his generosity being the total remodeling of the interior of Spoleto Cathedral. Less conspicuously but more extensively, Maffeo laid the foundations for extensive and enduring cultural and artistic exchange between Rome and Umbria that lasted throughout the 17th century.

One episode that illustrates well the close ties established in this way was the arrival of the spectacular altarpiece of St. Anthony by Veronese artist Alessandro Turchi ("Orbetto"), ordered by the pope's brother, Antonio, for the small Capuchin community of Trevi (now in the San Francesco Collection), a work that was out of all proportion to its context. No less surprising were the commissions carried out in Usigni, the birthplace of Fausto Poli, and in Poggioprimocaso, two towns in the Valnerina area in which Guidobaldo Abbatini worked, a painter who was, as it were, "exported" there from the milieu in Rome of which this area was an offshoot, among other things because of the presence of artists associated with the Crescenzi family circle.

As well as the influences from Rome, the cultural vitality of this Apennine area was also unexpectedly influenced by Florence: the Oblita valley to the northwest of Norcia formed a kind of Florentine "enclave" that led to an influx of a whole range of Tuscan art (paintings, sculptures, but also fabrics, silverware, books etc.), and other places were renowned for their specialist professions, highly valued in Florence itself (these included the surgeons of the "school" of Sant'Eutizio mentioned earlier and, in the 17th century, the well-known customs officials). The Tuscan idiom left its unequivocal mark on the Oblita valley for decades, as can be seen in works such as those produced in the 14th century by Giovanni del Biondo in Poggio di Croce and the paintings by Neri di Bicci and Piero di Cosimo (the latter now hangs in the National Gallery of Umbria) and the 18th-century masterpieces of Furini, Confortini and Caccini.

*The Marmore Falls*
*in a print from the 1800s*

## Umbria and the Grand Tour

The image of Umbria as a region with a landscape and culture of its own became particularly well defined in the 18th and 19th centuries, when it found itself included in the Grand Tour itineraries. Once again the Flaminian Way was a vital communications artery, taking travelers from or to Rome past towns like Otricoli, Narni, Terni, Spoleto, and Foligno. Assisi and Perugia soon acquired not-to-be-missed status for anyone wishing to get a real feel for the region. Naturally, these two cities were also seen by those arriving from Tuscany on the north–south route. So when Goethe left Florence for Rome, he passed through some of the main towns in the region. He singled out the Temple of Minerva in Assisi and the Ponte delle Torri aqueduct in Spoleto as two supreme examples in Italy of architecture in the classical "close-to-nature" sense, that is to say blending utility with beauty and grandiosity.

One of the highlights of the Umbrian itinerary was the visit to the *Marmore Falls*: the sight of these spectacular waterfalls inspired a new artistic genre, prompting artists to explore the atmospheric surroundings for other subject matter. While vista painters such as Hackert and Vasi limited themselves to rendering the landscape topographically, an even deeper sensibility came across in the canvases of painters like Joseph Anton Koch and, more notably still, Corot. Little did these artists realize that the totally unspoiled environment they were depicting would remain intact for just a few decades more. The peacefulness of this section of the Nera valley, whose perfect balance of nature and civilization Corot captured so masterfully (for example in his *Morning in the Papigno Valley*) was lost for ever with the arrival of industry in the late 19th and early 20th centuries. This is perhaps the most emblematic example of a series of developments, which in various ways and to varying extents altered the appearance of the Umbrian landscape and led to a new form of urban organization, as in the case of Terni, whose expansion was inextricably bound up with industrial growth, or in the redesign of whole sections of the region – the plain between Spoleto and Foligno and around Città di Castello are two examples – often in open contradiction to centuries-old production and social systems.

*Etruscan Venus of Cannicella*

The last century in particular has profoundly transformed the relationship between town and country, with mass exoduses to the places that gave new opportunities for work and the comforts of town life. The changes in production activities have greatly impoverished the countryside and led to a gradual abandonment of the historic centers, phenomena which have had a substantial negative effect on the cultural fabric in the widest sense of the term. Indicative of this is the slow but inexorable decay of many of the artistic and cultural treasures, especially movable works of art, the "migration" of which beginning in the early 19th century continued until a few decades ago in different but no less devastating ways.

## The region's museum system

No visitor to Umbria can hope to fully understand its art and cultural history without dedicating plenty of time to the region's museums. Among the most advanced in Italy, Umbria's museums form an extensive, well-structured network closely linked to the physical and historical environment to which they belong. Artworks are exhibited in a large number of small museums, rather than a small number of large collections under one roof that would be totally divorced from the context in which they were created. This approach satisfies the demand for close, visible contact between the preserved heritage and the places that spawned them, as well as doing justice to the great historical variety of the many distinct localities. It was precisely with the aim of making the removal of objects from their original sites less painful and to learn from the mistakes of the past (state confiscation of the cultural heritage in the 19th century being a case in point) that such care is taken nowadays to recreate on a small scale a comprehensive system of preservation that serves as a study center and workshop for cultural and social initiatives – first and foremost for the benefit of the local population – and as a place of research. The ambitious aim of organizing individual museums within an organically developed structure, in which each collection is both an entity in its own right and part of a whole, is the concrete result of the cultural policies the Umbrian regional authorities have been following for the last twenty years. As a result, all the

## A town, a museum

A region with such an age-old tradition of art, history and customs as rich as Umbria's certainly deserves the extensive, well-organized network of museums that has been created here. All the region's museums, even the smallest collections, are of great interest in terms of both the quantity and the quality of their exhibits.

Mostly housed in buildings that are themselves of architectural interest, they preserve a wealth of art and artefacts from centuries past that give a comprehensive picture not only of the artistic masterpieces the region has produced but also of social and economic life as it used to be.

Indeed many of the museums that have been created in recent years stem from a desire to give future generations the chance to learn about farming and peasant life as it used to be and see some of the tools the region's craftsmen once used, an opportunity that has been welcomed by those old enough to remember life in those days. Other museums are interactive, related in some way to the region's resources and its often still quite unspoilt natural treasures, involving visitors in the 'narrative" through a multi-media experience, or simple information panels. The hard work that has been done in recent years to restore local museums and protect their exhibits has led to the gradual setting up of a "Regional Museum System" complete with its own administrative rules and regulations and technical services designed to bring the best possible cultural, social and economic results. Preserving the cultural heritage in the places and for the communities they belong to in this way provides a public service in the truest sense of the term.

*An old spinning wheel at the Museo della Casa Contadina in Corciano*

museums offer valuable insights into the region's cultural heritage: they are by definition open structures which at the same time house notable examples of the art and history described on these pages. The museums of Spello, Trevi, Cascia, and Todi, for example, have several sections (archaeology, art, local history, coins, fabrics etc.) that present a centuries-old tradition in a manageable form. No less eloquent is the Municipal Museum of St. Francis in Montefalco, created to salvage a 14th-century Franciscan church whose collections are so rich they offer a complete overview of Umbrian figurative arts between the 14th and 16th centuries. The church contains frescoes by Giovanni di Corraduccio, and Benozzo Gozzoli's well-known cycle of the *Life of St. Francis* (1452), as well as paintings by Jacopo Vincioli and Pietro Perugino. There is also an interesting archaeological section in the in the crypt and a collection of paintings, fabrics, gold and wood furniture on the upper floor.

But there are also many other kinds of museum, some of which specialize in certain categories of exhibits that are large enough to warrant a collection of their own, including the "Claudio Faina" archaeology museum in Orvieto, the Museum of the Vine in Torgiano (a joint public and private enterprise) and the museum of the work of Alberto Burri in Città di Castello.

Today, the region's museum structures officially number 120, although many of these are still to open.

Of course the region does also have two large collections of the region's many and varied cultural treasures. The most important is the National Gallery of Umbria in Perugia, which ranks as one of the finest art collections in Italy. Recently reorganized to more modern museological standards, the gallery offers a synopsis of the salient moments of Umbrian art history and central Italian art from the 13th to the 18th centuries, in a state-owned collection that was started back in the 1860s. Umbria's National Archaeology Museum, the other main state-owned collection in Perugia housed in the former convent of *San Domenico*, has a noteworthy collection of protohistoric, Etruscan, and Roman finds.

# A visitor's guide

## Getting there

The best way to reach Umbria is undoubtedly by car: the main express highways are the Florence-Rome stretch of the A1 ("Autosole") freeway and the A14 ("Adriatica"), and there is an efficient network of fast roads connecting the towns of main interest, such as the E7 Cesena-Orte, which cuts through the region from north to south. Rail links follow three main routes: the eastern rail service connects Terni, Spoleto and Foligno, continuing north along the Valtopina as far as Fossano di Vico; the Central Umbrian Railroad runs from Terni to Città di Castello with a western line following the main Rome-Florence line; and a tourist line that branches off at Terontola to Perugia and on to Foligno (Italian State Railways, tel. 0755007467 Perugia – tel. 0744459741 Terni). Umbria can also be reached by plane: there are two flights a day from Milan to Perugia (except Sundays), which lands at the regional airport of Sant'Egidio, 12 km from Perugia (tel. 0756929447).

## Hotels

In Italy it is common practice (and Umbria is no exception) for the reception desk to register your passport, and only registered guests are allowed to use the rooms. This is mere routine, done for security reasons, and there is no need for concern. Room rates are based on whether they are for single ("camera singola") or double ("camera doppia") occupancy. In every room you will find a list of the hotel rates (generally on the back of the door). While 4- and 5-star hotels have double beds, most hotels have only single beds. Should you want a double bed, you have to ask for a "letto matrimoniale."

All hotels have rooms with bathrooms; only 1-star establishments usually have shared

*The abbey of Santi Severo e Martirio, near Orvieto*

bathrooms only. Most hotel rates include breakfast ("prima colazione"), but you can request no breakfast, thus reducing the rate. Breakfast is generally served in a communal room and comprises a buffet with pastries, bread with butter and jam, cold cereals, fruit, yogurt, coffee, and fruit juice. Some hotels regularly frequented by foreign tourists will also serve other items such as eggs for their American and British guests. The hotels for families and in tourist localities also offer "mezza pensione," or half board, in which breakfast and dinner are included in the price.

## Eating and drinking

The Italian "bar" is a multi-faceted, all-purpose establishment for drinking, eating and socializing, where you can order an espresso, have breakfast, and enjoy a quick sandwich for lunch or even a hot meal. You can often buy various items here (sometimes even stamps, cigarettes, phone cards, etc.). Bear in mind that table service ("servizio a tavola") includes a surcharge. Lunch at bars will include, but is not limited to, "panini," sandwiches with crusty bread, usually with cured meats such as "prosciutto" (salt-cured ham), "prosciutto cotto" (cooked ham), and cheeses such as mozzarella topped with tomato and basil. Often the "panini" and other savory sandwiches (like stuffed flatbread or "focaccia") are heated before being served. Some bars also include a "tavola calda." If you see this sign in a bar window, it means that hot dishes like pasta and even entrées are served. In Umbria, as in Italy, coffee is never served with savory dishes or sandwiches, and cappuccino is seldom drunk outside of breakfast (although the bars are happy to serve it at any time).

Whether at an "osteria" (a tavern), a "trattoria" (a home-style restaurant), or a "ristorante" (a proper restaurant), the service of lunch and dinner generally consists of – but is not limited to – the following: "antipasti" or appetizers; a "primo piatto" or first course, i.e., pasta, rice, or soup; "secondo piatto" or main course, i.e., meat or seafood; "contorno" or side-dish, served with the main course, i.e., vegetables or salad; "formaggi," "frutta," and "dolci," i.e., cheeses, fruit, and dessert; caffè or espresso coffee. Wine is generally served at mealtime, and while finer restaurants have excellent wine lists (some including vintage wines), ordering the house table wine generally brings good results. Mineral water is also commonly served at meals and can be "gassata" (sparkling) or "naturale" (still). The most sublime culinary experience in Italy is achieved by matching the local foods with the appropriate local wines: wisdom dictates that a friendly waiter will be flattered by your request for his recommendation on what to eat and drink.

The pizzeria is in general one of the most economical, democratic, and satisfying culinary experiences in Italy. Everyone eats at the pizzeria: young people, families, couples, locals and tourists alike. The acid test of any pizzeria is the Margherita, topped simply with cheese and tomato sauce. Beer, sparkling or still water, and Coca Cola are the beverages commonly served with pizza. Some restaurants include a pizza menu, but most establishments do not serve pizza at lunchtime.

## Regional cuisine

A broad range of gastronomic delights created using local cold cuts, meat, vegetables, oil and wine awaits visitors to Umbria. The region's simple, but wholesome and appetizing fare has developed out of the capacity of the local rural communities to turn their basic farm produce into mouth-watering dishes. On high days and holidays, goose and duck often form the main meat course. The many regional recipes, such as cheese pie, vary from village to village, with the basic ingredients – flour, water, salt, *pecorino* cheese, egg and yeast – appearing in any number of different combinations in keeping with the imaginative flair for which Umbrians are renowned. Many of the local delicacies can be sampled by simply stopping off at one of the area's many consortia and farms, which sell such specialties as neck of beef, sausages and ham cured by the "norcini", the butchers of Norcia whose work is almost an art form (Prodotto del Cavatore, tel. 0743816689). The Norcia area is also renowned for its prized black truffles;

white truffles are found in the Città di Castello, Orvieto, and Gubbio areas. Then there are Castelluccio lentils, Colfiorito red potatoes sold at stalls along the Colfiorito stretch of the road from Foligno to Macerata, and the sweet two-year oil made from well-ripened olives, which now must pass extremely stringent quality controls to receive the required seal

*The famous black truffle*

of approval (the regional consortium of Olio Extra Vergine d'Oliva Co.re.ol., tel. 0742344214, www.umbriadoc.com). A traditional salami from the Valnerina and Orvieto areas, known as *mazzafegato*, has an unusual combination of ingredients. As well as beef and pork, Umbrian cuisine makes quite extensive use of game, especially wood pigeon (*palombe*). Freshwater fish can be found just about everywhere. Arguably the most interesting traditional recipe, though, is the *regina in porchetta*, a large carp cooked in a mouth-watering array of herbs and spices. Many food products can also be bought at the region's many monasteries (Umbria Tourist Promotion Office, tel. 075575951), whose gastronomic delights can be washed down with wines of guaranteed origin (Quality Wine Consortium DOC, tel. 0762344214, www.umbriadoc.com, or tasted in the many local wine cellars.

## Communications

Nearly everyone in Italy owns a cellular phone. Although public phones are still available, they seem to be ever fewer and farther between. If you wish to use public phones, you will find them in bars, along the street, and phone centers generally located in the city center. Pre-paid phone cards can be purchased at most newsstands and tobacco shops, and can also be acquired at automated tellers. For European travelers, activating personal cellular coverage is relatively simple, as it is in most cases for American and Australian travelers as well. Contact your mobile service provider for details. Cellular phones can also be rented in Italy from TIM, the Italian national phone company. For information, visit its website at www.tim.it. When traveling by car through the countryside, a cellular phone can really come in handy. Note that when dialing in Italy, you must always dial the prefix (e.g., 02 for Milan, 06 for Rome) even when making a local call. When calling to cellular phones, however, the initial zero is always dropped.

## Everyday needs and general information

Tobacco is available in Italy only at state-licensed tobacco shops. This kind of vendor ("tabaccheria"), often incorporated in a bar, also sells stamps.

Medicines can be purchased only in a pharmacy ("farmacia"). Pharmacists are very knowledgeable about common ailments and can generally prescribe a treatment for you on the spot. Opening time is 8:30-12:30 and 3:30-7:30 p.m. but in any case there is always a pharmacy open 24 hours and during holidays.

Every locality offers tourists characteristic shops, markets with good bargains, and even boutiques featuring leading Italian fashion designers. Opening hours vary from region to region and from season to season. In general, shops are open from 9 to 1 and from 3 or 4 to 7 or 8 p.m., but in large cities they usually have no lunchtime break.

Banks are open from Monday to Friday, from 8:30 to 1:30 and then from 3 to 4. However, the afternoon business hours may vary.

Post offices are open from Monday to Saturday, from 8:30 to 1:30 (12:30 on Saturday). In the larger towns there are also some offices open in the afternoon.

Effective 1 January 2002, the currency used in all European Union countries is the euro. Coins are in denominations of 1, 2 and 5 cents and 1 and 2 euros; banknotes are in denominations of 5, 10, 20, 50, 100 and 200 euros, each with a different color.

Umbria, like the rest of Italy, is in the time zone which is six hours ahead of Eastern Standard Time in the USA. Daylight saving time is used from March to September, when watches and clocks are set an hour ahead of standard time.

When you sit down at a restaurant you are generally charged a "coperto" or cover charge ranging from 1.5 to 3 euros, for service and bread. Tipping is not customary in Italy. Beware of unscrupulous restaurateurs who add a space on their clients' credit card receipt for a tip, while it has already been included in the cover charge.

## Sites of the spirit

For many people Umbria has immediate associations of spirituality. *Umbria Santa* (Sacred Umbria) is one of the many epithets – this one dates back to the years following the Unification of Italy – that have been coined to establish a unified image for an otherwise quite dis-united area. A tour of Umbria's religious sites takes in so many different places, not least the home of the Franciscan movement, which also offers some exceptional art and architecture, and to which the regional tourist economy owes a great deal (see itinerary p. 197). Hardly any less important is the theme of popular religious devotion, well documented in the many shrines dotted around the countryside and villages that powerfully evoke a bygone age of legend, pagan ritual, visions, miracle waters, outbreaks of plague, powers of healing and even raising of the dead. An unusually frequent and intense phenomenon was the flourishing in the 15th and 16th centuries of shrines to the Virgin Mary around Lake Trasimeno and along Via Pievaiola between Perugia and Città della Pieve.

The *Madonna del Soccorso* at Magione, *delle Fontanelle* at Montecolgnola, *dei Miracoli* at Castel Rigone, *dell'Oliveto* a Passignano, *della Carraia* and *del Busso* at Panicarola, *della Stella* at Paciano, *di Mongiovino* and *delle Grondici* at Tavernelle are places of worship that tell not only their own story, but also that of a rural community which sought protection in ritual devotion. One particularly interesting glimpse of such country customs

## Knocking on the convent door

How many modern travelers dream of falling asleep in some ancient residence, where history is written into the very fabric of the place? In Umbria that dream can come true: a medieval fortress in the heart of Bastia Umbra, a 19th-century castle near Lake Trasimeno and an 18th-century convent just outside Perugia are just three places to stay that offer an opportunity to leave behind today's world and get in touch with the past. Restored to perfection, these historically evocative residences offer a wonderful blend of present-day creature comforts with all the sensations, smells and colors of an age gone by. Guests can now enjoy truffled trout where monks once consumed their frugal meals to the accompaniment of prayers and hymns.

*Dining in an old manor house*

In Umbria, stone is to the architecture what color is to the landscape. Visitors who venture inside the region's ancient residences and convents can enjoy the "pax monastica" as they drink in an atmosphere which bestows an inner sense of well-being, far from the hectic pace of modern existence, a feeling that creates an urge to live a more contemplative life. Anyone lucky enough to stay in a setting of herb gardens and peaceful cloisters in the middle of the countryside or protected by high walls in the center of town will feel sympathy for Alcuin, who as he left his cloister behind for the court of Charlemagne, uttered the words: "Oh sweet, beloved abode, farewell for ever!"

spanning three centuries is provided by the 17th-century *ex voto* majolica tiles left by worshipers whose prayers had been answered, at the shrine of the *Madonna dei Bagni* near Deruta (tel. 075973455).

## Endless shades of green

Everything in Umbria seems to be set against a verdant background of countryside rolling away to the horizon. The many different hues of green found in the region are created by the different types of soil – loamy in the northeast, clayey in the center, volcanic around Orvieto – and by the way man has transformed the land for farming. The gentle hills of the Valle Umbra are tinged with the silvery green of its olive plantations, the darker green of the ilex forms a backdrop to secluded monastic complexes (most notably the centuries-old groves around Sassovivo abbey and the Carceri hermitage) and covers the hills around Amelia and Narni, the Tiber valley offers the more opaque green of its tobacco plants, while the Martani mountains boast a whole palette of shades of green. But the leafiest parts of Umbria are, of course, its regional parks (www.parks.it), which were created to protect the varied landscape, one that is highly prized both for its sheer size and for its blend of natural scenery and man-made settlements. Parco del Lago Trasimeno (tel. 075828059) has at its disposal one of Europe's most advanced environmental documentation centers as well as providing an information service on water quality, which is monitored on a continuous basis. To increase the tourist potential of the surrounding hills, footpaths now retrace historical routes and one of the lake's three islands, *Isola Polvese*, has been set aside as a wildlife reserve. The Parco del Monte Cucco (tel. 0759177326) is famed for its vast beech woods, for its carse formations and natural beauty spots such as springs and narrow gorges (the Rio Freddo gorge is spectacular). The speleology center at Costacciaro (Centro di Speleologia, tel. 0759170236) provides a map of the footpaths. In the Parco del Monte Subiaso (tel. 075815181) is the *Eremo delle Carceri*, the forest hermitage that played an important part in the life of St. Francis, and stone-built hamlets that date back to medieval times (Collepino, Armenzano). A beautiful walk along the ridge takes ramblers beyond the hermitage through the protected park area across mountain pasture: discerning visitors will notice a clear difference in the vegetation hereabouts. In the mountains around Foligno, the Parco di Colfiorito (tel. 0742349714) offers a wealth of natural and cultural attractions: marshland with an abun-

## Nature parks and protected areas

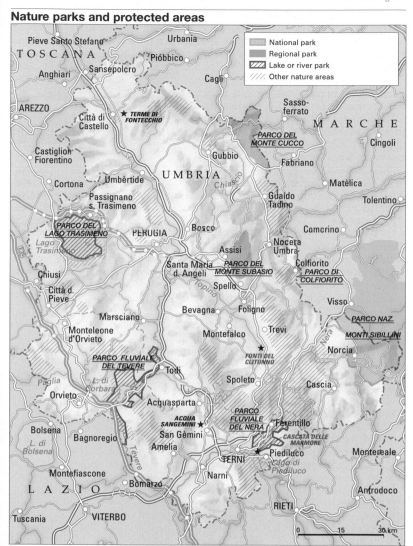

dance of flora and fauna, major archaeological and palaeontological finds on the plateau, whose system of fortified settlements in defense of a major communications network between the Tyrrhenian and Adriatic Seas, dated to as far back as the Iron Age. Finally, there are two river parks, the first stages in a more wide-ranging wetland protection project: the Parco del Tevere (tel. 0744950732), protected from Montemolino to Lake Alviano, and the Parco del Nera (tel. 0744583565), extending from the confluence of the Velino river to the Marmore Falls. Other areas of exceptional environmental interest are the Alviano wildlife reserve, which has bird watching facilities (Guardia Oasi, tel. 0744903715), the spectacular *Marmore Falls* (tel. 0744423047), waterfalls that were a must for 19th-century travelers on the Grand Tour, the Clitunno (or Clitumno) springs (tel. 0743521141), and the petrified forest of Dunarobba (tel. 0744933531), whose gigantic sequoia-like tree trunks date back between a million and two hundred thousand years. Then there are the valleys and basins (Valsorda, Valle del Fonno) of the Gualdese Apennines (IAT at Gubbio, tel. 0759220693, 0759220790), the entire Valnerina channel (Tourist Center at Valnerina-Cascia, tel. 074371401), the limestone Mt. Martani (Tourist Center at Todi, tel. 0758943395), and the Coscerno system, soon to become a wildlife park (Tourist Center at Valnerina-Cascia, tel. 074371401).

## Sport and outdoor pursuits

The region has seen a boom in outdoor pursuits in recent years with countless opportunities for sport and contact with nature through any number of activities, ranging from

the more traditional cycling tours (Umbria Tourist Promotion Office, tel. 075575951) and horse-riding through the unspoiled countryside, to new extreme sports such as bungee jumping, from the Canal Bridge in Rosciano (tel. 0744228105), and whitewater rafting along a 3-km stretch from the Marmore Falls along the Nera river rapids (Canoe Center www.raftingmarmore.com). Rock climbing for all levels of difficulty is on offer at Pale (Foligno), Mt. Tezio (Perugia), Mt. Vettore (Norcia) (Federazione Arrampicatori Sportivi Italiana, tel. 0744300946).

*Rafting on one of the many rivers*

Other water sports include water skiing on Lake Trasimeno (Services Department, tel. 075827125-075827168), and canoeing down the Rio Freddo, near Mt. Cucco, the Pago delle Fosse ravine (Mt. S. Vito, Scheggino), the Casco ravine (Le Cese, Spoleto), the Roccagelli gorge (Meggiano, Vallo di Nera) and the Parrano and Prodo ravines in Orvieto province (Umbria Tourist Promotion Office, tel. 075575951). Windsurfing and sailing remain the most popular sports on Lake Trasimeno where regattas are also organized (Tourist Center, tel. 0759652484). Those who prefer outdoor pursuits without special equipment can follow the many hiking routes organized by CAI (the Italian Alpine Club, tel. 0744286504) or follow the suggestions of the Umbria branch of the WWF (Perugia, tel. 0755058156).

### Music comes to town

The annual music festival Umbria Jazz takes place against some of the region's finest backdrops. The event is an intriguing blend of the music of the New World with the art and natural beauty found in and around Umbria's towns and cities, their medieval squares, theaters, wine cellars and gardens. The jazz festival is one of Italy's oldest, and has, since it was first held in 1973, acquired many dedicated followers both in Italy and abroad, thanks to its ability to attract the world's leading jazz musicians and to the way it brings together culture and tourism.

*Lionel Hampton at the Umbria Jazz festival*

From the very start, the festival broke free from the specialist musical confines to which jazz had been restricted until then, successfully bringing to the attention of musicologists and sociologists the compelling and often contradictory relationship between young people and music.

Over the years, as the festival has made a name for itself in the Italian and international press, Umbria Jazz has grown in size and complexity, offering almost an entire month of concerts in the event known as **Umbria Jazz Summer**: the first ten days of July are dedicated to concerts and musical events in the historic heart of Perugia, with a whirlwind of festivities at all hours of the day and continuing well into the night. Before the main Perugia event, the towns bordering on Lake Trasimeno play host to a smaller festival dedicated to the music of New Orleans, the waterside location itself a tribute the city where jazz was born.

**Umbria Jazz Winter** is held between Christmas and New Year at Orvieto. Quite unlike the summer festival in scope and spirit, this much quieter, offbeat event explores some of the more innovative aspects of contemporary jazz, appealing above all to true connoisseurs of the genre.

# A Guide to Umbria

Detailed descriptions
of the tourist sites

# 1 Perugia and Lake Trasimeno

## Area profile

One of the various bas-reliefs sculpted on Perugia's admirable *Fontana Maggiore*, in Piazza IV Novembre, portrays a woman holding a cornucopia from which, amid flowers and fruit, also fish issue. This, in fact, is how Nicola and Giovanni Pisano represented Perugia, ornate with Lake Trasimeno's major resource, thus symbolizing the close bond between the city and its lake; a bond rich in culture, art, and also trade. Not even the city's patron saint, Herculanus, managed to avoid being associated with fishing symbols, if it is true what Franco Sacchetti related, in one of his *novelle*, about a prank played on the inhabitants of Perugia at the hands of a Florentine painter, Buonamico Buffalmacco, who painted in the city's very central square not the image of the saint crowned with gold and gems, but with a "garland made of *lasche* [a fish typical of Lake Trasimeno], the largest to ever have come out of the lake." Castles and churches constructed by Perugia's ruling families are the most typical signs of the city's presence and importance in this lake area. In Giovanni di Piermatteo's *Madonna del Pergolato* (1447), the lake laps at the city's boundary walls, producing an image which, albeit slightly incongruous, perfectly captures Perugia's marked connection with the lake. This secular interest was of course prompted by economic advantages, both because fish in the lake were wondrously plentiful and also because of the extraordinary fertility of the surrounding countryside. This area, in fact, became a veritable grain house both for Perugia and its environs. Today tourism is the principal economic motor of the economy.

*Lake Trasimene front and, in the distance, the Isola Maggiore*

## 1.1 Perugia
**Itineraries along the Etruscan walls, and in the northern and southern boroughs**
*(maps on pages 42-43 and 44)*

With just over 150,000 inhabitants, Umbria's largest city (elev. 493 m) dominates a maze of valleys and major communication routes, between Val Tiberina and Valle Umbra. Here, the visitor is afforded various sights, the best being that which appears when arriving from Cortona, or from the expressway. Visitors arriving from other directions have only one access to the city, via the motorway (autostrada 75 bis). In order to have a more authentic visual impact, you have only to access the city by its more ancient roads, which wind up along the hill across Bulagaio da Ponte Felcino-Ponte Rio to the east, or the Montebello road to the south.

The historic link between city and countryside underlies the region's prevalently agricultural economy up to the 20th century. Industry, with is food and textile factories (Perugina, Buitoni, Spagnoli, Ellesse), developed markedly in the sixties, whereas the economic recession of the nineties, together with the taking over of local enterprises by foreign capital, threatened to further undermine the economic prosperity of the region. But Perugia is first and foremost a city of culture: its state university and its university for foreigners draw 30,000 students to the city each year, accounting for an economic windfall and, of course, socio-structural modifications within the historic center. This cultural vitality translates into high-level events, such as: Umbria Jazz (July); the Sagra Musicale Umbra (September), dedicated both to sacred and contemporary music; Rockin' Umbria (June and July); and Umbriafiction TV (late March early April).

Thanks to numerous archaeological finds unearthed in the area, we know that from the 9th cent. B.C. the hill's summit must have been occupied by clusters of huts, from the union of which the original primitive structure of the Etruscan center developed. Dating back to this period are the walls made of large travertine blocks (4th-3rd cent. B.C.) which, along a three-kilometer route, form a huge three-leaf clover of sorts girding two elevations, Colle Landone and Colle del Sole, separated by a "saddle" on which the city itself clusters. In the 1st cent. B.C., Perugia became a part of the Roman state and, at the behest of Augustus, underwent a structural rearrangement which focused primarily on the forum, the very heart of the city. During the imperial age building also took place outside the city's boundary walls; examples of which are the amphitheater outside the walls, the Conca thermal baths (2nd cent. A.D.), and possibly also a mausoleum beneath San Pietro bell tower. The city continued to spread outside the walled perimeter even during early Christian times. Growth was brusquely interrupted by the barbaric invasions which took place in the 6th cent. Urban development picked up again during the early Middle Ages, when the cathedral of Saint Peter (10th cent.) became enclosed within the city walls. By the close of the 11th cent. the communal government began the construction of public buildings; first that of the Palazzo dei Consoli (Consuls) and del Podestà (Mayor), then of the Palazzo dei Priori (1293-1443 ca.) which, together with the Fontana Maggiore (1275-78), radically changed the layout of the city's main square.

Between the 12th and 13th cent. the surrounding countryside extended all the way to the fertile lands around Lake Trasimeno, thus determining a profound change in the relationship between city and countryside. The rural aristocracy and the peasantry both took to dwelling within the city, thus giving rise to new boroughs (borghi), veritable appendices to the city which sprang up around the large monastic complexes, and which were absorbed within the urban perimeter walls between the 13th and 14th cent. With

*Corso Vannucci, Perugia main street*

the Peace of Bologna (1370), Perugia again fell under papal dominion. The city built a fortification system centering on the citadel of Porta Sole, soon demolished by a local uprising (1375). From the end of the 14th century, political instability gave rise to an alternating succession of various signorie (the domain of a lord, or signore). The government of Braccio Fortebracci (1416-24) is particularly noteworthy because of the public works achieved during this period.

From the second half of the 15th century, the Baglioni family, which staunchly backed the papacy, played a pivotal role in the city's political and cultural life. The refined and cultivated social class in power enhanced the city with artistically significant buildings.

Around the mid-16th cent. the papal state reaffirmed its dominion over the city and vented its ambitions for power by building the Rocca Paolina (1540-43), surmounting the medieval turreted Baglioni quarter which was swallowed up by the fortress. Perugia's medieval townscape was soon dotted here and there with Renaissance and Baroque facades, while its streets and squares were broadened. The 19th century marked the beginning of a "modernization" process, with the consequent decentralizing of service facilities and the building of an outer ring road, which clearly deprived the city's ancient boundary walls of any further practical significance. The historic center was redesigned after the destruction of the Rocca Paolina (1860), an area in which the broader expanse of Piazza Italia rose. During the first postwar period, the railway station (1867) attracted industry to the city (such as the Perugina chocolate company), whereas it was during the second postwar period that the residential areas and the historic center merged, thus giving rise to a new economic hub. During the years of major city planning (the first dates back to 1931), the city began to expand along its natural development axes (Monteluce in the northeast; Elce in the northwest; and the railway station in the city's southern area), without however giving to these expanding nuclei a definitive configuration. The outer quarters continued to grow while at the same time a new thoroughfare was built which, approaching the city at a tangent, intersects its more ancient streets as they radiate from the city center. Now Perugia is poised to invest in the overall recovery of its urban context and to iron out the contradictions that have arisen between new development tendencies on one hand and the need to preserve the city's historic heritage on the other.

## *The city within the Etruscan walls*

Our itinerary starts from Piazza IV Novembre, the city's monumental center, and proceeds almost entirely within its upper part as delimited by the Etruscan walls. Moving along the historic center axis, Corso Vannucci, we reach Piazza Italia, which was radically modified first by the building of the Rocca Paolina and subsequently by its destruction. From the square, once having crossed Via Baglioni, we turn right down Via Marzia, where the homonymous Etruscan gate abuts upon the medieval Baglioni quarter, "buried" inside the Rocca's subterranean remains. From here, via an escalator, we go down to the modern city where, proceeding along Via del Pario- ne, we reach the church of

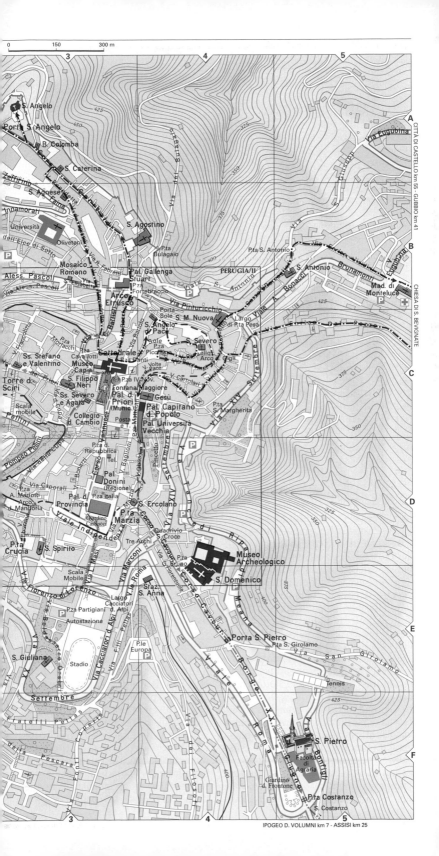

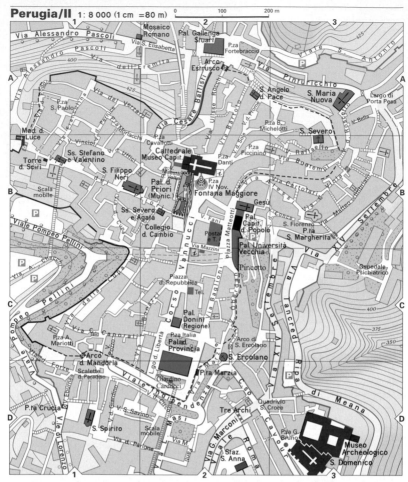

**Perugia/II** 1 : 8 000 (1 cm = 80 m)

Santo Spirito. The steps of Santo Spirito lead to Porta Crucia, from where we can make a brief detour to visit the church of San Prospero. Two streets, Via Eburnea and Via San Giacomo, link the Porta Crucia to Arco della Mandorla, through which we again access the città alta, or upper part of the city. From the next square, Piazza Mariotti, and following the curvature of the Etruscan walls upon which abuts Via della Cupa, we reach Via Sant'Agata, which takes us up to Via dei Priori, medieval Perugia's main east-west axis, linking the city center and Porta Trasimena, from which the roads leading to the lake and to Tuscany branched off. At the end of Via dei Priori, the monumental complex of San Francesco al Prato well exemplifies how the city took shape, especially as determined by the progressive setting up of the major monastic orders (Franciscan, Augustinian and Dominican). Next, we proceed down Via Pascoli, out-

side the città alta, to admire a mosaic in Via Santa Elisabetta, which was part of a Roman thermal complex. We are in the medieval Conca quarter, which rose at the base of the Etruscan walls, and of which there are significant remains along Via Battisti. Continuing along Piazza Cavallotti and Via Maestà delle Volte, we again find ourselves in Piazza Maggiore.

**Piazza IV Novembre\*** (II, B2). Broad and lively, this square constitutes the city's civil and religious center. It opens onto the area of the Roman forum and, since its origins, has represented the very hub of the city's street network, to the extent of becoming, in medieval times, the starting point of the five *vie regali* (royal roads) which provided access to the major routes in the area. The square's charm derives from the harmonious relationship between the various monuments fronting it: the Cathedral, the *Fontana Maggiore* and Palazzo dei Priori all playfully blend in alternating asymmetrical forms. The square began to take shape in the course of the early Middle Ages, after acting as the bishop's fortified citadel, but soon had to adapt to the dictates of urban expansion which determined its broadening and the construction of public buildings and the fountain. Ultimately, it took on its present layout with the building of a large access road (*Via Calderini*, 1591) which was to further modify its original layout.

Fontana Maggiore** (II, B2). The square's visible hub, it is the symbol of the medieval commune and of the entire city. Born of the need to transport water to the city, the fountain was built by Nicola and Giovanni Pisano in 1275-78 as the Monte Pacciano aqueduct terminal. A 13th-century masterpiece, the monument consists of two polygonal marble tubs surmounted by a bronze cup, from which rise the *three nymphs* (or theological virtues). The *formelle**, or marble slabs, of the lower tub reproduce an agricultural *calendar*, the *Zodiac signs* and the *seven liberal arts*; while those of the upper basin celebrate the mythical founding of the city and its political role in the area.

Cathedral * (II, B2). The long flight of steps upon which it rises is a favorite place for tourists to stop and enjoy a truly incomparable view of the square. The Cathedral, dedicated to St. Lawrence, features a complex stratification of construction phases. The initial structure, made a cathedral in 969, located on the site of the present transept, was redesigned by Fra Bevignate (1300), subsequently restructured in 1437, and consecrated in 1569. In the 17th century a surmounting brick structure was added. Its left side, in unfinished pink and white marble, features Gothic windows and many inserts from various periods: the 5th-century pul-

## The hidden fountain

In Perugia, water is almost as important an element as stone. Suffice it to recall the Etruscan wells, beginning with that at Sorbello, just a few dozen feet from the Fontana Maggiore, which probably consti-

*The Fontana Maggiore in an old print (top) and as it is today (bottom)*

tuted the city's main water supply, also during siege. Nor is it rare to come across ancient wells dug through the pavement of private houses and public buildings. Water gathered in cisterns, or brought to the city via an aqueduct dating as far back as the second half of the 13th century, was then distributed through a close network of fountains which fed the various quarters of the city. The hydraulic system – conceived by Fra Bevignate and Domenico Veneziano – was prolonged at the beginning of the 19th century to reach the borough of Sant'Angelo.

At any rate, the city's magnificence was celebrated not by one, but by two monu-

mental fountains. In fact, besides the Fontana Maggiore, at the foot of the Cathedral, a second fountain, completed in 1281 under the documented authority of such a master as Arnolfo di Cambio, was situated approximately midway along present-day Corso Vannucci. An idea of the monumental complexity of this fountain can be had by consulting the records documenting the craftsmen involved in its construction; other documents list the purchase of various materials used for the fountain itself and the basin.

The monument's splendor was short lived, however: at the beginning of the following century it was demolished for urban expansion. Of this "disappeared" fountain there remain only a few fragments carved in white Carrara marble, namely three reliefs and two sculptures now kept at the prestigious Galleria Nazionale dell'Umbria.

# Mechanically-assisted walkways in Perugia

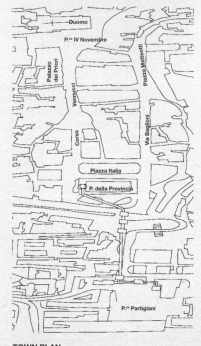

**TOWN PLAN**

In the early 1980s, the municipal authorities in Perugia created a mechanically-assisted walkway to overcome the problem of the town's steep streets and make the historic center more accessible to anyone arriving on foot from the new town below.

This series of covered walks, tunnels and moving stairways — from Piazza Partigiani to Piazza Italia, where it emerges underneath the portico of Palazzo della Provincia — flanks the historic Via del Circo before disappearing under the Rocca Paolina, the fortress built in the mid-16th century by Antonio da Sangallo the Younger for Pope Paul III Farnese. Here the route makes use of the hidden network of streets and squares of the old medieval quarter which Sangallo incorporated into the fortress, along with the Etruscan gateway known as Porta Marzia.

This archaeological journey into the bowels of medieval Perugia has become a part of everyday life in the town: each day some 20,000 people use the escala-

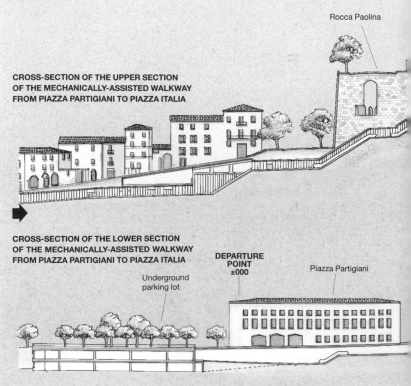

**CROSS-SECTION OF THE UPPER SECTION OF THE MECHANICALLY-ASSISTED WALKWAY FROM PIAZZA PARTIGIANI TO PIAZZA ITALIA**

**CROSS-SECTION OF THE LOWER SECTION OF THE MECHANICALLY-ASSISTED WALKWAY FROM PIAZZA PARTIGIANI TO PIAZZA ITALIA**

tors and tunnels to climb up 50 metres in barely fifteen minutes, and well away from city traffic.

Another similar system, the so-called "Cupa-Morlacchi" walkway created in 1989 in the northern part of the town, has long stretches of open-air moving stairways protected by glazed canopies. Two other routes are planned, one of which will connect the historic center with the expressway approach road and the Fontivegge shopping center.

*Right, the arrival (and departure) point of the moving stairways inside the Rocca Paolina, the fortress built over the 13th-century Baglioni quarter. The street of the same name was one of the main thoroughfares of the medieval town.*

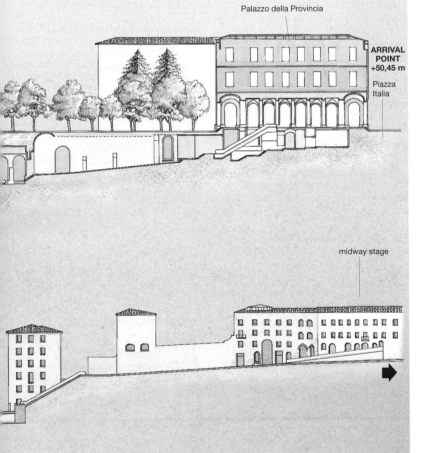

Palazzo della Provincia

**ARRIVAL POINT +50,45 m**

Piazza Italia

midway stage

47

pit from which preached San Bernardino da Siena, the travertine portal by Ippolito Scalza (1568), following a design by Galeazzo Alessi, the bronze statue of Pope Julius III (by Vincenzo Danti, 1555). Similarly unfinished is the bare facade, adorned with an elegant portal by Pietro Carattoli (1729). Its vast and luminous 15th-century interior is patterned after Nordic *Hallenkirchen*, with a tall nave and aisles of equal height, and divided by octagonal piers supporting pointed vaults. The structure, which was restored in the mid-19th century, is enhanced by 18th-century decorations and stuccowork. The decorations, consisting of paintings, frescoes and stained glass windows of different periods (16th to 19th cent.), make for a stylistically varied and harmonious whole. Particularly noteworthy are the *Chapel of San Bernardino* (under the first span of the right aisle); Federico Barocci's *Deposition* (1567-69); the sculpted wood **choir**\* by Giuliano da Maiano and Domenico del Tasso (1491) in the apse, the latter seriously damaged by fire in 1985. The entrance to the 15th-century *sagrestia,* frescoed by Gian Antonio Pandolfi (1573-76), is through the chapel to the right of the presbytery.

Connected with the sacristy are the inspiring **rectory cloisters**, with three superimposed arcades, where conclaves were held for some historic popes, including Celestine V, whom Dante placed at the entrance of Hell because he had abdicated.

**Museo Capitolare**\*. Annexed to the Cathedral, the museum houses art works and liturgical furnishings from the cathedral itself, from other diocesan churches and from private donations. Among the paintings, Luca Signorelli's famous **Virgin enthroned with Child, Saints John the Baptist, Onofrius, Lawrence, Hercolanus, a Musician Angel and a Bishop** (probably the patron) (1484). Particularly noteworthy are also a *Pieta\** by Bartolomeo Caporali (1486) and triptychs by Meo di Guido da Siena and Agnolo Gaddi. Among the sculptures, a *deacon's head\**, attributed to Arnolfo di Cambio. Also on show are illuminated codices (8th-9th cent.) and missals.

**Loggia di Braccio Fortebracci** (II, B2). A continuation of the left side of the Cathedral, the loggia formerly linked Perugia's seignorial residence (1423), which is no longer extant. Below the first vault are still visible the remains of a twelve-sided belfry, toppled in the 14th century, as it was believed that the mythical shield of Homeric legend (according to the tradition of the mythical search for the Palladium) was kept here.

**Museo di Storia Naturale "G. Cicioni,"** founded in the second half of the 19th century by naturalist Monsignor Giulio Cicioni and enlarged with various donations, since 1925 has been housed in the archbishopric. It is presently closed for reordering. Collections include mineralogy, paleontology, botany, and zoology, besides a plant collection with over 18,000 specimens.

**Palazzo dei Priori**\*\* (II, B2). Pride of the Perugia commune, this imposing and magnificent building dominates the area between Piazza IV Novembre and Corso Vannucci. The city's ancient administrative

## Perugia: Palazzo dei Priori

**PLAN**

1 Sala dei Notari    4 Collegio della Mercanzia
2 Portale Maggiore   5 Old Priori Chapel
3 Arco dei Priori    6 Collegio del Cambio

*The facade of Palazzo dei Priori*

seat presently houses the Town Hall and the Galleria Nazionale dell'Umbria. Its phase-by-phase construction (from 1293-97 to 1443), and its superimposition upon earlier structures, explain its irregular layout and asymmetrical facade. The structure's original body corresponds to the three windows overlooking the left side of the square and to the first ten overlooking Corso Vannucci, and was last broadened at the junction of Corso Vannucci and Via dei Priori.

The steps which fan out onto the square (1902) lead to a large portal surmounted by heavy consoles bearing copies of griffins and lions (the originals are inside the palace), and then into the austere **Sala dei Notari\*** (1582), with transversal arched ceiling and frescoes dating from the last decade of the 13th century. Here, of particular interest are the wooden stalls along the entrance wall and the 16th-century seats along the other walls (open 9am-1pm, 3pm-7pm; closed Mon and when concerts or other cultural events are held). On the side facing *Corso Vannucci* open out the handsome **portale\* maggiore** (1346), bearing an intricate allegorical decoration (the lunette contains portraits of *Sts. Lawrence, Hercolanus, and Constance*) and,

on the second floor, 19 superb Gothic **three-light windows\***. From the Gothic atrium a boldly pilastered staircase leads to the upper floor, where, in the communal council hall, are displayed the Perugia **griffin\*** and the Guelf **lion\***, the first Italian medieval example of large one-piece castings (ca. 1274), perhaps parts of a former fountain by Arnolfo di Cambio.

**Galleria Nazionale dell'Umbria\*\***. Developed out of the original nucleus of the Accademia del Disegno (second half 16th cent.), the national gallery was significantly expanded between the late 18th and early 19th centuries, when its collection of paintings was still housed in the Olivetan convent. In 1878, the art gallery was separated from the academy and transferred to the third floor of the Palazzo dei Priori (open 8.30am-7.30pm; closed first Mon of month). This important art collection, the most complete in the entire region, is ordered chronologically and di-

*Polyptych of San Domenico, by Fra Angelico (Galleria Nazionale dell'Umbria)*

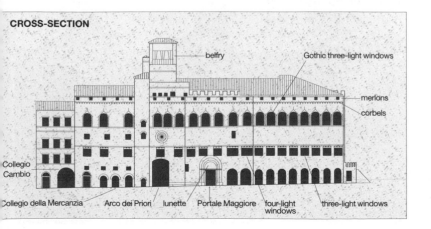

**CROSS-SECTION**

belfry     Gothic three-light windows

merlons

corbels

Collegio Cambio

Collegio della Mercanzia    Arco dei Priori    lunette    Portale Maggiore    four-light windows    three-light windows

vided by school, with works by artists active in this area from the 13th to the 19th centuries. Once the art gallery has been totally remodeled it will feature larger display areas, and will also occupy the lower floor. The new display areas will also include descriptive visual aids.

The visit to the gallery begins with 13th-century sculptures, which also comprise **five works**\*\* by Arnolfo di Cambio (1278-81) for a public fountain which is no longer extant. Pre-Giotto Umbrian painting has as its main representative the Maestro di San Francesco (**Cross**\*\*, 1272). Similarly important is Vigoroso da Siena's *dossale*\* (dossal, or altar ornament, 1291). Among the 14th-century works is a **Virgin with Child**\*\* by Duccio di Buoninsegna, and the **Montelabate polyptych**\*, by Meo da Siena, ca. 1317. Representative of the influence of Giotto in Assisi are an altarpiece by Marino da Perugia, Giovanni da Bonino's stained glass window (*Crucifixion*), and the statues of *Perugia's Patron Saints*\*, attributed to Ambrogio Maitani; and, among others, works by Mello da Gubbio and the Maestro della Dormitio of Terni (**Virgin and Child with Angels**). On display are many works by Sienese artists, such as Luca di Tommè (*Forsivo Polyptych*). International Gothic reached Perugia in the early 15th century: **Virgin and Child with Angels**\*\* by Gentile da Fabriano, the **Pietralunga polyptych**\* by Ottaviano Nelli (1404); showing early orientation toward new tendencies is Lello da Velletri, as may be seen in his *Virgin and Child with Saints*\*. The gallery's more significant Florentine Renaissance works include Fra Angelico's **San Domenico polytych**\*\* and Piero della Francesca's **Sant'Antonio polyptych**\*\*. One of Perugia's most important Renaissance works is the **Cappella dei Priori**\*\*, the chapel frescoed by Benedetto Bonfigli between 1454 and 1480. There are also numerous paintings by Bartolomeo Caporali and Fiorenzo di Lorenzo, exponents of Perugia's Renaissance school of painting. Particular relief is given to the works by Pietro Perugino, among which the **tavoletta**\* (1473), a part of the so-called niche of *San Bernardino*, and the **Sant'Agostino polyptych**\*\*, a masterpiece of the artist's maturity. One of his disciples, Pinturicchio, is present with such works as the imposing the **Santa Maria dei Fossi altarpiece**\*\* (1495-96). The Cinquecento is represented by local artists such as Domenico and Orazio Alfani, Raffaellino del Colle, and by the Florentine Giovanbattista Naldini. Similarly on display are such Seicento masters as Ventura Salimbeni, Orazio Gentileschi, Valentin de Boulogne, Pietro da Cortona. Representing the 18th century are works by Sebastiano Conca and Pierre Subleyras.

**Collegio della Mercanzia**\* (II, B2). It is not difficult to imagine, in the place of the numerous shops and bars along *Corso Vannucci*, the medieval workshops and warehouses which once lined this street. And this is how the ground floor of the *Palazzo dei Priori* must have looked, when in 1390 the *Mercanzia*, one of the city's most important trade guilds, was assigned the area to the right of the main portal. Inside, the rectangular **Sala delle Udienze** features precious pine and walnut *wood paneling*, carved by 15th-century woodcarvers from outside Italy.

*Frescoes by Perugino at the Collegio del Cambio*

**Collegio del Cambio\*** (II, B2). Next to the *Mercanzia* was located the seat of the just as powerful money-changers' guild (the *cambiatori*), built between 1452 and 1457 alongside the *Palazzo dei Priori*. Through a fine wood-carved portal (1501) you enter the *Sala dei Legisti*, with its inlaid counters by Giampietro Zuccari and assistants (1615-21). To the right, you enter the **Sala dell'Udienza del Cambio**, a vital testament to Italian Renaissance art. The rich wood counters inlaid by the Florentine Domenico del Tasso (1492-93) provide a backdrop to Perugino's **frescoes\*\*** (1498-1500) decorating the walls and the pointed vaults.

**Corso Vannucci\*** (II, B-C2). The city's busiest and most elegant street, meeting place, strolling and shopping venue, clearly evinces the Etrusco-Roman *cardo* (the Roman north-south axis). In medieval times, together with the square – the *Platea Comunis* – it was the vital core of town life. Opposite the Palazzo dei Priori, on the corner of Via Calderini, rises the **Palazzo del Collegio dei Notari** (1446), which was severely affected in 1591 by the opening of *Via Calderini*. Next to it rises the *Palazzo della Sapienza Vecchia* (1363). The medieval "piazza grande," bordered what is now *Piazza della Repubblica* (II, C2), which is faced by the former church of *Sant'Isidoro* (left) and by the *Teatro del Pavone* (right). Along the following stretch of the corso is one of the very best examples of 18th-century private home, **Palazzo Donini**, built on a Roman cistern.

**Piazza Italia** (II, C2). In the wake of post-Unification fervor, the area where once stood the *Rocca Paolina* was turned into a verdant square dominated by the monument to Victor Emmanuel II (Giulio Tadolini, 1890). Along its perimeter are buildings of various architectural styles, reflecting the middle-class tastes of the time: the 18th-century *Palazzo Antinori* (now the Hotel La Rosetta); *Palazzo Cesaroni* (1897); *Palazzo della Banca d'Italia* (1871); *Hotel Brufani* (1882-83); *Condominio Calderini* (1872). In the background, the imposing **Palazzo della Provincia** (by Alessandro Arienti, 1870).

The *Giardini Carducci*, a fine set of gardens lying behind the *Palazzo della Provincia*, offer a splendid *panorama\** of the city, of the Tiber valley and of the Valle Umbra. On Sunday mornings, these gardens come alive as they are the venue of an open-air modern-and-antique art market.

**Rocca Paolina.** In *Viale Indipendenza* (II, D1-2) and in *Via Marzia* (II, C-D2) you can still see the remains of the supporting ramparts of the *Rocca*, the imposing fortress demolished in 1860 after the city's annexation to the Kingdom of Italy. It was constructed at the behest of Paul III Farnese in 1540, after the Salt War and Perugia's incorporation within the papal state, to affirm the Church's dominion over the city.

**Porta Marzia\*** (II, D2). Gateway to the Etruscan perimeter (second half of the 3rd cent. BC), it was later encased within the east bastion of the fortress to decorate one of its entrances. Of the original gateway there remain only its semicircular arch and its crown. At the sides of the arch, two Corinthian pilasters support a capital, consisting of a loggia-like structure similarly resting on small Corinthian pilasters, amid which jet out the busts of three male figures (Jupiter, and Castor and Pollux), and, at the ends, two half-bust equine figures.

**The "buried city."** Porta Marzia affords access to the unusual subterranean **Via Bagliona\***, which penetrates the Rocca's underground structures amid the remains of the medieval quarter. Here can still be made out the ancient dwelling structures and street layout, the warehouses, the courtyards and the small squares, upon which a few windows can still be seen. Amid the tower-houses that once dominated the city from the Landone hill emerge the 13th-century *Casa di Gentile Baglioni* with its tower still intact, and the *block of houses belonging to Ridolfo and Braccio Baglioni.*

**Santa Giuliana** (I, E3). Continuing southward along Via Masi and Via Orsini, at the rear of the gardens in Piazza Partigiani (escalator from Piazza Italia), you come to the Cistercian church (1253), with its marble-clad 14th-century facade and geometric design typical of Perugia's churches.

**Santo Spirito and Porta Crucia** (II, D1). Gardens and terraced houses frame the church of the Holy Spirit, built in 1689 on a design by Francesco Vezzosi. Behind the rough facade, its interior features decorations by Pietro Carattoli and 18th-century paintings. From Santo Spirito a stairway leads to *Porta Crucia* (rebuilt in 1576), beneath which passed the "fish route," namely, the one used by the Trasimeno fishermen to reach the fish market in the Sopramuro area.

**San Prospero** (I, D2). Outside Porta Crucia, heading down *Via San Prospero*, you come to a very ancient church built around the 7th-8th centuries on an Etrusco-Roman burial area, as witnessed by the blocks of Etruscan stone encased in the outer walls. Inside the church (closed), with its low lateral arcades, the chapel on the right features frescoes by Bonamico (1225). The **ciborium** is believed to be from the 8th century.

**Arco della Mandorla\*** (II, C-D1). Also called *Porta Eburnea*, the archway was founded in Etruscan times, but remodeled during the Middle Ages, as can be seen by its ogival structure. Its upper stone blocks preserve traces of the original semicircular arch.

**Via della Cupa** (II, C1). It winds along the edge of a ridge which has always constituted a natural limit to urban expansion. The street, in fact, runs along the massive travertine Etruscan walls, upon which the medieval perimeter, thus showing the close link between the city's urban layout was superimposed, and the shape of the terrain that confers a deep recess to the walls themselves. At the base of this curvature, a *posterula* (a small rear door) offers passage only to pedestrians. From here, you have a good view of large sections of the modern parts of the city. To the right, in the old town area, almost encased in the Etruscan walls, the church of *San Benedetto* (its interior has 14th-15th cent. mural paintings) can readily be made out because of its unusual white-stone projecting apse. The following stretch of Via Cupa is taken up, on the left, by the **Collegio della Sapienza Vecchia**, today the Onaosi boarding school for girls, which in the 14th century was a model private boarding university, like those in Switzerland. Inside, still to be admired is a *Crucifixion* scene by a painter of the Giotto school, and a 14th-century *Annunciation*.

**Via dei Priori\*** (II, B1-2). This steep street descends from *Arco dei Priori*, beneath the Town Hall tower. The compact row of dwellings and religious complexes facing onto this thoroughfare is intersected here and there by very narrow, steeply stepped, winding streets, representing the most typical characteristic of the old city. To the left, the 14th-century church of *Santi Severo e Agata* (1290-1314), with its elegant Gothic-Romanesque portal and, inside, 14th-century fresco fragments.

On the opposite side, *Via Ritorta* cuts past houses with gabled-fronts and outside staircases.

Further on, the church of **San Filippo Neri\*** is the city's largest Baroque structure, with its facade by Vignola (1647-63) preceded by a double flight of stairs. Its aisleless interior, with side chapels, is richly decorated with frescoes by various artists active between the 17th and 18th centuries. Note above the main altar Pietro da Cortona's (1662) *Immaculate Conception*. After *Piazzetta degli Oddi* notice the **Torre degli Sciri\*** (II, B1), the only tower to have remained intact (with its 46 meters of smooth stone) among the many spires which in the Middle Ages towered over the city, symbolizing the power and wealth of the city's leading families.

Along the lateral Via degli Sciri stands the **Oratorio di San Francesco**, which is accessed via a 16th-century portal. The oratory houses valuable 16th-century wood artifacts, among which a carved and gilded coffered ceiling, and large paintings by Giovanni Antonio Scaramuccia featuring an important pictorial cycle on Christological themes.

**Piazzetta della Madonna della Luce\*** (II, A-B1). Via dei Priori bends right to disclose one of Perugia's most beautiful perspectives. Two 16th-century churches face one another on different levels: the church of the *Madonna della Luce* (1513-19) presents a travertine Renaissance facade, and its interior, with its vault frescoed by G.B. Caporali, a Baroque frame enclosing a fresco by Tiberio d'Assisi. To the right stands the church of *San Luca* (1586), designed by Bino Sozi for the Knights of Malta, whose palace (14th cent.) was located close by.

**Arco di San Luca**. To the right of the church of the *Madonna della Luce*, the Etruscan *Porta Trasimena*, of which remain only the supporting columns, is presently an ogival arch (14th cent.) beneath which passes the steep *Via del Piscinello*.

**Piazza San Francesco\*** (I, B-C2). At sunset the soft pink hues of the masonry enhance the appeal of this broad and luminous square at the end of Via dei Priori, which is overlooked by the statues of Sts. Francis and Bernardine. The friars minor installed themselves in the square around 1230, where they built the aisleless church of **San Francesco al Prato**, now in ruins and roofless after the collapse of its vaults. The unconsecrated church is accessible only for special events. The facade was restored in 1926, using local white and pink stone.

**The "Pietro Vannucci" Fine Arts Academy** was founded in 1573 by Orazio Alfani and Bino Sozi, and since 1901 it has been housed in the Franciscan convent. The museum section offers an impressive stuccowork collection (1st floor) with over 360 pieces, from the VI century BC to the 19th century; paintings by local artists active between the 16th and 20th centuries; a room of drawings and engravings dating from the 16th to the 20th century (9,000 drawings and over 5,000 prints). It is temporarily closed as a consequence of the 1997 earthquake.

Oratorio di San Bernardino** (I, C2). A Renaissance masterpiece, the oratory was built in 1452 in honor of St. Bernadine to the left of the church of San Francesco al Prato. Its facade, built by Agostino di Duccio (1457-61), has striking decorative work and delicate polychromy.

La Conca. From San Francesco, Via Pascoli runs along an area once occupied by the city's medieval craftsmen's quarter (especially by dyers, given the area's abundance of water) embedded in the depression (*conca*) bordering the Etruscan walls. In the 1960s, university buildings were erected on the garden site; in one of them (Via Sant'Elisabetta) is a fine white and black-tesserae *Roman mosaic* (2nd cent.) representing *Orpheus and the wild beasts*, which can also be admired from one of the windows facing onto the street.

A short detour along Via dell'Eremita (right of Via Pascoli) takes us to the 15th-century church of **Santi Sebastiano e Rocco**, also called *Madonna della Pace* because of a "miraculous" image on the main altar.

Via pensile (II, A2). This is the name by which *Via Battisti* is known. Built in 1901 and completely upsetting the area's preceding medieval layout, it skirts a rather long stretch of the Etruscan walls (3rd cent. BC), which are hidden by the street's ascending structure. Its travertine blocks are arranged in ordered rows without the use of mortar, and the street itself looks on-

to the northeast side of the city, from where the entire curvature of the walls from Verzaro (to the left) to Monteripido (to the right) can be taken in.

Archaeological area (II, B2). Located beneath the street level of *Piazza Cavallotti*, it conserves the remains of a paved Roman road, along which are still visible the furrows made by cart wheels, and of a semicircular fountain of the II century AD. Visits may be arranged through the Soprintendenza Archeologica.

Via Maestà delle Volte* (II, B2). Passing beneath this street's imposing archways, one returns to the main square, which contains a "period" fountain by Pietro Angelini (1927). This street, which winds along one of the city's most charming sections, once

*Lunette of the Oratorio di San Bernardino*

featured a *Maestà* painted beneath a supporting vault of the Palazzo del Podestà, the remains of which are still visible in its terminal section. The **Oratorio della Maestà delle Volte** was built in 1335 to protect the fresco, and was rebuilt in 1576 by Bino Sozi after having been destroyed by fire.

## *The northern boroughs*

Piazza Danti, on the right side of the Cathedral, leads northward beyond the Etruscan walls to the area of the city's expansion in medieval times. It is here, in fact, that the lower-class boroughs sprang up along the main thoroughfares, and which, between the 13th and 14th cent., filled with people coming from the countryside. Examples of such agglomerates are the boroughs of Porta Sant'Angelo, Porta Sant'Antonio and Fonte Nuovo. Although they have all been absorbed within the city walls, they nevertheless maintained their "low-class" dimension in contrast with the "upper" noble part of the city. Going down Via Rocchi, flanked by tall medieval boundary walls, you leave the ancient-wall perimeter passing under the Etruscan arch, which brings to Piazza Fortebraccio. From here, you continue along Corso Garibaldi, the central axis of the Porta Sant'Angelo borough, which rises to the temple of San Michele Archangelo, marking the boundary of the city's medieval expansion. Outside the walls is located the Monte Ripido convent, an important Franciscan institution. Retracing our steps along the corso, Via Benedetta and Via del Fagiano take us down the borough's western side. At the corner of Via Fabretti, a short detour to the right and we reach the University square (Piazza dell'Università) and the Olivetan complex. Scenic Via dell'Acquedotto and Via Appia take us back to the "upper" city. Once again in Piazza Danti, we can now approach the second part of our itinerary, which goes up to the Colle del Sole, the loftiest spot in the city's historic center. From Piazza Michelotti, to the hill's summit, Via dell'Aquila and Via Cesari lead to Piazza Piccinino, from where Via Bontempi descends toward the Etruscan perimeter. And from here, where Via del Roscetto ends, begins Corso Bersaglieri, the main axis of the narrow Sant'Antonio borough. Outside the walled perimeter, 20th-century Via Cialdini links the medieval city to the Santa Maria di Monteluce monastic complex, which was once outside the city walls. The final leg of our visit takes us all the way from the monastery, along Via del Giochetto and Via Dal Pozzo (axis of the modest Fonte Nuovo borough), to the church of San Bevignate. Via Dal Pozzo itself, in its opposite direction, takes us back to the historic center, before which however we again cross the city's medieval perimeter along Via dell'Asilo. At the beginning of this street once stood Porta San Simone del Carmine, destroyed in 1818 to make room for Via XIV Settembre.

**Piazza della Paglia** (II, B2). This was the medieval name for *Piazza Danti*, when oats and bread were sold here. Archaeological finds unearthed along the square's northern boundary point to similar trade activities even in Roman times. Thus, it is no wonder that, today, in the irregular area which took shape along the Cathedral's right side between the 14th and 16th century, every Thursday and Saturday morning the medieval Deruta-Ripabianca ceramics market is again held.

**Pozzo Etrusco**. At Piazza Danti 18 is located the entrance to this well, also called *Sorbello* because it is situated in the subterranean part of the Palazzo Bourbon-Sorbello (p. 56), once the Etruscan city's main water source. Dug in the vicinity around the second half of the 3rd cent. B.C., the well reaches a depth of approximately 36 meters from the present-day street level, with a 5.60 meter diameter and a capacity of 430,000 liters.

**Arco Etrusco\*** (II, A2). Also called *of Augustus*, the Etruscan arch was erected in the 3rd century AD, at the end of the Etruscan city's north-south axis (present-day Via Rocchi) as a main gateway through the walled perimeter, affording access to the extra-urban roads leading north. Practically intact, the arch features sturdy trapezoidal towers that protect the entranceway, and which are embedded in the colossal city walls.

**Piazza Fortebraccio** (II, A2). The natives continue to call it Piazza Grimana, after Cardinal Marino Grimani who had it built in 1536, thus filling the saddled depression which separated the walled city from the adjacent Sant'Angelo borough. On this vast and congested area stands the 18th-century *Palazzo Gallenga Stuart*, which today houses Perugia's Italian University for Foreigners (*Università italiana per stranieri*).

**Corso Garibaldi** (I, A-B3). Between rows of medieval houses and short narrow side streets intersecting in a spoke-like pattern, the corso, Borgo Sant'Angelo's former main street, winds in a northwesterly direction. The lower borough comprises the medieval churches and convents around which were to develop its populous lower-class quarter.

**Sant'Agostino** (I, B3-4). Located in Piazza Lupattelli, this church – built in 1256-60 and completely remodeled in the 18th century – used to be one of the city's major monastic complexes. The lower part of its facade is clad in pink and white marble (unusual for Perugia), whereas its upper section is in bare brick. The nearby **Oratorio della Confraternita** consists of two superimposed churches, the oldest dating from the 14th century (and featuring prized frescoes fragments of the same period); the other, which conserves superb examples of Baroque decorations and furnishings, dates from the second half of the 16th century.

**Other buildings along the corso**. The compact urban layout along this main artery, with its marked popular features, is graced with sundry architectural and decorative elements, porticoes, arches and external stairways clearly illustrating how tastes and styles evolved over the centuries. Used until recently as a hospice for the indigent, the former *Ospedale del Collegio della Mercanzia* (no. 84), with its 13th-century structure and 1507 restructuring, is architecturally offset by a 14th-century *casa* at no. 135 of the same street, boasting a stone slab facade and arched windows. Of yet another style are the church and monastery of *Santa Caterina*, restructured by Galeazzo Alessi in 1547. Tradition has it that, in 1220, St. Francis and St. Dominic met in the **Monastero della Beata Colomba** – the Dove clearly recognizable in the terracotta medallion over the portal. Branching off in Via Sant'Agnese, we come to the monastery of the same name (open 9am-11am, 3.30pm-5pm, ring for admittance). Founded in the 14th century, its small chapel conserves a *fresco\** by Perugino (1522).

**Sant'Angelo\*** (I, A3). Locally called "Orlando's Pavilion," it is one of Italy's oldest early Christian churches (5th-6th cent.). Backed against the urban walls, and surrounded by cypress trees upon a promontory facing the old city, it conferred a sacred character to this suburban area through which passed the major thoroughfare leading to Tuscany. The circular plan, with its elevated central area covered with a retractile roof, is internally supported by 16 ancient columns, the shafts of which differ in height and materials, and topped by Roman capitals.

**Porta Sant'Angelo** (I, A3). A close look at the wall texture of this gateway, located at the end of the corso, composed of a combination of sandstone,

limestone, and bricks, shows how many modifications this structure had undergone since 1326.

It was along the steep brick-paved upgrade leading to the convent of **San Francesco del Monte**, or *Monte Ripido* (I, A2) as it is also known, that the Via Crucis procession took place, of which remain eleven terracotta chapel stations (1633-36). Today, the effort of the ascent is rewarded by a broad view of the "star-shaped" city and of the imposing fortified Franciscan convent (1290), which in the 14th century became the seat of the order's general "Studium" (seat of learning).
Although the books themselves have been lost, the structure houses a handsome 18th-century library, with original furnishings and prized wood ceiling.

**Via Benedetta** (I, A-B3). As a result of the "spoke-like" structure of medieval boroughs, Corso Garibaldi is linked by a series of narrow streets to parallel Via Benedetta, along which rises the unusual orientalizing belfry of the former San Benedetto monastery (18th cent.). Next, with its many panoramic vistas, *Via del Fagiano*, once known as Via dei Condotti having been built upon the axis of the medieval aqueduct, eventually leads to the Piazza Maggiore.

The so-called **Monte Morcino Nuovo** church (I, B3), in Piazza dell'Università, designed in 1740 by Luigi Vanvitelli, is flanked by the *Olivetan monastery*, built by Vanvitelli himself with Carlo Murena. In 1811 the convent was ceded to the Università degli Studi.

**Via dell'Acquedotto** (I, B-C3). Via del Fagiano continues along its picturesque suspended course, built in 1812 when parapets were constructed over the archways of the medieval aqueduct. The aqueduct itself was built in 1254-76 by Fra Bevignate to convey water to the city from Mt. Pacciano.

*Panorama of Perugia, with the church of Sant'Angelo, Porta Sant'Angelo, and Monte Ripido*

**Colle del Sole**. Tradition has it that the Etruscans selected to erect their citadel (*arce*) atop this hill. On the most elevated spot of the hill opens *Piazza Michelotti* (II, A2-3), formerly *Monte di Porta Sole*, which can easily be reached from Piazza Danti along Via del Sole. Adjacent **Piazza Rossi Scotti**, commonly called *Porta Sole*, is supported by an ample arched enclosure wall (1374), from which is afforded a truly unique view* of the Sant'Angelo borough and the city walls. On the edge of the panoramic terrace, the church of *Sant'Angelo della Pace* (1540) faces the 17th-century *Palazzo Conestabile della Staffa*, adorned with frescoes by Giovanni Andrea Carlone and Felice Giani, and now the seat of the *Biblioteca Comunale Augusta*.

**San Severo** (II, A-B3). Legend has it that in the Sole quarter there rose a temple dedicated to a pagan deity. The sacred site, as indicated by tradition, was occupied in the 11th century by a Christian church (remains), next to which was erected in 1758 the church of *San Severo*. The upper part of the adjacent 15th-century chapel features a **fresco*** by Raphael, the lower part one by Perugino (1521).

**Piazza Piccinino** (II, B2). This is one of the three main public squares around which life gravitated in medieval times. It was broadened in the second half of the 16th century, and in 1575, on the east side of the square, was erected the church of the *Compagnia della Morte*. The Renaissance travertine well rim reveals the presence of an underlying Etruscan well. Next to it stands the 17th-century *Palazzo Bourbon-Sorbello*.

**Via Bontempi** (II, B3). Lined with aristocratic houses, this street runs along the same ancient road axis which terminates at the *Arco dei Gigli* or *Porta Sole*.

**Santa Maria Nuova** (II, A3). The church, which rises in Via del Roscetto, provided the impetus of the city's expansion in medieval times beyond the Arco dei Gigli. Dating as far back as 1285, it was rebuilt in 1376 after a fire. Its belfry (1644) is probably by Galeazzo Alessi. Inside, note the wooden *choir**, carved in 1456, and a *gonfalon* by Benedetto Bonfigli, 1472 (second altar on the right).

**Corso Bersaglieri** (I, B4-5). This thoroughfare is accessed through a rustic bare-sandstone gate, namely the 13th-century **Arco dei Tei.** The corso, the main street in the popular borough of Sant'Antonio, branches off into short narrow streets and is characterized by small dwellings interspersed with churches, the last of which is the church of Sant'Antonio Abate (13th cent.), remodeled in the 14th century and later in 1669. At the extremity of the corso stands *Porta Sant'Antonio* (1374), a gate which affords a splendid view of the city. Not far, recent diggings have uncovered the Etruscan tomb known as *Tomba dei Cai Cutu* (4th-3rd cent. BC), which is not open to the public.

**Santa Maria di Monteluce** (I, B5). *Via Cialdini*, a short street lined with medieval shops, leads to Piazza Monteluce, which in 1219 was the site of a nunnery devoted to St. Clare. In 1927 it was converted into a public hospital. The various colors of its facade tell of the successive phases of construction.

**San Bevignate** (I, B-C5, off map). Its massive and unadorned structure mirrors the "military" spirit of the Templar Order, which dedicated this church to Perugia's "mystery saint," a local hermit whose existence is not certain. Built in an isolated position in two successive phases (1256-85 and 1312), it has a single-apsed interior entirely covered with its original decorations featuring a 13th- and 14th-century **fresco cycle*** by local artists.

**San Fiorenzo** (II, B3). The church was perhaps built in the 8th century along the border between the aristocratic Perugia of Via Alessi and one of the city's popular boroughs, along the external edge of the Etruscan perimeter, and completely remodeled in 1768-70.

### *The medieval borough*

The itinerary begins from Piazza Matteotti which, linking the Piazza Maggiore and the corso, constitutes the city's most cen-

### A successful kiss

Let us try and imagine a huge jumbo jet parked inside Osaka airport, and all around a crowd of Japanese busy snapping pictures of that strange aircraft. The reason for their curiosity is

*The early Perugina chocolate factory*

and, above all, Francesco Buitoni, heir to a family of pasta makers from Sansepolcro, who transformed a small chocolate factory into a major manufacturing concern. In 1922, the company launched its famous

readily explained. That blue and silver painted airplane, with thousands of small stars dotting its wings and cockpit, immediately calls to mind one of Perugia's hallmark products: the Bacio Perugina, a chocolate with a hazelnut center, wrapped in starred silver paper. The jumbo jet idea was a publicity ploy, a good example of the dynamism of a firm which accounts for a significant part of the city's productive spirit. The Perugina company, in fact, is now over ninety years old. Francesco Andreani

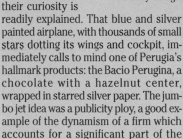

*The Perugina jumbo in Osaka, Japan*

Bacio Perugina, and between the wars expanded rapidly to become a leader in the sector of chocolate and sweets production. However, it is not only through the quality of its products that Perugina has obtained such popularity, but also through its well-orchestrated publicity campaigns. The company sponsored one of Italy's first successful radio broadcast serials, and each Bacio contains a little dose of home philosophy (like a fortune cookie); another particularly fortunate campaign launched in the 1930s involved collectors' cards. The character of the *Feroce Saladino* (Fierce Saladin), conceived by Angelo Bioletto, was the most sought-after card in the series, and thousands of collectors went to no limits in order to add one of these cards to their collections.

tral public area. From the eastern edge of the Etruscan city, we move along its perimeter tracing the line of the walls which remain interred beneath Piazza Matteotti and Via Oberdan. From here, along Via Sant'Ercolano, the course takes out of the upper city and into the borough of Porta San Pietro, the southern arm of the historic center. The elongated and wall-girded quarter developed in two distinct phases: the first expansion, linked to the church of San Domenico, is delimited by the 13th- and 14th-century walls and abuts upon Porta San Pietro. Starting outside the gateway, a later 14th-15th-century wall structure encloses Borgo XX Giugno, and ends at the basilica of San Pietro, a central hub in the city's historic layout flanked by Porta San Costanzo.

**The Sopramuro** (II, B-C2). One of the infinite inventions of medieval urban planning, the *sopramuro* structure is capable of adapting whatever natural structure to its own needs. The oblong *Piazza Matteotti* was erected upon the supporting wall structure beneath the hillside, and for this reason was once called *Piazza del Sopramuro*. In medieval times it was here that the basic "service" activities were held and located: the slaughterhouse, the "fishery" (later demolished to make room for the post office building, 1911), the public grain houses, lard processing, and tanning facilities. The latter involved the use of the covered niches located in the walls' foundations, which today house the elevators to the parking lot below. The square dominated the "battle field" where the public games were held, including the famous "stone war," consisting in a violent stone fight between teams from various city quarters. The importance of this square in the city's medieval layout is attested to by the pavement (1250), made up of quality bricks from Città della Pieve, which the rebel community was obliged to furnish free as a token of submission to the dominant city.

**Palazzo del Capitano del Popolo**\* (II, B2). From its portico resting on richly decorated consoles, the heralds would read official edicts and ordinances. Today, in remembrance of those public proclamations, the palace shares with that of the old university its destination as a court of law. An elegant Renaissance structure erected in 1473-81, it features a fine portal surmounted by two *Perugian griffins* and, in its lunette, a statue portraying *Justice*.

**Palazzo dell'Università Vecchia** (II, B-C2). Pope Sixtus IV decided to build the university's upper part (1483-1515), with its cross-shaped windows, following Fiorenzo di Lorenzo's design, as the seat of the city's "Studium," and here it remained until 1811. In the palace, which today houses the judiciary offices, have been brought to light the primitive archways upon which the square itself rested.

*View of Perugia, with San Domenico in the foreground*

An arcade leads to the 14th-century loggia, formerly the seat of the Wool Guild, and to the covered market terrace (1932), from where may be admired the massive supporting archways (over 15 meters tall) and a splendid view of Mt. Subasio with Assisi and the Valle Umbra.

**Chiesa del Gesù** (II, B2). This is one of the most popular places of worship in the city of Perugia. Built in 1571 (its facade, however, dates to 1934), it completes the east side of Piazza Matteotti and conserves in its interior, which was damaged by fire in 1989, frescoes by Giovanni Andrea Carlone. Beneath the church are three tower-like superimposed chapels: the oratory of the *Congregation of the Nobles* (1596); of the *Congregation of the Artists* (1603); of the *Congregation of the Sharecroppers* (1603), with frescoes from the 17th and 18th centuries.

Before leaving the square visitors are recommended to walk down **Via Volte della Pace**, at the end of Piazza Matteotti. The street is made up of a long and picturesque 14th-century gothic portico, where, as tradition has it, peace treaties between Perugia and nearby townships were concluded.

**Via Oberdan** (II, C2). A fine commercial thoroughfare in medieval times along the Etruscan wall (see remains), connecting the city center with the departure points for Rome and Florence, in the 14th century it was mostly the property of the hospital of Santa Maria della Misericordia (note the initials DME inscribed on the houses) and of the Monte di Pietà, founded in 1492. At number 54, the 14th-century former church of **Santa Maria della Misericordia**, restored for civic use, features two frescoed Madonnas on the facade (one by G.B. Caporali) and, on the upper floors, traces of the early hospital structure.

**Sant'Ercolano** (II, C-D2). The church is reached by proceeding along the street by the same name, passing under *Porta Cornea*, or as it is otherwise known, *Arco di Sant'Ercolano* (II, C2), a medieval reworking of an Etruscan gate. Backed against the ancient walls, this massive octagonal church was erected by the commune starting in 1297, on the presumed site of the saint's martyrdom. Originally built as a two-story church and mausoleum, and bounded by tall closed in and gently pointed arcades, its upper floor was demolished to make way for the Rocca Paolina. A double flight of steps dating from 1607 lead up to the church's original Gothic portal, beyond which the interior, with stuccowork decorations by Jean Regnaud and paintings by Carlone, is marked by its main altar resting on a 3rd-century Roman sarcophagus.

**Corso Cavour** (I, D-E4). The street is what remains of the ancient "royal road" to Rome; in the side street Via Podiani, stands the 16th-century **Palazzo della Penna**, built on the remains of a clearly identifiable Roman amphitheater. The building temporarily houses the *Dottori-Beuys Collection,* including works by Gerardo Dottori and six works by Joseph Beuys (1921-86), which belong to the municipality and will eventually be transferred to the Museo d'Arte Contemporanea e Moderna.

**Crocevia dei Tre Archi** (II, D2). On the site where this junction was built in the 19th century to ease the traffic flow in the city center, three arches (1821) were similarly erected, constituting the new Porta Santa Croce. The project entailed the demolition of part of the 13th-century church of *Santa Croce*, containing two 15th-cent. frescoes.

**San Domenico\*** (II, D3). Within the ambit of the city's 13th-century religious and political geography, the Dominicans acquired a significant location next to the since-demolished church of Santo Stefano del Castellare, formerly a gathering point for the city's ruling class. In this small square, now dedicated to Giordano Bruno (the Dominican who, accused of heresy, was burned at the stake), was built an initial church (1231-60), the remains of which are still visible in the cloister of the adjacent convent (today the Museo Archeologico Nazionale). In 1304, work began on the imposing Gothic basilica, completely restructured by Carlo Maderno (1632) after the collapse of its arched aisles. Its striking unclad facade is relieved by the portal (1596). Inside, the plainness of the nave and aisles is offset by the large Gothic stained glass window\* in the apse (1411), which, 23 meters tall, together with that in Milan Cathedral, is the largest of that period. The 4th chapel in the right aisle was decorated by Agostino di Duccio (1459); in the right transept stands the **monument to Benedict XI\***, who died in Perugia in 1304; in the apse is the wood choir\* of 1476; in the 5th chapel to the left are two frescoes probably by Benedetto di Bindo, and in the 3rd a *gonfalon* by Giannicola di Paolo (1494).

**Museo Archeologico Nazionale dell'Umbria** (II, D3). Relocated in 1948 to the Dominican convent complex, accessible from the left of the church, the museum is divided into two sections: Etrusco-Roman and prehistoric, which originally were housed respectively in the Palazzo dei Priori and the Palazzo

*The so-called Cippo di Perugia in the Museo Archeologico Nazionale*

Donini. The Etrusco-Roman section represents the museum's first nucleus, which was put together thanks to a donation (1790) by the local patrician Francesco Filippo Friggeri of his antiques collection, and subsequently enriched with material from archaeological digs in the area and from other donations. In 1921, the Bellucci Collection, comprising prehistoric and palaeontological material, and subsequently enhanced by finds from Umberto Calzoni's dig in Cetona (Siena), was donated to the city. The museum is open to the public 8.30am-7.30pm; it is closed on Mondays.

The *Etrusco-Roman section*, contains Villanovian material (9th-8th cent. BC) and black-and-red figure Attic ceramics. Particularly noteworthy is a *krater* from the Volterra works (from the Volumni hypogeum) by the Painter of Hesione. Of great interest is the **Cippo di Perugia\*** (3rd-2nd cent. B.C.), a stone with one of the longest Etruscan texts to have survived, sealing a property contract between two families. In a room is the suggestive recontruction of the Etruscan tomb of the Cai Cutu family, which was discovered in 1983. Among the material from Roman times, noteworthy is a *bronze statue of the emperor Germanicus\**, in triumphal attitude.

The *prehistoric section* is organized according to the places where finds were discovered, and to chronological-cultural criteria. The newly exhibited collection of amulets – donated by Giuseppe Bellucci – testify to the use of these objects up to the 19th and 20th centuries.

**The "Due Porte" San Pietro\*** (I, E4). At the end of Corso Cavour a "two-faced" gateway, also called *Porta Romana,* opens onto the medieval wall perimeter. On the corso side it appears as a plain 14th-century arch (originally it had two arches, whence its ancient name), surmounted by a sacred image painted in a niche (1765). Outwardly, it presents an elegant Renaissance facade. Built in 1475 by Agostino di Duccio and Polidoro di Stefano, it evokes Etruscan motifs in the lively figures on its two lateral structures, in the decorative patterns of the escutcheons, here alternating with rosettes, and in the plan to top the central arch with a large niche (never applied).

**San Pietro**\* (I, F5). The exterior fails to betray the complex architecture of this Benedictine abbey, founded (according to tradition, at the behest of nobleman Pietro Vincioli) at the end of the 10th century on an Etrusco-Roman burial site and over a pre-existing early-Christian temple, perhaps the city's original cathedral. The monastery (now the Faculty of Agriculture), which incorporates the basilica (of which the primitive structures still remain), is the result of various construction phases spanning the Middle Ages to the 18th century.

The entrance courtyard, by Valentino Martelli (1614), is dominated by the imposing **campanile**\*, which, respectively dodecagonal and then hexagonal in its lower parts, combines styles of various periods. The belfry cage (1463-68), designed by Bernardo Rossellino, is Gothic-Renaissance.

The entrance to the basilica is at the left rear corner, near the portico which conserves frescoes by Maestro Ironico, and which formerly decorated the original facade. The 16th-century portal, surmounted by a frescoed lunette attributed to Giannicola di Paolo, opens onto the nave and aisles; the nave with its 16th-century coffered ceiling, is supported on 18 ancient columns. Its simple medieval architecture is enhanced by rich decorations executed between the late 16th century and early 17th. Of particular interest: ten large canvases\* by L'Aliense (*Scenes from the Life of Christ*, 1592-94) on the walls of the nave; five **quadretti**\* (little paintings) by

Perugino (1496) in the 15th-century sacristy; the wooden **choir**\* in the apse, with its elegant incised carvings and inlays (1526-35). Also featured are works by Sassoferrato, Guercino, and Guido Reni.

The former **convent** (today another seat of the Faculty of Architecture) develops around a Renaissance main cloister, and a smaller cloister otherwise called *Chiostro delle Stelle*, built by Galeazzo Alessi (1571). In the ancient *pescheria* of the friars an **Orto Botanico Medievale** (medieval botanical garden) has recently been instituted, where the fascinating medieval symbolism linked to plants is particularly evident.

In the 15th century troops drilled in the **Giardino del Frontone** (I, F4-5); today, after the area was restructured (1780-91), what remains are the shapes of the monumental holm-oaks, which line the three parallel lanes that lead to the small amphitheater with its triumphal arch.

**San Costanzo** (I, F5, off map). The XX Giugno borough abuts onto the 16th-century *Porta San Costanzo* (I, F5), beyond which rises the church dedicated to Perugia's patron saint, whose feast day is celebrated with a traditional local sweet, called the "*Torcolo di San Costanzo*." In front of this church, the young women of Perugia would await a sign (a wink) from the saint, assuring them that they would marry within the year. Documented as dating from the 11th century, but revised in neo-Romanesque style by Guglielmo Calderini, the church still preserves an altar from 1205. To the right of San Costanzo extends the *Orto Botanico*, the botanical garden founded in 1530 and transferred here in 1896.

## 1.2 Perugia's environs
**Excursions from Perugia to the Volumni tombs, Corciano and Marsciano, 49.3 km**

These three itineraries all follow the historic thoroughfares that branch out of the city walls and into the countryside. The first reaches the fascinating Etruscan necropolis on the road that linked the city to the Tiber. A chance discovery in 1840 triggered a series of important excavation campaigns which shed new light on the city's early history, a discovery that triggered an appreciable tourist trade, even in those days. The way to Corciano runs along a road formerly known as the Cortonese, or the Tuscan road, which already existed in Etrusco-Roman times. In the Middle Ages, having become the royal road (*via regale*) of the Trasimeno, it ran over once fertile lands, the appearance of which has now been modified by urban expansion. Our last excursion, to Marsciano, takes us along the modern road (no. 317), which corresponds to the initial stretch of the *via regale* to Rome: a ridged course far from the valley floor of the Tiber.

*A period photo from the Museo della Casa, Corciano*

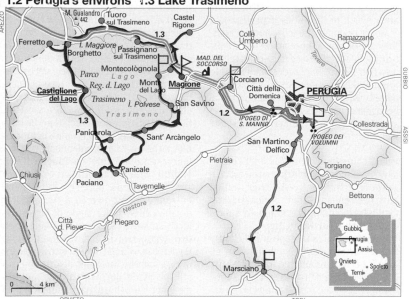

### Ipogeo dei Volumni**

From Perugia, first Viale Roma and then the scenic state road (75bis) to Assisi, skirting the village of San Giovanni, lead to the delightful 19th-century structure, which serves as a vestibule to the hypogeum, the most important of those so far explored in the vast Palazzone necropolis. The large chamber tomb which belonged to the Velimna (Volumni, in Latin) family, found by chance in 1840, is one of the best-known Hellenistic-age examples of a noble Etruscan tomb. Dating from the second half of the 2nd century BC, it reproduces the plan of a aristocratic home. The tomb is accessed via a steep descending stairway (modern) which leads to a pitched-roof rectangular area (*atrium*), onto which open three cells (*cubicula*) on each of its longer sides. On the walls hang escutcheons extolling the martial virtues of the deceased.

The rear side abuts upon the main room (*tablinium*), which contains **seven cinerary urns**\* in marble and travertine. In line with the entrance is placed the urn of the head of the family, half lying on a drape-covered bed supported by winged funerary demons that hold vigil above the painted doorway to the Beyond; all around are minor urns bearing the recumbent figures of other defunct family members.

The 19th-century building contains numerous cinerary urns found in chamber tombs dating from the latest period of the Etruscan city. The urns are mainly travertine, with pitched roofs and smooth front, carved or decorated with mythological themes.

### Via Cortonese

From the Fontivegge train station, Via Cortonese runs through the new residential areas and continues along the Trasimeno road (75 bis).

The ancient road crossed countryside quite different from that of today, which has been radically altered by unplanned urban expansion, and fostered by the major road networks built during the seventies, such as the four-lane link road between Perugia and the Autostrada del Sole motorway.

The road runs along the vast green picnic area of *Pian di Massiano* and the "R. Curi" municipal stadium, beyond which there is a sign indicating the turnoff to Città della Domenica. Next, we come to Ferro di Cavallo, a small community linked to the 14th-century church of *San Manno*, which features an Etruscan hypogeum as its crypt. The state road continues through the Ellera-Olmo industrial area, at the end of which, and to the right, you come to the medieval castle of Corciano.

### Fontivegge

Located near the railway station (1860), Fontivegge derives its name from the ancient Veggio sources (the present dates from 1615-42). In the early 20th century, the Perugina chocolate factory was the first industrial complex to settle in this area, which in the fifties experienced a building boom. In the following decades, the city took on a more marked administrative, financial and service-oriented dimension. *Piazza Nuova*, designed by Aldo Rossi, symbolizes this development: brick paved, with a central fountain and the Perugina company's old smokestack, it is surrounded by multi-function and office facilities.

### Pian di Massiano

In recent years, the city's southwest outskirts near the Fontivegge train station have been enhanced with regional sports facilities, including a stadium, a sports complex and "fitness" paths.

The uncluttered landscape is a backdrop to the various activities which can no longer be accommodated in the historic center: business activities and trade fairs, among which the most famous is the annual *Fiera dei Morti* (1-3 November), which since the 13th century has involved the exchange of farm produce and animals, and various amusement-park attractions between the months of October and November.

### Città della Domenica

Also called *Spagnolia*, after industrialist Mario Spagnoli who created it in 1955, *Città della Domenica* (Sunday City) is an amusement park on Mt. Pulito, a barren lower elevation of Mt. Malbe, replanted with several thousand olive trees. Its look is that of a small homespun Disneyland, with its fabled environments (the village of Pinocchio, the house of Snow White, Swan Lake, the witches' forest, the castle of Sleeping Beauty), its "chunk" of Africa and the Wild West, its lake, and "shaky" rock bridges.

Lastly, there is also a *Serpentarium* with live reptiles, a rich shell collection and numerous animals free to roam about at will, and which can be comfortably and safely viewed from a small train that crosses the entire park area (open mid-March to mid-Sep, 9am-7pm; from mid-Sep to Nov 3, only on Sat and holidays).

### Ipogeo di San Manno*

*Ferro di Cavallo* (278 m) is a complex which developed in the early 20th century over a former nucleus resting on the church of San Manno, which despite its 14th-century aspect is entirely decorated with fresco remains of the preceding century. Around the church, which was purchased by the Order of Malta, a rural fortified monastery was erected in the Middle Ages. Under this complex is hidden one of the major monuments of Etruscan funerary architecture, the **Ipogeo di San Manno**, which was utilized as a crypt and cellar. Steps, opposite the original entrance lead down to a rectangular dome-vaulted room made of large perfectly squared blocks, upon which open two symmetrical cells. On the door to the left cell, which contained the cinerary urns, a lengthy three-line inscription can still be made out, which, although its meaning is obscure, has contributed to the tomb's fame.

### Corciano

The town (elev. 408 m, pop. 13,623) is a typical medieval castle town of the Perugia countryside, enclosed within a massive turreted 15th-century perimeter. It preserves its original layout, with streets and lanes clinging to the sloping hillside of olive trees, together with the stone houses arranged in typical "crown" fashion. Facing elevated and centrally located Piazza Coragino is the church of **Santa Maria**, Gothic in layout, but radically transformed in the 19th century; on the altar is Perugino's *Our Lady of the Assumption*. Slightly further up, stands the church of *San Cristoforo*, built upon the remains of an Etruscan burial site, which houses a small *Museo di Arte Sacra* or *della Pievania* (visits may be arranged with the local town authorities), with frescoes and furnishings from the parish church. To the left of the church is located the *Museo della Casa Contadina*, which, with its period tools, utensils and furnishings, is a replica of a typical rural dwelling. The castle played a pivotal strategic role along the Via di Toscana, acquiring a sizable economic and administrative importance in this fertile agricultural area. All this is evident from the numerous palazzi that line Corso Rotelli, the town's main thoroughfare: *Palazzo dei Priori* and *Palazzo della Mer-*

*Puppet from the village of Pinocchio, in the Città della Domenica near Perugia*

*cunzia* (15th cent.), followed by *Palazzo del Capitano del Popolo*, or *del Contado*, of the same period, with it characteristic terracotta decorations. Next, the **Palazzo Comunale**, the 16th-century residence of the Della Corgna, wherein are conserved local Bronze Age and Etruscan finds.

**Agosto Corcianese.** Since 1965, art and crafts fairs, concerts, theater performances, and the now-famous historical *Gonfalone* pageant have enlivened this medieval borough during the month of August. No less picturesque is the Christmas *presepe*, or crèche, which involves the town's population in a pageant of domestic and artisanal life, colorfully played out against the historic center's narrow streets.

**Pieve del Vescovo.** Two kilometers north of Corciano, this 14th-century castle, now in disrepair, became the summer residence of Perugia's bishops, and was restored (1560-70) to designs by Galeazzo Alessi. Here sojourned future pope Leo XIII, who at the time was Perugia's bishop and cardinal. If you need to restore your energy, a good idea is to stop at the *Associazione Enogastronomica*, near the castle itself, where you can sample traditional fare adapted to more modern tastes. Proceeding along the hill road amid olive groves and vineyards you will reach the **Santuario della Madonna del Soccorso**, an elegant little temple, made of local stone, erected in 1719-29 to house a "miraculous" image of the Madonna, originally frescoed on the wall of a hayloft.

### The Strada Marscianese
This road leaves Perugia by *Porta San Pietro* and, at the Pallotta crossroads. It becomes state road 317. Driving along this still charming area, dotted with small boroughs and castles, one can take in the rolling hills that, to the west, constitute a natural backdrop to the Tiber valley floor.

### Villa Alfani e la Madonnuccia
Proceeding in this direction, we come first to San Martino Delfico, with its 18th-century *Villa Alfani*, next to Silvestri, characterized by its double stairway which can be seen from the road. Once beyond the turn-off for *San Martino in Campo*, where of interest is a small chapel called the *Madonnuccia*, our itinerary takes us through a few small villages geared essentially to the crafts, until we come to *San Valentino* (304 m), a small hillside *nucleus* with a longstanding tradition of loom-woven fabrics. At km 22.3, **Cerqueto** (311 m) well deserves a visit because of its parish church, where, in 1478, Perugino painted his first documented work (*San Sebastiano\**, the only figure that remains of the fresco).

### Marsciano
Once an important castle town in Perugia's rural surroundings, Marsciano (184 m, pop. 15,973) is one of the valley's most productive and busy centers. Between the 19th and 20th centuries Marsciano enjoyed marked growth and undertook urban renewal, which also involved the parish church, wherein is conserved a fresco by the school of Perugino, portraying the *Madonna and Child* with *Sts. Francis and Bernardine*.

# 1.3 Lake Trasimeno
**A circular 68.2-km itinerary** *(map on page 61)*

Early maps show Lake Trasimeno as "Perugia's lake," which underscores how this area, long contested by Cortona, Arezzo, and Perugia, felt the influence of the area's principal city. A similar lot fell to other centers along the lakeside, among which only Castiglione del Lago managed to emancipate itself, between the 16th and 17th centuries, during the marquisate of the Della Corgna family. Greatly varied and changing depending on the vantage point, the landscape is always dominated by the opaque green of the lake – "a veil of water on a meadow," as the art critic Cesare Brandi defined it – which reflects its light over the delicate setting, and which so inspired Perugino.

*Lake Trasimeno has a wonderful variety of birdlife*

Our suggested itinerary runs counterclockwise around the lake, from Magione to Passignano. From Castiglione del Lago, you can take short detours to Castel Rigone, Paciano, and Panicale.

*San Feliciano on Lake Trasimeno*

The parish church of the *Annunziata*, reworked in 1946-47, preserves a part of its 15th-16th-century decorations, and an *Annunciation* on Deruta majolica tiles (1584) located above the triumphal altar.

## The lake**

Lake Trasimeno offers an unlimited number of hues ranging from the soft yellow of the primroses to the bright yellow of the water lily, from the bright red of the cornel fruit to the orange of the *Lilium bulbiferum*. Lake Trasimeno is the largest inland lake in peninsular Italy, and the country's fourth (126 sq. km) in size. Surrounded by a plain and by rolling hills, where woods are sporadically interrupted by fields of corn or sunflowers, vineyards and olive groves, its laminar aspect it is reminiscent a huge flock of birds. In fact, the lake originated from the filling of a tectonic valley, and is never more than 6 meters deep. With its very slow water reflux rate, it is one of Italy's most fragile and precious humid areas. In the past, the Romans had tried to regulate the lake's water level by digging a tunnel in the San Savino area. The present canal was built in 1898. Having definitively set aside 18th- and 19th-century plans to drain the lake, from 1950 to 1960 the basin itself was broadened to offset prolonged drought periods. A veritable paradise for botany and water-fowl lovers, the three islands that surface from the waters (*Maggiore*, *Minore* and *Polvese*), are home to various wild duck and bird species. You can easily see cormorant families skimming over the water, while the kite stalks among the reeds and the lake sparrow sports its elegantly soft hued livery. With a little luck, you will also catch sight of the spectacular plunge of the osprey. The waters themselves are populated by pike and carp. Eels are documented as far back as 1342; whereas the *lasca* (roach), highly prized in the Middle Ages, has become extinct. In March 1995 the **Parco del Lago Trasimeno** was constituted, a natural preserve aimed at protecting and exploiting the lake and its surrounding delicate natural environment.

## Magione

This locality (elev. 299 m, pop. 12,015) owes its name to the fortified **Badia\***, the abbey built by the Order of St. John of Jerusalem (13th cent.) as a hostel for pilgrims headed for Rome; it was later fortified in the 15th century, probably to designs by Fioravante Fioravanti. With its square layout and corner towers, it features an elegant inner courtyard skirted by three rows of superimposed loggias and a "throne hall." Since the 14th century, the complex has belonged to the Knights of Malta and is not open to the public. The parish church, dedicated to St. John the Baptist, was commissioned by the Knights of Malta in the 16th century and remodeled in the 19th (only its facade is 18th century). Its interior is decorated with frescoes by Gerardo Dottori (1947), who is also the author of the *tavola* that adorns the council hall in the *Palazzo Comunale* and features Fra Giovanni, a native of this area, who told of his journey to the Far East in his *Historia Mongolorum* a sort of early travelogue. On the main street is located the church of **Santa Maria delle Grazie**, where visitors can admire a *Maestà* attributed to Andrea di Giovanni (1371). Above the town stands the so-called *Torre dei Lombardi*, a military vantage point for the ancient road leading toward the lake's north shore. The plain at the foot of the town is known as **Pian di Carpine**, because of the thick hornbeam woods that once covered it.

## Toward the lake

Having crossed Magione, and before reaching the lake shore, you can make a slight detour to the left and visit the church of the *Madonna delle Fontanelle* (1508), which was erected upon a "miraculous" font, and the battlements and towers of **Montecolognola** (elev. 410 m), an elliptical hillside castle.

## Castel Rigone

This magnificent natural vantage point (elev. 653 m), which, according to tradition, was founded by Rigone, Totila's lieutenant, can be reached via a scenic route off the state road to the right, after the *Monteruffiano* tower, which winds upward amid olive groves. The borough, restructured so as to better accommodate tourist needs, is medieval (having been fortified in 1297), but its major monument is the sanctuary of the **Madonna dei Miracoli\***, among Umbria's most significant Renaissance structures. Erected in 1494 with the help of the Perugia Commune, in thanks for the prodigies attributed to an image of the Blessed Virgin during a plague period, this graceful sandstone structure is set off by a squat bell tower which in 1831 replaced the former *campanile* (1531). Its facade, by Domenico Bertini (1512), features a portal with lunette and candelabrum motifs. The second altar to the right, along the only broad nave, features Bernardo di Girolamo Rosselli's *Madonna del Rosario* (1558); housed in a bluish-gray stone chapel (frescoed by Tommaso Papacello) along the left arm of the transept there is a splendid wood crucifix,

part of a traditional crucifixion iconography; in the apse, contained within a splendid frame by Bernardo di Lazzaro (1528), there is a copy of the Epiphany painted for this church by Domenico Alfani on cartoons by Rosso Fiorentino. In the left transept chapel, similarly in *pietra serena*, there is a painting of the *Virgin and Child* (late 15th century); and, in the second altar to the left, G. B. Caporali's *Coronation of the Virgin*.

From Castel Rigone, trekking enthusiasts can proceed along a magnificent route which leads to the highest point of the Trasimeno hills, Mt. Castiglione (802 m).

## Passignano sul Trasimeno

From atop its 289 meters, the ancient *Passum Jani* (Janus' oasis, pop. 4,981) overlooks the north shore of the Trasimeno. From the lake shore, and through a maze of narrow streets amid the 15th-century houses of the town's most ancient quarter, you reach the towers of its most elevated section, among which rises the 14th-cen-

## Water culture

The fishing nets, the humble *vallaioli* fishermen's huts, boats and sweep-nets, the replicas of some of the most ancient Trasimeno fishing techniques, such as the *tuori* and that utilizing the *arelle* (a trellis system for catching fish) – all these instruments provide a general view of a trade which in the past meant the livelihood of those who peopled the shores of Lake Trasimeno, and which is still present in the traditions and the diet of this lake district. The *Arte dei Pesciaioli*, the guild that laid down the rules for territorial division for fishing the lake, dates all the way back to the 13th century.

*Fishing nets on Isola Maggiore*

Nowadays, modernization can be noted in the motor boats, which have long substituted oar-powered craft. In addition, the depletion of the lake's fauna has drastically undermined the fishing trade to the advantage of more profitable agricultural activities.

San Feliciano's *Museo della Pesca del Lago Trasimeno* was set up to document life on the lake, for centuries the primary activity of the locals; with its extensive displays of objects and utensils, the museum also demonstrates the techniques once used by the lake fishermen, conserving a heritage which would otherwise be lost.

The presence of the lake and its products is clearly perceived in the gastronomic specialties of the area, consisting primarily of pike, carp, tench (the *risotto* made with this fish is excellent), eel, and perch; whereas the shores are an ideal habitat for canes, which grow in abundance. From these canes come wicker and other cane articles made by local craftsmen.

San Feliciano is the best-known locality for the working of lake reeds and the manufacturing of mats, baskets, and wicker chairs.

tury triangular *Torre di Ponente*. The atmosphere of the ancient borough's bygone age was altered in 1923, when the Italian Aeronautics Company (makers of hydroplanes) – later converted into a naval shipyard – set up operations in this area. With the industrial crisis, attention has focused on tourism, and the fact that Passignano has become the seat of the province's navigational services has surely enhanced the local economy.

From the new parish church (1937), you enter the historic center, where is located the 16th-century Renaissance-style church of *San Rocco*, with its unusual twin portal. Retracing your steps, you ascend to the church of *San Bernardino*, with its sandstone facade (1573), upon which is superimposed the Oratory of the Most Holy Sacrament. Thus, you reach the top of the town, dominated by the imposing ruins of the fortress. Next to the cemetery, the ancient parish church of **San Cristoforo** (10th-11th cent.), now reduced to a cemetery church, features in its interior a collection of ex-voto saint figures, which were frescoed in the first half of the 15th century. Once outside the town, you come to the *Santuario della Madonna dell'Oliveto*, erected in 1582-86 to honor the sacred image of a *Madonna and Child* attributed to an assistant of Bartolomeo Caporali, and today hung above the church's magnificent main altar, by Mariotto Radi (1603).

### From Passignano to Tuoro

Once over Mt. Montigeto one enters a valley furrowed by the long cypress-lane leading to **Villa del Pischiello**, built by Uguccione di Bourbon-Sorbello around 1799. The area took its name from the *Bastia Corgna manor*, a fortified farm estate successively turned into a palazzo. Dotting the surrounding hillsides place names recall the presence of fortifications which were built to protect this strategic area. Still standing, albeit in ruins, is the late 14th-century hanging tower of the **Castello di Vernazzano**, to which in 1457 was added a fortress. Similarly in ruins is the manor church of *San Michele Arcangelo*, restructured during the Renaissance, with its characteristic rest facility for wayfarers.

### Tuoro sul Trasimeno

This late-medieval center (elev. 309 m, pop. 3,617) rises in an area which was theater to one of the most disastrous and legendary battles of antiquity (217 BC), in which over 16,000 Roman soldiers lost

their lives at the hands of Hannibal's Carthaginian army. Upon the mausoleum of the Roman commander, Caius Flaminius, who fell in this battle, legend has it that the Capra palace was built. Remodeled during the Renaissance, it contains a fresco attributed by some to Perugino. Today it

*The Campo del Sole at Punta Navaccia*

belongs to the University of Perugia.

The phases of the battle have been reconstructed in a "Hannibal itinerary," organized by the local authorities. By way of a historical footnote, it seems that the locality's name (Tuoro), derives from a fishing technique once practiced hereabouts.

Upstream from the town are situated sandstone quarries which are well known throughout the Perugia area. And, to this stone the local authorities have dedicated the **Campo del Sole**, at the lakeside area of *Punta Navaccia* (soon to become a nature park); that is, a series of column-shaped stone sculptures, designed by Pietro Cascella and sculpted by numerous artists between 1985 and 1989

### Isola Maggiore

In the 13th century, the peace and quiet of this environment, rich in holm-oaks, olive groves, and cypress trees, attracted a community of friars minor who, a few years later, welcomed St. Francis himself for an entire Lenten period. The island (elev. 309 m) today, the lake's second largest and the only one still to be inhabited, is a favorite destination for boat tours (for information, contact: APT del Trasimeno, tel. 075 9652484; APM SNT, tel. 075 827157). The village, located on the west bank, consists of only one paved street, running between 14th- and 15th-century houses, and a 17th-century parish church. At the end of the town stands the romantic church of *San Salvatore*, featuring within a fragmentary polyptych by Sano di Pietro, from the church of the nearby Franciscan monastery. The island's southern tip is occupied by the **Castello Guglielmi**, or *Villa Isabella* (in disrepair), ordered by the Marquis Giacinto Guglielmi and built in 1885 upon the remains of the Franciscan monastery, of which remain traces both in the cloister and in the church itself. It was the Marquise Elena Guglielmi who contributed to its fame thanks to the lacework laboratory she instituted in 1904, teaching local women, who were already expert fish-net weavers, how to apply the "Irish stitch," which to this day constitutes the island's most typical craftwork. The island is dominated by the Gothic church of *San Michele Arcangelo*, with frescoes dating from the 14th-16th centuries. Above the altar, there is an altarpiece painting of the Crucifixion, tentatively attributed to Bartolomeo Caporali. The *Isola Minore,* instead, is completely covered with a typical Mediterranean vegetation and is no longer inhabited.

## Toward Castiglione del Lago

Once having crossed the bridge over the Macerone, the Trasimeno state road turns left from the short detour to the church of *Santa Maria,* better known as the *Pieve di Confine* (or, *dei Confini*), built in the early 12th century in Romanesque style along the confines between papal territory and the grand duchy of Tuscany. After some years as a farmstead, today it is in a state of total abandon. If, instead, you wish to emulate such illustrious travelers as Michelangelo, Goethe, and Lord Byron, you can stop at the *Dogana,* the building (restructured in the 19th century) which housed them, and which today has been turned into an eco-tourist facility. The summit of the surrounding hillside is totally girded by the wall remains of the 13th-century *Castello di Monte Gualandro,* which in the past was used as a customs house. Once having gone beyond *Borghetto* (elev. 259 m), a fortified borough which in the 16th century was equipped with an artificial harbor, you reach a wooded area south of the state road, known as *bosco del Ferretto*. Its name comes from the wealth of ferrous compounds found in its soil, which in turn fosters a luxuriant vegetation consisting of low oaks, Turkey oaks, farm lands, ponds and heaths covered with heather and broom – the myriad colors of the Trasimeno. On the southern edge is located *Casale Pieracci,* a 14th-century agricultural complex.

## Castiglione del Lago*

The limestone promontory on which this town rises (elev. 304 m, pop. 13,722), was, in the days of the Etruscans and Romans, an island on the lake. The populated area, enclosed within the vast walled perimeter, is one of the most interesting in the entire lake district. The impress is that left by the Della Corgna family, who, in 1550, and with the help of Pope Julius III, became the lords of the Trasimeno.

**The borgo**. Entering the historic center through the 19th-century *Porta Senese,* on your left you immediately come upon the parish church of the *Maddalena,* a Neoclassical structure by Giovanni Carponi, with its outside portico dating from 1867. Its interior features decorations by Mariano Piervittori and a *tavola* by Eusebio da San Giorgio (1500). Proceeding along *Via Vittorio Emanuele* you come to a square at the end of which stands the church of *San Domenico di Guzman* (presently being restored), which, built in 1683, has a fine 18th-century wooden ceiling.

**Palazzo della Corgna\*.** Situated at the center of the town, this building, incorporating a former hunting pavilion belonging to the Baglioni family, was built by Ascanio della Corgna in 1563. Its L-shape construction (later enlarged by Cardinal Fulvio, Ascanio's brother) was originally

*The fortifield walls of the Castello del Leone, Castiglione del Lago*

surrounded by a beautiful garden, admired for its floral and fruit and vegetable decorations, of which very little now remains. Its look is that of a noble residence which survives only to exemplify the lifestyles and decorative tastes of a bygone age, together with the family's economic and political fortunes. The fresco motifs that decorate the room, by Niccolò Circignani and Giovanni Antonio Pandolfi, and which celebrate the family, are among the most significant examples of late Umbrian mannerism.

The ground floor (closed to visitors) was the "secret" part of the palace, and was used for leisure purposes. It is here that the building's most refined paintings are to be found, among which the odd *Storie del mondo alla rovescia* (literally, *Backward Histories of the World*), presumed the work of Salvio Savini. In the former gardens stands a modern hospital, whose chapel conserves a fresco attributed to G. B. Caporali.

**Castello del Leone**. A long passage, which was covered in the 17th century, connects the *Palazzo della Corgna* to the castle, which was to give the town its name. In the 13th century, Frederick II of Swabia ordered the castle built as an army observation post, utilizing a previous fortification which also included a parish church (remains visible). Its pentagonal plan, surmounted by a triangular battlemented tower, is today a charming backdrop for shows and other performances.

Every two years, in spring, the international kite flyers meeting is held in Castiglione, a truly spectacular event which brightens the sky with a multitude of colors.

### Panicarola and its sanctuaries

A short drive takes you to *Panicarola* (269 m), where an early Iron-Age necropolis has been unearthed. Northwest of the town lies the sanctuary of the *Madonna della Carraia* (1686), contained inside the dome by Giovanni Caproni (1867). Its vast Greek-cross interior features a main altar carved and gilded with a "miraculous" image of the *Madonna* (16th cent.). Southeast, instead, stands the sanctuary of the *Madonna del Busso*, whose name probably derives from the boxwood plants common in the area.

### Paciano

According to a local legend, with his temple, two-faced Janus "watched" over the Petrarvella spur, where today rises Paciano (elev. 391 m, pop. 937), a fortified borough which has conserved its original layout (14th cent.), built upon three parallel streets within the six-towered, three-gated perimeter (still intact). At the center of the town lies the church of *San Giuseppe*, founded in the 11th century, where hangs the local *gonfalon* executed by craftsmen of Benedetto Bonfigli's workshop (*Madonna della Misericordia* or *delle Grazie*, ca. 1480). The *Confraternita del Santissimo Sacramento* is a confraternity which houses a precious art collection known as *Raccolta d'arte San Giuseppe*, with paintings from the 15th to the 18th centuries, vestments, Etruscan ar-

chaeological finds, and a fresco by Francesco di Castel della Pieve, considered Perugino's master. Leaving by the Rastrella Gate, beside which rises the 17th-century *Palazzo Cennini*, you reach the sanctuary of the *Madonna della Stella* (1572-79), decorated by Scilla Pecennini. The sacristy features frescoes (1590-1620) that relate the history of the sanctuary.

After visiting these boroughs, you can penetrate into the oak and chestnut tree woods in the **Mt. Pausillo** area; a 300 hectare natural park area crowed with deer, mountain sheep, and a mushroom-rich underbrush.

### Panicale*

Founded upon one of Umbria's most beautiful natural terraces, Panicale (431 m, pop. 5,278) looks over the Trasimeno from one side and, from the other, over the broad Nestore river valley. The environmentally rich hillside town preserves intact its 13th-14th-century layout, which centers on three main squares, at three different levels, and all linked by the main street.

**Outside the town walls**. The tree-lined thoroughfare leading to the walled town center runs by the church of the *Madonna della Neve*, also called *della Sbarra*, in memory of the erstwhile customs post. Amid the houses you can just make out the facade of the former church of *Sant'Agostino* (14th cent.), in Piazza Regina Margherita, today utilized as an art venue.

**Piazza Umberto I**. Skirting the walls you come to *Porta Perugina*, rebuilt in the late 19th century, through which you pass into the square characterized by an octagonal limestone cistern (1473), which in 1903 was turned into a fountain, and by the *Palazzo Pretorio*, with its stone coat of arms (14th cent.) Nearby, stands the *teatro "C. Caporali,"* a 17th-century structure, remodeled and fitted with three tiers of boxes in 1858 by Giovanni Caproni. The stage curtain is by Mariano Piervittori (1869).

**Collegiata\***. This collegiate church rises in Piazza San Michele, where it was founded between the 10th and 11th century. Enlarged in 1546 and rebuilt in the 17th century, it features two Renaissance portals framed by an unfinished facade. Inside are to be admired a *Birth of Christ* by G.B. Caporali (1519), and a 16th-century wooden crucifix with moveable arms.

**Piazza Masolino**. The street opposite the *collegiata* quickly takes you to a scenic square dedicated to painter Masolino da Panicale, who however was born in Panicale of the Tuscan Valdarno region. Here stands the 14th-century *Palazzo del Podestà*, by now reduced to a mere shell, with its triangular-vaulted 1769 bell-tower.

Once back in Piazza Umberto I, and passing under *Porta Perugina*, you reach the church of San Sebastiano, wherein are two frescoes by Perugino: the famous **Martyrdom of Saint Sebastian**\*\* (1505) and the *Blessed Virgin and Child with Sts. Augustine and Mary Magdalene.*

## Sant'Arcangelo
Includes the ancient fortified dwellings collectively subsumed under the name of the homonymous **Badia** (abbey, 286 m), the result of various construction phases, and recently remodeled and destined to residential purposes. Slightly further on lies the church of *Santa Maria di Ancaelle,* an ashlar building with a 12th-century apse hidden behind a late 15th-century altar, and 13th-century fresco fragments.

*Cane cutting at San Savino*

## San Savino and La Valle
At the Mt. Buono fork, turn left toward *San Savino* castle (314 m), built around the year 1000 and reconstructed in the 14th century. With its triangular tower and high walls its dominates the arm of the lake called *La Valle*, characterized by vast cane fields and turned into a Nature Oasis by the provincial authorities. Fishing, however, is not allowed so as to protect the fish species that come to breed near its shores.

## San Feliciano
The village (elev. 279 m) testifies to the fishing tradition of the lake. Among tourist initiatives, worthnoting is the *Museo della Pesca del Lago Trasimeno* (open, summer, Tue-Sun, 10am-12.30pm, 5pm-7pm; winter, Tue, Thu, Sat, 9.30am-12.30pm, 2.30pm-4.30), which illustrates the history of the lake from a naturalistic point of view.

## Isola Polvese
From San Feliciano, by seasonal ferry, you can reach the lake's largest island (1.5 km long). Abandoned by the fishing community and by the Olivetan monks who colonized it in the 13th century, the island was bought

in the mid-19th century by Counts Panciani of Spoleto, to be used as a farm and hunting reserve. Having changed various hands, it was set aside in the 1960s as a park. Since it was purchased in 1975 by Perugia's Provincial Government, it has been transformed into a nature sanctuary and as an environmental educational facility for local students. There are numerous remains of churches which were built by the various religious orders that settled in this area. Especially worth visiting is the former convent of *San Secondo*, which belonged to the Olivetan monks from 1404 to 1624. Of the ancient medieval village there remains only the 14th-century castle and the nearby church of *San Giuliano*, built on the remains of a Roman villa.

## Monte del Lago
Before the borough itself stands the eerie *Castello di Zocco* (13th cent.), enclosed within by 15th-century walls. Above, two towers mark the presence of the *Rocca Baglioni*, later property of the Pompilj family, a massive edifice which was enlarged in 1372. Hence, you come to *Monte del Lago* (295 m), which appears fan-like atop a promontory overlooking the Trasimeno opposite Castiglione del Lago. A point of interest is the garden of *Villa Palombaro*, restructured in the late 19th century by Senator Pompilj, who opposed with all his might projects aimed at draining the lake. He also transmitted his love for this area to his wife Vittoria Aganoor, who dedicated her poetry to Lake Trasimeno. From 1922 the area has housed a hydrobiological station, transformed in 1955 into the Hydrobiology and Fish Farming Institute. From Monte del Lago you return to Magione (p. 64) and to the end of our itinerary.

# 2 The Val Tiberina

## Area profile

"Fancy an extended and spacious valley surrounded by mountains, the summits of which are crowned with ancient and luxuriant forests [...] You almost have the impression of finding yourself before an unreal, indeed an imaginary, landscape, issued from the brush of an exquisite painter." So wrote Pliny the Younger to his friend Apollonius (v, 6) from his villa near Tifernum Tiberinum (present-day Città di Castello). And, in fact, still to this day this entire area, which from the late Pliocene and for over a million years was invaded by the waters of the erstwhile Lake Tiberinum, appears in all its uniqueness. A part of the upper course of the Tiber, it extends in a north-south direction from Albiano to Umbertide. The border between Tuscany and Umbria, and which runs between Sansepolcro and San Giustino, dates from 15th-century political reorganization, and now has a purely administrative significance. In fact, as Ernesto Guevara aptly put it, valleys formed by large rivers – and this one is no exception – are, historically, powerful vehicles of cultural exchange.

In medieval times, the area was traditionally divided into two levels: "Piano di sopra" and "Piano di sotto." The former centered on the Sansepolcro-Città di Castello area; the latter on Perugia. *Piano di sotto* was long under the influence of the major Benedictine abbeys (11th-12th cent.) which, by colonizing vast plain and mountain areas, left their typical mark on the land. The work of the abbots was to be continued by the Perugia Commune, which extended its dominion up to Umbertide in the 13th-14th century, implementing land reclamation and deforestation strategies. To a political agreement between the Church and the Florentine State (1441) is due the definitive administrative division of the valley as marked by its present regional extension. The only truly unifying element has always been the river, surrounded by narrow stretches of plainland and ridges that become more pronounced toward the northeast. Favorable environmental conditions have fostered intensive farming, both on the water-rich valley floor and along the hillsides, which is broad and sunlit on its left side, and forestry on its other. Besides vineyards and olive groves, tobacco has been a mainstay crop for centuries. Introduced to Sansepolcro in 1575, starting in the 19th century tobacco became a source of wealth for the entire surrounding area, while its extensive cultivations and characteristic drying facilities – today largely abandoned but recognizable from the numerous chimneys – left a marked impress on the surrounding area. Industrialization has contributed to further enhance still vital artisanal output in such sectors as paper manufacturing, typography, period furniture, and textiles, and has gone hand in hand with modernizing plainland agricultural processes.

*View toward the Val Tiberina*

# From Perugia to Città di Castello

**Excursions along the Tiberina and Pantano roads, 101 km** *(map on page 72)*

With this itinerary we leave expressway no. E45 and follow the old parallel Tiberine state road which runs along the Tiber valley from Perugia to Umbertide, and from here to Città di Castello and San Giustiano (for a total 71 km). You leave the provincial capital from northeast, proceeding along Via Eugubina until you reach Ponte Felcino, one of Perugia's four historic outskirts (the others being Ponte San Giovanni, Ponte Valleceppi, Ponte Pattoli). Medieval castles, boroughs, and abbeys, among which stand out the Santa Maria di Montelabate complex and Civitella Benazzone, accompany you along the route which runs through the lowland fields to the left and the Apennines on the opposite side. The most evident mountain reaches beyond the Tiber are Mt. Tezio and, further on, at a distance of 27.8 km from Umbertide, tree-covered Mt. Corona. From Perugia to Umbertide, an alternate route is the historic "Pantano" road (30 km), along the western side of the valley that cuts between Mt. Acuto and Mt. Corona, passing by Colle Umberto I, Antognolla and the abbey of San Salvatore. After Umbertide, an approximately 8-km upgrade off the Tiberina state road climbs to the charming borough of Montone, and continues on to Trestina, to the right of the Tiber. From here, a 9.5-km detour takes you to the Petroia abbey and the church of San Crescentino in Morra. Continuing toward Città di Castello, after little more than 3 km, in San Secondo, you leave the Tiberina and climb left to the castle atop Mt. Santa Maria Tiberina, from where you again

*Raphael's gonfalon of the Santissima Trinità, Pinacoteca Comunale, Città di Castello*

descend toward the valley along a winding road that touches Uppiano. Before reaching Città di Castello, it is worth stopping at Villa La Montesca, from where you have a wonderful view of the city. After visiting the largest center in the upper Tiber area, the state road takes you to Cisterna and, after an additional 12.6 km, to San Giustiano, close to the Tuscan border.

## To Umbertide via the old Tiberine road

### Montelabate
You approach this area accompanied by the Apennines rising on your right. Until the 14th century the abbey of *Santa Maria in Val di Ponte*, better known as *Montelabate* (elev. 387 m) was one of the principal centers of Benedictine power, upon which were dependent thirty parishes and twenty castles.
The abbey, today a farm belonging to Genova's Gaslini Foundation, was badly damaged by the 1984 earthquake and is still awaiting restoration. The convent complex features the imposing Gothic-Romanesque church of *Santa Maria* (11th cent.), which was rebuilt in 1281 and reinforced in 1569 with the addition of supporting buttresses. Its *campanile* (1269) was reduced by a third in the 19th century. In the early 14th century, its facade was adorned with a pointed portal and a large rose window. Following the death of the last abbot (1404), the abbey lost its territorial power, but did not cease to enrich its church with art works. Fiorenzo di Lorenzo painted his *Crucifixion with Saints* fresco in 1492, Bartolomeo Caporali a *Virgin with Sts. Anthony, Bernardine, Sebastian and worshipers* (1488).

## 2 From Perugia to Città di Castello

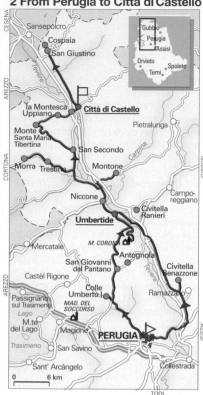

### Civitella Benazzone

This castle was part of the abbey's territorial organization. *Civitella Benazzone* (elev. 440 m), a medieval borough strategically situated so as to control the Tiber, was under the jurisdiction of the nearby abbey of *San Paolo in Val di Ponte*, or *Badia Celestina* (12th cent.), now no more than a ruin with the exception of its still intact Romanesque crypt.

### Civitella Ranieri*

There stands out, in the close network of fortifications marking the valley, a particularly elegant complex which is supposed to have been constructed upon the citadel erected in 1078 by Raniero, brother of Guglielmo, the duke of Monferrato. In its present form given it by Ruggero Cane Ranieri (15th cent.), the castle features a square layout with cylindrical corner towers and a huge keep. Its interior, which still belongs to the Ranieri family and is not open to visitors, conserves finely worked 16th-century fireplaces.

*View across Umbertide*

## Toward Umbertide via the Pantano road

### Colle Umberto I

You sense you are approaching this ancient walled borough (elev. 268 m) when you reach the *Osteria del Colle*, which conserves only the name of its former function as a way station. The beauty of the surrounding countryside inspired Cardinal Fulvio della Corgna to have himself built a sumptuous villa in the vicinity of the town. Designed by Galeazzo Alessi (1580), **Villa del Cardinale** features a magnificent Italian garden, and, in its interior, fresco decorations by Salvio Savini.

### Antognolla

From atop a rocky spur, this 13th-century castle (elev. 416 m) garrisoned a transverse road linking the Tiber valley. Houses and walls constituted a considerable fortified complex, which is presently being restored and will be turned into tourist residential facilities.

### Badia di San Salvatore di Monte Corona

Against the green backdrop of an oak wood on Mt. Corona, the abbey, which up to the 16th century was known as *San Salvatore del Monte Acuto*, was the seat of the local Camaldolite order. Founded in the 11th century, perhaps by Ro-

muald himself, it became the principal economic hub of the district, including vast agricultural estates, pastures and forests which, despite the many property transfers ensuing upon the convent's suppression in 1863, constitutes one of the area's major agricultural concerns. The upper aisled Romanesque church, consecrated in 1105, was subsequently modified and enlarged in the 16th and 17th centuries. Its interior conserves remains of 14th-century Umbrian school frescoes, and in the presbytery, an 8th-century *ciborium*\*. The underlying **crypt**, perhaps dating from the 11th century, is a vast chamber with a nave, four aisles and three apses wherein were extensively reutilized materials from Roman times, which were taken from the early Christian temple upon which it rose. Annexed to it is a small museum featuring ancient liturgical objects.

### Umbertide

At the point where the Reggia flows into the Tiber, amid hills dotted with the remains of medieval fortifications, Umbertide (elev. 247 m, pop. 14,779) occupied a position of strategic importance for the control of communication routes. The first document attesting to the feudal castle of Fratta dates from 1189, and describes it as a Perugian outpost in the Tiber valley which rose upon the hypothetical Roman *pagus*

(rural district) of *Pitulum*, also mentioned by Pliny. It long remained under the control of Perugia, and only in 1863 acquired its current name in memory of its early medieval founder. The historic center was damaged by air raids in 1944, which largely destroyed the walled perimeter that branches off from the *Rocca*, or fortress.

**Piazza Mazzini**. The very core of the historic center, this vast square sprawls out of the city walls, overlooked by the *Rocca* (fortress) and the collegiate church of *Santa Maria della Reggia*, which face one another from the opposite banks of the river. In 1559, Galeazzo Alessi and Giulio Danti designed the church's octagonal layout, which was completed around the mid-17th century by Bernardino Sermigni. In its brightly lit interior is conserved a *Virgin with Child and Saints* (15th cent.), and a *Transfiguration* by Niccolò Circignani (1578).

**Rocca** or fortress. In the late 1980s the city decided to recover a part of its historical heritage: the square tower, the two circular towers and a third rampart of the 14th-15th-century Rocca. Here, the *Centro per l'Arte Contemporanea* organizes art exhibits and periodically displays the "Collezione Giovanni Ciangottini," with works by the artist himself, and by Renato Birolli, Mino Maccari, Luciano Minguzzi and Toti Scialoja. In nearby Piazza Forte-

bracci (Braccio was a prisoner here in 1393) stands the *Teatro dei Riuniti*, rebuilt in 1808 upon a previous 18th-century theater.

**Piazza Matteotti**. Linked to *Piazza Mazzini* by short and narrow *Via Stella*, this central square opens onto the walled city heart, where rises the 17th-century *Palazzo Comunale*, former residence of counts Ranieri di Sorbello, with its interior sculpture and painting decorations dating from the late 17th century.

**Borgo inferiore**. Separated from the historic center by the railway, this "lower borough" focuses on the oblong *Piazza San Francesco*, the most ancient and characteristic of the city's squares, with three churches lining its left side. The Baroque church of *Santa Croce* (1610) has been turned into a museum, and houses, among other works, Luca Signorelli's *Deposition from the Cross\** (1516), executed for this church and placed in a wood frame in 1612, and *Virgin and Child in Glory* by Pomarancio (1577), from the adjacent 14th-century church of *San Francesco*, with its trilobed arched portal. The adjacent former convent houses the *Archivio Storico Comunale* (the Archives with Fratta Statutes, and 14th-century notarial titles) and the municipal library. Lastly, closed and awaiting to be restored is the church of *San Bernardino* (1426), which was restructured in 1768 (inside, a *Last Supper* by Muzio Flori, 1602).

Once in the northern periphery of the city, a short detour in the vicinity of the neoclassical *Ospedale Civile* (by Giovanni Santini), takes us to the church of **Santa Maria della Pietà** (1486). The lunette above its portal features a fresco attributed to Pinturicchio, or to Bartolomeo Caporali.

**Montone\***
The development of this fascinating elliptical borough (elev. 482 m, pop. 1,561), with its original medieval layout still intact, is closely linked to the two hills on which rise a Franciscan monastery to the north, and the *Rocca di Braccio*, or frotress, to the south. After having

been under the dominion of the Del Colle and Del Monte margraves in the high Middle Ages, in the 13th century it became a fief of Andrea Fortebracci, called Braccio da Montone, a soldier of fortune and lord of Perugia. To his memory is dedicated the main square in the town center, where once stood the feudal manor, and which today is the *Palazzo Comunale* (the Town Hall). A strikingly panoramic stairway leads to the Gothic church of **San Francesco**, built in the 14th century, featuring a portico and a striking carved wood portal protected by a grating (by Antonio Bencivenni, 1514). The church and the adjacent former Franciscan monastery were restored in 1995 and converted into a **municipal museum**, whose main attraction are the church's own decorations.

On Easter Monday, Montone holds a costume pageant celebrating the "Holy Thorn Donation," made to the city by Carlo Fortebracci, Braccio's son, in 1473. On this day, the relic is displayed in the collegiate church of *Santa Maria e San Gregorio Magno*, a single-aisle 17th-century structure situated on the highest spot in the borough. In the nearby grassy clearing are found the remains of the *Rocca di Braccio*, destroyed in 1478 by order of Sixtus IV.

Outside the borough, at the foot of the hill, rises the **Pieve Vecchia** (the old parish church), dedicated to St. Gregory. This Byzantine-Romanesque structure, which was erected in the 11th century and modified in the 16th, features two Renaissance tabernacles and frescoed aisles.

From Montone, proceeding northeasterly along the Valle del Carpine, you go beyond the picturesque **Rocca d'Aries** (property of the municipality). After proceeding for 17 km along this road you reach **Pietralunga** (elev. 566 m), located amid a richly wooded area. Situated in the Candeleto pine wood, the *Raccolta della Fauna Umbra* features a well-stocked zoological collection by Silvio Bambini. Southwest of the town rises one of the most ancient churches in Città di Castello diocese, the **Pieve de' Saddi**, dating from the 11th century.

**Abbazia di Petroia**
In the 11th century, the Nestore valley, bordering the Tiber near Trestina, was the seat

*The Rocca at Umbertide*

of a Benedictine abbey, which flourished up to the 14th century. After being successively restructured, what remains of this Romanesque church are the columns along the nave, whereas the wall of the ancient choir is today its facade, and highlights the precious terracotta plaques that were embedded in its surface shortly after the year 1000. Another significant religious structure in the valley is the church of *San Crescentino*, near the town of *Morra* (elev. 306 m), built in 1420 and frescoed by Luca Signorelli and assistants.

## Monte Santa Maria Tiberina

It is difficult to distinguish the summit of this cone-shaped hill from the shape of the castle tower and belfry of the ancient parish church of Santa Maria. The village (elev. 688 m) blends perfectly with its hillside surroundings, in turn overlooked by the feudal castle of the Del Monte family (13th cent.) and by the parish church of *Santa Maria*, with its crypt containing members of the noble family.

## Villa La Montesca

Occupying a scenic position above Città di Castello, the villa was built in the late 19th century by Leopoldo Franchetti, and is now the property of the regional government. Around the Tuscan-style manor house there extends a beautiful park (visitable) with much local flora and exotic plants.

# Città di Castello

Green rolling hills and brightly sunlit farmlands are the backdrop to the main urban center (elev. 288 m, pop. 38,223; map on page 76) of the Tiberine valley, which unexpectedly breaks the spatial geometric pattern of medieval towns and appears to the visitor in all the sober beauty of its broad, straight streets and aristocratic 16th-century palaces. Exactly like the local dialect, the city is a cultural blend of elements and influences from Umbria, Tuscany, the Marche region, and Rome. The crafters of this small arts capital were the refined and cultivated Vitelli, lords of Castello from the 15th to the 16th centuries, who renewed both the city's urban layout and the dwellings of its medieval walled borough, the latter a remnant of the Roman *Tifernum Tiberinum*. They left their mark in the large family palaces, one for each quarter and all splendidly decorated, which involved entire parts of the

city where streets and squares were broadened so as to endow the Renaissance ideal to the city. The taste for what is beautiful has always been strong, and continues to underlie and bolster the local crafts activities, including typography, which was introduced in the 16th century, plus furniture and textile manufacturing. Textiles are still made on hand looms in the "Tela umbra" workshop.

Our visit to the city starts from the Cathedral in Piazza Gabriotti and continues along Corso Cavour up to Piazza Matteotti. In this short stretch are concentrated the town's principal public buildings. The next street, Via Angeloni, is the city's most representative, with its palaces of the Vitelli family and San Francesco. Via Lanari leads to Via San Bartolomeo, which skirts Palazzo Vitelli in the Sant'Egidio area, and also Palazzo Albizzini (containing a part of the Burri collection) in Piazza Garibaldi. From here we cross Piazza Costa, where one can admire Palazzo Bufalini and Palazzo Bourbon del Monte, and then along the entire Corso Vittorio Emanuele up to the Renaissance church of Santa Maria Maggiore. After Via Borgo Farinaro we proceed to Largo Muzi, where stands the entrance to the Vitelli Palace garden alla Cannoniera, which houses the municipal art gallery. On the corner, at the end of this street, is located the church of San Domenico. Through Via Signorelli and Via Casceri we again return to Piazza Gabriotti. At the end of the pedestrian walk it is well to visit the tobacco drying facilities (located in the southern part of town) with the fine works comprised in the Burri Collection. Going along in the same direction, we come to Villa Garavelle with its Museo delle Tradizioni Popolari.

**Duomo,** or **Cathedral** (B1). In *Piazza Gabriotti* (formerly known as *Piazza di Sotto,* or *Delle Donne*), funnel-shaped around the vertical hub of the civic tower, in the 11th century a church dedicated to Sts. Floridus and Amantius was erected. The complex was enlarged in 1365 and remodeled between the 15th and 16th centuries. Its facade however is incomplete. Of the Romanesque church there remains an airy cylindrical bell-tower bearing traces of Byzantine influence, whereas the Gothic style can be seen in the left-side portal, adorned with wreathed columns and reliefs. The aisleless interior, with its 18th-century coffered ceiling, is embellished with sumptuous 16th-17th-century altar statues, paintings and frescoes. Particu-

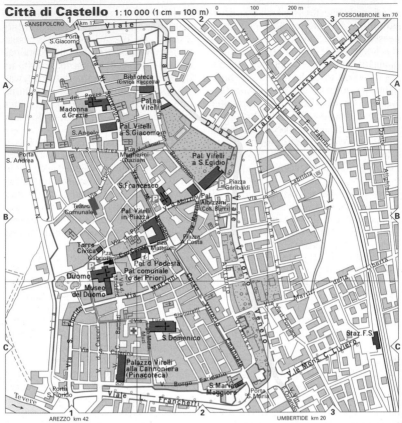

**Città di Castello** 1 : 10 000 (1 cm = 100 m)

larly noteworthy are the frescoes by Niccolò Circignani in the San Paolo Chapel (on the left).

**Museo del Duomo\***. To the right of the Cathedral, the former rectory houses the chapter's art collection. Particularly interesting is the **Tesoro di Canoscio\***, a treasury including rare embossed silver articles used during the Communion service, dated 5th-6th century. Other highly prized articles are the *bronze censers* (12th-14th cent.); a group of Romanesque relic-holders (*capselle*); an embossed silver and gilded *altar frontal\**, a Romanesque silver-wrought masterpiece; and a 14th-century Sienese-school pastoral staff; among the paintings, a *Virgin with Child and the Young St. John Baptist,* by Pinturicchio, and the **Christ in Glory\*** (1529-30) a masterpiece by Rosso Fiorentino.

**Palazzo Comunale\***, or *dei Priori* (B1). Located in the same *Piazza Gabriotti,* the building is an unfinished work by Angelo da Orvieto (1322-38), with an ashlar facade, an elegant portal and fine mullioned

windows on the upper story. The *Archivio Notarile*, containing deeds dating from 1328, is housed in this building. Opposite stands the **Torre Civica**, decorated with coats of arms, and affording an excellent view from its summit. Next to it rises the former bishop's palace, dating from the 12th century (remodeled).

**Piazza Matteotti** (B2). The heart of the city's social life, this square rose in the 16th century as an extension to the noble **Palazzo Vitelli in Piazza**, which was begun in the late 15th century and completed, in Tuscan style, around the mid-16th century. The 14th-century former *Palazzo del Podestà* (now the *Pretura*), attributed to Angelo da Orvieto, looks onto the square with its Baroque 1686 facade, whereas, along Corso Cavour, it has maintained its austere Gothic forms.

**San Francesco** (B2). Erected in 1273, this church was almost completely remodeled in the course of the 18th century. Of its early construction there remain the right side with its pointed portal and three polygonal apses. In its interior, near the entrance, there is an important Renaissance addition, the *Vitelli Chapel\** , built by Giorgio Vasari and enclosed by an iron railing designed by Pietro di Ercolano (1566). The chapel contains 26 inlaid stalls portraying the *Scenes from the Lives of Mary and St. Francis* and, above the altar, a *Coronation of the Virgin with Saints*, also by Vasari (1564). Raphael's *Wedding of the Virgin*, on the left altar under the forth arch, has been replaced by a copy, the original having been recklessly given by the local authorities (defined by a contemporary as a "vile troop of ignorant fanatics") to one of Napoleon's generals in 1798. The original is now preserved in Brera, in Milan.

**Palazzo Vitelli a Sant'Egidio\*** (B2). The power of the Vitelli family is fully symbolized by the size of this palace (now a bank), erected in the city's Sant'Egidio quarter by Paolo Vitelli in the second half of the 16th century. At the rear of the garden there is the *Palazzina*, with a beautiful loggia.

**Palazzo Albizzini** (B2). This Florentine Renaissance building (second half 15th cent.) is the seat of the **Fondazione Palazzo Albizzini "Collezione Burri,"** instituted in 1978 by Alberto Burri, a major contemporary artist. The collection includes 130 pieces carried out between 1948 and 1989, arranged chronologically. The collection is completed by works on display in the former tobacco-drying facilities (p. 78). The foundation also features an archive, a library specialized in modern art, and a photographic collection which documents the entire output of the artist, a native of Città di Castello.

**Piazza Costa**. To the left of Palazzo Albizzini, *Via Mazzini* leads to a square where is located the 16th-century *Palazzo Bourbon del Monte*, seat of the *Tela Umbra* textile laboratory, instituted in 1909 by Baroness Alice Franchetti

for the study and preservation of ancient craft techniques. Today it belongs to the regional government, which has set up a permanent exhibition (*Collezione Tessile di Tela Umbra*) featuring historical tools and instruments for spinning and weaving, embroidery and laceworks.

**Parrocchiale dei Vitelli** (C2). This parish church is located in the popular medieval *Farinario* quarter (the so-called *Mattonata*), where the noble Vitelli family originally resided. Toward the close of the 15th century, Niccolò Vitelli ordered the construction of the church of *Santa Maria Maggiore*, which features an unusual combination of Renaissance forms on its outside, and Gothic forms on the inside, along with 15th-century frescoes.

**Palazzo Vitelli alla Cannoniera\*** (C2). Built by order of Alessandro Vitelli, starting in 1521, on the spot where there formerly stood a cannon foundry after which it is named. Enlarged in successive stages, it is a fine Florentine-style construction which well exemplifies the 16th-century model of aristocratic homes. The garden, once renowned for its exotic plants, is overlooked by Vasari's elegant facade (1532-35) and decorated with graffiti by Doceno. The interior decorations

Christ in Glory *by Rosso Fiorentino, Museo del Duomo, Città di Castello* are partly by Doceno himself and in part by Cola dell'Amatrice.

**Pinacoteca Comunale\***. Instituted in 1860, the municipal art gallery was finally given a suitable home only in 1912, when restorer-antique dealer Elia Volpi donated Palazzo Vitelli alla Cannoniera to the municipal authorities, along with its collection. Among the works of major interest: a *Virgin Enthroned with Child\** by the Maestro di Città di Castello; the finely fashioned *Reliquary of St. Andrew\** (1420), from the workshop of Lorenzo Ghiberti. The **gonfalon of the Santissima Trinità\*\*** is the only work by Raphael to have remained in the city. Between the late 15th and early 16th century, Luca Signorelli exercised a vital influence on local art. Of this artist are conserved a fresco fragment of *St. Paul* (1474) and the **Martyrdom of St. Sebastian\*** (1497-98). Tusco-Roman mannerism is documented by five works by Raffaellino del Colle. The display also includes a *collection of sculptures*, among which a terracotta group from the Della Robbia workshop, works by a contemporary native of Città di Castello, Bruno Bartoccini, and from the Ruggeri donation (including works by Carlo Carrà, Giorgio De Chirico and Mario Mafai).

*One of the works on display at the Collezione Burri*

**San Domenico** (C2). The Dominicans preferred to construct for themselves sumptuous buildings, so as to visually affirm their supremacy over all the other monastic orders. The church of San Domenico is no exception; begun in the 14th century and completed in 1425, its facade however remained unfinished. Its rectangular nave conserves 15th-century frescoes, whereas the Renaissance altar on the right, at the extreme

end of the nave, once displayed a *Crucifixion* by Raphael, now in the National Gallery, London. Similarly, the left altar was once embellished by a *St. Sebastian* by Luca Signorelli, now on display in the Pinacoteca.

**Collezione Burri agli ex seccatoi tabacco\*** (C3, off map). At the city's southern border (in the direction of Umbertide) there lie the factory facilities which, up to the 1970s, dried locally-produced tropical tobacco. In this abandoned industrial complex, in 1978 Alberto Burri put on a magnificent exhibit of 128 large-scale works, which completed the *Palazzo Albizzini* collection (page 77).

Proceeding in the same direction, after approximately 2 km you come to *Garavelle*, where a typical farm house of this area houses the **Centro di Documentazione delle Tradizioni Popolari**. Utilizing period materials, dwellings, tools and typical furnishings of peasant civilization have been reconstructed. In the adjacent *Villa Capelletti* an iron-model collection is currently being set up. The state road toward Arezzo is the direction to follow to reach, after 11 km, **Citerna** (480 m, pop. 3,050). Atop one of the town's hills, of interest is the considerable art collection of the church of **San Francesco** (1316), subsequently remodeled in 1508 in simple Renaissance style. Also worth visiting is the church of *San Michele Arcangelo*, especially for its large *tavola* portraying the *Crucifixion* (1570) by Niccolò Pomarancio.

**San Giustino**
The town (336 m, pop. 10,049) extends, in perfect feudal fashion, around the **Bufalini castle\***, which in 1988 was purchased by the state and converted into a museum (presently being restored). It was constructed between 1480 and 1492 for defensive purposes, as is clear from its quadrangular shape and corner towers connected

*The former tobacco-drying plant of Città di Castello, now home of the Collezione Burri*

## When tobacco is good for you

The most dramatic, and perhaps the most curious event probably took place in 1966 when, subsequent to the Florence flood, which destroyed precious documents of European history and civilization, the *Fattoria Autonoma Tabacchi* rose to the occasion offering the use of its technical facilities and staff to dry out the invaluable books of the Biblioteca Nazionale Centrale, documents of Florence's civil and penal Court and of its newspaper concern *La Nazione*. In those days, from improvised means of conveyance, hundreds of volunteers unloaded thousands of volumes, muddied beyond recognition, which after the initial cleaning were hung in the large drying rooms.

*Tobacco drying, a typical sight in the valley*

Here, thanks to a special airing system, began the slow process of drying out the pages damaged by the waters of the Arno river. The sodden pages took the place of tropical tobacco leaves, the product of a crop which after the second world war transformed vast areas of the Val Tiberina, over which a white gauze covering was stretched creating underneath the right hot and humid climate conditions required by the tobacco plant to thrive.

It appears that tobacco crops were introduced to Umbria back in the 16th century, and later, the small Republic of Cospaia, a duty-free area on the border between the Grand Duchy of Tuscany and the Papal State, became a flourishing center of contraband. Later, in the 1970s, tobacco cultivation, no longer profitable, was gradually abandoned, and so was the use of the drying rooms. Thus, in 1978 Alberto Burri was afforded a first building in which to display his works; and later, with the purchase of the entire complex by the *Palazzo Albizzini Foundation*, a general recovery project, geared to converting the structures into a museum, got underway. The use of these special structures has made it possible to display similarly unique works of art; unique also in their dimensions, such as those recently donated by Burri, who in this way has endowed his city with a complete collection of his works.

by battlemented gangways. In the 16th century, the Bufalini family transformed the castle into their residence, adding loggias and windows and entrusting Doceno with the decoration of its interior (1537-54), which still has its rich period furnishings and a picture gallery mirroring the tastes of the noble Umbrian family. In the style of the period is also the splendid garden, with its boxwood maze. The nearby parish church

has canvas paintings (16th-17th cent.) commissioned by the Bufalini, and, below the rectory, an ancient crypt (9th cent.).

Excavations at **Colle Plinio** (368 m) have unearthed the remains of Pliny the Younger's villa *"in Tuscis,"* a grand country villa complete with wine cellar, vats for the pressing of grapes and a thermal system. Mosaic and marble fragments provide some indication of the pomp of this dwelling.

# 3 The Eugubine valley and the Umbrian Apennine

## Area profile

"Oh emerald Eugubine!" Maecenas defined the stone city which stands out at the foot of steep Mt. Ingino, almost as if it were carved in gray limestone blocks, "of a sublime monochrome" as Guido Piovene observed "which only in the Renaissance was enhanced with sandstone." Gubbio rises in the middle of a mountain-surrounded valley which westwardly connects it to the Val Tiberina, and eastwardly to the Gualdo Tadino valley. From whatever direction in Umbria you arrive, the compact mass of monumental buildings heralds the town's typical medieval character, whose special charm is also enhanced by ancient local traditions, like the Candle Race, which give the impression that this city is bent on embedding itself in a second layer of archaic memories. Even the surrounding area, which corresponds to the region's northwest quadrant,

*Crossbow competition at Gubbio*

is influenced by this city's "stony charm." Delimited at the east by a compact steep limestone mountain range, it opens toward the Adriatic through the Fossato di Vico pass, while to the west the area slopes toward the Tiber valley with a series of rolling sandy and marly hills. Via Flaminia fueled the settling of areas between Fossato and Scheggia, while the abbeys and military garrisons fostered the development of areas surrounding the main thoroughfare.

## 3.1 Gubbio
**A circular itinerary starting from Piazza Quaranta Martiri** *(map on page 82)*

Founded by the Umbri who had settled on Mt. Ingino and the nearby Mt. Calvo, probably in the early millennium BC, the urban layout of ancient *Ikuvium* is documented by the Tavole Eugubine (bronze plaques today in the *Palazzo dei Consoli*), an exceptionally valuable epigraphic testament carved in Umbrian characters between the late 2nd and early 1st century BC. Thanks to descriptions of ceremonial rituals, in fact, it is possible to establish the city's confines and its civic composition: the *Arce Fisia*, occupying a dominant position, and the *Tota Ikuvina* (the city) along the city's slopes, collectively protected by a perimeter wall. Gubbio continued to be a center of primary importance even in Roman times, as can be seen by the remains of thermal baths, a theater, and a mausoleum. After the barbaric invasions and phases of Visigothic destruction (early 5th cent.), the peace treaty of 605

marked Umbria's division between the Longobard duchy of Spoleto and the Byzantine duchy of Perugia. Under the regency of Bishop Ubaldo Baldassini (ca. 1130-60), Gubbio consolidated its hold over a vast area, repelling the league of the nearby cities headed by Perugia (1151). Between the 12th and 13th century there ensued a period of significant urban development, involving the construction of the city's gateways and its aqueduct, besides its administrative subdivision into four administrative neighborhoods. In 1384 the city passed to the Montefeltro family of Urbino, and the transfer of the communal magistratures to seigniorial power was reflected in the construction of the Ducal Palace opposite the Cathedral. Subsequently, when power had passed into the hands of the Della Rovere (1508), the city, absorbed by the duchy of Urbino, underwent a period of decay, and in 1624 became a part of the Papal State, thus accentuating its isolation, and speeding the city's economic and urban decline. In the 19th century, while the city's walls were destroyed, a campaign aimed at restoring its medieval layout got underway. After World War II, new urban schemes were approved to rationalize the building of the city's outskirts, and to requalify the medieval core on the other. This was manifested in the Gubbio Charter (1960), which

azza della Signoria. Proceeding along Via Galeotti and Via Ducale you ascend to the city's loftiest spot, dominated by the Cathedral and the Palazzo Ducale. From Piazza della Signoria you reach the church of Santa Maria Nuova along Via Savelli della Porta, through the quarter of Sant'Andrea. Outside Porta Romana, which opens onto the medieval perimeter, is located the vast complex of Sant'Agostino. Continuing along Corso Garibaldi, you first reach the church

*Gubbio perched on the steep sides of Mt. Ingino*

focused on the functional restoration of the city's historic areas.

Our itinerary takes us along the same road that the inhabitants of Gubbio cover during the Corsa dei Ceri, a festivity whose origins are lost in time (page 87), with the only variation of its starting point, Piazza Quaranta Martiri, where today it is practically obligatory to park. After a short visit to the remains of the Roman Theater, you reach the convent of San Domenico, crossing the feudal quarter of San Martino along Via Cavour. Via Vantaggi and Via Gabrielli take you to the 13th-century palace of the Capitano del Popolo, in the vicinity of Porta Metauro, outside which stands the church of Santa Croce della Foce, the starting point for the procession that retraces the passion of Christ. Through the quarter of San Giuliano, beyond the Camigano river, and along the characteristic Via dei Consoli, you come to the broad open space of Pi-

of San Pietro, in the quarter of the same name, and then Via della Repubblica, which opens onto the left in Piazza San Giovanni with the church of San Giovanni Battista. Lastly, you conclude your visit by returning to Piazza Quaranta Martiri.

**Piazza Quaranta Martiri** (B1-2). A medieval market situated on the edge of the city's most ancient core, today the area is part parking lot and part public gardens. Also, it is from here, where the main regional roads meet, that you have the best view* of the upper city standing out against the mountain. The square is dedicated to the city's victims of 1944.

Its northern side is delimited by the elongated 14th-century structure of the former "Spedal Grande," a hospital built by the brotherhood of the Blessed Virgin Mary, and ceded in 1452 to the lay Brotherhood of the Bianchi (the Whites). In the

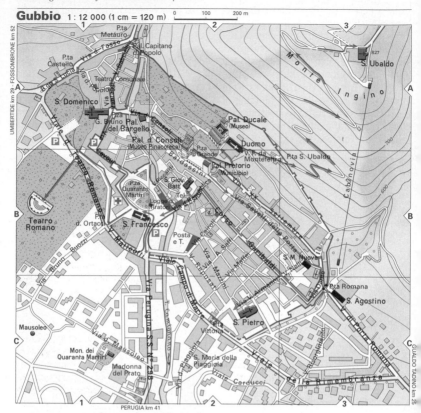

**Gubbio**  1 : 12 000 (1 cm = 120 m)

17th century, the wool-weavers' guild added on an open gallery, the *Loggiato dei Tiratori dell'Arte della Lana*, which surmounts the entire length of the preceding structure, utilizing it as a pressing facility. The portico that leads to the edifice was once adorned with mural paintings, of which there remains a *Virgin between Sts. Peter and Paul* by Bernardino di Nanni (1473). To the hospital was annexed the church of **Santa Maria dei Laici**, built in 1313, and enlarged, perhaps to a plan by Francesco Allegrini, when the complex was being restructured. The building, damaged during the latest earthquake (1997), is undergoing restoration and its movable art patrimony is temporarily stored in the Palazzo Ducale.

**Convento di San Francesco**\* (B1-2). Near the Spadalonga warehouse, where tradition has it that St. Francis, after leaving his paternal home, was welcomed and clothed, there rose in 1255 the Franciscan complex which today closes off the square's southern boundary. The church is a Gothic structure, featuring a simple but unfinished facade, a Gothic portal and a

small rose window from Foligno's church of San Francesco. A double portal and small rose window (14th cent.) adorn the church's left side, which is embellished with pilaster strips and tall single-light windows (partly walled). Its exterior is completed by three polygonal apses which belonged to the original vessel, upon which rests a similarly polygonal bell tower (15th cent.). Inside, there are a tall nave and spacious aisles resting on cross-vaults, which in 1720 substituted the open-beamed roof, still visible in the remodeled section toward the apse. In the right apse, the *Chapel of San Francesco* evinces traces of the ancient Spadalonga house incorporated within the church. The central apse is decorated with 13th-century frescoes dating from the church's construction. The left apse, dedicated to the Madonna, is decorated with **Scenes from the Life of Mary**\*, frescoed in 17 frames by Ottaviano Nelli (ca. 1408 and 1413); on the altar, similarly by Nelli, a *Our Lady of Mercy*, within an embossed silver frame. The 14th-century sacristy leads to the cloister with its 14th-century frescoes. The sacristy gives access to the *cloister*, with 14th-century frescoes. Elegant mullioned windows flank the portal which leads into the *capitular hall*, where is conserved a fresco (probably 14th-cent.), originally in the cloister and portraying the *Transport of the Holy House of Loreto*, the earliest known representation of the theme. The recently arranged **Raccolta d'Arte di San Francesco** includes archaeological finds, 14th- to 18th-century goldwork, 16th-century vestments and vessels, and paintings. Particularly noteworthy is the seal known as *Sigillo dell'antica custodia di Gubbio*.

At the end of the short street to the left of the church stands the *Porta degli Ortacci*, so called because here were located the vegetable gardens of the convent. Turning down *Via Buozzi* you come to the **Mausoleo** (C1), what remains of a Roman tomb, containing a barrel-vault sepulchral chamber. From the doorway, skirting the walls on the right, you come to the **Roman Theater** (B1), dating from the 1st century AD. Digs and restoration work have been ongoing since 1789 and have brought to light exceptionally finely crafted and well-preserved mosaics. In summer, classical dramas are performed in this unique setting.

**San Martino Quarter** (A-B1). *Via Cavour* cuts through this quarter which is marked by a goodly number of aristocratic homes. At the end of the street stands *Palazzo Beni*, an austere edifice built by the noble Beni family in the late 14th century, and which incorporated pre-existing structures. The portal dates from the 16th-17th century. From here you proceed to *Piazza Giordano Bruno*, dedicated to the Dominican friar who was burned at the stake as a heretic. Here rises the Dominican complex; an area where a feudal settlement had developed in the 11th century, which was to give rise to the city's first medieval layout.

**San Domenico** (A1). Having relocated in the nearby monastery in the early 14th century, the Dominicans enlarged the smaller church of San Martino (which dated from 1180), changing the church's name to San

*The arches of the Roman Theater in Gubbio*

Domenico. Remodeled in the 16th and 18th centuries, its aisle was shortened, but its facade still remained unfinished. Massive quadrangular columns support the apse. The interior (undergoing restoration) features frescoes of the 15th-century Gubbio school, carved choir-stalls dating from 1563, and an admirable *lectern** attributed to Terzuolo. The left arm of the crossing contains works by Felice Damiani (*Circumcision*, 1603), Giovanni Baglioni (*Magdalen*), and a *Virgin with Child* attributed to Raffaellino del Colle (1546).

To the right of San Domenico, proceeding along Via Borromei and Via Popolo, where stands the *Teatro Comunale* (1713-38), which was restructured in the mid-19th century, you come to the church of **San Secondo** in Via Tiferante. The church was originally built between the 12th and 14th century, and remodeled in the early 15th. Inside hang works by Bernardino Nocchi, Stefano Tofanelli, Bernardino di Nanni, and Giacomo di Benedetto Bedi. The main altar (Gothic) dates from 1336, whereas the Lord's table is of the 8th century.

**Toward Porta Metauro**. We now proceed along Via Vantaggi and Via Gabrielli, where stood a huge *palazzo* with a tall medieval defensive tower; this brings us to the so-called **Palazzo del Capitano del Popolo** (A1), which currently serves as an exhibition facility. A typical late-13th-century structure in the Gubbio manner, its curved facade follows the curvature of the street, and is graced by three tiers of ogive windows. Opposite the building's entrances stands an oval stone, commonly known as the *Pietrone*, where the cross bearers pause during the procession of Holy Friday. Inside the palace there is a rather unique lavabo, or stone basin. The street ends at **Porta Metauro**, the only gate of the city to have a wooden door, and the remains of a mural painting in its lunette.

The main entrance to **Parco Ranghiasci**, which has preserved its original structure as determined by the Ranghiasci-Brancaleoni family in the mid-19th century, opens on Via Gabrielli. Higher up one can still see a tower and a part of the city walls.

**Santa Croce della Foce** (A1). Situated outside the gate, the church has always been the starting point of the Holy Friday procession. Built perhaps upon late-Roman foundations, and remodeled in the 16th and 17th centuries, its interior has an impressive gilded coffered ceiling from the 17th century.

*Palazzo dei Consoli, overlooking Piazza Grande*

**Via dei Consoli*** (A1-2). One of the city's most characteristic streets, it was probably built upon the course of pre-Roman fortifications. Rising broad and curvilinear, and flanked by ashlar-fronted buildings which, with their fine masonry and the ample street-level openings of the shops and warehouses, give an exact picture of what Gubbio was like in the late Middle Ages. The narrow ogival doorways (see house at no. 49) at street level are known as *porte del morto* (deadman's doors), and through external wooden stairways (now in stone, where they still survive) provided access to the upper stories. A magnificent example of these homes is the so-called **Palazzo del Bargello** (1302), which faces a square by the same name. Its well-preserved facade consists of three ashlared tiers and scalloped-stone framed windows. Opposite is the 16th-century *Fontana dei Matti* (the Madmen's Fountain), remodeled in 1862. According to a popular tradition, it is sufficient to circle the basin three times, splashing yourself with its water, to deserve the title of "madman." The square, where once stood the Umbrian Tessenaca gate, is the heart of the *San Giuliano quarter*, which takes its name from the church (now extensively remodeled), and which is documented in a papal bull of 1182.

**Piazza Grande**** (A-B2). A bold medieval architectural achievement, this "hanging" square was conceived as a grandiose monumental churchyard connecting the two seats of the civil magistratures: the Palazzo dei Consoli, the only one to have been completed, and the Palazzo Pretorio, which remained unfinished after the advent of the Gabrielli lordship (1350) and the end of communal autonomy. In 1321, the decision was made to build this "artificial" square in the very center of the

city, an undertaking which involved placing supporting structures beneath the suspended area and the buildings themselves, decidedly oversized with respect to their "historic" setting. Particularly impressive is the "terrace" which juts toward the surrounding countryside.

**Palazzo dei Consoli**** (A-B2). The palace is one of Italy's chief examples of civic architecture. As indicated by an inscription above the portal, it was built between 1332 and 1349 by Angelo da Orvieto (who however probably executed only the portal and the stairway), with the help of Gattapone, acting as his surveyor. It is rectangular in layout and faces the square with an ashlared facade offset at intervals by tiers of sturdy pilasters. A slender tower rises on the left.

A fan-shaped stairway leads up to the Gothic portal and thence to the *Arengo*, a magnificent barrel-vaulted hall where once the communal popular assemblies were held (open winter, 10am-1pm, 2pm-5pm; summer, 10am-1pm, 3pm-6pm). The ground floor is occupied by the **Museo Civico** featuring finds unearthed up to the 19th century: inscriptions, fragments, statues, and marblework dating from Roman and early medieval periods. Of particular interest is a Roman sarcophagus upon which are carved bacchanal scenes and an inscription by Gneus Satrius Rufo describing works carried out in Gubbio in the time of Augustus. The palace's former sacristy contains a **coin collection** with specimens minted in Gubbio from the Umbrian period to the 18th century. In the rooms, which are accessed from **Via Gattapone**, are on display more recent finds tracing Gubbio's evolution from pre-historic times to the early Middle Ages. In the palace's former chapel are placed the famous **Tavole Eugubine**, found in 1444 in the vicinity of Scheggia by Paolo di Gregorio, who in 1456 ceded them to the Commune in exchange for grazing rights. These are seven bronze plaques of varying size inscribed partly with Umbrian characters of Etruscan derivation (2nd cent. BC), and partly in Latin (late 2nd-early 1st cent.) treating such themes as worship, legal systems, the religious ceremonies of the Gubbian community and of the Atiedii brotherhood. On the upper floor, preceded by the *Sala della Loggetta*, are displayed ceramics made in the Gubbio area from the 16th to the 19th century. Arranged in chronological order, the works in the **Pinacoteca***  illustrate local artistry from the Middle Ages to the Baroque. In its five rooms you can admire a *Crucifixion* by Maestro della Croce di Gubbio, and a *gonfalon of the Confraternita della Misericordia*, Sinibaldo Ibi's highest achievement. Of outstanding workmanship are the furnishings, the 16th-century fireplace with andirons (Room 2) and the stone wall font of the same period (the palace was directly linked to the aqueduct).

*One of the so-called Tavole Eugubine, kept at Palazzo dei Consoli*

**Palazzo Pretorio** (B2). Standing opposite Palazzo dei Consoli, this building appears as an unfinished Gothic structure (1349), subsequently remodeled from 1475 to the 17th century, and enlarged in the 19th (it now houses the Town Hall). Originally it consisted of three vast halls, one above the other, covered by cross vaults supported by a sole central pillar. To the left, the Neoclassical *Palazzo Ranghiasci-Brancaleoni* with its park to the rear (page 83) which, in accordance with English garden design, links pre-existing buildings; inside is conserved a Roman mosaic.

Before starting our climb toward the Cathedral, it is well to take a quick look at **Via Baldassini**, which runs parallel, albeit at a lower level, to *Piazza Grande*. Lined by numerous antique shops, the street is dominated by the sheer front of the *Palazzo dei Consoli* and by a compact row of 13th-century houses, amid which stands out the so-called **Casa dei Baldassini**, where tradition has it that Ubaldo Baldassini, the city's patron saint, was born in 1084. The

square can be reached from Via Gattapone, opposite the house.

**Toward the Platea Communis**. A narrow passageway (on the northeast side of Piazza Grande) leads to the *Via Galeotti** steps, a picturesque medieval street, which links overlying *Via Federico da Montefeltro*. The street is overhung by the 13th-century **Palazzo del Capitolo dei Canonici**, with its elegant mullion-windowed facade. Through an iron grating on the ground floor can be seen a large 16th-century wooden barrel, called the *botte dei canonici* (the priests' barrel), with a 387 barrel (200 hectoliter) capacity. Dominated by the Palazzo Ducale and the Cathedral, this vast area was the political and religious center in the days of Bishop Ubaldo.

**Cathedral*** (A2). Dedicated to Sts. James and Marianus, the Cathedral's design is attributed to Giovanni da Gubbio and built in an area granted by bishop Bentivoglio (1190-94). Completed in 1229, enlarged in 1336, and still again in the mid-16th century, it has a simple facade with an ogival portal and a rose window surrounded by symbols of the Evangelists and the mystical lamb, which were parts of the former church. The effect created by the church's broad nave, with its ten large pointed transversal roof-supporting arches (a typical local model), is truly magnificent. Of particular interest, in the archway on the right, a *Pietà* by Dono Doni; after which comes the *Chapel of the Santissimo Sacramento* (18th cent.), which was frescoed throughout by between 1654 and 1656 by Francesco Allegrini, who achieved one of his best works. In the *presbytery*, there are two organs with intaglios by Gubbio artists Luca and Giacomo Maffei (1550). An example of particularly fine workmanship is the *tavola*, with a gilded background, by Sinibaldo Ibi (1507).

The **Museo Diocesano**, housing art collection from the cathedral has been arranged in the nearby *Palazzo dei Canonici*. Among the valuable works is a magnificent 16th-century Flemish cope in gold brocade (parts of which were stolen in 1990) and the *Virgin in Glory* from the church of Agnano, bearing the signature "Opus Melli Eugubii" (i.e., Mello da Gubbio). The recent discovery of this signature during restoration work has shed some doubt on Guiduccio Palmerucci as the earliest 14th-century Gubbian painter. The section devoted to incriptions offers Roman and medieval examples as well as expressive representations of the patron saints. Among painterly works, frescoes by the Maestro Espressionista di Santa Chiara and by Guido di Palmeruccio.

**Palazzo Ducale**\*\* (A2). Also called *Corte Nuova*, this palace, whose construction was ordered by Federico da Montefeltro, subsumes areas and medieval public buildings, transforming them in Renaissance style. Almost certainly designed by Francesco di Giorgio and completed in 1480, the building consists of two central structures, one facing the valley and the other the mountain; the two blocks are connected by a magnificent courtyard known as **Corte d'Onore**\*, with elegant Renaissance forms, and accessed via a plain stone portal.

State property, the building was restored and converted into a museum (open 8.30am-7pm; closed Mon). The various rooms, despoiled in the early 19th century of their original furnishings, now house also temporary exhibitions. Especially striking are the two cabinets located in the first room (1493 and 1627); the doors of the main portal\*, carved and emblazoned with symbols of the Montefeltro family, and attributed to Mariotto di Paolo Sensi – called *Il Terzuolo* – one of the major exponents of the art of wood carving.

In 1977, beneath the Renaissance complex an **archaeological area** was unearthed (10th-13th cent.), featuring remains of streets, a tower, a *palatium*, a warehouse, and two cisterns, besides a fired-brick paved surface and an underpass which linked the Cathedral's churchyard with the road that leads to Mt. Ingino. However, still more interesting, especially from a historic viewpoint, is the finding of a village presenting a stratification which goes from the early Middle Ages to the Renaissance (visiting hours same as museum).

Following the steep and winding *Corso delle Candele*, which climbs up Mt. Ingino amid pine and cypress trees, a demanding detour will take you to the **basilica of Sant'Ubaldo** (A3). Alternative, and much less demanding, routes are the cableway near the Roman gate (page 87), which in a few minutes takes you to the church; or the 6-kilometer road from *Porta Metauro* (page 83), which goes up the Bottaccione ravine

and touches the *Parco del Coppo* (elev. 900 m), which is a recreational facility. 827 meters high, the basilica is essentially an enlarged version (1511-14) of the medieval church of San Gervasio, and offers an elegant cloister with octagonal brick columns that lead to the church's nave and four aisles, embellished with 16th and 18th-century paintings. On the main altar there is a Renaissance urn which contains the body of St. Ubald, which was transferred to the basilica in 1194, in honor of whom every year is staged the *Corsa dei Ceri,* or Candle Race (page 87). The candles themselves are kept in the first right-hand aisle.

Mt. Ingino becomes the theater of a fabulous Christmas reenactment when, on its slopes, the world's largest **Christmas tree** comes alive. The mountain's southern slope is lit up by 450 colored lights and 16 kilometers of wiring which continue up to the mountain top, describing a dazzling comet shape.

**Sant'Andrea quarter** (B-C 2-3). From Piazza Grande we proceed along *Via XX Settembre*, where it is thought the old Umbrian wall ran, with its rows of characteristic 17th-18th-century houses. After a few steps, *Via Mastro Giorgio* to the right quickly takes you to *Via Savelli della Porta*, with its 17th-century church of the *Muratori*, otherwise called **San Francesco della Pace**, where, during the night, as related in Saint Francis's *Fioretti*, the famous wolf tamed by the saint used to seek refuge. Inside is conserved the stone upon which St. Francis of Assisi preached to the people, and the three statues which make up the Ceri. Along the same street (no. 16) stands **Palazzo della Porta**, attributed to Francesco di Giorgio, with its elegant Renaissance portal. At the end of the street rises the church of **Santa Maria Nuova**, built between 1270 and 1280, and now state property. Its single nave, remodeled in the 17th century, is accessed via a plain ogival portal, which is asymmetric with respect to the facade. Of the fine 14th and 15th-century frescoes which once embellished it, there remains only a *Madonna del Belvedere*\* by Ottaviano Nelli (1413), encased in a sandstone tabernacle dating from 1510. The church also conserves furnishings from various local churches. Once having gone beyond 14th-century *Palazzo Falcucci* (no. 79), where tradition has it that Dante stayed, you come to *Via Dante* which, to the left, leads to the Umbrian *Porta Vehia* (4th-3rd cent. BC), remodeled in the Middle Ages. Nearby stands the *San Marziale monastery*, formerly Benedictine and now Carmelite, with the church of *Sant'Andrea*, whence

## Saint Ubaldo and the ceri

The objective of this traditional race is not that of crossing the finish line first, since the order of the procession is always the same. In lead position, the *cero* of Saint Ubaldo, in the center that of Saint George, and in the rear that of Saint Anthony. Instead, in the ten or so minutes it takes the bearers of the three imposing structures to cover the climb from the city gate to the basilica of Sant'Ubaldo (elev. 827 m), the Saint

*Bright colors and crowds at the Corsa dei Ceri*

Ubaldo *cero* bearers must manage to close the portal of the church leaving the others out. The latter, on the other hand, have to try and stick at least a part of their *cero* through the doors.

This ritual, which never changes, is repeated every year on 15

May, on the eve of celebrations in honor of Gubbio's patron saint.

The *ceri*, taken by the regional government to symbolize Umbria, are three 4-meter tall wooden devices weighing approximately 200 kilos, each consisting of two superimposed hollow octagonal prisms, joined by a central mast.

Each *cero* is fixed to a *barella* (stretcher) which the bearers carry on their shoulders.

To be chosen for the task, which, contrary to appearances, does not require great strength but a lot of training, is a source of pride.

The *ceri* are crowned with statues of Saint Ubaldo, protector of masons and stone-cutters, Saint George, patron of craftsmen and haberdashers, and Saint Anthony, patron of both peasants and students. The rituals which mark this event, the procession, and the race, are all very spectacular, involving not only the entire population of Gubbio, but also the numerous tourists who flock to this Umbrian city.

*Contestants raise one of the heavy Ceri in the initial stage of the race*

the name of the neighborhood. The apse is made up of materials from other structures. Turning right, we come to medieval tower-shaped **Porta Romana**, a gate featuring in its interior (open 10am-1pm, 3pm-7pm; closed Mon) an interesting collection of reverberation-furnace majolicas (16th-19th cent.), which boasts pieces by Maestro Giorgio Andreoli and his school. Immediately outside the gate is the complex of **Sant'Agostino** (1251), with its 18th-century facade and beamed ceiling supported by eight large arches, an arrangement that was fairly common in Gubbio. The apse is entirely covered with frescoes of the Nelli school, portraying *Scenes of the Life of Saint Augustine* in 26 pictures. The triumphal arch is decorated with an imposing scene of the *Last Judgment*.

**San Pietro** (C2). Continuing along the sloping Via Neri, which is a particularly de-

manding stretch of the Corsa dei Ceri because of its gradient and curvature, you come to the church of one of Gubbio's most ancient convents. Here are evident traces of the successive phases of construction, such as a small five-arched portico (late Roman period), the transformation of the church's layout from a three to single arched nave (13th cent.), and lastly the various Renaissance transformations to the interior by the Olivetan Benedictines (1519), who closed the central rose window and opened two lateral windows to make room for the new *organ*, by Vincenzo Beltrami. The frescoes in the chapel, such as the *Crèche* at the 5th right altar, are by Raffaellino del Colle.

After San Pietro, through medieval *Porta Vittoria* we come to *Borgo della Piaggiola*, characterized by the 15th-century church of *Santa Maria della Piaggiola* (C2), which was rebuilt in 1613.

## 3.1 The Eugubine valley 3.2 The Nocera-Gualdo Apennine

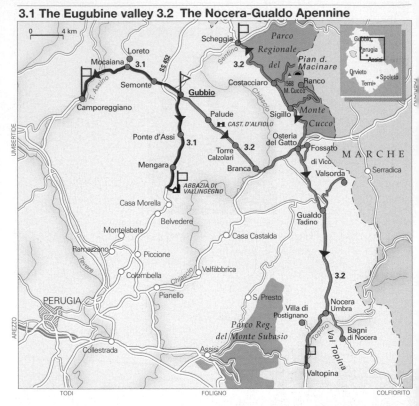

Although it is unfinished on the outside, it boasts some extraordinary Baroque decorations and stuccowork in its interior, which include a *Pietà* by Domenico di Cecco (1444) and a *Virgin and Child*, attributed to Ottaviano Nelli.

**Toward San Giovanni Battista**. Saint Ubaldo's tabernacle (1761) marks the beginning of the broad and straight **Corso Garibaldi** (B2), the main thoroughfare of the San Pietro quarter, developed in the early 13th century and characterized by a regular street grid. At the beginning of the avenue stands the church of the Santissima Trinità, built in 1410 by the Augustinian brotherhood. At the end and to the right, Via della Repubblica leads to the church of **San Giovanni Battista**, in the very heart of medieval Gubbio. The church, with its limestone Gothic facade and Romanesque campanile, was built between the 13th and 14th centuries. The hexagonal Gothic chapel of the baptistery contains a Renaissance majolica *baptismal font*, and, above the altar, a *Baptism of Christ* by Perugino (school of).

Every year on 15 August, the city celebrates the **Palio della Balestra** (crossbow competition) a nocturnal challenge amid torches and dazzling purple and black costumes, in remembrance of the unending struggle between the city's various quarters (Sant'Andrea, San Pietro, San Martino, and San Giuliano).

Leaving Gubbio along Via Perugia, one can admire the elegant square-stone facade of the **Madonna del Prato** (C1), a church built in 1662-78, most probably to designs by Francesco Borromini. Bishop Sperelli, who wanted the church built, commissioned Francesco Allegrini with the fresco decoration of the interior.

In little over 2 km from Porta Metauro, along the state road (298) to Scheggia, one comes to the **Gola del Bottaccione**, a gorge carved by the Camignano river between the cliff walls of Mts. Ingino and Calvo. The gorge is particularly interesting from a geological standpoint, and presents a complete carbon sediment in which "magnetite needles" (iron oxide) have been identified, a fossil "compass" of sorts. Unusual platinum-type minerals have also been discovered in this area, which are thought to be residues of meteorites.

## *The Eugubine valley*

### The Assino Valley

This valley connects the Gubbio depression with the upper Tiber valley, transversely cutting the Mt. Civitello dorsal. Leaving Gubbio along Via Tifernate (state road 219), we go beyond the former *Capuchin convent*, today a hotel (which boasts a fresco by Ottaviano Nelli), and head toward a woody valley deeply cut by a river. Where the Contessa state road branches off in the direction of the Marche region, we come to the Romanesque church of *San Donato*, restructured in the 18th century. In *Monteleto* (elev. 454 m) have been unearthed the remains of a large ashlar-block wall, identified as having constituted the foundations of a temple dedicated to the Roman goddess Diana (Republican age). Continuing along this road, we reach *Loreto*, with its church of San Giovanni (12th cent.). Again on state road 219, we follow the river course: on our right the *Castello di Carbonara* (12th cent.) one of the most intact fortified buildings of the entire region. At km 17 we come to *Camporeggiano* (elev. 316 m), where in 1057 St. Peter Damian erected the abbey of **San Bartolomeo** with an interesting crypt.

### From Gubbio to Perugia

State road 298 Eugubina crosses the Gubbio valley, on the edge of which stands the church of **Santa Maria Maddalena**, which boasts mural paintings dating from the 15th-16th centuries. This small temple was one of a series of hospices located along the "Via Municipalia" to Assisi, renamed *Via Francescana* because, according to tradition, it was the way followed by St. Francis to reach Gubbio after leaving his father's house. During his journey, Francis stopped at a monastery traditionally identified as the abbey of **Vallingegno** (at km 14.3). Rebuilt by the Benedictines in the 13th century, the crypt conserves a late imperial ark containing the remains of the holy martyr after whom the church is named. After an overall 41-km drive we come to Perugia.

## 3.2 The Nocera-Gualdo Apennine

**An excursion from Gubbio to Gualdo Tadino and to Nocera Umbra, 40.3 km** (*map on p. 88*)

The first leg of this itinerary winds along state road 219, marked by small varying settlements, and alternately dotted with defensive castles. Having crossed the Chiascio river, after Branca we head along the Gualdo Tadino valley, which opens at the foot of the Apennine dorsal that divides the Umbrian and Marche regions. After skirting a small industrial area, the road comes to the Osteria del Gatto crossroads (19.5 km) where it runs into the Via Flaminia. On the hillside opposite stands Fossato di Vico. From Osteria del Gatto, you can head in a northwestern direction along the Flaminia, which, to the east and up to the regional border, delimits the mountainous Mt. Cucco park area, classified as a natural regional park. Included in the area are the villages of Sigillo, Costacciaro, and Scheggia (the latter at a distance of 16 km from Osteria del Gatto). This expansive mountain area is characterized by Benedictine hermitages and monasteries. From the Osteria del Gatto crossroads, take state road 3 (Flaminia) in the direction of Nocera Umbra, crossing the Gualdo plain which, to the left, is dominated by Mt. Maggio, whose slopes, in the 1930s, were replanted with black pine. The Flaminia, to the right of which runs the former Roman roadway, now occupied by Gualdo's in-

*A farmstead nestled in the greenery of the Valtopina*

dustrial area, is flanked on its left by a piedmont road linking a series of small settlements that arose around churches. After Gualdo Tadino, you continue on in Nocera Umbra territory (14 km), amid visible remains along the ancient Via Flaminia. Recovery from the extensive damage caused by the 1997 and 1998 earthquakes will have to go hand in hand with strategies geared to tapping the area's significant historic, natural, and traditional resources.

### The Eugubine valley castles
Proceeding along state road 219, in the area of the Eugubine and Assino valleys, you come in sight of **Castel d'Alfiolo**, or *Badia*, erected as a watch and defensive tower by Counts d'Alfiolo in the 11th century. Between the 12th and 13th centuries the complex was converted into a Benedictine monastery, subsequently (16th cent.) to become the residence of Cardinal Cervini, the future Pope Marcellus II. These numerous castle structures tell us that the ridges dominating the plain to the northeast constituted a noteworthy line of fortification. *Torre Calzolari* (elev. 522 m) is actually a neogothic transformation (19th cent.) of a former feudal complex. The *Branca* castle (elev. 385 m), which belonged to the family of that name, is documented in the 12th century; between the 18th and 19th century the castle was turned into a residence. Lastly, *Castello di Colmollaro*, built near the Saonda river, is where Dante is said to have stayed during his difficult pilgrimage.

### Fossato di Vico
After crossing the *Chiascio* river, one of the Tiber's major left-bank tributaries, you leave the Gubbio valley and come to Fossato di Vico (elev. 581 m, pop. 2,403), the northernmost boundary of the Gualdo Tadino valley. Around the fortified castle, of which scant ruins remain, there developed a medieval settlement which was hotly contested by Perugia and Gubbio (13th cent.). Proceeding along the steep ascent from the Borgo to the center, you come to the church of *San Benedetto*, which vaunts frescoes of the Gubbian school. The **Piaggiola Chapel** is adorned with mural paintings by the school of Ottaviano Nelli. Thereafter you come to the church of **San Pietro**\*, founded in the 11th century, and featuring two ogive aisles and barrel vaults. Famous are Fossato's "Rughe," covered urban walkways built for defensive purposes, but a useful system for obtaining extra building space.

### Mt. Cucco Natural Park
In the townships of Sigillo, Costacciaro, and Scheggia, this natural (and regionally protected) area covers a surface of some 10,000 hectares. Exceptionally rich in terms of vegetation, fauna, and geological deposits, the park reaches to the boundaries of the Marche region. The core of this area is the massive limestone **Mt. Cucco** (elev. 1,566 m), which, with its conical shape, dominates the Umbro-Marche landscape. Here, excursion buffs will find their "paradise" (a trail map can be obtained at Costacciaro's national speleology center), besides being able to admire the various fascinating effects of soil erosion, along with numerous springs and ravines cut in the course of centuries by the force of the river. Among these, **Rio Freddo** is particularly spectacular, where a rock-cut canyon 5 km long and 200 meters deep has been carved out by the river.

From Sigillo, take the scenic route which climbs the 9-km mountain slope, after which you come to the *Val di Ranco* (elev. 1,040 m), amid woods and prairies that afford ideal walks. However, the area's major attraction is the **Mt. Cucco grotto**, the entrance to which (elev. 1,390) is sheer above the Acqua Fredda canal. Discovered in the 16th century, and systematically explored starting in 1890, with its 922 meters in depth it ranks 5th in the world. The most fascinating feature is the so-called *Sala Margherita*, a space which owes its name to the countless stalactites and stalagmites, which create a peculiar floral impression. Caution, however, is necessary: excursionists descending down to 30 meters need to be well equipped; indeed, the ensuing leg of the descent is reserved for experienced speleologists only.

### Sigillo
The town (elev. 490 m, pop. 2,403) rises along the Via Flaminia at the foot of Mt. Cucco, in an area which was already populated during Roman times. After the 1751 earthquake, the town underwent extensive rebuilding which altered the fortified appearance it had previously assumed when Perugia was the area's dominating city (1274). The town's center is Piazza dei Martiri, faced by the *Palazzo Comunale*, whose facade was redone in 1802. The church of **Sant'Agostino**, was restructured in 1761; the church conserves an *Annunciation* by Ippolito Borghese (1617), the only canvas that the painter, otherwise active in Naples, left his native city; other notable works include a gilded copper *cross* by Enrico Piamonte (1494). The church of **Sant'Anna**, today included in the ceme-

## Of towns and cakes

Anyone so persuaded can try the following experiment. Take a traditional product and ascertain how its composition and presentation vary from place to place, sometimes differing markedly, but at times in ways which are barely perceptible. A case in point is the *torta al testo*, a typical recipe whose origins, some claim, go as far back as to the Etruscans, and which takes its name from the terracotta pan used in its preparation. Its basic ingredients – flour and water, salt and local *pecorino* (sheep cheese), eggs and yeast – combine in infinite variations. The cake becomes thinner the further north you go, and almost becomes colorless in its Romagna variety (where it is known as *piadina*), while still retaining its typical consistency and flavor. The *torta al testo*, excellent with a drop of genuine olive oil, can be enhanced by a vast selection of ingredients (such as ham, salami, or other types of sausage meats, cheese, or the various types of fresh radish, which are especially tender and fragrant), depending on local gastronomical traditions. Of course, the same goes for olive oil, the taste and acidity level of which varies depending on soil composition and on how much sunlight the olive trees receive.

*The* torta al testo, *a typical Umbrian recipe*

tery, has a facade which dates from 1507, preceded by a 17th-century portico. The inside is decorated by votive frescoes by Matteo da Gualdo.

Other monuments to be admired in the vicinity of Sigillo is the imposing **Roman Bridge** over the Flaminia, called "Ponte Spiano," and spanning the Fonturci river. Built probably in the Augustan Age, it has survived the passing of the centuries, together with its arch composed of 13 pentagonal wedge-shaped stone blocks. Above the bridge the small church of *Santa Maria del Soccorso* was built in the 16th century.

At **Scirca** (elev. 505 m) can be seen the remains of another *Roman bridge* dubbed the "ponte dei pietroni" because of the huge size of its stones (2nd cent.); the bridge was blown up the retreating Germans in 1944. Also in the village is the Romanesque church of *Santa Maria Assunta*, with fresco decorations by Matteo da Gualdo.

### Hermitages and monasteries

Mt. Cucco's mountain area park is not only an important source of natural features. It also has many hermitages and monasteries, which, although partly abandoned, still bear witness to the intense monastic activity that once characterized this area. Near Pascelupo one can visit the *Eremo di San Girolamo* (hermitage), otherwise known as the Mt. Cucco hermitage (11th cent.), nestled inside a picturesque stone amphitheater, and restructured by the Camaldolites in the 20th century. At the spot where the Rio Freddo flows into the Sentino, on the border between Umbria and the Marche, stands the interesting abbey of **Santi Emiliano e Bartolomeo in Congiuntoli**, founded by the Benedictines, with a church dating from 1286. To the left of Isola Fossara, a woodland road (2.8 km) leads to the abbey of **Santa Maria di Sitria** (elev. 528 m), founded by St. Romuald in the 11th century, and dependent upon the abbey of Fonte Avellana.

### Costacciaro

Perched on the hillside, this village (elev. 567 m, pop. 1,307), with its regular orthogonal street pattern, partly still enclosed by walls, belies its ancient castle origins. It in fact was a Gubbian presidium along the Flaminia (13th cent.). Worth visiting is the church of **San Francesco** (14th cent.), with its nave and aisles terminating in a recessed apse and adorned with frescoes in the manner of Matteo da Gualdo; the wood altars date from the 17th century.

### Scheggia

Beyond the Sentino river, the Flaminia highway enters the town (elev. 580 m) across the *Scheggia bridge*, which was rebuilt after World War II respecting the bridge's original 1789 design; the bridge is also known as the "Botte d'Italia" (Italy's barrel) because of its vaguely barrel-shaped appearance. Scheggia developed as a way station at the junction between Gubbio, Sassoferrato, and Flaminia. The town's small *Antiquarium Comunale* is currently preparing an exhibit of Roman finds. The center acquired importance when, in the 12th century, it passed under the patronage of the Fonte Avellana hermitage (in the Marche), a powerful Benedictine abbey upon which depended many monasteries and abbeys, constituting the only human presence in these green solitary valleys between the 11th and 13th centuries.

## Gualdo Tadino

The double name of this town (elev. 536 m, pop. 14,380), which rises at the foot of Mt. Serra Santa on the edge of the broad valley created by draining a lake, synthesizes the checkered history of the town, which was repeatedly razed and then abandoned; first it was transferred above and then on the plain. The primitive Umbrian settlement of the "Tadinates," who were considered damned in the Tavole Eugubine, was located on the nearby Mori hill, as documented by recent finds; in Roman times, *Tadinum* supposedly located on the plain, along the same axis as the Flaminia (present-day Sant'Antonio di Rasina). Subsequent to disastrous arrival of King Totila of the Ostrogoths, who met his death here while attempting to flee, and the transfer of the bishopric to Nocera (1007), the settlement was rebuilt along the Feo river as a Benedictine center, known in Longobard as the *Wald*, meaning forest. Between the 11th and the 12th centuries, the abbey of Saint Benedict exercised its jurisdiction over many churches and lands, and over the very community of the Tadinites (the inhabitants of Tadino), who up to 1210 remained under its protection. Only in the early 13th century was Gualdo transferred to its present site. Having become a free commune (1237) under the protection of Frederick II, it was circled with walls and endowed with a powerful fortress. In the Middle Ages the town extended over the hillside, pivoting on the central square, which is presently occupied by two churches, one Benedictine

and the other Franciscan, and by an 18th-century public building. The 1751 and 1832 earthquakes utterly destroyed the remaining structures. Gualdo was particularly struck by the recent succession of earthquakes in September-October 1997, and again in April 1998. One of the area's most thriving economic centers, Gualdo is especially renowned for its majolica production, which is documented as far back as the 14th century, but which began to flourish in the 16th.

Our itinerary takes us along the ridge road which, from Porta San Benedetto, the only one of the four situated along the 13th-century perimeter, to be well preserved, and climbs up to the Rocca Flea. To the right opens Piazza del Mercato, now Piazza Mazzini. There follow in rapid succession Piazza XX Settembre, with its church of Santa Maria dei Raccomandati, and Piazza Grande, which lost its two medieval public buildings in the 1751 earthquake, with its church of San Francesco. Of the Palazzo del Podestà there remains only the topless civic tower which barely manages to emerge above the other buildings which were subsequently constructed around it. Next comes 19th-century Piazza Garibaldi, where the city decidedly changes its appearance; where the town's orthogonal layout gives way to the curvilinear pattern of the hillside. In the background rises the Rocca Flea, restored in the 1990s.

*The Giochi delle Porte procession during the pageant at Gualdo Tadino*

**Santa Maria dei Raccomandati**. The church, situated in Piazza XX Settembre, is the seat a Brotherhood by the same name, wherein are conserved a triptych by Matteo da Gualdo (Madonna and Child with Sts. Sebastian and Roch) and two paintings (an Annunciation and a Saint Bonaventure) by Avanzino Nucci. Facing the same square is the 13th-century church of San Donato, which boasts a painting by F. Mancini.

**Piazza Martiri della Libertà**. Completely remodeled after the 1751 earthquake, it still presents the 13th-century tower, which formerly belonged to the Palazzo del Podestà. Opposite is the *Palazzo Comunale*, erected in 1768-69 on the ruins of the Palazzo delle Arti e dei Priori.

**San Francesco***. Rises on the western boundary of the square, which it faces with its right side. The Franciscans settled here in the 13th century and reconsecrated the church in 1315. Frequently restored, it presents a bell-shaped facade, Gothic portal and trilobate lunette which faces *Corso Italia*; an unusual position for the construction of a mendicant order which preferred more open spaces. We need not be misled by the fact that it is the church's left side that faces the square; this is so as the square itself is where the convent's cloister once stood (subsequently demolished). The interior is decorated with 14th- and 15th-century frescoes, among which a large unfinished *Dormitio Virginis* by a 14th-century Umbrian painter. Suspended in the apse is an altarpiece **Crucifix***  dating from the 12th-15th century. The choir, main altar and the pulpit on the left date from the 14th century. The pilaster between the first and second chapel features a *Virgin and Child,* by Matteo da Gualdo, the earliest known work by this artist.

**San Benedetto**. With its 13th-century facade, this church dominates the side of the square opposite the church of San Francesco. Elevated to a cathedral by Benedict XV in 1915, of the original structure (1256, and subsequently remodeled during the 18th and 19th centuries) it conserves the facade with its three portals and a splendid rose window with a double ring of small columns. Against its right side leans a 16th-century *fountain*, which was built at the same time as the aqueduct (1573). Its aisled interior was rebuilt in 1875 by Virginio Vespignani, and frescoed by Ulisse Ribustini (1907-24).

**Rocca Flea**. Dating from the early Middle Ages, rebuilt by Frederick II, and restored in 1394 by Biordo Michelotti, in the 16th century this fortified castle was converted into a residence for cardinal legates, who enlarged the structure and decorated its interior. It subsequently became a prison, and in the 19th century it was given to the municipality of Gualdo Tadino, which used it for the same purpose. Its present-day structure is the result of the many uses it was destined to: walls with corner towers close the central courtyard (open Jul-Sep, 10.30am-12.30pm, 3pm-6pm; closed Mon; other months, close Mon-Wed). In the 1990s the complex was restructured and is now used as a facility for cultural and multimedia activities, as weel as a musem. The *Pinacoteca Comunale* includes works from churches in the town and the Gualdo area, among which of particular note are a polyptych* by Niccolò Alunno (1471) and three triptychs by Matteo da Gualdo. The planned *Museo della Ceramica Storica* will display pieces found during restoration of the Rocca, and works executed during the annual International Ceramics Contest, thus providing a significant overall view of local ceramic production starting from the 15th century.

Continuing beyond the Rocca for about 2 km, you come to the foot of Mt. Serra Santa (elev. 1,421 m), where rises the **Convento dell'Annunziata**, built in 1521 for the order of the Observants Minor and restructured along with the church in the 17th century. Proceeding along the *val di Gorgo*, or *di San Marzio*, you come to the solitary hermitage of *San Marzio* (12th cent.) and to the *sorgente della Rocchetta,* from which springs the mineral water bottled in a nearby plant. An early Iron Age chamber was unearthed in this valley; the chamber yielded the two gold disks which are now in Perugia's *Museo Archeologico.*

For a truly enchanting view, take the road which climbs northward through a forest of conifers until you reach the 16th-century *Santuario della Madonna del Divino Amore,* a pilgrimage site, and then the beautiful **Conca di Valsorda*** prairies, situated at an elevation of approximately a thousand meters, and which are further embellished by two tiny mountain lakes.

## Nocera Umbra

Umbrian "Nuokria" became a Roman municipality, with the name of "Nuceria Camellaria," and with the purpose of defending the stretch of the *Via Prolaquense* which branches off toward the port of Ancona. The town (elev. 520 m, pop. 5,977), being strategically situated on the border of the Spoleto duchy, played a role of primary importance even during the period of Longobard dominion. After a very short period as a self-governing commune, Nocera Umbra submitted itself to Perugia in 1202, and in 1248 was destroyed by Frederick II. Before passing under papal dominion (1439), in the late 14th century the town experienced the Trinci seignory. Tapping of the nearby thermal springs dates from the 16th century. Up to the 19th century, these renowned springs brought new prosperity to the city's traditionally agricultural economy. Having transferred its settlement from the plain, where formerly the Roman settlement was located, to the hillside, from where it could dominate the Topino valley, in the Middle Ages Nocera developed its present perimeter wall, which converges toward the Rocca and the Cathedral, and which face one another on the highest point of the spur. The city's real urban hub became Piazza Grande, seat of the local magistratures (transferred to the Rocca in the 15th century), the episcopal authority, and of the Franciscans. Nocera Umbra was damaged by repeated earthquakes which rocked the area in the fall of 1997. We suggest you visit the city also as a token of trust in its rebuilding and restoration of its artistic, civic and historic heritage.

**Historic center**. Through 16th-century *Porta Nuova*, or *Garibaldi*, widened in 1929 to make room for the "Mille Miglia" automobile race, you access tree-lined Viale Matteotti, which in turn leads to *Porta Vecchia*, the main opening in the city's 13th-century perimeter wall. The gate is flanked by two fountains (1866) bearing inscriptions extolling the properties of Nocera's water. Proceed along the main street (now *Corso Vittorio Emanuele*), which leads to the upper part of the city amid houses which were renovated in the 16th-17th centuries, whereas those along side streets date from the Middle Ages. On the right, you descend toward the **Portico di San Filippo**, a typical arcaded street built in

the 17th century on the medieval walls. A small square at the end of the arcades is the location of the neo-Gothic church of **San Filippo** (Luigi Poletti, 1864-68), featuring neo-Renaissance decorative elements and a painting by Francesco Grandi (*Death of St. Philip, with the Apparition of the Virgin*). Across the square and to the left, return to the *corso* and to the church of **Santa Chiara** (13th cent.), completely restructured in the 17th century, and which contains a *Birth of the Virgin* by Carlo Maratta (1643).

**San Francesco**\*. When Frederick II destroyed the Franciscan convent outside the walls (1319), the friars moved to their seat in Piazza Grande, occupying a small oratory adjacent to the Palazzo dei Priori. In 1494-97, the church was totally restructured and turned into a one-aisle structure, oriented northerly toward the convent which had been enlarged at the expense of the palazzo dei Priori. Its interior decoration, begun in 1497, took place in two successive phases: in the early years of the 16th century in the style of Matteo da Gualdo, and, starting in 1530, under the influence of masters from the Marche. First re-

*The polyptych by Niccolò di Liberatore painted for the Cathedral of Nocera Umbra in 1483*

stored in 1950, and again in 1981-97, the edifice has a fine stone facade with a late-Gothic portal, and an even earlier side door. In 1997, a **Museo Civico** was set up in its interior, featuring a series of frescoes painted between the 15th and 16th centuries, paintings and sculptures from the Cathedral and the surrounding area, and archaeological finds. Everything moveable was transferred elsewhere after the earthquake. Among the frescoes, of particular interest are those by Matteo da Gualdo (*Virgin and Child, Annunciation*, 2nd arch toward the right-hand apse). Among the paintings, an altarpiece **Crucifixion**, portraying the Virgin, Sts. John and Francis at Christ's feet, by a later 13th-century Roman-Umbrian painter; a **polyptych**\* made especially for the Cathedral by Niccolò di Liberatore (1483), and featuring a magnificent carved and gilded Gothic-style frame. Archaeological materials include finds from the **Portone necropolis**, dug in the 19th century and yielding 166 Longobard tombs (late 6th-later 7th cent.) richly furnished with weapons, gold objects, ceramics, and other articles.

Located in *Via Pontani*, off *Piazza Caprera*, is the church of *San Giovanni Battista*, in which hang 17th-century paintings at its Baroque altars. Slightly further on there opens the semicircular **Piazza Torre Vecchia**, which in the communal age was where the People's Council held its assemblies.

**Duomo**, or Cathedral. *Via San Rinaldo*, which ascends toward the upper part of the city, is flanked on the left by the 18th-century *Palazzo Comunale* and the *Palazzo Vescovile* (19th cent.), and on the right by the former *Seminario Vescovile* (1760), which houses the *Biblioteca Piervisani*, with some 40,000 volumes, including rare editions and illuminated hymnals. Dedicated to the Assumption, the *Duomo* rises on the same high hill where once stood the Rocca, the fortified castle belonging to the local counts. Originally Romanesque, the Cathedral was completely rebuilt in 1448, and remodeled in the 18th and 19th centuries, whereas its stone-ornamented facade is early 20th century (1925). The bell tower is 16th century. Its interior, characterized by a large nave and semicircular apse, features three canvases and murals portraying Marian themes, commissioned to Giulio Cesare Angeli (1619) by the municipal government.

Near Nocera (8.5 km proceeding southwesterly) are the remains of the **Rocca di Postignano** (elev. 778 m), founded in the 10th century to guard the Valtopina area, and, in the 15th-century, domain of the Trinci family.

### Bagni di Nocera

Linked to Nocera by a road that branches to the right off state road 361 Septempedana, which in part runs along the ancient Via Prolaquense that connected Nocera to Ancona via the Potenza valley, *Bagni* constitutes a municipal district together with *Stravignano* (elev. 577 m). From the 16th century, the local Angelica Spring is well known for the curative properties of its water. In 1611, an initial spa facility was built, and was later expanded in 1714. When this health spa foundered in the 19th century, the Bisleri family decided to market its mineral water, building a bottling plant near its Cacciatore spring.

The road upward along the tree-covered slopes of Colle Croce leads to a plateau which provides a divide between the Tyrrhenian and the Adriatic. Slightly below the pass of Colfiorito (elev. 821) lies the **Palude di Colfiorito**\* (elev. 752 m), the most characteristic area of the regional Park by the same name.

### Valtopina

The Topino river (77 km), which flows into the Chiascio near Bettona, descends abundantly from Mt. Pennino (east of Nocera Umbra), giving life to an extensive cultivated area along the valley floor. Situated on the state road, **Valtopina** (elev. 360 m, pop. 1,371) developed in an area of ancient colonization, which is documented by the remains of a rural Roman settlement. In medieval times, the locality was called Villa di Cerqua, an important agricultural and commercial hub for the various valley settlements which had been established during the Trinci seignory. The church of the successive *Pieve Fanonica* (elev. 327 m), built on the remains of a sacred Roman site, recycled numerous blocks of Roman stone, thereby greatly enhancing its structure. From the Pieve Fanonica-Capodacqua station, to the left of the municipal highway, you have a good view of a Roman aqueduct. Other Roman remains are in *Pontecentesimo* (elev. 325 m), located one hundred miles from Rome (hence the locality's name), which have been identified as belonging to a former bridge that once spanned the ancient road.

# 4 The Valle Umbra

## Area profile

The "fruitful fields, adorned with rows of trees and interspersed with vineyards, with many and abundant rivulets of clear fresh water," the "multitude of olive trees" and the particular luxuriance of "grain and other crops," the bounty of "excellent wines and other fruits," according to the early 15th-century architect Leon Battista Alberti, comprise the pleasant landscape of Italy's central regions, and of the Umbrian Valley in particular. The beauty of the Valle Umbra countryside, which has been often and variously described in literature, is the result of millenary transformations wrought by man, who has dwelled here since time immemorial, as is witnessed by stone materials found both in Spoleto and Spello. Both natural and artificial transformations undergone by the Tiberine lake basin, which in the plio-quaternary period extended for 125 km from Sansepolcro to Terni, with a surface area of 1,800 square kilometers, progressively resulted in a landfill which, initially, gave rise to a marshy plain, and then to a reclaimed area of great fertility. The Valle Umbra is the most vast vestige of the ancient lake. To the northwest, it joins the Tiber via the so-called Torgiano "threshold," believed to have been built by the Etruscans, whereas outwardly it opens through the Chiascio, Topino, and Menotre valleys, which cut through the Apennine dorsal in the north, and extend all the way to Spoleto. Even the mountain ranges that delimit the valley vary both in terms of formation and height. To the east and northeast the valley is dominated by Mt. Subasio, with its steep spurs and the mountain range between Spello and Spoleto overhung by Mt. Maggiore (1,428 m). To the west it is closed by low-lying marl and sandstone hills. The valley's particular configuration has inevitably influenced its road network, which in the past centered on rectilinear Via Flaminia (220-19 BC), whereas today it follows state road 75 Centrale Umbra, which only in Foligno again joins the ancient Roman road. The desire to establish widespread settlements dates from the I century BC, that is, when parcels of land were confiscated from the local population to be given to the veterans who had fought for the Roman Empire. Between late antiquity and the Middle Ages, this arrangement underwent profound changes, resulting in a reduction in the number of settlements and their subsequent relocation on the surrounding heights. With the close of the 16th century and a renewed interest in the land, reclamation of the low level areas got under way, prompting a return of the inhabitants to the plains. Thus, there took shape a process of rural colonization marked by dwellings, ranging from modest to very modest, which spread over this vast plain area often mixing with the villas of the wealthy landowners. The surrounding hills were dotted with olive trees, a plant capable of sinking its roots even in the most unfavorable terrains.

Over the past fifty years the plain has changed radically, particularly due to industrialization, which has practically erased all signs of the area's history. Only the hillside has manage to preserve its pristine soft-colored beauty.

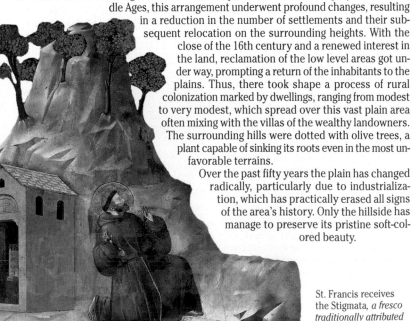

St. Francis receives the Stigmata, *a fresco traditionally attributed to Giotto, in the basilica of San Francesco*

*The facade of the upper church of the basilica of San Francesco*

## 4.1 Assisi

**A circuit through the town** *(map on pages 98-99)* **and excursions to the Franciscan sites**

To those arriving from the Valle Umbra, which has become practically the only access route, the town appears spread out on terraces along the Mt. Subasio incline, which dominates the countryside between Topino and Chiascio. Entering the town one inevitably breathes a Franciscan atmosphere, fed in part by literature, which has always considered this small Umbrian town "the city of St. Francis," and in part by the monuments which embellish its every corner. Dante was the first (Canto XI of the *Paradise*, lines 52-54) to stress the symbiosis between topography and the narration of the lives of saints. Assisi is "[...] transfigured by the charm and enchantment that Saint Francis and ancient Umbrian art have transfused in this land," as Herman Hesse wrote in 1907, and by the numerous signs of its rich history. The latter is documented by archaeological finds from the late Bronze and Iron ages, through the Bronze age and on up to the Hellenistic age, when the town took on a terraced urban form of Greek derivation. The Roman layout, on the other hand, was reutilized in the 12th century by the free Ghibelline commune, centering around the market square, the imperial castle fortress, Santa Maria Maggiore and San Rufino. In the 13th century, the market square became the hub of the city's civic activities, and again, in 1228, construction began on the Franciscan basilica outside the walls, offset by the church of Santa Chiara (1257), situated at the opposite end of the city. Meanwhile, the town experienced a period of economic growth which coincided with a population increase, together with subsequent structural changes and a significant extension of the town's perimeter (1260 and 1316). Also much in evidence was the mark of papal power, which, in the 14th century, expressed itself in the construction of two fortified castles. If the 17th and 18th centuries were characterized by the building of civil and religious structures within the city's medieval perimeter, the 19th century, on the other hand, promoted a radical transformation in terms of how those buildings were to be used. In addition, the convents' rich art heritage became municipal property. The Franciscan movement, from an academic standpoint and also in terms of physical mobility (the flow of pilgrims and tourists), managed to end the isolation to which it had been relegated only thanks to the exhumation of St. Francis (1818) and St. Claire (1850). After the Unification of Italy, and during the twenty years of the Fascist regime, public buildings underwent a drastic neo-medieval "facelift," and the stuccowork from their facades removed so as to create a more picturesque, but largely fake, visual effect. In September and October 1997, the town was struck by a series of earthquakes, causing structural damage to numerous monumental buildings now being systematically restored.

Our visit starts from Piazza del Comune and, down Via Rufino, continues up to the Cathedral, and from here to an area that still preserves signs of the town's Roman period. Via di Porta Perlici delimits a quarter configured on the ancient urban layout, and includes an amphitheater (in Piazza Matteotti) and a theater (in Via del Torrione). Detouring from Via di Porta Perlici to the hilltop, you come to the Rocca Maggiore. Once back in Piazza San Rufino, go down Via Doni and Via Sermei, two steep side streets connecting the main streets in the town's northwest and southeast sections. Piazza Santa Chiara is structured so as to complement the basilica, which, in order of importance, is the town's second religious hub. Proceeding along Via Sant'Agnese you reach Piazza del Vescovado, where stands Santa Maria Maggiore, the former cathedral built upon the town's first medieval walls. Via Sant'Apollinare, narrowly flanked by the monastery on one side and by that of San Quirico on the other, leads to borgo San Pietro, a terraced area inside the town's most ancient perimeter and the 1316 walls. The Romanesque church of San Pietro, which, when constructed, lay outside the town walls, is linked to Benedictine monasticism, similarly present in Assisi with the church of San Paolo within the walls. Through Porta San Francesco and down Via Frate Elia, you come to the basilica, which, from the lower square is a truly imposing sight, with its two superimposed vessels resting upon the Sacro Convento. Next, proceed down Via San Francesco, a street connecting (both physically and ideally) the Franciscan basilica with Piazza del Comune.

**Piazza del Comune** (B3-4). The city's former terrace structure is well exemplified by this "piazza grande," with its ample rectangular shape. In medieval times the square was the town's hub; it was here that the main streets met, and where, from the early 13th century, the people gathered and devoted themselves to trade and exchange. Starting in 1212, the ab-

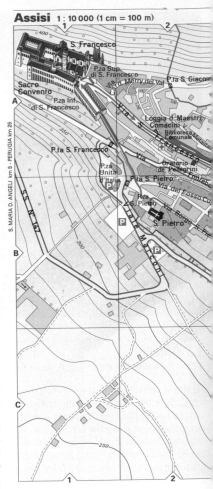

**Assisi**  1 : 10 000 (1 cm = 100 m)

S. MARIA D. ANGELI km 25 - PERUGIA km 25
S.S. N° 147

bot of San Benedetto ceded to the municipal government the "cell" of the ancient temple of Minerva, together with other structures along the square which were to house the consuls' magistrature. Between the mid-13th century and 1282, along the entire upper section of the square was built the **Palazzo del Capitano del Popolo**, which in 1927 was restored and equipped with embattlements, together with the extremely high (but now unsafe) *Torre del Popolo* (1305) which looms nearby. The construction of the *Palazzo dei Priori* (1475) completed the square's southern side. The fountains with three lions gracing the square dates from the 16th century, whereas the *Palazzo delle Poste* (on the northwest side) is the result of restructuring in 1926, when a medieval fervor gripped the town as it celebrated the seventh centennial of the death of its saint.

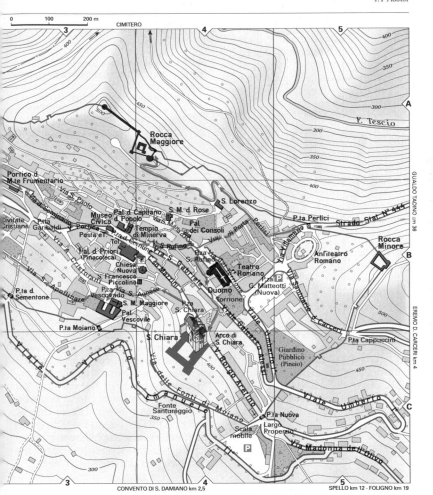

0  100  200 m

CIMITERO

F. Tescio

GUALDO TADINO cm 36

Rocca Maggiore

Portico d. M.te Frumentario

Via S. Paolo

S. M.d. Rose

S. Lorenzo

P.ta Perlici   Strada Stat. N° 444

civitate cristiana

P.ta Garibaldi

Pal. d. Capitano d. Popolo

Museo Cívico

Porticu

Posta e T.

Pal. dei Consoli

Tempio di Minerva

S. M. d. Rose

Rocca Minore

Pal. d. Priori (Pinacoteca)

Chiesa Nuova

S. Francesco Piccolino

Cso Mazzini

Piazza S. Rufino

S. Rufino

Anfiteatro Romano

Teatro Romano

Duomo

G. Matteotti (Nuova)

P.ta d. Sementone

S. M. Maggiore

Pal. Vescovile

P.ta S. Chiara

Torrione

P.ta Moiano

S. Chiara

Arco di S. Chiara

P.ta Cappuccini

EREMO D. CARCERI km 4

Via delle Fonti di Moiano

Giardino Pùbblico (Pincio)

Fonte Santuréggio

V. Borgo Aretino

P.ta Nuova

Largo Properzio

Scala mobile

P

Via Madonna dell'Olivo

Viale  Umberto

B

C

CONVENTO DI S. DAMIANO km 2,5

SPELLO km 12 - FOLIGNO km 19

**Tempio di Minerva\***. The sanctuary, built between the early 1st century BC and the Augustan age in the very heart of the town, is erroneously held to have been dedicated to the goddess Minerva. Utilized in the Middle Ages as a dwelling for monks, and later as a municipal prison, in 1539 it was turned into a church, with the name of *Santa Maria sopra Minerva*. Subsequently it was given a Baroque facelift and dedicated to St. Philip Neri.

**Palazzo dei Priori** (B3). The characteristic (albeit extensively restored, especially the windows and its simulated embattlements), construction of this very long building involved incorporating four pre-existing structures since 1275. Beneath this complex, and to the right, opens the so-called *Volta Pinta*, a barrel-vault passage so termed because of its 16th-century decorations.

By taking *Via Arco dei Priori* to the left of *Palazzo dei Priori*, you soon come to the **Chiesa Nuova**, built in 1615 upon the presumed remains of St. Francis birthplace. Completely decorated with mural paintings (1621), it features frescoes by Cesare Sermei, Giacomo Giorgetti and Andrea Polinori. Left of the presbytery there is access to what remains of the so-called *Casa del Santo* (restored).

**San Rufino\*** (B4). The churchyard's tapering shape creates a "magnifying-glass" effect for those viewing the Cathedral from the square. Probably founded in the 8th century, the church was first reworked in 1036 by Bishop Ugone, who also raised it to the rank of cathedral. In 1140, reconstruction of the church got under way (design by Giovanni da Gubbio), but it was only in 1253 that it was officially consecrated by Innocent IV. The **facade\***, an Umbrian Romanesque masterpiece, is horizontally divided into three registers, with geometric and ornamental decorations from various periods. It is flanked by a squat but imposing **campanile**, it too Romanesque, which rests upon a perfectly conserved 2nd-century BC Roman cistern. Its interior was completely renovated in 1571 by Galeazzo Alessi, and features, at the beginning of the right aisle, the *baptismal font* in which tradition has it that St. Francis, St. Clare and perhaps Frederick II of Swabia were baptized. The apse features a wooden **choir\*** carved by Giovanni di Piergiacomo (1520). A small doorway to the left of the sacristy leads down to the *Oratorio di San Francesco*, a subterranean oratory where the saint is said to have prayed before

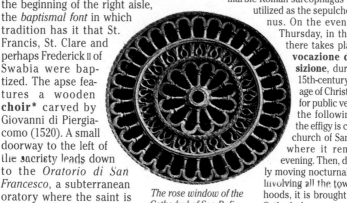

*The rose window of the Cathedral of San Rufino*

preaching to the faithful. Adjacent to the right aisle is the **Museo della Cattedrale**, founded in 1941, which contains paintings and sacred furnishings from the Cathedral and other churches in the diocese. Of particular artistic significance: Puccio Capama's **Deposition\*** and a triptych by Niccolò Alunno, **Virgin and Child with Four Saints\***, dated 1470. Adjoining the museum is the *Archivio Capitolare*, the archives rich in documents dating from 963 and in illuminated codices (13th-15th century).

To the right of the facade there is access to the **crypt\***, which contains painting fragments from the 11th century, a bishop's chair and a Luni marble Roman sarcophagus (III cent. AD), utilized as the sepulcher of St. Rufinus. On the evening of Holy Thursday, in the Cathedral there takes place the **Rievocazione della Deposizione**, during which a 15th-century wooden image of Christ is displayed for public veneration. On the following morning, the effigy is carried to the church of San Francesco, where it remains until evening. Then, during a highly moving nocturnal procession involving all the town's brotherhoods, it is brought back to the Cathedral.

**Porta Perlici quarter** (B4-5). Northeast of the Cathedral lies an area which belies the Roman origins of its regular road network. Here developed the popular medieval quarter, which has conserved its 14th-cent. layout. On the northeast side of *Piazza Matteotti*, where medieval animal fairs were held, rise the convent of *Santa Caterina* (13th cent.). The complex flanks the area of the former **Roman amphitheater**, whose elliptical plan gave shape to the small houses which later clustered in this area.

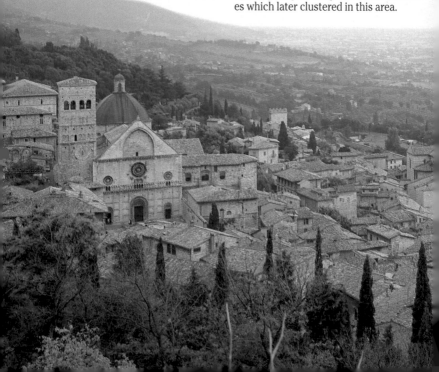

**Rocca Maggiore\*** (A3-4). This fortified castle, on a summit overlooking the city and the valley, makes an extraordinary landmark. Its striking visual effect is enhanced by the sinuous lines of the town walls which rise all the way to the corner towers, forming a trapezoidal perimeter that encloses a tall quadrangular fortress. Frederick Barbarossa and Frederick II, when still a child, are said to have sojourned in the fort. Destroyed during a popular uprising in 1198, it was rebuilt in 1356 by Cardinal Albornoz according to the original plan (open: 10am to sunset). Its 14th-century walls weld the Rocca Maggiore to the **Rocca Minore**, otherwise known as the *Cassero di Sant'Antonio*, the smaller fortress which was likewise commissioned by Albornoz in 1360 to defend the castle's northward prospect.

**Santa Chiara\*\*** (B-C4). In the hearts of Assisi's inhabitants the "struggle' between St. Francis and St. Clare is always open; a rivalry which also takes shape in the temple which, from 1260, preserves the mortal remains of the saint. Its characteristic facade, in pink and white Subasio limestone, features a finely wrought **rose window\***, with a double row of small columns and arches, and a tympanum. Its narrow front is emboldened by three colossal rampant arches (late 14th cent.) which seem to balance the thrust of the vaults. The church's single nave, adorned with precious art works, has four spans (corresponding to the external arches), and ter-

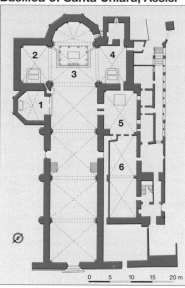

## Basilica of Santa Chiara, Assisi

1 St. Agnes' Chapel
2 Madonna and Child by Maestro della Santa Chiara
3 Crucifix by Maestro della Santa Chiara
4 St. Clare and Eight Scenes from Her Life by Maestro della Santa Chiara
5 Chapel of the Sacrament
6 Oratory of the Crucifix

minates in a polygonal apse with three simple windows. Among the many fine works in the church's interior (closed), particularly noteworthy are an altarpiece by Maestro della Santa Chiara (*Virgin and Child*, 1265) located in the left transept; an altarpiece **Crucifixion\*** by the same author, in the apse; various *frescoes* in the style of Giotto, in the vault compartments, by the Maestro Espressionista di Santa Chiara; **St. Clare and Eight Scenes from her Life\*\*** in the right transept, attributed to the same Maestro (1283). To appreciate the aura of St. Francis, enter the **San Giorgio Chapel** (open on the right side of the aisle), which is divided in two chambers by a stained-glass partition that was part of the original church. Besides a fresco by Puccio Capanna (**Virgin and Child Enthroned with Saints\***), the church also features an altarpiece **Crucifix\*** (late 12th cent.) which, according to tradition, spoke to St. Francis in San Damiano.

*The rooftops of Assisi with the churches of San Rufino (left), and Santa Chiara (right)*

Passing under the 13th-century *Arco di Santa Chiara* along Via Borgo Aretino, to the left of the basilica, make a short detour toward the *Fonti di Moiano*, a set of freshwater springs known as early as the 12th century for their curative properties, and then on to **Porta Moiano** (B3), a gate open in the 14th-century perimeter, whose name derives from the ancient "Mons Iani," as it was here that once stood a temple dedicated to Janus. A spring, the waters of which are said to have curative properties, and the remains of Roman structures are located on the incline that slopes beneath the road.

Piazza del Vescovado (B3). Situated outside the first town walls, as the center of religious power, in the 11th century **Santa Maria Maggiore** lost its status as cathedral to San Rufino. The Romanesque church has a plain facade, enhanced by a rose window bearing an inscription indicating that the church was restructured by one Giovanni (1163), identified as the builder of the new cathedral. In the interior, there are remains of frescoes dating from the 14th and 15th centuries. The *crypt\** (closed) is all that has survived of the primitive church (9th-10th cent.), and leads to a subterranean chamber containing the remains of a *Roman house*, featuring fine mosaic pavements and wall paintings. From the adjacent garden can be seen the remains of the Roman wall perimeter, in Subasio limestone. After the cathedral was transferred, the only edifice symbolizing religious power in the square was the *Palazzo Vescovile* (the bishop's palace), where St. Francis made his vow of poverty and where, many years later, when he was seriously ill, he returned to be conveyed to the Porziuncola.

San Pietro\* (B27). Proceeding along Via Sant'Apollinare and then *Via Borgo San Pietro*, the main axis of this popular 14th-century quarter, you come to a Benedictine church consecrated in the early 13th century and reconsecrated by Innocent IV in 1253. Its beautiful rectangular facade is marked by three portals, each with a rose window; whereas its aisled interior conserves 14th-century funeral monuments and frescoes of the 13th and 14th centuries.

Basilica of San Francesco\*\* (A1). St. Francis died on 3 October 1226, and two years later work began on the grand church which was destined to become both a spiritual reference point for Assisi and for all of Christianity. Brother Elijah, St. Francis's successor, was a dynamic director of the building works, and Gregory IX laid the first stone on the Colle dell'Inferno, where capital executions are believed to have been carried out, and which subsequently changed its name to Colle del Paradiso. The architectural peculiarity of this magnificent complex is largely due to the superimposition of two churches, each one signifying a separate construction phase; this detail is enhanced by the double rows of very high arches of the *Sacro Convento*, the monastic complex that protects the rear of the temple toward the valley, thus materializing both that sense of strength and lightness which are perhaps one of the main prerogatives of the Franciscan order. Uncertain are the documentary sources of the successive construction phases after 1230, when the saint's body was translated to the lower basilica, up to its consecration by Innocent IV (1253). In 1367, the chapel of St. Catherine was completed, and with it the entire church, which was to undergo no change over the centuries that followed. The church was decorated by the leading painters of the time, who turned it into a "document" of exceptionally high quality, especially as regards 13th- and 14th-century Italian fresco painting. The 1997 earthquake produced serious lesions in the upper basilica, causing the collapse of two segments of the vault, and the loss of two of Cimabue's frescoes (restoration work ended in 1999). In sharp contrast with the interior, the basilica's facade, Gothic but readapted to local tastes, features plain lines broken by a twin portal and splendid double **rose window\***. Along its left side rises the tall quadrangular Romanesque Umbrian-style **campanile** (1239), despoiled of its crown in 1530.

Chiesa Inferiore, or lower church. A double **portal\*** dating from the second half of the 13th century, and preceded by a Renaissance portico, leads into the church's nave, which is divided in three arched spans, the focal point of which is the saint's sepulcher. The walls along the nave, whose pavement inclines toward the main altar, are covered with frescoes\* by the Maestro di San Francesco, among the first to be painted (ca. 1253), which were partly destroyed after the opening of the lateral chapels. To the right remain **Scenes from the Life of Christ** and, on the left, **Scenes from the Life of St. Francis**, stressing the link between Christ and the saint of Assisi. Midway along the nave, two stairs descend to the crypt where, in 1818, was discovered the body of St. Francis, laid to rest by brother Elijah beneath three slabs of travertine. The plain stone urn in which the saint's body was found continues to house the saint above the altar, surrounded at its four corners by the bodies of his closest companions (Leone, Rufino, Masseo, and Angelo). The niche on the landing connecting the two rooms contains the remains of the Blessed Jacopa dei Settesoli, a noble Roman woman, and devout counselor of Francis who called her "brother Jacopa." Back in the nave, to be visited are the lateral chapels: the 3rd on the right is completely decorated with **frescoes\*** by Giotto and assistants. The two-sided, Gothic-style high altar in the presbytery, consecrated in 1253, features a white-stone Lord's table donated by the emperor of Constantinople, Jean de Brienne. Famous are the **frescoes\*** in the vault's four compartments (1322) depicting the *Allegories of Franciscan Virtues* (*Poverty, Chastity, Obedience*), and the *Glory of St. Francis*. Recent critics attribute these works to various helpers working under Giotto's direction. Two distinct characters are identifiable in the vault compartments, the so-called Parente di Giotto (a Tuscan follower) and the Maestro delle Vele, an Umbrian Giotto-style painter. The vault of the right crossing arm is entirely covered by two large rows of frescoes\* painted by Giotto's assistants. The **Virgin and Child enthroned, with four Angels and St. Francis\*\*** is the only painting of the preceding decorative system, by Cimabue, to have survived. The *Crucifixion* is attributed to Giotto; whereas the *five saints*, of which the 4th figure is a beautiful image believed to portray **St. Clare\*** (actually, St. Margaret), on the rear wall are attributed to Simone Martini. The semicircular apse contains a fine Gothic **choir\***, carved and inlaid by Apollonio Petrocchi and helpers, and, on its wall, a *Last Judgment* by Cesare Sermei (1623). The left arm

crossing is decorated with frescoes painted in 1315-20 by Pietro Lorenzetti and helpers, among which stand out, on the left, a **Crucifixion\*** and a **Virgin and Child between Sts. Francis and John\*** by the Sienese master. The **frescoes\*** in the 1st left chapel along the nave, a masterpiece of mysticism and grace (1312-20), telling of the life of St. Martin, are the work of Simone Martini.

**Chiesa Superiore**, or upper church. Leaving the dimly lit lower church, we ascend to the Chiesa Superiore, which the French historian Hippolyte Taine saw as "suspended in air and light." In fact, the rose window, the windows along the archways,

*Detail of the* Crucifixion *by Pietro Lorenzetti, in the lower church of the basilica of San Francesco*

and those of the apse all recall Nordic light-pervaded models, while to a certain extent blending Italy's architectural style with the pure forms of French Gothic. Our visit begins with the transept, entirely deco-

## Basilica of San Francesco, Assisi

The basilica, which was built in two stages in the 13th century, is in fact two churches in one. The *Chiesa Inferiore*, or lower church, built around 1230, consists of a single nave with side chapels, a central barrel-vaulted ceiling, cross-vaulted transept and the crypt where St. Francis was buried. Above is the *Chiesa Superiore*, or upper church, which dates back to the second half of the 13th century. This church, also with a single nave, is an ensemble of strikingly Gothic elements that converge on the transept and its polygonal apse.

The facade of the basilica takes its inspiration from the French Gothic style, and features a large rose window surmounted by a smaller, but the monument's main attraction is without doubt its lavish fresco cycles that entirely cover the interior walls, in keeping with the didactic aims of the Franciscan order.

### Giotto's frescoes

Beneath the gallery of the central nave of the upper church is the cycle of the *Life of St. Francis* (1296-1300), attributed to Giotto but executed with the help of assistants. The 28 frescoes that make up the cycle (in roman numerals, I-XXVIII, on the plan) depict the main scenes from the account of the saint's life by St. Bonaventure of Bagnoregio (the *Legenda Maior*). The most noteworthy are: *St. Francis gives his Cloak to a Pauper* (II), *St. Francis drives the Demons out of Arezzo* (X), *St. Francis celebrates the Feast of the Nativity at Greccio* (XIII), *St. Francis creates a Spring to slake a Wayfarer's Thirst* (XIV), *St. Francis preaches to the Birds* (XV), *St. Francis receives the Stigmata* (XIX).

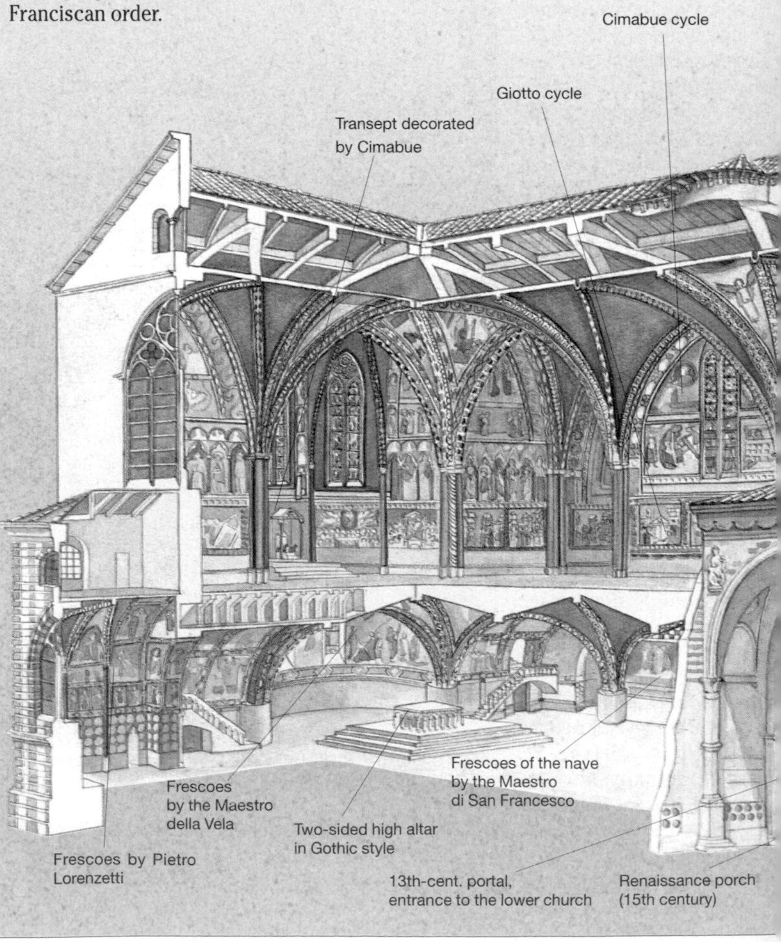

Cimabue cycle

Giotto cycle

Transept decorated by Cimabue

Frescoes by the Maestro della Vela

Frescoes by Pietro Lorenzetti

Two-sided high altar in Gothic style

Frescoes of the nave by the Maestro di San Francesco

13th-cent. portal, entrance to the lower church

Renaissance porch (15th century)

## Basilica of San Francesco, plan of the frescoes in the nave of the upper church

## Cimabue's frescoes

The other frescoes in the upper church, attributed to Cimabue and his team, flank the two-light windows above the gallery and show *Scenes from the Old Testament* (on the right, 1-16) and *Scenes from the New Testament* (on the left, 17-32). To either side of the rose window on the inside wall of the façade are the *Ascension* (33) and *Pentecost* (34).

Upper rose window

Central rose window

Renaissance tower

Romanesque gallery

Two-light portal, entrance to the upper church

rated by Cimabue (the frescoes are badly worn). The **Crucifixion\*** is particularly striking, and is one of the master's most powerful and dramatic compositions. In the apse, there is a magnificent wooden **choir\***, by Domenico Indivini and assistants (1491-1501), consisting of 102 stalls. Extensively deteriorated are the frescoes in the right arm depicting *Scenes from the Life of St. Peter* by the Maestro Oltremontano and Cimabue's team. The upper walls of the nave are decorated with 34 frescoes depicting **Scenes from the Old Testament** (right) and **New Testament** (left), painted by various helpers who substituted Cimabue. Instead, beneath the gallery, there is a stupendous 28-fresco cycle depicting the **Life of St. Francis\*\*** (p. 104), attributed to Giotto both as the principal artist and as supervisor of the various helpers who contributed to the project. The scenes, which start from the right wall and continue uninterruptedly up to the end of the left wall, are inspired by the account of Francis' life written by St. Bonaventure of Bagnoregio, and constituted a model for successive figurations of the saint. The terrace behind the apse affords access to the **Museo-Tesoro\*** which includes paintings, goldcraft, and textile artifacts linked to the history of the basilica. Even if often pillaged, the museum's collection continues to be of great interest, due to the 13th-century masterpieces of French goldwork and textile artifacts. The adjacent "red room" hosts the Perkins Collection, donated to the city in 1955 by the American art historian Frederick Mason Perkins, who, in his Assisi home, had collected 56 paintings mostly by Florentine and Sienese masters of the 14th and 15th centuries (Fra Angelico, and Niccolò Alunno).

The convent, with cloister built by Sixtus IV in 1476, houses an important **library**, with many illuminated codices, incunabula, 16th-century printed editions; besides a musical archive, the *Fondo Antico* and the *Archivio Vescovile* (episcopal archive).

*Horseman from the Calendimaggio pageant in Assisi*

The basilica of San Francesco, and with it all of Umbria, is the vibrant core of a more far-reaching and loftier "nation": that of humanity itself. The **Marcia della Pace** (Peace March), a colorful procession which periodically unfolds for kilometers between Perugia and Assisi, uniting races and religions, embodying this ideal of united humankind.
Colorfulness and merrymaking, albeit of a lay character, can be admired during the festival of **Calendimaggio**. Having lost its original function as a propitiatory rite, which consisted in planting a "May branch," this feast has remained in the collective spirit as a way of welcoming the arrival of spring. On 30 April and 1 May, colorful costume pageants are staged, including *sbandieratori* (flag wavers) who open a musical contest with songs imitating those once performed by medieval minstrels, who dedicated them to damsels and ladies.

**Via San Francesco** (A2). In medieval times this was Via Superba, which recalls the basilica in Piazza Grande, with its souvenir shops; the square shows evident signs of the successive transformations it underwent. The Gothic-style dwellings were subsumed within the large building complexes of the 17th-century aristocratic palaces, among which (no. 19A), **Palazzo Bernabei** (by Giacomo Giorgetti, 17th cent.), now the seat of the Università di Perugia. After a row of medieval-looking houses, you reach the *Loggia dei Maestri Comacini* (13th cent.), so called because of the coats of arms that appear on the architrave. Climbing amid old houses up to the small square in which stands the church of *Santa Margherita* (13th cent.), *Vicolo Sant'Andrea*, to one side of the *Loggia*, takes you to this quiet and peaceful corner of the town, from where you have a magnificent view from the basilica. Back in Via San Francesco, you come in view of the long facade of **Palazzo Giacobetti** (no. 12), with its monumental balcony and 17th-century railing, now home of the *Biblioteca Comunale*, together with the *Accademia Properziana del Subasio*, which contains statutes dating from 1554. During restoration work on the building, the library has been temporarily transferred to another location.

**Pinacoteca Comunale**. The municipal art collections have been recently arranged in Palazzo Vallemani, at no. 10 of Via San Francesco. They were originally set up in 1912 in order to collect all the frescoes (mostly by the Umbrian school from the 13th to the 17th cent.), which had been removed from churches, brotherhoods, oratories, and city gates, in both the town and its environs. The most significant

## Jens Johannes Jørgensen, the pilgrim poet

Anyone walking through Assisi in the early years of the twentieth century might well have come across a stern-looking gentlemen with a pince-nez, a handlebar moustache and a bushy goatee beard. This was Jens Johannes Jørgensen, one of the leading Danish poets of the day, who in the summer of 1894 had left his native island of Fyn to spend the rest of his life in Assisi, where he became known as "Sor Giovanni". So strong was his attachment to the town he could hardly bear to be separated from it: "When I left Assisi this morning, to be sure, I left my heart there; my heart belongs to Umbria; what sense is there in leaving without it..." he wrote. As a devout follower of St. Francis (this Protestant poet eventually converted to Catholicism) he had begun going on mental pilgrimages to the sites associated with the saint when he was still in Copenhagen, an activity that became a reality

*The portico of the Sacro Convento in Assisi*

"one fine April day", and took him to the ivory-yellow walls of the Sacro Convento, where a child was playing at 'processions' "with a gilt wooden candlestick and a rustic cross." But it was not only the spiritual and artistic places that charmed the Danish poet: he also captured pleasant little slices of the life of the day (of the kind the patient observer may still find today among the crowds of pilgrims), with his description of such characters as Signora Filomena and her tasty hams in Piazza del Vescovado, the coppersmith of Via San Francesco, or the town's only pastry cook, along the Strada Maestra. With his travel books, Jørgensen "built a bridge" between Denmark and Assisi: his writings on St. Francis and his town are among the best known of all Danish literature, and some of them have been translated into twenty languages, including Chinese and Japanese.

works include fragments of a fresco cycle inspired by medieval chivalry (late 13th cent.) from the Palazzo del Capitano del Popolo, as well as a *Virgin in Glory* from Giotto's workshop; frescoes by the Maestro Espressionista di Santa Chiara, Ottaviano Nelli, Tiberio d'Assisi, and Dono Doni (*The Stigmata of St. Francis*, and an *Annunciation*); a processional gonfalon by Niccolò Alunno and workshop.

In the following stretch of Via San Francesco is the **Oratorio dei Pellegrini\*** (1457), with its plain facade on which remains a worn fresco by Matteo da Gualdo, whereas its interior features 15th-century frescoes. To the rear, the fine **Portico del Monte Frumentario\***, which was part of Assisi's earliest public hospital, founded in 1267 and, in the 18th century, converted into an Agricultural Credit Institution. Adjacent is the *Fonte Oliviera*, a fountain whose building was ordered by Oliviero Lodovici in 1570. Beyond the 13th-century *Arco del Seminario*, called the "portella di Panzo" in the Middle Ages and boundary of the Roman walled town, Via San Francesco becomes **Via del Seminario**,

where **Palazzo Seminario** has swallowed up the *Sant'Angelo di Panzo* Benedictine monastery (1270).

**Museo Civico** (B3). Located in the *crypt of San Niccolò* (1097), a church which was demolished in 1926 to make room for the construction of the *Palazzo delle Poste*, the museum (entrance from no. 2 Via Portica) was instituted in 1934 and exhibits materials from pre-Roman and Roman times found in and around Assisi. A long corridor leads to the archaeological area, commonly known as the Roman Forum, but actually an area connected with the overhanging temple of Minerva. Still visible are the pavement with a furrow for draining away water, and a tabernacle containing the statues of Castor and Pollux donated to the city in the time of Tiberius by two wealthy *liberti* (freed slaves).

### Franciscan sites

The countryside around Assisi is where Francis sought and found his own spirituality (map on page 110). At a distance of 2.5 km from Porta Nuova (C4) lies the picturesque convent of San Damiano. Porta dei Cappuccini (B-C5) is the starting point of our second, highly recommended, excursion to the Eremo delle Carceri, which can be reached via a 3.8-km scenic route. Beyond this locality, proceed across the Subasio natural park in the direction of Collepino and the Armenzano hermitage. Our last recommended excursion takes us, after 5 km from Largo San Pietro (A-B1), to the renowned basilica of Santa Maria degli Angeli, nestled at the foot of Assisi.

**San Damiano\***. After *Porta Nuova*, and a pleasant walk among the olive trees, you come to the *San Damiano* convent (elev. 310 m). It is here that, as St. Francis's biographers relate, in 1205 the *Crucifix* (now in the basilica of Santa Chiara) spoke to the saint, calling upon him to restore the edifice, which in 1212 was to welcome St. Clare with her first companions. In the winter of 1224-25, Francis composed here his *Canticle of the Creatures*. After the

**Eremo delle Carceri\***. First among the olive trees, then upward along the slopes of San Rufino hill, while enjoying a magnificent view of the plain amid fine oaks, you come to a place particularly steeped in Franciscan atmosphere (elev. 791 m). It was in this little church, surrounded by grottoes which had always been frequented by hermits, that Francis and his companions would withdraw in prayer. In the 15th century, Bernardino da Siena built a convent, or hermitage, here (open 6.30am-5pm; 6.30am-7.30pm, daylight-saving time) which today consists of a small triangular courtyard and a 15th-century church.

Descending a stairway and passing through numerous tiny doors, you enter the *grotto of St. Francis*, where the saint came to rest and meditate.

It is worth strolling down the so-called "viale di San Francesco," leading through the **selva\***, picturesque both in terms of the landscape and the hermit grottoes that line it.

*The Eremo delle Carceri in the woods near Assisi*

death of St. Clare, her companions remained there until 1260, when they relocated to the city, ceding the convent to the cathedral capital. In its interior, the apse is decorated with 14th-century frescoes, while the wooden *choir*, which dates from 1504, in part covers a small window through which the Clarissan sisters communicated. The vestibule leads out onto the small terrace, called the *Giardinetto di Santa Chiara*, from which there is a wonderful view of the plain.

**Parco del Monte Subasio.** The Subasio mountain range (elev. 1,290 m), which extends over 7,500 hectares, has become a protected area. Along its piedmont stretches are olive groves that have largely taken the place of the former forest covering which had been depleted by more or less legal deforestation practices. On the top is a plateau with vast meadows and pastures. Slightly down began the large woods of secular oaks both deciduous and evergreen.

## Santa Maria degli Angeli

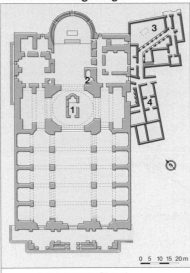

```
0  5  10 15 20 m
```

1 Porziuncola Chapel
2 Transito Chapel
3 Roseto Chapel
4 Museum

This environmental variety is particularly apparent as you proceed beyond the Eremo delle Carceri, along the ancient road which, after the Madonna della Spella sanctuary (elev. 978 m), descends 21.5 km to **Collepino** (elev. 600 m), a pink stone village with the layout of a medieval "borough". Next, heading northward, you come to the church of *San Silvestro*, with its 11th-century crypt*. Amid splendid views of the Valle Umbra, the road takes you to **Armenzano** (elev. 759 m), which also felt the effects of the 1997 earthquake. The town, perfectly circular in layout, (it was originally girded by a double concentric wall), is a typical example of a small fortified peasant village.

**Santa Maria degli Angeli**\*\*. The modern buildings surrounding it detract from that atmosphere of religious solace that St. Francis sought and enjoyed in this area. In 1205, Francis chose the abandoned little church of the **Porziuncola** (10th-11th centuries), then situated in a forest, as his home, restoring it and founding here the Franciscan order. This

*The Porziuncola chapel at Santa Maria degli Angeli*

is where the saint was most wont to live, where he gave his frock to St. Clare, and where he established his so-called chapter *delle stuoie*, to which over 5,000 monks flocked. Around this plain rectangular structure, decorated with 13th- and 14th-century frescoes, between 1569 and 1679 was built the magnificent **basilica**. Designed by Galeazzo Alessi, it has an aisled nave and a soaring dome, which was girded after 1832, and emerges from the surrounding plain from whatever spot it is viewed. Housed in its interior is the most complete collection of Umbrian 16th- and 17th-century paintings. At the front of the presbytery is located the **Cappella del Transito**\*, the infirmary cell where Francis died; featuring frescoes by Spagna and an enameled terracotta piece by Andrea della Robbia, author of a magnificent **dossal**\*, similarly in enameled terracotta, which is preserved in the crypt. Do not leave the basilica without having visited the *roseto*, the tiny rose garden of thornless roses, linked to a legend of the saint's life. Immediately after comes the **Cappella del Roseto**\*, consisting of three rooms, including the *Oratorio di San Bonaventura*, with wall frescoes by Tiberio d'Assisi (1506).

Five rooms annexed to the basilica, house a **museum** featuring sacred art works and liturgical articles, among which an altarpiece **Crucifix**\* by Giunta Pisano (ca. 1236) and a portrait of **St. Francis** by a master painter who, after this painting, became known as the Maestro di San Francesco. A huge theater has been built in the nearby village.

An 8.5 km drive along the road leading to Perugia takes you to **Bastia Umbra** (elev. 202 m, pop. 17,256), the ancient *Insula Romana*, so called because it was surrounded by the waters of the *Lacus Umber* (subsequently drained). The medieval nucleus developed around an important castle contended both by Assisi and Perugia.

In Piazza Mazzini stands the 14th-century former church of *Santa Croce*, with its characteristic white-and-pink banded facade; inside, 15th- and 17th-century works by Tiberio d'Assisi and Cesare Sermei. Noteworthy are also the churches of *San Rocco*, which features two paintings by Dono Doni, and *San Paolo*, where St. Clare sought refuge.

## 4.2 From Assisi to Foligno  4.4 From Montefalco to Trevi and to Spoleto

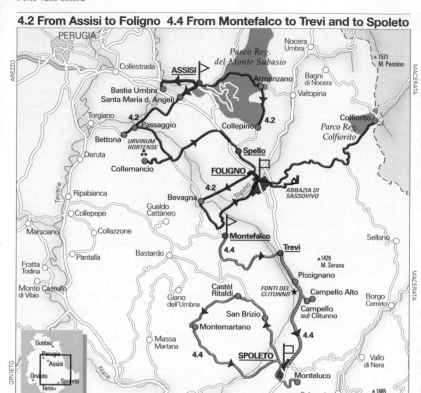

# 4.2 From Assisi to Foligno

**An excursion along a minor road (35 km) and two walks through Spello** *(map on page 112)* **and Bevagna**

In order to grasp the complexity of this area's fertile landscape, it is best to leave the state road that runs along the valley floor, and head down a secondary road, which, from Assisi, heads straight to Santa Maria degli Angeli (page 109), and toward the hills that skirt the Valle Umbra, through land that was reclaimed by the local municipality as far back as 1466, and which now supports corn and sunflower crops. Once across the river Topino, our itinerary next touches Passaggio, a district belonging to the nearby municipality of Bettona, from which it is separated by low hills. Proceeding in the direction of Collemancio, we come to an area which is especially interesting from an archaeological standpoint. Turning back across the plain, after 30 km we come to Spello. Continuing along secondary roads that crisscross the plain, here furrowed by parallel courses of the Timia, the Teverone and the Clitunno, our road deviates from

the main thoroughfare to Foligno (see section 4.3 on page 116), and again to the more typical landscape around Bevagna. This secondary road, enables us to ramble between the plain and the rolling hills, in search of the historic links between the hillside towns (Spello) and those situated along the low western hills (Bettona, Bevagna).

### Passaggio

This village (elev. 202 m) is characterized by intense agricultural and crafts activities. Here stands the former abbey of **San Crispolto**, founded by the Benedictines to preserve the remains of the saint, and in the 19th century converted into an agricultural complex. Subsequently, it was turned into a private residence, which however still conserves a crypt older than the 11th century. Not far off is the elegant 18th-century *Villa del Boccaglione*, with its late-Baroque layout.

## Bettona

A picturesque road among the olive trees takes us to charmingly situated Bettona (elev. 353 m, pop. 3,644), called, because of its panoramic position, the "Etruscan balcony," defended by ellipsoidal walls, which were ordered rebuilt in 1367 by Cardinal Albornoz. The town was the only Etruscan center on the left bank of the Tiber, as witnessed by finds from ancient *Vettona*. The inhabited area extends along the highest point of the hill around the medieval perimeter linking *Piazza Cavour* (formerly the Roman forum), and *Piazza Garibaldi*.

The first building to appear is the collegiate church of **Santa Maria Maggiore**, rebuilt in the 13th century and remodeled in the 19th, which features a fresco by Gerardo Dottori. Opposite stands **Oratorio di Sant'Andrea** (14th cent.), completely transformed between the 17th and 18th century, and characterized within by a coffered wooden ceiling and lively decorations (17th-18th) on the back wall. To visit the oratory, inquire either at the *Pinacoteca* or contact the custodian in the house next door.

To the left of the Collegiata stands the *Palazzo della Podestà* (1371), seat of the **Pinacoteca Civica**, the municipal art gallery, instituted in the early part of this century and remodeled in 1996; the works on display include 14th- and 18th-century paintings, and include paintings by Perugino and Dono Doni, Della Robbia terracottas, and a collection of archaeological finds. In the adjacent *Piazza Garibaldi* rises the church of **San Crispolto**, erected in the 13th century (together with the contiguous Franciscan convent), and restructured in 1797.

## Collemancio

At an elevation of 507 m, the structure of this small medieval walled "borough," which in the 13th century became a free commune, has remained intact, as can be seen in the *Palazzo del Podestà*. Whereas the **Pieve di Santo Stefano** was restructured in 1539. Slightly north of the town are the remains of an ancient settlement, identified as *Urvinum Hortense*, a Roman *municipium* of the 6th Augustan region, mentioned in the writings of Pliny the Elder. The importance of this site is confirmed by the remains of a Republican temple, and by a large spa decorated with polychrome mosaics featuring Nilotic scenes (first half of the 3rd cent.).

## Cannara

Its name is nothing but a remote echo of the numerous marsh reeds (*canne* in Italian) that once grew in this area of stagnant swamplands. The town (elev. 191 m, pop. 3,741) has kept the regular layout of an ancient agricultural center, with its characteristic small square, overshadowed by a 14th-century cylindrical tower, upon which face the church of **San Giovanni**, with frescoes by Niccolò Alunno, and that of *San Francesco* (13th-14th cent.). Not far from here rises the church of the *Buona Morte*, where St. Francis is said to have founded the Third Order. Particularly elegant is the 18th-century church of **San Matteo**, which contains a *triptych* by Alunno and a rich polychrome wooden *cantoria*.

# Spello*

An ancient hillside "borough," Spello rises on a narrow extension of Mt. Subasio overlooking the Valle Umbra. Situated at an elevation of 280 m (pop. 8,042), this town has more traces of its former Roman presence than any other Umbrian site, from its walls and its Imperial-age city gates (which were reutilized in medieval times), the remains of the amphitheater and the spa, all blending in a unique interplay of styles and colors. The town's plan is simple and rational, developed along a sole central artery linking two main gates (Porta Consolare and Porta dell'Arce), which gradually rises up to the hilltop. The importance of this former Roman municipium (*Hispellum*, in Latin) derived from its close association with the Via Flaminia, which greatly facilitated the area's land reclamation and settlement. Taken over by the Longobards, it became part of the Spoleto Duchy, conserving all the while its Roman wall boundaries. Between the 12th and 13th century, subsequent to the various struggles between the papacy and the Empire, the town expanded to the extent of absorbing within its wall perimeter a northerly situated

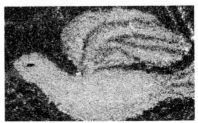

*A composition for the flower display at Spello*

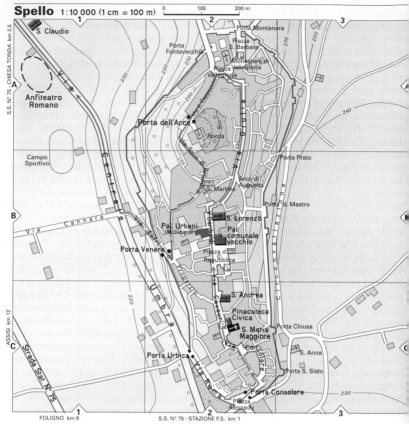

**Spello** 1:10 000 (1 cm = 100 m)

historic settlement. When it passed under the control of the papal state, the only structures to be remodeled were its churches. Our visit continues along the main thoroughfare from south to north, crossing the three quarters of Borgo, Mezota, and Posterula, corresponding to the town's popular quarter, its central area where the public buildings are located, and to its early medieval citadel respectively. Having reached Piazza Umberto I, proceed along Via Giulia, which crosses the Prato quarter, situated between the Roman walls and those of the late Middle Ages. On the hill stands the Vallegloria monastery, from where, proceeding along Via Arco Romano, Via Torre Belvedere, and Via Sant'Agostino, which runs parallel to the Roman walls, you come to Porta Venere. From here, descend approximately 1.5 km along Via Central Umbra and visit the archaeological area and the church of San Claudio. Continuing northward, you come to the entrance to Villa Costanzi.

**Historic Center** (C27). From *Porta Consolare* – the main entrance to the Roman city, flanked on the right by a square medieval tower crowned with an olive tree that is at least 500 years old – you reach the *terziere* (quarter) situated along the Via Consolare, which winds upward separating the symmetrical area of the Roman layout (to the left) from the medieval (to the right). Situated along the way is the **Cappella Tiga,** with important, if incomplete, frescoes by Alunno (1461). A chain hanging on the ancient house to the left indicates that you are about to enter the Mezota *terziere*.

Before passing under the *Porta Consolare*, it is worth turning left down *Via Roma* (C2) to skirt a beautiful stretch of the **Mura Augustee**\*, one of Italy's best conserved fortified structures, in Subasio limestone. At the end of the street stands Imperial-age **Porta Urbica**, with its Tuscan-style arch, and on the opposite side the 12th-century church of *San Ventura*.

**Santa Maria Maggiore**\* (C2). Together with the collegiate church of *San Lorenzo*, this church delimits the Mezota quarter. Founded in the 11th-12th century, its facade dates from 1644 and boasts a Romanesque pyramidal bell tower, opposite which are two ribbed Roman column shafts. The second bell tower, to the rear, was made higher in the 16th century. Its stuccowork decoration, extending over all the interior walls, is by Agostino Silva. In the **Baglioni Chapel\*\***, the visitor's eye is attracted by the finely wrought Deruta majolica pavement (1566), and especially by Pinturicchio's **frescoes\*** (1501), considered one of the artist's highest achievements. By the same Perugia master is also the *Virgin and Child\**, placed above a small altar in the former *Chapel of the Canonici*. The church's *Archivio Storico* includes rare musical editions (15th-18th cent.) and manuscripts from the 18th-19th centuries.

In 1994 a **Pinacoteca Civica** (public art gallery) was set up in the Palazzo dei Canonici (1552). The collection, which will be enriched by other additions, displays in chronological order paintings, sculptures, and local gold artifacts dating from the 13th to the 18th century (opening hours due to changes during the year).

**Sant'Andrea** (C2). Continuing along the main thoroughfare of Via Cavour, you come to the church and convent where Andrea Caccioli, a follower of St. Francis, founded one of the first Friars Minor communities. Built in 1258, it underwent various successive renovations (17th-18th cent.), although the facade and its elegantly simple Romanesque portal were preserved. The interior is neo-gothic (1913).

**Piazza della Repubblica** (B2). An area rich in stratifications which the intensive construction activity of the 20th century has profoundly modified, transforming it into a featureless tree-lined rectangle. To the rear of the square stands the **Palazzo Comunale Vecchio**; built in 1270, it was enlarged and radically transformed in the 16th century. The fountain bearing the coat of arms of Pope Julius III was added in the 16th century. On display in the atrium is a collection of Roman stone tablets and other finds, while the **Sala Emilio Greco**, on the upper floor, contains sculptures and graphic works by the Sicilian artist. The palazzo also houses the *library*, with painted-wood book cabinets dating from the 17th century; two archives, the *Archivio Comunale* and *Notarile*, with documents dating from 1370, and the *Accademia Romanistica Costantiniana*, with historic and legal texts.

**San Lorenzo** (B2). The history of this church is entirely told by its facade. The walled *loggetta* above the portal's upper right corner dates from the 12th century (when the church was built), as does the row decorated with white and pink medallions; the portal, the three rose windows and the upper molding are of the 16th century: the decorations above the left door date from the 8th and 9th centuries. Of the works on display inside the church, particularly noteworthy is the late 15th-century *tabernacle\** for storing holy oil.

**Contrada Prato** (A-B 2-3). This borough developed outside the Roman wall and was later absorbed by that of the 14th-century, the central thoroughfare, Via Giulia. Besides the remains of the Roman gate, called the **Arco di Augusto**, situated opposite the tabernacle known as *Maestà di Fonte del Mastro*, the area is also characterized by the *Teatro Comunale Subasio* (1787) and by

*Porta Venere in Spello, with its two twelve-sided towers*

the *Oratorio San Biagio*, the latter decorated with frescoes of the 15th and 16th centuries.

**Monastero di Vallegloria.** Located at the end of Via Giulia, and built by the Clarissans around the year 1320, its interior carries a 16th-century pictorial cycle by Marcantonio Grecchi, Ascensidonio Spacca, and Cesare Sermei.

**Posterula** (A-B2). The town's most elevated point and, according to documentary sources, its most ancient quarter. After Porta dell'Arce, the Roman arch built in the Republican age (also called dei Cappuccini), with a tower to its left that belonged to the Rocca erected by Cardinal Albornoz in the 14th century, our descent takes us down Via Torre Belvedere to the **Belvedere***, from where there is a truly spectacular view of the Topino plain and of the hills.

**Porta Venere** (B1-2). So called in the 17th century because of a temple dedicated to the goddess of love, which once probably stood in the vicinity, the gate originally (in Imperial times) had three openings, one of which afforded access to a partly subterranean street leading to the *Porta Urbica* along the inside of the town walls. The twelve-sided towers flanking the gate are Romanesque.

**The archaeological area** (A1). Of the *Roman amphitheater* (1st cent. BC) are still visible the shapeless remains of the northern entrance. Here, the late 12th-century church of **San Claudio*** also rests upon a Roman edifice.

**Villa Costanzi, formerly Fidelia** (A1, off map). A quite spectacular villa, constructed upon a Roman sanctuary by the Urbani family in the 16th century as the center of an olive and vineyard plantation. Worth visiting is the villa's park, with its centuries-old trees and terracing, and naturally the 18th-century pavilion which, since 1985, houses the **Straka Coppa Collection**. The fruit of the Coppa family's collecting activity, the gallery includes a section dedicated to modern and contemporary artists such as Orfeo Tamburi, Renato Guttuso, Giacomo Manzù, and Antonio Ligabue; and a classic section with works by Titian, Ludovico Carracci, and Giovanni Fattori (open Apr-Jun and Sep, Thu-Sun, 10.30am-1pm, 2.30pm-5.30pm;

Jul-Aug, Mon-Sun, 10.30am-1pm, 4pm-7pm; Oct-Mar, Sat-Sun only, 10.30am-1pm, 2.30pm-5.30pm).

Masterpieces of local craftsmanship are the **Infiorate del Corpus Domini**. After weeks of intense work, it takes only one evening to prepare the floral compositions that will grace the Corpus Domini procession. The flowers last only a few hours: from 9am to 12am, and constitute a colorfully fragrant "carpet" of blooms representing sacred motifs. The procession is a truly unique and unforgettable event.

## Bevagna

Nestled on a ridge on the western side of the valley, surrounded by waterways which have always provided a natural defensive system, lies Bevagna (elev. 225 m, pop. 4,719). The town is crossed by the *Via Flaminia*, which is still the town's principal thoroughfare, from *Porta del Salvatore* to *Porta Foligno*. Ancient *Mevania* became an important leg along the Consular Road, and consequently urbanized quite rapidly, spilling outside the old town walls. The Roman legacy is so deeply rooted that the town's layout remained unaltered even in medieval times. It was in the 12th century that the public square began to take shape, a scheme that was completed in 1270 with the building of the *Palazzo dei Consoli*. Reclamation of the surrounding plains began in the 15th century with the excavation of the Topino river bed, but was not enough to encourage development of a primarily hemp-based agricultural economy. As a consequence, this area remained of secondary importance compared with developments elsewhere in the Valle Umbra.

**The Corso**. Following the unchanged tract of the Flaminia, we enter the city through **Porta Foligno** (or *Flaminia*), which was altered when the roadway was widened. The structures that can be seen above the arch are medieval, whereas its crown dates from the 18th century. Impressive remains of the original Roman walls, however, are visible at either side of the gate. From here we proceed down *Corso Matteotti*, which retraces the Roman thoroughfare. On the left are the remains of a *Roman edifice*, with a fine black-and-white mosaic pavement. On the right, the facade of a former church boasts decorative pillars originally part of the former church of *San Vincenzo* (12th cent.), now in ruins. The most important Roman landmark, however, is the *Roman theater* (1st cent.), the remains of which constitute the foundations of the houses set around it in a semicircle, reproducing the circular structure of the theater.

**Toward San Francesco**. Branching off to the right of the corso is Via Crescimbeni, it too featuring the remains of a **Roman temple**, built perhaps in the 2nd century AD. When in *Via di Porta Guelfa*, contact the custodian of no. 2 for admission to the temple, which conserves a **mosaic** from the first half of the 2nd century AD, featuring lively marine scenes depicted in black and white tesserae, originally part of a Roman thermal bath facility. After the Roman temple, the street leads to long and narrow *Piazza Garibaldi*, where a stairway ascends to the church of **San Francesco**, built after 1275 upon the most elevated spot in the city. The facade of stone slabs, the portal, and part of the square bell tower, give us some idea of what the original building must have been like. The interior, restructured in the 18th century, features a *Pietà* by Ascensidonio Spacca (1596) and a *Crucifixion with Angel and St. Francis* by Dono Doni. Walled beneath an iron grating is the stone upon which, according to a legend, St. Francis stood when preaching to the birds in *Pian d'Arca*.

We return to **Corso Matteotti**. On the left of the corso is the **Chiesa della Consolazione** (1735), which houses a wooden statue of *Christ Resurrected* (16th cent.), which, on Easter Sunday, is carried in a procession through the town. On the right, you come to *Palazzo Lepri*, now the Town Hall, rebuilt by Andrea Vici in the 19th century. The ground floor houses the **Museo Civico** (instituted in 1996), featuring archaeological finds, paintings, maps, and documents illustrating the town's history from an-

cient times to the 18th century (open Oct-Mar, Fri-Sun, 10.30am-1pm, 2.30pm-5pm; Apr-May and Sep, Tue-Sun, 10.30am-1pm, 2.30pm-6pm; Jun-Jul, Tue-Sun, 10.30am-1pm, 3.30pm-7pm; Aug, Mon-Sun, 10.30am-1pm, 3.30pm-7.30pm). The collection includes a **Virgin and Child** by Dono Doni, originally in the church of St. Francis, besides works by Ascensidonio Spacca and Andrea Camassei. At the end of the corso, set amid a compact row of houses, stands the 14th-century church of **Santi Domenico e Giacomo**, together with the former Dominican convent donated by the township to the order in 1291. The church's interior, modernized in 1737, conserves works by Ascensidonio Spacca, Andrea Camassei, and G. B. Pacetti. In the subterranea of the former convent still visible are the remains of a large barrel-vaulted Roman edifice.

**Piazza Silvestri**\*\*. The square constitutes one of the region's most interesting medieval urban achievements: an area lacking symmetry and frontal alignments, and totally consisting of "corner-edge" perspectives which are further enlivened by the monumental presence of two churches, the Palazzo dei Consoli, the *Colonna di San Rocco* (the shaft of a Roman column), and by a pseudo-medieval fountain (1896). The **Palazzo dei Consoli** (1270) stands out with its ground-level loggia surmounted by ribbed vaults. The broad staircase leads to the small but harmoniously proportioned **Teatro Francesco Torti**. An ample vault links the *palazzo* to the **basilica of San Silvestro**\*, a jewel of Umbro-Romanesque architecture (1195), whose unfinished facade features an ornate marble triforium. On the opposite side of the square stands the collegiate church of **San Michele Arcangelo**\* (late 12th or early 13th

*The Teatro Francesco Torti at Bevagna*

cent.), which, from 1951 to 1957, was cleared of its 18th-century additions. In the process, its large circular "eye," which once probably housed a rose window, was restored. The jambs framing its magnificent central **portal**\* are made from Roman moldings, whereas the solid pointed bell tower which rises to its right is of a later period. The next church, **Sant'Agostino**, was built in the 14th century, with Umbrian-school

frescoes of that period and others of the 16th century.

As a reminder of the town's past, it was decided recently to hold an annual re-enactment of medieval trades in the main square. The **Mercato delle Gaite** entails the craftsmen of Bevagna's various quarters in a contest for the "gaita," the honor, that is, of watching over the town.

## 4.3 Foligno
**A circular itinerary starting from Piazza della Repubblica**

Because it lies in the plain, Foligno (elev. 234 m, pop. 52,930), differs from the region's typical historic centers, usually situated on the hillside. The city developed before the year 1000 near *Fulginia*, a small Umbrian center that entered the sphere of Roman influence in the early 3rd century BC. From the 11th to the 12th century the city began to expand, reaching its period of greatest development

around the mid-14th century. After being occupied by the papal army of Eugene IV (1439), Foligno ceased to have an autonomous history-making role. Between the country's unification and the 1930s, the urban walls were completely razed, thereby enabling the city center to spill outward into the countryside and give way to progressive urbanization.

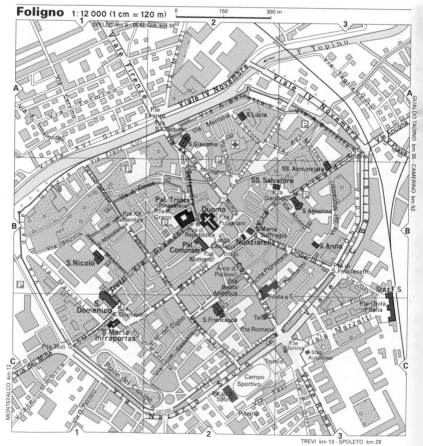

**Foligno** 1:12 000 (1 cm = 120 m)

Foligno is usually described as being "egg-shaped". Right in the middle is Piazza della Repubblica, upon which are located the main buildings representing the city's principal civic and religious authorities. This layout is offset by the network of narrow streets and secondary squares which constitute the city's rather modest periphery, a chaotic maze lying just beyond the linear facades of its main buildings. Our recommended itinerary will attempt to recompose a unitary image of the historic city, fragmented by the many lacerations which have particularly affected the city's historic center, by capturing the significance of areas which may be of lesser importance, but which nevertheless have a fascination all their own, even though they have been partly overshadowed by more recent architectural modifications.

From Piazza della Repubblica, Via XX Settembre leads toward the modest Poelle quarter, skirting from within, along the banks of the Topino, the tract of the medieval walls all the way to where it runs in-

*The main facade of Foligno Cathedral*

to Via Garibaldi, the city's main east-west axis. At the central three-street junction, take Corso Cavour and the Via Rutili until you come to San Francesco, continuing on to Canapè park. Again proceeding along the walls, you come to the main western gateway (Porta Santa Maria) and, once having crossed Piazza San Domenico, Via Gramsci again takes you back to the main square. Turning off from Via Gramsci and

proceeding down Via Scuole Arti e Mestieri, Via del Reclusorio, Via San Giovanni dell'Acqua, Via delle Conce, and Piazza del Grano, you enter one of the city's most secluded quarters, through which the Topino once flowed.

**Piazza della Repubblica** (B2). Together with adjacent Piazza del Duomo, Piazza della Repubblica is the city's hub. The vast rectangle square dating from the communal age took shape around the 13th century with the building of three public buildings: Palazzo del Podestà, Palazzo dei Priori and Palazzo del Capitano del Popolo. In the following century, the Trinci erected their prestigious family palace on the northern side of the square.

**Duomo***, or Cathedral (B2). Here, in the 9th-10th century there probably stood a temple of some kind, which offered a good site for a church dedicated to San Feliciano, one of the city's martyrs. Over the centuries, the church was progressively enlarged; from 1772 and 1819 the church's interior underwent a neoclassical transformation by Giuseppe Piermarini, who modified Vanvitelli's original design. Among the works on display inside the Cathedral, tempera paintings by Pietro di Giovanni di Corraducci and by Niccolò Alunno in the sacristy; while in the semicircular vault of the apse hangs works by Francesco Mancini. The facade of the Cathedral, facing Piazza della Repubblica, richly adorned with decorations, seems to outwardly prefigure the transept as a church in its own right, whereas the magnificent **portal*** by masters Rodolfo and Binello (1201) features classicizing decorations.

Next to the Duomo's left aisle stands the **Palazzo delle Canoniche** (11th cent.), restored in 1923-26. The building is to contain a collection of diocesan art, with paintings from the 15th to 18th century, and documents of Christian archaeology. Opposite, the 13th-century **Palazzo Comunale** was totally restructured between 1546 and 1642. The only building to survive from the Middle Ages is the fine tower, the upper part of which was modified in the 16th century, but suffered serious damage during the 1997 earthquake.

**Palazzo Trinci*** (B2). In the late 14th century, the powerful Trinci family purchased houses and towers from the rich merchant Giovanni di Ceccarello that bordered on their property, and radically restructured them to give them their present appearance. In the rooms of this palace, set up as a **Museo della città**, one still breathes the cultural atmosphere which the family promoted with its circle of scholars and humanists, and which is well represented by the frescoes\*, an encyclopedia of cultural life in the early 15th century. The interior (open 10am-7pm; closed Mon) boasts a striking *Gothic staircase\** (once unroofed), with curious architectural solutions and late-Gothic decorative work. The first-floor comprises rooms with frescoes dating from the 15th and 16th centuries: the **chapel\***, completely adorned with mural paintings by Ottaviano Nelli (1424); the **Sala delle Arti Liberali e dei Pianeti\***, with paintings by an accomplished 15th-century Venetian master, whose identity has yet to be established; the *Sala dei Giganti*, frescoed with 15 (originally 20) incomplete figures representing illustrious characters of Roman history.

The **Pinacoteca Comunale**, instituted in 1870, was relocated in the building in 1935. The gallery documents Umbrian and Folignate painting from the 14th to the 16th century. The collection includes paintings by Bernardino Mezzastris, Dono Doni and Ascensidonio Spacca; also many frescoes detached from buildings and churches in the town.

The **Museo Archeologico** collection was set up by the Accademia Fulginia in 1762 to illustrate the history of Foligno territory and its Roman early settlement. Particularly interesting is the section devoted to ancient sculptures collected by the Trinci family in the 15th century (Sala dei Giganti and Sala delle Arti Liberali) and organized according to didactic criteria. Also note the finds from the necropolis of Santa Maria in Campis.

**Quartiere delle Poelle**. Developed in the Middle Ages between the former Topino river bed (today Via Gentile da Foligno, AB 2-3) and the 13th-century canalization, the neighborhood is still characterized by narrow streets which branch into the rectilinear *Via Mentana*. The church of **San Giacomo** is one of the three religious poles around which the quarter developed. Documented since the 13th century, it features a characteristic white-and-red banded facade and an ogival portal. The church of *San Giovanni* contains various attractive 15th-century frescoes, while the **Santa Lucia** monastery includes a church dating from the 14th-15th centuries, preceded by a graceful portico over a portal surmounted by a lunette featuring a fresco by

Pier Antonio Mezzastris (1471). At the end of the street stands a long tract of the medieval walls bordering the Topino river, with the characteristic *Torre dei Cinque Cantoni*, soon to be converted into a small astronomical observatory.

**Via Garibaldi** (B2-3). One of the axes of the "crossing" characterizing the layout of the medieval city still recognizable despite postwar transformations. Along this street are located some particularly significant religious buildings in terms of the architectural renewal that the "old city" underwent during the 18th and 19th centuries. After the unfinished former church of the **Annunziata**, by Carlo Murena (annexed to the police department), you reach Piazza Garibaldi which is fronted by the church of **Santissimo Salvatore** (1138), formerly a Benedictine abbey, and later a collegiate. (Both the church and the 14th-century bell tower were damaged by the 1997 earthquake.) The interior of the church was restructured, according to a design by Pietro Loni, in 1747. Opposite stands the church of **Sant'Agostino**, the brick facade of which likewise by Pietro Loni, is particularly striking. The interior is enhanced by an impressive altar by Gioacchino Grampini (1678), upon which is placed a sacred wooden image of the *Our Lady of Sorrow* (1700). Slightly further on, the 18th-century church of **Santa Maria del Suffragio** with its facade dating from 1826.

**Oratorio della Nunziatella\*** (B2). Built by the local municipality in 1490-94 in honor of a miracle, this graceful rectangular Renaissance temple features a *tabernacle* richly decorated by Lattanzio di Niccolò and two works by Perugino (a **Baptism of Christ** and a *God the Father*, 1507). The adjacent rooms house the civic *Centro di Documentazione della Stampa*, illustrating the early introduction of the printing art, by the Orfini brothers, to the city of Foligno in 1470.

A short detour takes us in *Corso Cavour*, to the late 17th-century church of **Santa Maria di Betlem**, and, in *Via dei Monasteri*, to the monastery of **Sant'Anna\***, otherwise known as the *Monastero delle Contesse*, originally a circle for women only. It was founded in 1388 and decorated by Pier Antonio Mezzastris, Feliciano de Muti, and Giovanni di Corraduccio (see the *chapel of the Beata Angelina*, 14th cent.).

**Corso Cavour**. Facing the corso, immediately on the left, is the late-16th-century

## The printing of the Divine Comedy

Typography in Foligno dates from 1470, only five years after movable type was introduced to Italy. The protagonists of this undertaking were Johann Numeister and two other Germans, Craft (a type composer and punch setter), and Stephan Arndes from Hamburg, later active in Perugia and Lübeck. They were called to the city and funded by the Orfini brothers (Emiliano, Mariotto, and Antonio), formerly papal engravers and minters, who also ran a typography from their own home in Piazza Grande. The Foligno printing presses turned out some extraordinary masterpieces, such as the first edition of Cicero's *De bello italico adversus Gothos*, and the *Epistolae ad familiares*, the first edition of Dante Alighieri's *Divine Comedy*, printed on 11 April 1472 (with a print run of between 200 and 300 copies), of which 14 originals are still extant. This first printing house, however, was short lived, perhaps because, in those early days, it wasn't yet easy to rely on a well-organized distribution network. The seed however had been sown, and many a qualified printer was to have later contributions to Foligno's fame as a leading typographical center. Today, the buildings connected to the Nunziatella oratory house the *Centro di documentazione della Stampa*, which illustrates the various developmental phases of the printing art in Foligno. Also on display is an ancient printing press which, according to tradition, was the one utilized to print Dante's *Divine Comedy*. Although scholars do not all agreed on this attribution, the press continues testify to an artistic tradition which Foligno has preserved at the highest level.

*Dante Alighieri*

**Palazzo Iacobilli-Roncalli**, in which, after successive building modifications, only the *Sala della Musica* with its artful stucco decorations has preserved its original look. Next comes the facade of the former **Teatro Apollo-Piermarini** (1827), destroyed by air raids in 1944. Its only surviving room houses the *Centro di Documentazione del Teatro*, instituted by the Mancinelli (1827-1913) and Loreti (1894-1932) foundations.

Near the municipal stadium off *Corso Cavour*, on the second and third Sunday in September the **Giostra della Quintana** race is run, preceded by a historic pageant featuring some 600 costume-wearing participants. The *Quintana* re-enacts a tournament dating from the 17th century, during which men on horseback showed their ability to ride while holding their lance at rest.

**Piazza San Francesco** (C2). Here too is an example of an urban area clearly defined by the presence of two churches: the church of the **Madonna del Gonfalone** (1724), with its plain unfinished facade, now used as a venue for exhibits and other events, and the church of **San Francesco**, a 19th-century re-edition of a medieval church featuring early 14th-century frescoes and a late 13th-century *Crucifixion*.

**Santa Maria Infraportas**\* (C1). As its name suggests, the church was built outside the city walls, with a white-and-pink stone facade and a small portico flanked on its right by a tabernacle (1480). Numerous votive frescoes grace its interior, al-

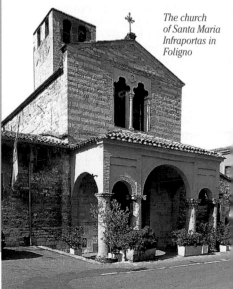

*The church of Santa Maria Infraportas in Foligno*

ternating with works by Pier Antonio Mezzastris and Ugolino di Gisberto. Adorned with frescoes from the second half of the 12th century, the **chapel of the Assunta**\* is well worth a visit.

**Via Gramsci** (B1-2). The former Via dei Mercanti continues to be one of the city's most representative streets, especially because of the aristocratic palaces with which it is lined. On the edge of the old city stands the former convent church of **San Domenico** (1285), which was converted into an auditorium by Franco Antonelli (1994). Through its fine pointed portal you pass into a modern room whose walls are hung with an extensive series of votive frescoes. Among the street's civic buildings, of particular interest are: 16th-century **Palazzo Brunetti-Candiotti**, restructured in 1797 by Filippo Neri; *Palazzo Vitelleschi* (no. 52-54), a building with richly-decorated rooms (17th cent.) that now houses the municipal offices; and *Palazzo Guiducci*, with 16th-century decorations.

**Rione delle Conce**. Taking Via della Scuola d'Arti e Mestieri, and going beyond the little church of *San Tomaso dei Cipischi* (1190) – today the Museo Scout – you come to a square fronted by the church of **San Nicolò**, restructured by the Olivetans in the 14th century and by the Augustinians in the following. The adjacent Piazza XX Settembre, affords access to the medieval craftsmen's *rione* (quarter) with its network of narrow little streets. Once having crossed the *Topinello* canal, flowing along the old river course, you reach the characteristic, albeit run down, **Portico delle Conce**, with its ancient workshops facing the canal.

For a rewarding excursion (6 km) that blends the sacred with a natural environment, proceed beyond *Via Garibaldi* in the direction of Camerino, until you come to the Sassovivo abbey (elev. 520 m). Before venturing into the abbey's solitary wooded landscape, stop and admire the church of **San Bartolomeo**, a Franciscan complex erected in 1415 upon a castle fortress formerly of the Trinci family. Even the **abbey of Sassovivo** was built upon a fortified residence (of the Monaldi family, second half of the 11th cent.). It attained such a degree of importance in the 13th century as to have under its control 92 monasteries, 41 churches and 7 hospitals. It fell into decline and was eventually suppressed in 1860. Today it is the seat of Father Foucauld's *Jesus Caritas Community*. Particularly striking is the church's Romanesque *cloister*\* (damaged by the 1997 earthquake), built in 1229. From the courtyard you can proceed to the *loggia* (1442) and the 11th-century **crypt**\*, Sassovivo's initial nucleus. From here, paths branch off into a centuries-old wood of holm-oaks.

## 4.4 From Montefalco to Trevi and to Spoleto

**An excursion of 43.8 km** *(map on page 110)* **and two walking tours in Montefalco and Trevi** *(maps on pages 121 and 123)*

After Foligno, a 12-km drive along a vineyard and olive grove-studded countryside takes you to Montefalco, one of the region's major art centers. Going beyond the Castello dei Fabbri, you again cross the valley through its narrowest stretch. At the 25.8-km junction with the Flaminia, a short upgrade shoots off toward the Trevi summit. From here to Spoleto, the busy state road is choked by the business and industrial complexes lining it (cement works, furniture factories, olive-oil plants; the latter turning out high-quality products). Breathtaking landscapes are to be glimpsed along the slopes of the Mts. Serano and Maggiore, at times reaching elevations of 1,500 m covered with olive groves and oak, maple and chestnut forests, in an environment still marked by small, well preserved historic "boroughs." Especially impressive is the Pissignano castle, a medieval structure (today private property) spiked with turrets overlooking the Flaminia. On the opposite side of the street, and at a lower level, the Roman Clitumno temple. From the Fonti del Clitumno, a short tract leads to the medieval village of Campello Alto.

**Montefalco**\*
From atop a 472 m elevation the town dominates the Topino and Clitumno plains, offering vistas of exceptional beauty, as to have deserved the appellative of "Umbria's Balcony." The symbiosis of this town (pop. 5,592) with its surrounding area is not only aesthetic, because of its characteristic roads branching off from the town's circular square downward to the valley below, but also economic and political. The town's detached position from the Flaminia thoroughfare has always pre-

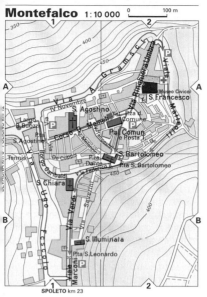

**Montefalco** 1 : 10 000

SPOLETO km 23

vented it from playing a leading role in the area, but not from being a significant cultural landmark, thanks especially to the many works commissioned to local artists by the Franciscans. This role by the Friars Minor is well exemplified by Benozzo Gozzoli's fresco cycle in the church of San Francesco, converted into an art gallery in 1890, and today a living testament to Umbria's cultural heritage. You enter the town through Porta Sant'Agostino, a gate which opens in the medieval walls, and head down Corso Mameli, the main axis of the Castellare "borough," at the end of which you come to the circular central square. From here, sloping narrow streets take you to the lower "borough" of San Leonardo. Via dei Vasari (Potters' street) still bears visual witness to its typical local production of vases and earthenware. Returning to the square, take Via Ringhiera Umbra, the main thoroughfare of the Colle Mora quarter, the salient feature of which is the church of San Francesco. From Porta della Rocca you can enjoy a splendid view of the Topino valley and the Clitumno plain. Viale Matteotti flanks the medieval walls which lead to the borough of San Leonardo, with, at the end of Via Verdi, and Porta Spoleto. At a distance of approximately one and a half kilometers outside the town walls, situated on Viale Marconi, is the church of San Fortunato, which well deserves a visit.

**Borgo del Castellare** (A1). Entry to the historic center is through *Porta Sant'Agostino*, situated in a well-preserved tract of the 13th-century walls and surmounted by a battlemented tower. It is here that *Corso Mameli*, the medieval axis of *Borgo del Castellare* (early 13th cent.), begins its ascent. *Casa Angeli*, to the right, has an interesting facade set with remains or urns, chunks of Roman marble, and coats of arms. The entire quarter is dominated by the church of *Sant'Agostino* (1279-85), with its plain but elegant stone facade and handsome late 13th-century portal, through which you pass into the church's interior, its walls covered with frescoes by Maestro Espressionista Gozzalesco, Pier Antonio Mezzastris and G. B. Caporali, dating from the 14th, 15th, and 16th centuries.

Before reaching Piazza del Comune, the Corso broadens into small Piazza Mustafà, where stands **Palazzo Tempestivi** (16th cent.), with an ashlar framed portal. **Palazzo Langeli**, in nearby *Via Tempestini*, is attributed by some to Vignola.

**Piazza del Comune** (A2). This is the highest spot in the town, and the hub of its civil and religious power. The *platea rotunda*, as it was defined in the early 14th century because of its almost circular shape, in the Middle Ages became the center of town life

*The 13th-century Porta Sant'Agostino, at Montefalco*

and a point of convergence of the five principal streets that divide the town into segments. **Palazzo Comunale** (1270) is the square's main building, the facade of which was remodeled in the 19th century. Today it houses the *Biblioteca Civica*, with approximately 10,000 volumes (16th-century juridical and scholastic treatises, incunabula, and manuscripts) and the *Archivio Storico Comunale*, containing documents from the 15th to the 19th centuries. Also facing the square are the former church of **San Filippo Neri** (1705), converted into a theater in 1895, the *Oratorio di Santa Maria di Piazza*, dating from the 13th century and featuring a fresco by Francesco Melanzio, and the elegant 16th-century *Palazzo de Cuppis*.

**San Francesco**\* (A2). A few steps down from the square, we come to this former church, built together with the convent between 1336 and 1340. The chapels to the right, which form a minor aisle, were added in the 17th century. Over the centuries this church has served as a religious and political focus.

Here public gatherings were held and priors (chief magistrates) elected, in an atmosphere of perfect harmony between temporal and civil power. It was also here that in the second half of the 15th century the Friars Minor summoned Benozzo Gozzoli to the town, and commissioned him to paint scenes from the life of St. Francis, a work which was to influence Umbrian painting for the entire second half of the century.

In 1895 the church was turned into a **Museo Civico**; the display was reorganized in 1990; besides the decorations belonging to the former church, there is now a Pinacoteca (art gallery) housed in various rooms of the former convent (open Mar-May, Sep-Oct, 10.30am-1pm, 2pm-6pm; Jun-Jul, 10.30am-1pm, 3pm-7pm; Aug, 10.30am-1pm, 3pm-7.30pm; Nov-Feb, 10.30am-1pm, 2.30pm-5pm, closed Mon during these last months).

Starting our visit from the church, we can admire frescoes by Benozzo Gozzoli in the **San Girolamo Chapel**\*, and by Jacopo Vincioli (together with an assistant) in the *San Bernardino Chapel*. The **Crucifix**\* in the third bay is by the Maestro Espressionista di Santa Chiara, whereas the fourth and fifth spans feature frescoes by Giovanni di Corraduccio. It is the central apse, however, that captures the visitor's attention, with a fresco cycle depicting **Scenes from the Life of St. Francis**\*, painted in 1452 by Benozzo Gozzoli upon commission by Fra Jacopo da Montefalco. The *Bontadosi Chapel* (1589), off the nave, features an altarpiece by Ascensidonio Spacca; there follows the *Nicchia di Sant'Antonio di Padova*, frescoed by Jacopo Vincioli.

A first floor area houses the **Pinacoteca**, with tempera paintings and detached frescoes by the Montefalco painter Francesco Melanzio; 14th-16th-century works, among which a *Crucifixion with Mourners* by an artist from the school of Niccolò Alunno. There follow 17th- and 18th-century works, and, in two separate rooms, a collection of everyday articles, together with religious artifacts. The semicircular crypt houses a **tablet collection** featuring archaeological finds and stone tablets from the 1st century onward.

**Borgo San Leonardo** (B1). A 14th-century extension of the city that lines the road to Spoleto. After a cylindrical tower situated along the perimeter wall, you come to the church of **Santa Chiara** and the convent founded by the saint from Montefalco (Chiara di Damiano). The church (13th-14th cent.) was radically remodeled by Valentino Monti in the early 17th century, except for the *Santa Croce Chapel*\* (contact sisters for a visit), which was frescoed by Umbrian artists in 1333. At the far end of the borough stands the church of **Sant'Illuminata**\*, a harmonious Renaissance house of worship built in 1491 and frescoed by Francesco Melanzio and Bernardino Mezzastris.

**San Fortunato**\* (B1, off map). After 12 km along *Viale Marconi* you come to the church dedicated to Montefalco's evangelizer, who died in 390. The Longobard court, complete with its own *castellum* and church, dating from 749, became an important center in the 13th century, until the castle was destroyed by a popular uprising in 1439. The present church is preceded by a 15th-century arcaded courtyard, featuring four ancient columns and a *portal* frescoed by Benozzo Gozzoli and Tiberio d'Assisi. Inside hangs a **St. Fortunatus enthroned**\* by Benozzo Gozzoli, in addition to other fresco fragments by the same author. Worth visiting, in the surrounding wooded area, are the so-called *Grotte di San Fortunato*, dug in the terrain and linked, according to tradition, to episodes in the saint's life.

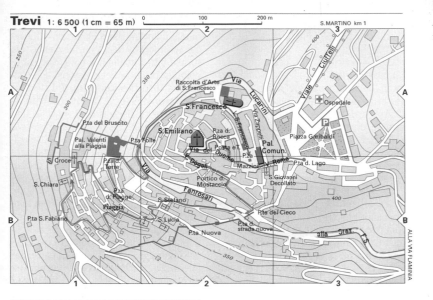

**Trevi** 1: 6 500 (1 cm = 65 m)

S.MARTINO km 1

# Trevi

A broad stretch of olive trees accompanies the ascent to this town (elev. 412 m, pop. 7,595), perched on a hill overlooking the Spoleto plain. The town spirals round the hillside, sloping valleyward over terraces which were added during the 13th and 14th century. Trevi has always taken advantage of the fertile plain and the major communications route along the valley floor, around which developed modern-day Borgo Trevi. The beautiful mountain to the rear of the town has become depopulated; there remain however highly prized olive crops, thanks to the quality of the soil which has always favored the production of olive oil, as well as lime, another traditional local product.

Piazza Garibaldi is located on the edge of the medieval town, which is accessed by Via Roma, which quickly leads to centrally located Piazza Mazzini. From here, Via del Duomo climbs to the top of the hill, where stands the Cathedral of Sant'Emiliano. The early medieval town centered entirely around this compact and closed urban sector, surrounded by a wall with a 70 meter radius. Cobble stones and bricks pave the streets forming ancient traditional patterns. Take Via Dògali down to the Portico del Mostaccio, which opens onto the town's earliest stretch of wall, which probably coincides with the original Roman perimeter. Continuing downward, you cross an area built up between the two medieval walls up to the Porta del Cieco, situated in the 13th-century walls. This ex-

cursion can however be extended by going down into the Borgo di Piaggia, featuring a few medieval Romanesque churches. From here, the climb along the steep upgrade takes you back to the "strada nuova," with its ample view of both the valley and the mountain. The church of San Francesco, which also in Trevi occupies a position of urban significance, concludes our visit to the town. Outside the historic center, other points of interest are the church of San Martino, the Sanctuary of the Madonna delle Lacrime (along the road from Trevi

*View of Trevi, with Sant'Emiliano on the hilltop*

123

down toward the Flaminia), and, in the plain, Santa Maria di Pietrarossa.

**Piazza Mazzini** (A-B2). Leaving broad *Piazzale Garibaldi*, from Via Roma you reach the *piazza*, passing under an archway in the public palace. This is the center of city life, dominated by the **Palazzo Comunale**, documented for the first time in 1273, and radically modified during the following centuries. An underpass leads to the *Torre del Comune*, a solid 13th-century construction.

**Sant'Emiliano** (A2). The hub of Trevi's most ancient settlement, this church was built between the 12th and 13th century, and totally rebuilt in 1867, preserving however some parts of the previous structures. The three small **apses**\* of the Romanesque church are considered the most interesting structures of their kind in the region. The centerpiece of its aisled interior is the **altar of the Sacrament**\*, especially because of its extremely fine decorations by Rocco di Tommaso (1522).

Facing Sant'Emiliano is the 15th-century *Palazzo Lucarini* that houses the **Trevi Flash Art Museum** (tel. 0742381818), where contemporary art exhibits are organized. Periodically the museum's permanent collection is displayed, consisting of works by Italian and foreign artists, from the 1970s to the present.

**Piaggia** (A-B 1-2). Narrow streets, winding downward below the ancient city walls, descend to this area which developed in the 13th century, enclosed by medieval walls and arranged fan-fashion along the steep slope. As usual, churches constituted the area's first basic architectural reference points (the church of **Santa Lucia**, founded in the 14th century and entirely restructured in 1635; along the western edge of the walls, the elliptical-plan church of **Santa Chiara**; and not far away, the Benedictine church of *Santa Croce*, totally rebuilt in late 17th century). You come thus to *Piazza della Torre*, that represents almost a private area belonging to the Valenti family. The main **palazzo**, 16th century but transformed in the following century, contains finds from Roman times and detached 14th-century frescoes.

**San Francesco** (A2). The former convent, documented in 1285 as an important settlement, has undergone numerous modifications. After being abandoned by the monks following the suppression of the religious orders by Napoleon, the church was turned into a communal barn. The entire complex has now been restored and converted into the **Raccolta d'Arte San Francesco**, joint to the Pinacoteca Civica, instituted as far back as 1869. Its collection comprises paintings by local artists (from the 15th to the 18th century), archaeological finds, sculptures and documents pertinent to the city's history (open Oct-Mar, Fri-Sun, 10.30am-1pm, 2.30pm-5pm; Apr-May and Sep, Tue-Sun, 10.30am-1pm, 2.30pm-6pm; Jun-Jul, Tue-Sun, 10.30am-1pm, 3.30pm-7pm; Aug, Mon-Sun, 10.30am-1pm, 3pm-7.30pm). Visits start on the second floor, with works by Giovanni di Corraduccio, Pinturicchio, and Alunno. Of particular interest on the lower floor is the **Coronation of Mary, with Angels, St. Francis and Saints**\* by Spagna. In the interior of the church there is a large *altarpiece cross* (early 14th cent.) and a precious Renaissance wall organ (1509).

The *Museo della Città e del Territorio*, display archaeological finds, sculptures and local historic documents from Roman times to the 19th century.

**San Martino**\* (A3, off map). A ten-minute walk from Piazza Garibaldi along tree-lined pedestrian *Viale Ciuffelli*, which affords a wonderful panorama\* of the valley, takes you to the ancient *Pieve di Trevi*, in place of which the Observants Minor erected the church of *San Martino* in the late 15th century. The lunette fresco over the portal is by Tiberio d'Assisi, who also decorated parts of the interior in collaboration with Pier Antonio Mezzastris. On the opposite side of the square stands the **San Girolamo Chapel** (1512), which contains one of Spagna's best frescoes (1512).

**Madonna delle Lacrime** (B3, off map). After 1 km along a road that descends through olive trees, you reach this church (1487-1522) which was built (design by Francesco di Pietrasanta) to harbor a "miraculous" image of the Madonna, painted in 1483. Its vast and luminous interior (to gain access, inquire at the nearby *Istituto medico-psicopedagogico*) contains frescoes by Angelucci da Mevale and an **Epiphany of Sts. Peter and Paul**\* by Perugino (1521), and a chapel decorated by Spagna (1520).

After 5.2 km along the state road in the direction of Foligno, you come to the church of **Santa**

**Maria di Pietrarossa,** which owes its name to a red rectangular stone, with a hole in the middle, from which curative water is said once to have sprung. The many archaeological finds to have surfaced here justify the assumption that this was the center of the imperial-age town of *Trebiae.*

### Pissignano and the Fonti del Clitunno

Here, where the valley narrows, after the octagonal *Chiesa Tonda* (16th cent.), you find on your right an elegant early-Christian structure dedicated to the Holy Savior, and better known as the **Tempietto del Clitunno**\* (open Apr-Oct, 9am-8pm; Nov-Mar, 9am-4pm; closed Mon). There is clear evidence of the elements that were part of the typical pagan *sacelli* (stone altars and burial sites) mentioned by Pliny the Younger, which were located along the nearby river spring. The temple overlooks the Clitunno from a rise which was formerly reached via two lateral stairways. The frieze decorating the facade bears a dedicatory inscription to the God of angels. Leaving to the left the *Castello di Passignano* (elev. 280 m), with its triangular plan superimposed upon a tower, you come to the **Fonti del Clitunno**\*, the springs from where the Clitunno rivulet that flows into the Teverone issues. Pools of clear, cold water form a placid lake which, although not very deep, is dotted with verdant islets whose grassy shores are pleasantly shaded by weeping willows (open Jan-15 Mar, 10am-1pm, 2pm-4pm; 16 Mar-Apr, 9am-7pm; May-Aug, 8.30am-8pm; Sep, 9am-1pm, 2pm-7.30pm; Oct, 9am-1pm, 2pm-6.30pm; Nov-Dec, 10am-1pm, 2pm-5pm). Even in Roman times, the beauty of the setting stimulated tourism which, as Pliny relates, prompted the building of hotels, baths, and villas.

### Campello Alto

Proceeding toward Spoleto, you come to *Campello sul Clitunno* (elev. 290 m, pop. 2,312), with its 16th-century church of *Santa Maria della Bianca*, overlooked by the **Castello di Campello Alto** (elev. 514 m), perched at the summit of a hill which can be reached via a winding road bordered by a circular wall.

*Sundown on the Fonti del Clitunno*

## 4.5 Spoleto
**Walks along the Traversa Interna and in the upper town** *(map on page 126)*

Spoleto's (elev. 396, pop. 37,743) charm derives not only from its varyingly renowned monuments, but in particular from its rather special relationship with the surrounding environment. Monteluco not only functions as a scenic backdrop, but has also played a leading role in Spoleto's history, with its oakwood forests which from antiquity have been protected by special laws. Being able to control the valley, rightly called the "valle spoletina," from its hillside vantage point enabled the city over the centuries to play a leading role which would be difficult to explain from a strictly economic point of view. In the 4th century BC, Cyclopean walls were constructed in the town center, which however was given a Greek-model layout starting only in 241 BC, after the foundation of a Roman colony. After the decline of the Roman Empire, there ensued various barbaric dominations, until the Duchy of Spoleto was instituted by the Longobards. In 1155 Spoleto "highly fortified, defended by a hundred towers," was razed to the ground by Barbarossa, a destruction which sparked a process of political autonomy, giving rise to an unprecedented period of urban renewal. It the second half of the 13th century Piazza del Mercato took shape in the area formerly occupied by the ancient Roman forum, including the construction of the Palazzo Comunale. Successively, with the arrival of the Mendicant orders, large and imposing churches begin to appear, whereas settlements along the town's access roads triggered the development of "boroughs" and later of a new urban wall complete with watch tower and city gates (1296). The layout which for centuries had characterized

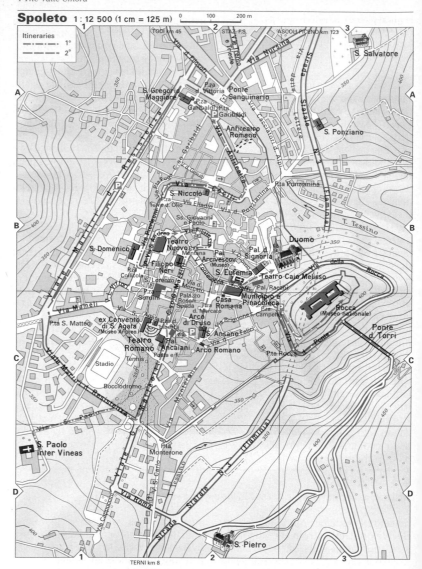

**Spoleto** 1 : 12 500 (1 cm = 125 m)

the town was altered in 1834 by the architect Ireneo Aleandri, who designed the thoroughfare known as the "Traversa nazionale" in order to ease the flow of vehicle traffic into the town.

It was, however, only after World War II that the town began to experience some sort of cultural revival, thanks to the Centro Italiano di Studi sull'Alto Medioevo, a center for early medieval studies (1951), the Teatro Nazionale Sperimentale (1947), and the Festival dei Due Mondi, instituted in 1958 by the composer Gian Carlo Menotti – now one of the world's most prestigious cultural happenings.

Our visit to the town follows two itiner-

aries: the Traversa interna and the upper city. There follows a visit to the churches lying beyond the river, and another to Monteluco and the fortified villages.

## *The Traversa interna*

Our first itinerary takes us along the Traversa interna, which from Piazza Garibaldi intersects the city from north to south, ending at the church of San Paolo inter vineas. The shape of the hill upon which the town rests had formerly made for a compact urban layout together with a rather steep vertical road network, which greatly hampered vehicular traffic. Such constrictions entailed buildings much higher than the area's seismic nature would otherwise allow. As a result, in 1834 Ireneo Aleandri designed a roadway which was to function both as a postal route and communications artery connecting the palazzi of the town's major aristocratic families and, naturally, the churches. Today it is simply an automobile thoroughfare, almost totally lacking in shops.

Piazza Garibaldi (A2). After stopping to admire the broad tree-lined area of *Piazza della Vittoria*, and having visited the remains of the **Ponte Sanguinario**, the so-called Bloody Bridge as it was in its vicinity that Christians were martyred. *Porta Garibaldi,* beneath which we access the square, was first rebuilt in the 15th century, and again in 1825 by Leo XII (this is why it is also called *Porta Leonina*). Destroyed by the retreating Germans in 1944, it was subsequently rebuilt as a double-span bridge. Many are the Roman remains to be found in the foundations of some of the square's public buildings.

San Gregorio Maggiore* (A2). Often, Christian churches were built on sites of earlier cult worship, like this Romanesque church, built in 1079 over a pre-existing church lying next to a cemetery. The building underwent various alterations; the facade was completely restored in 1907, and the interior in 1947-50. Opening onto the portico that was added in the 16th century is the 13th-century *Cappella degli Innocenti*, probably frescoed by the Angelucci from Mevale. Its ponderous bell tower (12th cent.), on the other hand, was raised in the late 15th century. Restructuring has brought to light medieval frescoes which formerly adorned the interiors – at the expense of the church's successive Baroque decorations.

Via dell'Anfiteatro. The initial stretch of the *Traversa interna* runs along a street which, in medieval times, was called "delle Grotte," because of the large niches flanking it – used as shops, but formerly part of a **Roman amphitheater**. Built in the 2nd century outside the perimeter wall, the amphitheater was probably built with two arched tiers, as indicated by the remains of broad sections of the structure's external covered passageway. Restructured as a fortress by the Goths in 545 AD, it was subsequently dismantled to provide building material for the Albornoz' Rocca. In the Middle Ages this area was occupied by the former monasteries of the *Madonna della Stella* and of *San Gregorio Minore,* subsequently, and until recently, used for military purposes, and featuring two impressive cloisters: one late-medieval and the other late-16th-century. The Stella monastery church, dedicated to Sts. Stephen and Thomas, dates from the late 18th century.

Via Cecili (B2). In the initial stretch of this tree-lined street appears the tall polygonal apse of the 14th-century church of **San Nicolò**, accessible via the cobbled *Misericordia* incline. Erected in 1304 together with the Augustinian monastery, it was severely damaged by the 1767 earthquake and subsequently abandoned by the monks in the 19th century. Restoration

*The outer portico of the Roman amphitheater in Spoleto*

has aimed to transform the church's vast and imposing interior into a convention center and theater area. Back along Via Cecili, lies an impressive tract of the first city walls. If we look carefully, we notice three layers of different wall-building techniques: large limestone blocks constitute the most ancient stratum (4th cent. BC); a squared buttressing section dating from 241 BC; and elongated parallelepiped sections dating from restoration work carried out in the 1st century BC.

Piazza Torre dell'Olio (B2). The area was an important junction in the old town, as it marks the junction of the *cardines* (the north-south axis) with the *decumani* (the east-west axis). Similarly, it was here that, according to tradition, Hannibal was routed by the besieged Spoletans, who showered him and his troops with boiling oil. The square is preceded by a secondary facade of **Palazzo Vigili**, itself the result of a fusion of 13th and 16th-century structures, and today the location of a restaurant. In one of its rooms one can still see the remains of walls dating from the 14th century BC. Soaring above the *palazzo* is the *Torre dell'Olio*.

**San Domenico** (B1). The *Traversa* extends beyond the square through *Via Pierleone*, featuring a characteristic medieval tower with its megalithic slabs, all the way to a tree-lined square faced by this Dominican church, which was built between the 13th and 14th century on the spot where the Dominican order had settled in 1247. In 1915, the Franciscans took over the church; they restored its Gothic interior which involved removal of its 17th-century decorations and altars. The first altar features an important early 15th-century fresco (**Triumph of St. Thomas Aquinas**); of the same period are the frescoes in the *Santa Maria Maddalena Chapel*. Similarly noteworthy is a silver *reliquary* by Ludovico Barchi (1726), featuring a nail from the Holy Cross, which tradition holds was brought here by the Blessed Gregory. The underlying *crypt* is decorated with 14th- and 15th-century frescoes.

**Piazza Collicola** (B1). As with other squares in the city, this piazza results from the nobility's desire to occupy an area suited to the prestige of its dwellings. The square is, in fact, dominated by the grand **Palazzo Collicola** (by Sebastiano Cipriani, 1737), rich in art works by Liborio Coccetti and now the seat of the **Galleria Civica d'Arte Contemporanea**. The art gallery is arranged in three sections. The first comprises paintings and sculptures form the Caradente donation, including international artists who took part in the 1962 sculpture exhibition (works by H. Moore, A. Penalba, L. Chadwick, E. Colla and others). A room will be devoted to Calder's mobiles. The second section includes works which competed in the "Spoleto Prize," a national figurative-art exhibition held from 1953 to 1968 (such artists as Arnaldo Pomodoro, Giulio Turcato, and Lorenzo Vespignani). The third section is dedicated to the sculptor Leoncillo.

Among the works of many other artists are the "wall drawings" of Sal Lewitt.

From the steps facing the *palazzo* it is a short walk to the former Romanesque church of **San Lorenzo**, which conserves Umbrian School frescoes from the 15th and 16th centuries.

**Teatro Nuovo** (B2). Where once stood the church of Sant'Andrea (in turn built on the remains of the Roman baths of the 2nd century BC), between 1853 and 1864 was erected a theater designed by Ireneo Aleandri. The hall, with its five tiers of boxes, was decorated by Giuseppe Masella and Vincenzo Gaiassi, whereas the stage curtain (representing the *Flight of Hannibal*) is by Francesco Coghetti. Annexed to the theater is the *Museo del Teatro*, containing posters of first performances, autographs, photographs, and a variety of other related theater documents. Since 1947 the theater has hosted the Teatro Lirico Sperimentale (from 1947) and performances associated with the Festival dei Due Mondi.

**Via Filitteria** (B2). Paved in the 19th century, it conserves in its name (*phylakteria*) was one of the twelve late-medieval Greek-Byzantine districts into which the town was administratively subdivided. Inwardly situated along *Vicolo Corvino* (on the right) stands the church of **Santi Giovanni e Paolo**, a plain 12th-century structure; the interior has one of the earliest representations of *St. Francis* and a *Martyrdom of St. Thomas à Becket* attributed to Alberto Sozio (12th cent.). In the *crypt,* by the same artist, a fresco representing the *Martyrdom of Sts. John and Paul\** (detached and temporarily on loan to the *Pinacoteca*). After a picturesque bend in the road, we come to the **Palazzo Zacchei-Travaglini**, built in the 16th century and enlarged in the 18th. From here, proceed to *Via Walter Tobagi*, on which faces **Palazzo Pianciani**. Its construction involved razing adjacent houses, so as to confer greater space to the narrow but elegant square of the same name. An impressive stairway, designed by Ugo Tarchi (1922-23), links the square with overhanging *Via di Fontesecca*, to which, *Palazzo Leoncilli*, with its *loggia* and small balcony, constitutes a graceful backdrop.

**San Filippo Neri** (B2). Begun in 1640 upon a design by Loreto Scelli, it features a grand travertine facade and Roman-style dome. Its interior is enhanced by frescoes by Gaetano Lapis, Sebastiano, Conca and Lazzaro Baldi. In its elegant sacristy there is a fine marble bust of *San Filippo Neri* by Alessandro Algardi.

**Corso Mazzini** (B-C2). The building of the *Traversa* roadway radically modified this rectilinear street which is characterized by an unnatural alignment of collectively uniform building fronts. The first structure we encounter is the former *convent of the Filippini* (1671), from 1871 seat of a tribunal. From here, proceed along several side streets which once formed the town's ancient network, such as *Via del Mercato* and the narrow *Via San Gregorio della Sinagoga*, where the Jewish community had its houses and temple. Especially interesting is the 20-meter long corridor of a Roman building, together with a mosaic-paved room, the purpose of which however remains a mystery.

**Piazza della Libertà**. This is the spot of the court of the Ancaiani nobles, the leading Umbrian landowners; the square underwent radical changes during 19th-cent. restructuring work. Of the many family *palazzi* which enlivened this area, **Palazzo Ancaiani** (17th cent.; restored in 1960), is the only one to have survived. Since 1951, it has been the seat of the *Centro Italiano di Studi sull'Alto Medioevo*.

**Sant'Agata** (C2). Built as a Benedictine monastery at the end of the 14th century next to a former church by the same name (11th cent.), Sant'Agata is partly superimposed upon a site previously occupied by the stage of the Roman theater (see following paragraph). The limited space afforded by the hillside has inevitably involved a certain amount of structural stratification: convents cannibalized the materials of medieval houses of the Corvi family, of which only the *palazzo* remains. After a spell as a prison from 1870 to 1954, today the complex is the seat of the **Museo Archeologico Nazionale**

(also including the site of the Roman theater). Still in the remodeling phase, the museum houses material from the civic museum and from more recent finds, arranged in chronological order (open 9am-7pm). Displayed are rare Bronze Age finds from recent digs in the vicinity of the Campello grotto and the *Rocca di Spoleto*. The museum's Roman section (from the Republican to the Imperial age) features an interesting series of portraits from the 1st to the 3rd century.

**Roman Theater** (C1-2). Built within the town perimeter in the second quarter of the 1st century, the theater was seriously damaged by landslides, and was subsequently concealed and altered by the building of Sant'Agata, the Corvi houses and by the broadening of the Benedictine monastery (from the 14th to the 16th cent.). Further spoliations were due to the plundering of quality materials for the building of aristocratic homes.

Starting in Via Sant'Agata, the long curvilinear *Via Madonna di Loreto*, along which a portico was built in the late 16th century to shelter pilgrims, leads to the sanctuary of the **Madonna di Loreto**, begun in

*The Roman theater in Spoleto*

1572 by Annibale Lippi to house an image of the *Blessed Virgin* by Jacopo Siciliano. Of the painting, considered miraculous, there remains only a fragment.

**Viale Matteotti** (C1-2). Lateral *Via Egio*, off the last stretch of the *Traversa*, features remains of the initial wall perimeter, which can be seen inside a hanging garden, and runs through the *Giardini Pubblici* amid fragrant essences, which call to mind the gardens of the no longer extant Servite monastery. Here, the edge of the 13th-century walled city is marked by Richard Fuller's light-alloy *Cupola*.

**San Paolo inter vineas**\* (D1). The church was rebuilt together with the nunnery in the 10th century and remodeled before 1234, the year of its consecration by Pope Gregory IX. Through its plain arched portal you pass into the aisled interior, with its ample transept featuring a series of 13th-century **frescoe cycle** (*prophets, scenes from the creation*); these were detached from a previous structure and rearranged without following their original order.

## The upper town (città alta)

This second itinerary starts from Piazza della Libertà along Via Brignone, which leads to the upper part of the historic center, where one can see the most significant remains of the Roman town, among which the Arco di Druso (Drusus). From Piazza del Mercato, Via dei Duchi and Via Saffi take you to sloping Via dell'Arringo, built in the Middle Ages to provide a spectacular access route to Piazza del Duomo. Here, with the transformation of its early medieval religious settlement, took shape the town's first and most significant constructions. Centering on the building of the Cathedral, which continued in the 13th century, they were to mark Spoleto's basic and long-term layout and structures. At the end of Via Saffi, our visit takes us to the Palazzo Comunale museum complex, and then, along Via del Municipio, to Piazza Campello, at the foot of the Rocca.

**Via Brignone** (C2). A palimpsest of the town's history, the street is dotted with the remains of dwellings and structures dating from Roman times, preserved in the basement of houses, and frequently reutilized from medieval times, and still even today. A visit to one of the upper town's public places provides an unusual assemblage of

architectural elements. To the left, the street leads to *Piazza Fontana*, with its sparkling 16th-century fountain; whereas to the right it is graced by *Palazzo Mauri* (early 17th century, closed to the public after the 1997 earthquake).

**Arco di Monterone** (C2). Coming from Rome, the Flaminia entered the town through this arch (3rd cent. BC), which spans *Via Monterone* with its massive limestone blocks. Further on, *Arco delle Felici* is similarly a large-block structure featuring fragments dating perhaps from the 4th century.

**Sant'Ansano** (C2). Superimposed in the 12th century upon a house of prayer dedicated to Sts. Isaac and Martial (7th cent.), which in turn had absorbed part of the Roman forum. Renovated in the late 18th century by Antonio Dotti, the church comprises sections of the former edifice in its left flank. A stairway to the left of the main altar leads to the Roman temple and to the crypt of St. Isaac. The **temple** was probably built by the second half of the 1st century along the southern side of the forum, and, according to a traditional layout, comprised a cell preceded by a four-columned portico. The **crypt of Sant'Isacco**\*, instead, dates from the 12th century; it features a rectangular plan set off by columns (from a previous structure) surmounted by roughly hewn capitals, and interesting fresco fragments on the walls.

**Arco di Druso**\*. Still another tangible remain of Roman Spoleto. To the left of Sant'Ansano stands what was the monumental entrance to the forum, built in the year 23 in honor of Drusus Minor and Germanicus (son and nephew of Tiberius) and buried over in the Middle Ages. The arch is simply decorated with pillars topped with Corinthian capitals. After leaving 17th-century *Palazzo Leti* on the left, Via dell'Arco di Druso, the *cardo maximus* of the Roman town plan, which rose in the place of the Palazzo del Podestà (and to the rear the similarly 17th-century facade of *Palazzo Parenzi*), leads to the heart of the Roman town.

**Piazza del Mercato** (C2). The fact that still in the Middle Ages it was called Piazza del Foro, sheds light on the leading role this area played over the centuries, even if, after the intensive building that went on during the Middle Ages, very little remains of its broad Roman-age perimeter. The ornate

**Fonte di Piazza**, the fountain built by Costantino Fiaschetti in pure Roman style, dates from 1746-48 (its coats of arms belonged to a previous structure, 1626).

**Via del Palazzo dei Duchi** (B-C2). The charm of this street stems from the medieval-looking shops that line it, though they actually date from the 16th century, when the arcades beneath the surviving spans of the church of San Donato were converted to shops. These still feature their original display counters. To the left stands the 13th-century *Casa Spiga*.

**Via Fontesecca**. Via del Palazzo dei Duchi abuts upon Via Fontesecca, where stands the *Casa dei Maestri Comacini*, with its characteristic pointed-arch doors and arched windows. Proceeding along a front of aristocratic dwellings, renovated between the 15th and the 16th century (among which the facade of the Palazzo Comunale, p. 132), we move toward the Cathedral and the fortress. To the right, Via di Visiale affords access to a Roman house below the western, 20th-century side of the Palazzo Comunale.

Brought to light in 1885-1912 by Giuseppe Sordini, the **Casa Romana** (C2) probably belonged to Vespasia Polla, emperor Vespasian's mother. Worth seeing are the remains of floor mosaics, with their geometric patterns and white and black tesserae.

**Palazzo Arcivescovile** (B2). Preceded by the "bridge" of 16th-century Palazzo Martorelli-Orsini, the bishop's palace is the result of several building phases, particularly significant among which the 15th and 16th-century restoration of the structure's southern wing and the 17th-century renewal of its inner courtyard. Today it is the seat of the diocesan museum (see below). The structure is believed to rest upon a large public building dating from the age of Silla, then subsequently reutilized by Theodoric and then again by the Longobards. In the 10th century it was converted into a Benedictine monastery by decree of the abbess Gunderada.

The **Museo Diocesano di Spoleto-Norcia** (open, summer, 10am-12.30pm, 4pm-7pm; winter, 10am-12.30pm, 3pm-6pm) was instituted in 1976 and houses the diocese's art heritage, a collection begun in the

## A Festive Town

In an interview of August 1956, the contemporary composer Gian Carlo Menotti, known the world over for his originally modern conception of opera, told of his travels through the Italian peninsula in search of a dream, namely to find a small city in which to organize an annual chamber-music, opera, theater, and ballet festival. After stopping at various towns, and taking stock of the run-down state of provincial theaters, his choice fell on Spoleto, a tranquil town, with a long-standing cultural tradition, already the seat of the *Teatro Sperimentale Lirico*, to which many young musicians owed their careers. The town's mayor, furthermore, guaranteed that no "engine would roar or buzz either around or near the theater, and that there would be complete silence and peace." And so it was. On 5

*Carla Fracci at the Festival of Spoleto*

June the Festival got under way with Verdi's opera *Macbeth*, under the direction of Luchino Visconti. It was a resounding success. Since then, there have been over forty editions of this event which every year has sparked interest, enthusiasm, and even heated debates. And though it has been threatened many times with closure (for economic or artistic reasons), it has sprung to life again, attracting tens of thousands of spectators and the attention of critics from all over the world. The festival's revolutionary aim of having the most diverse art forms side by side, albeit respecting the broadest possible spectrum of cultural perspectives, each year renews its magic, with Spoleto's squares, churches, and theaters again celebrating the event.

1920s. It includes paintings and sculptures datable from the 13th to the 18th century, arranged in the five rooms that made up the cardinal's apartment (open 10am-12.30pm, 3.30pm-7pm). Among the works displayed, an *Virgin and Child* by Bartolomeo di Miranda, wood sculptures and paintings by Neri di Bicci, Filippini Lippi and Domenico Beccafumi.

**Sant'Eufemia\*** (B2). Situated inside the enclosure of the bishop's palace, the basilica, rebuilt (in Spoleto Romanesque style) in the 12th century and restored between 1907 and 1953, features a plain facade surmounted by a sloping roof. Its interior is characterized by its marked verticalism and also for being the only church in Umbria to have a *matroneum* (an open *loggia* above the central nave reserved for women). Particularly striking is the marble **altarpiece** at the back of the main altar (13th cent.).

**Palazzo Comunale** (B-C2). The only surviving feature of the original 13th-century *palazzo* is the rectangular tower, the upper portion of which was completed in the 18th century. The palace was first renovated in the 15th century as the residence of Pope Nicholas V. Since the 19th century, its upper rooms, decorated by Giuseppe Moscatelli and Benigno Peruzzi (1896-1900), have housed the Pinacoteca Comunale (the municipal art gallery).

**Pinacoteca Comunale\***. The first series of works to be conserved in the municipal art gallery were taken from the Rocca in 1867, followed by works belonging to the religious corporations subsequent to their suppression. The gallery's first display layout dates from 1871, whereas its second from 1904 (open 10am-1pm, 3pm-6pm; closed Mon). Plans are under way to transfer a number of works (from the 12th to the 15th cent.) to the future *Museo Nazionale* to be housed in the Rocca. In the second room is displayed the oldest painting in the Pinacoteca, a **Crucifixion\*** (on canvas applied to an altarpiece) by a late 12th-century Umbrian artist. Similarly noteworthy are two painted *Crosses\**, one dating from the 13th century, the other by Maestro di Cesi (late 13th-early 14th cent.). This same room also contains two frescoes\* by Spagna, including a **Virgin and Child with Saints\*** commissioned by the Ridolfi. Representative of the art production between the 16h and 18th century is, among others,

a *Magdalen\**, probably by Guercino. On display in showcases are illuminated codices and other items crafted by Italian goldsmiths.

The *Palazzo Comunale* is fronted by a typical row of houses built in different periods. Between two 16th-century dwellings, the result of preceding 13th-14th-century renovations, there opens the *Vicolo della Basilica*, so called for the presence of a Roman **basilica**, presumed to have been a temple on a square plan with ashlar base (the lower part dates from the 1st cent., the upper from a subsequent period).

**Piazza del Duomo** (B2-3). *Via dell'Arringo* directly connects Via Saffi to the square, affording a fine view of the Cathedral. The "cut" of this new street radically altered the geometric layout of the Roman *insula*, becoming tangible evidence in the city of episcopal power which, in the late 12th century, prompted construction of a larger church and the transfer of the episcopacy to the area of Sant'Eufemia. The artificial terrace upon which it opens dates from Roman times; but it was only between the 12th and 16th centuries that the area took on its definitive layout. Standing on its left side are the 14th-century *Casa Fabricolosi* and the *sarcofago* featuring a hunting scene (3rd cent.), now converted into a fountain. To the left, the red and white molded stone slabs of the *Casa dell'Opera del Duomo* (1419) and the small but elegant **Teatro Caio Melisso** (1664, but renovated in 1880), featuring a stage curtain by Domenico Bruschi. The following (former) church of **Santa Maria della Manna d'Oro** is built on an octagonal plan, here and there reminiscent of Bramante, built in 1527 as a votive offering after the Sack of Rome, and completed in 1681. Today, its interior is used for staging exhibitions.

**Duomo\*\***, or **Cathedral** (B2-3). This Romanesque structure, erected in the late 12th century upon former Santa Maria del Vescovato (8th-9th cent.), immediately catches the eye of those entering the square. You cannot but admire the large rose window gracing the facade, surrounded by *symbols of the Evangelists*; equally remarkable is the majestic Byzantine-style mosaic (*Christ blessing between the Virgin and St. John*), signed by Solsterno and dated 1207, located in an arcade of the upper tier. Completing the picture, to the left stands the ponderous **bell tower** built in the 12th century with material recovered from previous Roman structures.

# Spoleto Cathedral

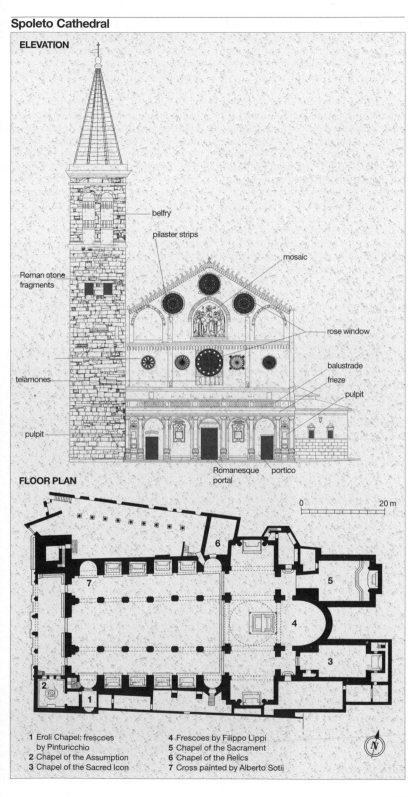

## ELEVATION

belfry

pilaster strips

mosaic

Roman stone fragments

rose window

telamones

balustrade

frieze

pulpit

pulpit

Romanesque portal

portico

## FLOOR PLAN

0          20 m

1 Eroli Chapel: frescoes
  by Pinturicchio
2 Chapel of the Assumption
3 Chapel of the Sacred Icon
4 Frescoes by Filippo Lippi
5 Chapel of the Sacrament
6 Chapel of the Relics
7 Cross painted by Alberto Sotii

The magnificent Romanesque **portal***, with its impressive jambs and architrave decorated with a vine-leaf motif, and preceded by an elegant Renaissance portico, leads into the Roman-cross interior and to the semicircular apse, which was extensively modified by the official architect of Pope Urban VIII, Luigi Arrigucci (17th cent.). The nave conserves most of the original floor mosaic. To the right lies the *Eroli Chapel*, with frescoes by Pinturicchio (**God the Father with Angels, Virgin and Child with Sts. John the Baptist and Stephen**), and a *Pietà* on the altar dossal. It is connected to the following *Chapel of the Assunta*, totally frescoed. In the right arm of the crossing stands *Giovanni Francesco Orsini's funeral monument* (by Ambrogio da Milano, 1499). By order and at the expense of Lorenzo il Magnifico was erected the *Tomb of Fra Filippo Lippi* (which no longer contains the painter's body, perhaps lost when the tomb was restored in the 17th century), designed by Lippi himself and bearing an epigraph by Agnolo Poliziano. The archway below the organ leads to the *Chapel of the Santissima Icone*, the ancient sacristy redesigned in 1626 by G. B. Mola, which houses a silver tabernacle containing a venerated image of the *Virgin*, which, according to a legend, was saved from the fury of the Iconoclasts in Constantinople and donated to the town of Spoleto by Barbarossa in 1185. Truly admirable are the **frescoes*** that adorn the *presbytery*, painted by Filippo Lippi (1467-69) with the assistance of Fra Diamante and Pier Matteo d'Amelia (*Annunciation, Dormitio Virginis, Crèche*, and the magnificent *Coronation of the Virgin Mary*). To the left of the presbytery, the 17th-century *Chapel of the Sacrament* and the former *Chapel of Sant'Anna*, built in the 14th century as an extension of the transept, and from which its late 16th-century frescoes were removed in order to highlight its 14th-century

decorations. Along the left aisle, the *Chapel of Relics* (1540) houses a **Virgin and Child**; a finely crafted polychrome wooden sculpture (early 14th cent.); and a rare autograph letter (to brother Leone) by St. Francis. Built to conserve the icon and other sacred objects, it also has handsome wardrobes, carved and inlaid in the mid 16th-century by Giovanni Andrea di ser Moscato and Damiano di Mariotto. Placed at the beginning of the aisle is Alberto Sozio's **Cross***, a splendid parchment painting applied to a *tavola* dating from 1187. The rectory houses the **Archivio Capitolare**, which contains important documents, parchments and codices. Among the latter, three late 12th-century *Leggendari* (medieval accounts of saints' lives) from the churches of San Felice di Narco and San Brizio. From the rectory you can descend to the **crypt of San Primiano**, a rare example of a 9th-century semicircular crypt containing fresco remains of the same period.

To the left of the Caio Melisso theater, a brief departure off *Via del Duomo* takes you to *Via dello Spagna,* where recent restoration work has unearthed an **ambulacrum** dating from the age of Silla, and consisting of a sharp-bended, ap-

*The huge Ponte delle Torri, near Spoleto*

proximately 30-meter-long passageway with imposing arcades facing the valley. It is believed to have been built as a terrace to accommodate northward expansion, though this was never carried out.

**Piazza Campello** (C2). This vast sloping square links the walled city to the Rocca. The trees planted in the 20th century have altered the square's original perspective while concealing its complex access routes; the site was chosen by the Franciscans in the 13th century to build the former church of **Santi Simone e Giuda**, which, together with the convent, was converted into barracks (1863), and then into male boarding facilities. Next to it stands the *Fontana del Mascherone* (1763). In place of the medieval homes of the local aristocratic family was erected the **Palazzo Campello** (1597-1600), which greatly ennobled the square.

The **Rocca**\* (B-C3). At the high end of Piazza Campello is the lane leading to the Rocca, or fortress. The hill's summit (elev. 453 m) had already been leveled in ancient times to make room for the building of the acropolis; in the 5th century it housed an Italianate temple, and in the following century was surrounded by a perimeter wall. In 1359 Cardinal Albornoz decided to erect a castle here as a stronghold of papal power, commissioning Matteo di Giovanni, called Gattapone, with the design of a ponderous rectangular six-towered structure, divided into two quadrangles by an imposing transversal arm (the Weapons courtyard to the North; the honors courtyard to the south). Subsequently, the castle was often enlarged and decorated with frescoes and coats of arms which testify to the many illustrious personages who came to stay (such as Lucretia Borgia, governess of the duchy from 1499 to 1502); the complex was turned into a penal colony in 1817 by the papal state. Utilized as a prison facility up to 1983, it is now state property (and still in the process of being restored); plans involve its conversion to a national museum, with housing restoration workshops, and venues for cultural events and conferences. Thanks to this project, certain late 14th-century decorations have been brought to light, such as those found in the **Camera Pinta**, inside the main tower, entirely frescoed with courtly and chivalric scenes.

The rooms on the first and second floors looking onto the honors courtyard will house the **Museo Nazionale di Spoleto**, wherein will be displayed, in chronological and thematic order, inscriptions and archaeological finds from late antiquity to the late Middle Ages (until now kept in the civic museum). Also on display will be the fresco series detached from the church of San Paolo inter vineas (12th-13th cent.) and from the former Palazze monastery (late 13th cent.), besides a group of altarpiece paintings dating from the 12th to the 15th centuries, now on display in the Pinacoteca Comunale.

A splendid itinerary starts from Piazza Campello and proceeds down *Via del Ponte*\*, flanked by a stretch of polygonal Roman walls, which first takes us to an open area affording a marvelous view\* of forest-covered *Monteluco*, and then to breath taking **Ponte delle Torri**\*, a bridge that spans the chasm between Monteluco and the hill upon which the *Rocca* is perched. Seventy-six meters tall and 230 wide, with its nine pillars connected by ten arcades this imposing limestone structure dominates the valley. The function of this aqueduct-bridge (whose construction is tentatively set between the 13th and 14th cent.) was to convey water to the upper part of the town and to the Rocca, while at the same time provide access to Monteluco and to the small Mulini fortress. Its two tower pillars (hence the bridge's name) are hollow, with one featuring two superimposed windowed rooms, and the other a room with an arched doorway, probably a former guard post.

## San Pietro\*

Leaving the city by *Porta Monterone*, along *Via San Carlo*, we cross the Tessino river and the state road, from where there is a magnificent view of the Rocca and of the Ponte delle Torri, and we reach the steps leading to a scenic esplanade. The area was once occupied by a villa and a necropolis, but from the 5th century it became the seat of a church built by Archbishop Achilleo to house a relic (parts of St. Peter's chains). The church's facade was rebuilt in Romanesque style (12th-13th cent.), and, because of the **reliefs**\* that adorn the three rows in which it is divided, is considered a masterpiece of Umbrian Romanesque sculpture. Its central portal is surmounted by a horseshoe-shaped lunette flanked by two eagles, whereas its jambs and architrave feature ornamentation of a more classical type, with two small side columns, stylized animal and geometric figures alternating with pairs of symbolic sculptures. The church's aisled interior, completely restructured in 1699, features on the entrance wall a 15th-century votive fresco portraying the patron, kneeling in prayer.

## Basilica of San Salvatore\*

Taking from Piazza della Vittoria the road that leads to Norcia, and once on the oth-

*The figured reliefs of the portal of San Pietro, near Spoleto*

er side of the Tessino river, you come to the so-called *basilica of the Crocifisso*, formerly known as *San Concordio*. This is a most interesting early Christian structure (late 4th, early 5th cent.), repeatedly defaced and then restructured over the centuries, which has however preserved its original (and rare) architectural features – similar to those of the *Tempietto del Clitunno*, in which classical art is blended with oriental motifs. The lower level of its **facade\***, restored in 1997, presents three marble portals decorated with floral motifs, and its upper level three broad windows: the central one surmounted by an arch, those on either side by tympanums. Its narrow nave and aisles produce a marked sense of verticality, divided by Doric columns. The quadrilateral plan of the presbytery is clearly set off by the nave, the ceiling of which has preserved its original beam structure. At its four corners rise pairs of tall ribbed Corinthian columns. The central portion of the apse features a fresco of a monogrammed and gemmed cross, dating from the previous decorative program; its upper part presents fresco fragments from the 13th century and a 15th-century *Crucifixion* (painted by an artist of Spagna's school).

## San Ponziano

Tradition has it that it was here that Spoletan martyr, Ponziano, was buried in 175 AD. A coat of arms (located in a niche in the entrance arch to the monastery) portrays the town's patron saint on horseback holding a shield bearing the figure of a cross. The area was declared a sacred Christian burial ground by St. Sincleta and Syriac monastics, and subsequently a convent for Benedictine (11th cent.) and Clarissan (16th cent.) nuns. The jambs flanking its elegant portal are supported by two *lions* resting on Roman urns, and surmounted by a fine rose window (parts of which are missing), circled by *symbols of the Evangelists*. A room in its interior, entirely renovated in 1788 by Giuseppe Valadier, houses a *sarcophagus* from an early-Christian cemetery and, in the crypt, three other sarcophagi similarly from the ancient cemetery, and 14h- and 15th-century votive paintings, including an *angel and two praying figures* by Maestro di Fossa.

## Monteluco

The excursion to Monteluco (8.3 km), particularly interesting because of its landscape, starts from Spoleto along Viale Matteotti and takes us across the Tessino. After 5 km we reach the Romanesque church of **San Giuliano** (elev. 628 m), built in the 12th century in the place of a former edifice (6th cent.), similarly dedicated to the martyred saint. Inside are frescoes by the Master of Eggi (1442). Continuing along the wooded area, we come to the **sanctuary of Monteluco** (elev. 773 m), a pilgrimage destination, built upon a primitive Franciscan settlement, of which remains a fresh-water spring traditionally believed to have been made to issue forth by the saint. The convent, which has been restructured and expanded several times, houses the small chapel where St. Francis prayed, and 18th-century wardrobes with Murano vases containing relics donated by Urban VII. After a short stretch along the wooded area, we come to attractive scenic spots and tiny grottoes whose particular atmosphere calls to mind the former sacredness of these venues (the very name, in fact, comes from "lucus"or sacred wood), protected by Jupiter in Roman times and subsequently chosen by hermits and mystics.

## The fortified towns

Over the years, the land lying between the fertile Maroggia stream and the Martani mountains has been frequently reclaimed, starting from Roman times up to the late 19th century. These improvements involved channeling the stream and its affluent, the Tessino, which run parallel for a long stretch. After the extensive building of fortified castles in the second half of the 16th century, the new sociopolitical climate favored the conversion of these fortresses into agricultural units, thus fostering the economic recovery of an area which is admired not only for the beauty of its landscape (especially the Martani limestone massif, page 140), but also because of its rich historic and artistic heritage, fueled by an eventful sequel of centuries. Our circular (and counter clockwise) 40.2 km itinerary leaves Spoleto along Viale Trento e Trieste and takes us (northwesterly) in the direction of Castel Ritaldi, from where it returns to the city proceeding along the eastern side of the Mt. Martani massif, amid chestnut trees and oak woods.

### Pontebari and San Brizio
After reaching the verdant hill of *San Tommaso* (elev. 360 m), with its former 13th-century church, we come to **Pontebari** (elev. 266 m), whose name derives from a 19th-century bridge built upon a structure dating from the 12th-13th century. One road branches off to the church of **San Sabino**, constructed in the late 6th century upon a burial site and characterized by the presence of numerous Roman stone tablets. The 13th-century *Castello di Maiano* (elev. 253 m) precedes the fortified town of **San Brizio** (elev. 246 m), still protected by late-medieval walls, with its 12th

cent. *parish church* which houses a Roman sarcophagus containing the remains of the saint after whom the town is named. After 11 km, you reach **Bruna** (elev. 242 m), overlooked by the *sanctuary of Santa Maria della Bruna* (1510), with its unusual orientalizing forms.

### Castel San Giovanni
The town, rising at an elevation of 225 meters, is closely linked to the 14th-century castle which, with its square and cylindrical corner towers, dominated the surrounding countryside. Worth visiting is the 14th cent.parish church, the interior of which is decorated with 16th-century frescoes and a *Virgin and Saints* by Gaspare Angelucci da Mevale. North of Castel San Giovanni lies the town of *Picciche* (elev. 226 m), with its 13th-century castle and the church of *Santo Stefano* frescoed by Francesco Melanzio. Heading northwest we come to **Castel Ritaldi** (elev. 297 m, pop. 2,656), with its typical quasi-circular 13th century castle. The parish church has frescoes by Lattanzio di Nicolò (1509) and Tiberio d'Assisi (1512).

### Montemartano
Our itinerary now takes us in a southwesterly direction along the Ruicciano stream where the most interesting stretch of landscape begins. Beech and chestnut woods accompany us along the way to *Montemartano* (elev. 586 m), a fascinating natural setting that enhances the mystery of its 14th-century castle remains, complete with towers and walls. From here, excursion enthusiasts can climb up to the top of *Mt. Martana* (elev. 1,094 m), which affords a splendid view of the Valle Umbra and its surrounding elevations. The stretch from Montemartano to Spoleto gives an exact idea of what is meant by "fortified territory": the area is dappled the remains of castles, such as the 14th-century *Castello di Terzo la Pieve* (elev. 387 m), or the vestiges of the successive castles of *Uncinano* and *Morgnano*, and, before returning to Pontebari, the small castle community of **Sant'Angelo in Mercole** (elev. 415 m), whose 14th-century walls and towers can be reached via a winding hillside road. State road 418 intersects **San Giovanni di Baiano** (elev. 313 m) – where Galileo once sojourned. The site is watched over by the 14th-century *Castello di Baiano*. The road back to the Galileo winds along low rolling hills.

# 5 The central Tiber valley and the Martani mountains

## Area profile

Over the centuries the Tiber has played a double role as link and divider between Etruria and Umbria. Today, in the heart of Umbria, the river – whose course wends its way amid weeping willows, black alders, poplars and locust trees – continues to play a vital role. Important water courses such as the Nestore and the Puglia flow into the main river bed together with the Naia, a stream linking this area to that around Terni, recreating on a reduced scale the same layout as the main valley: mountain elevations on one side (the Martani) and rolling hills on the other (the plateau between Acquasparta and Amelia). Overlooking the commercial and industrial areas located along the main roadway and more recent modifications in the area's agricultural makeup, the Tiber valley continues to boast a large variety of rural structures that derive from Umbria's former sharecropping system. In addition, crop diversification strategies have given these lands a colorfully varied "garden-plot" appearance. The area's urban centers, although closely dependent upon the surrounding countryside, nevertheless play a dominant role with respect to the latter. In the second half of the 20th century, town and country, coupled with the development of agricultural mechanization, have given rise to a new figure, that of the farm worker. The only real town of any size in the area is Todi, which "has as its base a hill that is surpassed by no other, triangular in shape, standing alone and separated; indeed, according to Silvius Italicus, a preminent mountain; and yet so pleasant and so fertile as not to be compared even with Parnassus itself" (Laurus, 1). Todi has long contended dominion of its territory with Perugia; a dominion which materialized in the stones of the numerous castles which still today dominate the countryside.

*The abbey of Santi Fidenzio e Terenzio set in the countryside of Massa Martana*

# 5.1 From Perugia to Todi
**Excursions along the Tiberina road (SS 3bis) and through the Martani mountains, 82.5 km**

As in the past, villas and medieval castles keep watch over the highway, and have catalyzed the gradual reclamation of the marshy valley floor. The landscape takes on a more rugged look as we approach the limestone Peglia massif, with its closed fields and crop lands alternating with wooded areas, remnants of former sharecropping arrangements. Leaving Perugia from Porta San Pietro, follow the signs to Rome, which lead to the highway turn-off, and from here to the road that eventually ends in Todi: a long straight thoroughfare running along the right side of the river, marked by tall and slender poplars. The first leg of this itinerary still bears the influence of Perugia, whereas the crossroads leading to Torgiano takes us to a luxuriant agrarian landscape, rich in vineyards that constitute the area's main resource. A stop at the Madonna dei Bagni sanctuary is an absolute must. Located on the valley floor, and formerly submerged by the flooding waters of the Tiber, the area was reclaimed by the Benedictine monks of San Pietro di Perugia, who, up to 1860, owned vast land holdings in the area. Upon reaching Ripabianca, you can leave the four-lane expressway and head in the direction of Todi along the route (follow road signs to Gualdo Cattaneo) which winds along the western side of the Martani mountains. This historic itinerary touches Ponte di Ferro (13 km), Bastardo, San Savino and (after 12 km) Giano dell'Umbria. From Giano, a road leads down to Castagnola. Turn left at the crossroads, and continue for approximately 14 more kilometers to Massa Martana. Southward, after 5.5 kilometers, the road joins route E45, which rapidly takes you to Todi.

## Torgiano
*Castrum Torsciani*, located on a rise at the confluence of the Tiber and the Chiascio, is today a well-known premium-wine producing area. The town's medieval appearance (elev. 219 m, pop. 5,158) stems from the castle founded by Perugia upon Roman remains in the 13th century. The vast expanses of quality vineyards (DOC and DOCG certified wines) that cover the surrounding hillsides are visual proof of this area's historic link with wine production. Tellingly, the municipal es-

cutcheon consists of a tower wrapped in a grapevine motif. Torgiano also has an important **Museo del Vino\***, which boasts the most complete collection of documents, implements and crafts associated with grape growing and wine producing. Founded in 1974 by the Lungarotti winery

## 5.1 From Perugia to Todi
## 5.3 From Todi to Terni

(one of the leading local wine producers), the museum is housed in twenty rooms of the Palazzo Graziani-Baglioni. The *archaeological collection* features prized pieces such as Cycladic pitchers and Hittite ceramics (3rd-1st millennium BC), Attic *kylikes*, Etruscan vases and bronzes, and glass from Roman times. The ceramics collection includes over 400 artifacts from various periods and locations (including works by the Della Robbia masters, and other renowned 16th-20th-century *botteghe* (workshops). Particularly noteworthy are the apothecary vases and the collection of period engravings featuring grape, mythological and biblical motifs, with works ranging from such artists as Mantegna and Picasso.

Changing techniques and customs are documented by a rich collection of "waffle irons" (comparable to wine in terms of preparation and consumption), comprising numerous pieces from the 13th to the 17th century. Among the various farm implements on display, of particular interest are two large wine presses dating from the 17th century. A rich *oenological library* completes the collection.

## Deruta

Rows of ceramic works and exhibition outlets tell us we are approaching Deruta (elev. 218 m, pop. 7,860), for centuries economically linked to the production of ceramic artifacts. The town's ancient origins are borne out by the unearthing of a Hellenistic-age necropolis and a Roman-age agricultural community, lying not far from the present town center. And, as early as the 14th century, there are documents attesting to the use of local clays in the production of ceramic goods; an output which reached its peak on the European market in the 16th century. After a fall in interest, the art of ceramics became once again popular thanks to Gregorio Castelli, and has come down to our days constantly diversifying itself in terms of quality and style, and is fostered by the State Institute for Ceramic Arts.

The town's core is the long *Piazza dei Consoli*, bordered on one side by the *Palazzo Comunale*, which still conserves on its facade the Venetian lion in Traù travertine donated by the Dalmatian city of Zadar. The first-floor rooms house the **Pinacoteca Civica**, featuring frescoes detached from local churches, and paintings dating from the 15th and 18th centu-

*A ceramic work from Deruta*

ry. Works from the 17th and 18th century are from the Lione Pascoli collection, donated to the municipality in 1931. Works on display from previous centuries include, among others, paintings by Niccolò Alunno, Pietro Perugino, and three sketches by Baciccia. In 1998 the former convent of *San Francesco*, adjoining the church, was restructured to house the **Museo Regionale della Ceramica**, partly already contained in the *Palazzo Comunale*. The collection was begun in the late 19th century by Francesco Briganti, and from the 1980s new acquisitions were made which document ceramic output from the Middle Ages to 1930. The *Pecchioli* and *Milziade Magnin Collections* respectively include 130 works from the antique dealership market (16th-17th cent.), and approximately a thousand pieces from Umbria and Puglia. Particularly important are the precious so-called "archaic" and "glossy" majolicas, the latter being the fruit of a middle-eastern technique which impresses ceramic artifacts with an iridescent gold-pink finish. In its interior, the adjoining church of **San Francesco** conserves 14th- and 15th-century frescoes and a bronze bell cast in 1228 to celebrate the canonization of St. Francis.

### Madonna dei Bagni

The sanctuary was erected in 1687 on the spot where a ceramic fragment and an oak tree commemorated a miraculous healing. Since then, Madonna dei Bagni has never ceased to welcome the prayers of the faithful, symbolized by the approximately six hundred votive majolicas that constitute an unusual wall covering, and also a precious testimony of three centuries of religious devotion, and of the evolution of ceramic-making techniques.

## The western side of the Martani mountains

Slightly beyond Madonna dei Bagni, at Ripabianca, our alternative itinerary to route E45 branches off, enabling us to reach Todi proceeding along the bed of the Puglia river. The area, which offers a bounty

*A Deruta craftsman at work*

of different landscapes and environmental vistas, is dotted with small fortified settlements which, owing to the relative marginality of their locations and poor road networks, managed to develop independently with respect to nearby and more powerful townships.

### Gualdo Cattaneo
The town (elev. 446 m, pop. 5,949), garrisoned with a border castle atop a hill between the Puglia and Attone rivers, conserves from that period its walled and towered perimeter.
Dominating centrally located *Piazza Umberto I* is the huge bastion of a triangular fortress, built in 1494-98 according to a design by Francesco di Bartolomeo di Pietrasanta.
The **parish church**, in the apse of which is conserved a *Last Supper* by Ascensidonio Spacca, was restructured in the 19th century. The presbytery leads to the chapel, decorated with frescoes by Ferraù Fenzoni; the crypt dates from the 13th century. Below the *Palazzo Comunale* you descend to the church of **Sant'Agostino**, with frescoes by Andrea Polinori (*St. Catherine of Alexandria*), Pietro

Paolo Sensini (*Virgin of the Rosary*) and Francesco Providoni (*Purgatory*).

### Giano dell'Umbria
To enjoy a truly panoramic vista of the Clitunno valley and of Mt. Martano, climb the 546 meters to *Giano* (pop. 3,200), a castle once contested by Todi and Spoleto. The site was first fortified in Roman times. Still today the town continues to be closely linked to its hill, with at its summit its fine main square, built around the churches of *Santa Maria delle Grazie* and *San Michele Arcangelo*, and surrounded by medieval houses.
The former developed as the result of an 18th-century renovation of an earlier building, the orientation of which was modified (it features a *Virgin and Child with Saints* by Andrea Polinori), whereas the latter, being the castle's main church, underwent frequent modifications. From Giano, an interesting excursion takes you up to *Mt. Martano*, which, 1,094 meters above sea level, affords magnificent vistas of the plain below.

An approximately two-kilometer excursion, proceeding northwesterly, takes you to the abbey

## Not by wine alone

What do a Cycladic-age pitcher and a work by Picasso, a Hittite tray and a ceramic cup by Mastro Giorgio da Gubbio have in common? The easiest answer is: wine. A more complex answer lies in the highly articulated cultural initiatives which, for almost a quarter century, have been animating the Lungarotti Foundation, of which the *Museo del Vino* at Torgiano is a part. Initially, it was an avant-garde Umbrian agricultural concern, capable, among other things, of renewing wine producing strategies, based essentially on traditional Sangiovese and Cannaiolo varieties (for red wines), and Trebbiano (for whites), by experimenting with new grape types and marketing new wines which readily met with wine drinkers' favor. In 1974 a museum was inaugurated; one that has little to do with local specimens, but which approaches the theme of wine production from an artistic perspective, especially as expressed in and by the so-called minor arts: ceramics, engravings, publishing, glassware, the art of iron making, etc. This is one of Umbria's most significant museums for the quality and breadth of the collections, and the way they are displayed. Over the years, the foundation has broadened its sphere of activity by promoting exhibitions, conventions, and publishing initiatives, thereby becoming a crucial reference point for the region's cultural panorama. And, before taking your leave from the splendid decor of *Palazzo Graziani-Baglioni*, which houses the museum, it is well worth visiting its adjoining restaurant. Here you can taste classic Umbrian cuisine, it too the fruit of careful research in the vast field of gastronomy.

*A glimpse of the archaeological section in the Museo del Vino at Torgiano*

of **San Felice**, erected, according to local lore, in the 11th-12th century on the site of the saint's martyrdom. Evident are the traces of Lombard influences on the Umbrian Romanesque forms of the church, with its aisled nave (barrel-vaulted), and its presbytery raised up over the crypt. The latter houses a sarcophagus containing the saint's remains. Standing nearby is the **Castello di Castagnola** (elev. 483 m), long contested in the Middle Ages between Foligno, Spoleto, and Todi.

## Massa Martana

An ancient fortified centre, situated at the foot of the Martani mountains, which constitute one of the settlement's major attractions. This area's particular appeal stems from the typical Mediterranean vegetation and from the many remains bearing witness to an extremely ancient civilization. The town (elev. 351 m, pop. 3,579), enclosed within its ancient perimeter (note the 10th-century gate), was seriously damaged by the May 1997 earthquake, and is presently closed to visitors. The church of the *Madonna della Pace*, a Renaissance temple built on an octagonal plan outside the old walls, was also damaged by the earthquake in May.

Taking the road west to the Todi-Foligno provincial road, you reach the abbey of **Santi Fidenzio e Terenzio**, now private property, erected in the 11th century with material retrieved from a Roman settlement that had been excavated in the vicinity.

The facade is in banded red and while stone, with a Romanesque portal surmounted by mullioned windows and a broad mutule. Inside the church (open Sun, 10am-12am) are conserved a Roman sepulchral stone and a 13th-century pulpit; bas-relief decorations featuring symbolic Longobard motifs adorn the walls of the apse. Off to one side of the church stands a battlemented tower.

Proceeding southward, after a few kilometers we come to the church of **Santa Maria in Pantano**, one of the most ancient churches in Umbria, thought to have been built by St. Severus. It may have been the site of a Roman edifice that formed part of the *Vicus Martis Tudertium*, a way station along the Via Flaminia in proximity to Todi.

The church presents an inclining facade with portal and rose window dating from the 13th century, and apse perhaps of the 8th. The altar was crafted from an inscribed Roman sacrificial altar. In the nearby locality of *Ceceraio* can be seen temple-structure tombs belonging to the *Vicus Martis* necropolis.

# 5.2 Todi

**Walking tour from Piazza del Popolo to Porta Perugina** *(map on page 143)*

Still today, Todi (elev. 400 m, pop. 16,876) strikes us for the way it boldly grips and adjusts to the hillside upon which it rests, and because of its well-preserved bastions rising out of a plinth of olive trees that has provided a natural defensive system for centuries. The city's recent but consolidated tourist industry is greatly aided by the Todi Festival, which, instituted in 1987, takes place in the last ten days of August, and has significantly contributed to enhancing the town's status as an international venue. The special relationship between the town and its site is borne out by its complex water system, as old as the town itself. Consisting of a series of wells and tunnels, the system is an eloquent demonstration of how it is possible

*The medieval public palaces at Todi*

to turn a hydro-geomorphological disadvantage into a strategic environmental plus. Todi's most ancient core corresponds to the Umbro-Etruscan *arce* (citadel), spanning the two summits of the hill and enclosed within the first defensive walls, and which in the name *tular* (boundary) stresses the town's primary characteristic. Once absorbed within the political sphere of Rome, in the Augustan Age it became the *Colonia Julia Fida Tuder*, and underwent a profound urban transformation, the traces of which are still evident. Between the 13th and 14th centuries the city experienced political and economic growth, which determined its expansion toward the outlying countryside essentially along preexisting access routes. As a consequence, four "boroughs" developed,

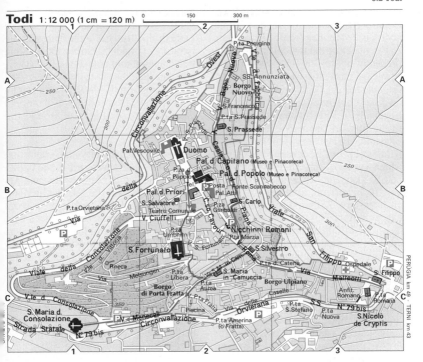

**Todi** 1 : 12 000 (1 cm = 120 m)

three of which were comprised within the third perimeter (1244) and hence an integral part of the *forma urbis*, which remained unchanged up to the second half of the 20th century.

Our itinerary starts from the centrally located Piazza del Popolo and proceeds from the center in the three directions of urban expansion. Piazza Maggiore lies at the confluence of the main streets, with Via Salara leading to the western quarters, which have undergone radical transformations. In order to reach San Fortunato from Palazzo dei Priori, follow Via Mazzini up to Piazza Jacopone, after which, continuing slightly to the right, you come to picturesque Piazza Umberto I, dominated by a broad and tall stairway leading to the church. To the left of San Fortunato, Via Leoni skirts the Roman boundary wall all the way to Porta Aurea. From here, a short detour to the right leads to the church of Santa Maria della Consolazione (elev. 338 m), standing in an isolated position outside the medieval wall. Proceeding to the end of the street, bearing right after Porta Catena, you reach Borgo Ulpiano, a 13th-century quarter extending to Porta Romana. From Porta Catena, Via Roma and Via Mercato Vecchio lead to Piazza del Mercato, located in the town's eastern sector between the two Roman wall perimeters. Nearby Via della Pia-

na extends along the axis of the lower walls. The second perimeter ends at Porta San Prassede, from where you proceed along steep Via di Borgo Nuovo (intersecting Via Amerina within the perimeter walls), which constitutes the Perugia-oriented axis along which the medieval city developed.

**Piazza del Popolo**\*\* (B2). Occupying a level area in a context of steep inclines, the square rests on large Roman cisterns that act as foundations. This, in fact, was the heart of the Augustan city. Between the 13th and 14th centuries, the square was redesigned to accommodate the symbols of the communal city's political status: on one side the three civil magistrature buildings, on the other the Cathedral.

**Palazzi Pubblici**\*\* (B2). The public magistrature buildings appeared during the 13th century, with the construction on the square's eastern side of the **Palazzo del Popolo**\*. One of Italy's most ancient public buildings, the part facing Piazza Garibaldi was begun in Lombard style, probably as the seat and residence of the *podestà* (mayor). Its present appearance is the fruit of restoration work carried out between the 19th and 20th centuries, which also topped the structure with battle-

143

ments. The **Palazzo del Capitano\*** was constructed in 1293. Its graceful Gothic-style facade is enhanced by a broad stairway connecting the two buildings which presently house the Town Hall and the municipal museums. On the first floor of the *Palazzo del Capitano* is located the *Sala del Capitano del Popolo*, featuring fragments of 14th-century frescoes; opposite this lies the *Salone del Consiglio Generale*. The last floor of the two *palazzi* is taken up by the **Museo Pinacoteca**, which was reorganized in 1997 (open Oct-Feb 10.30am-1pm, 2pm-4.30pm; Mar and Sep 10.30am-1pm, 2pm-5pm; Apr-Aug 10.30am-1pm, 2.30pm-6pm; closed Mon except in Apr). Our visit begins with the *Museo della Città*, which illustrates the city's most significant historic events, from its legendary origins to the *Risorgimento* (the political movement which brought to Italy's Unification). The museum's *archaeological section* includes material from digs in the area, and from antique collections. Among the most interesting pieces, a series of red-figured Attic *kylikes*, besides a collection of Roman ceramics and inscriptions. The *coin section* boasts almost 1,500 pieces, with some specimens dating from the 4th-3rd centuries AD to modern times. There follow the *textile section*, with sacred vestments and rare silk, velvet, damask, and linen apparels (15th-18th cent.), and a *ceramics section*, arranged in the *Sala del Consiglio dei Priori* (on the walls, frescoes by Sensini and Ignazio Mei), with 18th-19th century artifacts of various origin. Lastly, we come to a large hall housing the *Pinacoteca*, featuring an altarpiece by Spagna (**Coronation of Mary, with Choir of Angels and Saints\***, 1511); a *Deposition* by Pietro Paolo Sensini (1608); six works by Faenzone and paintings by Bartolomeo Barbiani, Andrea Polinori and Giacinto Boccanera.

**Palazzo dei Priori\*** (B2). Standing on the short side of the square, opposite the Cathedral, is the seat of the *Pretura* (magistrature). Originally Gothic, the building was enlarged and completed in 1334-47, and again modified in 1513. Its trapezoidal tower dates from 1334-47. Of particular interest is the fresco decoration of the *Sala delle Udienze*, dating from around the 14th century.

**Duomo\*\*** (B2). Twenty-nine travertine steps lead up to the facade of the Cathedral, dedicated to Maria Santissima Annunziata, begun in the 12th century and completed in the 14th. The central upper portion of the facade is graced by a magnificent **rose window\***, which was begun in the time of Bishop Basilio Moscardi (1515) and completed under his successor (1517-23). Particularly noteworthy is the carved wooden **portal\***, the four upper panels of which are by Antonio Bencivenni da Mercatello, whereas its six lower oak panels (replacing the badly damaged originals) are by Carlo Lorenti. In the church's three-part interior hangs a detached fresco fragment attributed to Spagna (*Trinity*, ca. 1515) and two altarpieces representing *Sts. Peter and Paul* by the same artist; an altarpiece by Giannicola di Paolo (1516); suspended above the altar a painted altarpiece **Crucifix\*** (Umbrian school, second half of the 13th cent.); and frescoes by Faenzone (1599) decorating the vault of the *Cesi Chapel\**. Also worth visiting is the *crypt*, which contains **three sculptures\***, originally adorning the facade, and attributed

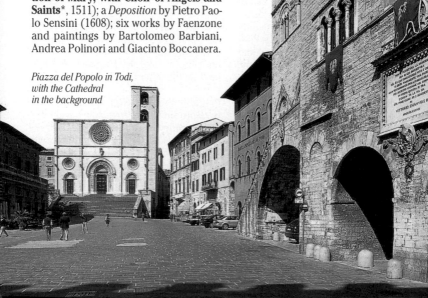

*Piazza del Popolo in Todi, with the Cathedral in the background*

## Jacopone, a troublesome friar

Jacopo dei Benedetti, better known as Jacopone, a notary by profession, having married an aristocratic girl by the name of Vanna, enjoyed all the privileges which could attend a rich man of the day: money, power, culture, and a busy social life. However, at the peak of his maturity, he was struck by a grave family tragedy: the sudden death of his wife. During a ball, the floor on which the young woman was dancing collapsed, burying her beneath a heap of stone and dust.

Now free of all matrimonial constrictions, Jacopone vented his long-concealed resentments toward the exuberance of the society about him, and embarked on a personal battle against its vices. Legend has

*Bronze monument to Jacopone da Todi*

it that he wandered through the streets, so crazed and wild that even his fellow friars of Todi eventually wondered whether it would be best to censure him. Political events often forced Jacopone to take sides, to take up arms; he found himself enchained in the city jail. When he was finally set free, he took refuge in Collazzone, in the convent of *San Lorenzo*, where he died on the night of 25 December 1306. Jacopone was a figure totally foreign to the reassuring spirit and image of Franciscan monasticism, a difficult character, whose personal drama surfaces in the pages of his poetry, replete with the man's inner lacerations and strivings toward an impossible terrestrial redemption.

to Giovanni Pisano (the first two) and to the sculptor Rubeus.

In a small courtyard behind the *Duomo* have been unearthed the remains of an imperial-age **domus**, with a mosaic floor of polychrome symbols. Also on this side of the hill a stretch of the ancient city walls is still visible.

Taking *Via Rolli* to the left of the Cathedral, you come to the **Monastero delle Lucrezie**, which, from the cloister, affords one of the best views of the town. In the adjoining church of *San Giovanni Battista*, recent restoration work has brought to light a fresco series dating from the first two decades of the 17th century.

**San Fortunato**\* (B-C"). In order to stress the importance of Todi's Franciscan settlement, in 1292 the municipal authorities decided to build this church on the site of an existing temple (1192). Its facade, which remained unfinished, is by Giovanni di Santuccio di Firenzuola (1415-58), and has as its fulcrum the main **portal**\*, with a pointed arch and sculptures decorating its outer frame. The interior, with a nave and two aisles surmounted by intersecting vaults, presents a fresco fragment by Masolino da Panicale (**Virgin with Child and Angels**\*, 1432); an altarpiece by Andrea Polinori, signed and dated 1618, and a carved and inlaid wooden *choir*\* by Antonio Maffei (1590). The

*Chapel of the Assunta* (left aisle) is entirely decorated with **frescoes**\* and paintings by Andrea Polinori.

**Santa Maria della Consolazione**\* (C1). Erected along the outer (southwest) edge of the 13th-century walls, the church (plan on page 147) has an interesting central plan, and was begun in 1508 to celebrate a cult surrounding the sacred image of an enthroned Madonna, and completed only in 1607. Though there is no concrete evidence, in the late 16th century the church's design was attributed to Bramante, whereas precise documents exist attesting to the involvement of other masters (Cola da Caprarola, Vignola, Ippolito Scalza). The central plan of the church pivots around four apses, three of which polygonal and a fourth semicircular. Crowning this composition is a tall dome, the circular structure of which creates a strong sense of vertical thrust. The interior is particularly well lit, and is embellished with decorative cycles by Filippo da Meli and Francesco Casella, and by a magnificent altar, perhaps designed by Andrea Polinori.

**Santa Maria in Camuccia.** This two-story structure, erected in the 7th-8th century and rebuilt in the 13th, is the fulcrum of the *Camuccia* quarter, which extends between

## Todi: Santa Maria della Consolazione

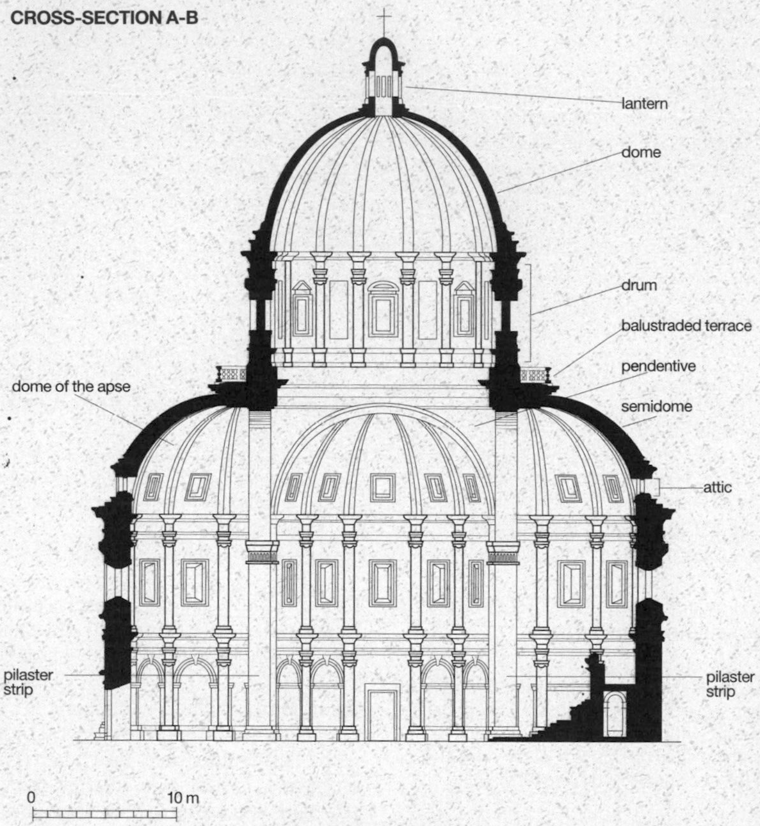
CROSS-SECTION A-B
lantern
dome
drum
balustraded terrace
pendentive
semidome
dome of the apse
attic
pilaster strip
pilaster strip
0
10 m

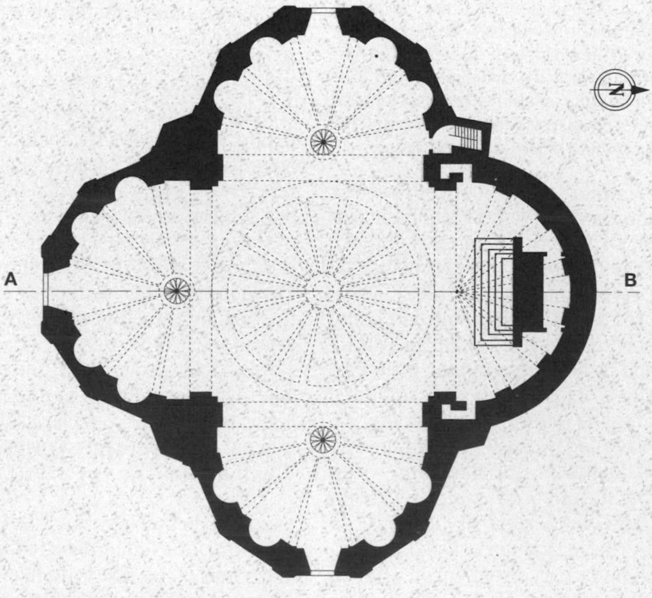
N
A
B

the two Roman perimeter walls. Of interest, along the church's nave, is a wooden statue with polychrome traces portraying a late 12th-century **Virgin and Child**\*, called *Sedes Sapientiae*.

Branching off outside *Porta Aurea*, beyond the church, is the medieval borough of **Porta Fratta**, whose core is represented by the church of *San Giorgio* (1017), embellished by a fresco attributed to Spagna (*Madonna and Child*). The street leads to *Porta Fratta* (or *Porta Amerina*), which was formerly located in the 13th-century perimeter.

**Borgo Ulpiano** (C2-3). Erected in the 13th century between *Porta Catena* and *Porta Romana*, the borough gravitates around the former church of the **Trinità**, which was renovated in the 18th century and converted into a museum. Besides the churches of *San Nicolò* (15th cent.) and *San Filippo Benizi* (15th-16th cent.), both possessing frescoes by Andrea Polinori, also worth visiting is the ancient little church of **San Nicolò de Cryptis**, built in 1093 on the site where once stood a Roman amphitheater. Still visible in the church's courtyard are remains of the imposing Roman theater, which with all probability featured two tiers of spectator bleachers.

**Piazza del Mercato Vecchio** (B2). Dominated by the four so-called Roman **nicchioni** (niches), this monumental substructure was built in the late Republican and early Imperial ages. A *via tecta* (covered street), along the right side linked the square ground level with the upper terrace. After the church of *San Carlo*, formerly *Sant'Ilario* (1112), you come to the **Fonte Scannabecco** (or Scarnabecco, 1241), comprising an arcade supported by seven columns surmounted by variously wrought capitals. Particularly characteristic are the medieval houses along the final stretch of the street.

**Borgo Nuovo** (A2). Rising outside *Porta San Prassede* in the early 13th century, the borough developed along a steep incline amid typical medieval buildings once occupied by craftsmen's workshops, and strategically marked off by monastic complexes situated at the two ends of the road to Perugia, the borough's main axis. To the Clarissan convent was added the church of **San Francesco al Borgo**, which was renovated in the 18th and 19th centuries, and whose interior is graced with decorations by the Agretti brothers. Slightly further on stands the complex of the **Santissima Annunziata**, with an *Annunciation*\* by Corrado Giaquinto.

The street ends at *Porta Perugina*, the best preserved gateway in the third perimeter wall.

A brief excursion in the locality of *Badoglie di Todi* takes us to the **Museo della Civiltà Contadina**, founded by Tersilio Foglietti as an exhibition space for rural "work and life" up to the 1950s. The museum also contains replicas of rustic homes, complete with period furnishings and tools (tel. 0758989402).

By a 1994 regional decree, presently being implemented, the stretch of the Tiber from the Montemolino bridge to the artificial Alviano lake reservoir has been classified a nature and wildlife park, the **Parco Fluviale del Tevere**. *Baschi* state road 448 crosses the rugged *Gola del Forello* (Forello gorge), classified as an area of major interest for its flora and fauna. From here we come to the broken shoreline of **Lake Corbara**, an ample reservoir embedded in the valley.

# 5.3 From Todi to Terni along the Tiberina Road

**An excursion from Todi to Terni along the Tiberina state road, 39 km** (*map on page 139*).

The Naia stream basin links the Tiber valley with the Ternano, in an extremely favorable context from a climatic and geographical point of view. This and the abundant water supply have fostered the expansion of agriculture. The abundant hot springs – especially in the Massa Martana, Acquasparta and San Gemini areas – have led to the growth of spas and health centers. For these same reasons the area was already well known in Roman times. Our itinerary leaves Todi from Porta Romana and takes us across the Rio and Naia stream valley in the direction of Terni. After a broad bend in the road we come in sight of the hill upon which, at a distance of 19.7 km, stands Acquasparta. Along the following stretch, which is only a few kilometers long, lie the archaeological site of Carsulae and the renowned San Gemini spa.

## Acquasparta

Proceeding along the provincial road, flanked by wooded ridges, before entering the town you come to the **Catacomba di San Faustino**, Umbria's only Christian catacomb (3rd cent.). From here, the ancient consular road leads to *Ponte Fonnaia*, a bold bridge that carries the Via Flaminia over the modest Naia river. Thus we come to *Acquasparta* (elev. 320 m, pop. 4,411), a center renowned from Roman times for the curative properties of its water, and later a fortified borough known as the *Terre Arnolfe*, which was granted to Arnolfus in 966 as a fief by Otto I. Between the 16th and 17th century, the Cesi purchased the holding from Pier Luigi Farnese to erect a splendid residence, thus affecting the urban layout of the town. In the town's center stands the majestic **Palazzo Cesi***, erected in 1565 to designs by Giovanni Domenico Bianchi. In 1606 this building became the seat of the *Accademia dei Lincei,* founded in Rome in 1603 by Prince Federico Cesi. Noteworthy are the splendid carved coffered **wood ceilings*** – of special note is the first-floor *salone,* featuring a series of impressions of Hercules, and considered one of highest examples of this prized Roman craft. The building is now the property of the University of Perugia and used as a venue for cultural events and conventions.

*The little church of San Damiano at Carsulae*

## Carsulae

Originally a Roman junction serving the Via Flaminia Antica, the first settlement developed in the 3rd century BC after the opening of the consular road that crosses the town from south to north. With the loss of importance of the Flaminia's western branch to its eastern counterpart, Carsulae fell into abandon and was subsequently invaded by barbaric populations which, together with the earthquakes that repeatedly struck the area, hastened its destruction. The town "resurfaced" in the 1950s. Its layout is virtually intact, thanks to the lack of successive structural stratifications. Its places and public buildings opened directly onto the Flaminia, with the sole exception of the slightly decen-

tered theater (or games) quarter. The water supply depended on a series of cisterns, wells, and conduits. Current plans include an Antiquarium, which will illustrate the features of the archaeological area and display the main finds. A visit to the area (always open) begins from the little church of **San Damiano** (1), built in the 11th century with material from Roman remains, which can partly be recognized along the church's left side and facade. From here, along Via Flaminia, you reach the remains of the aisled and apsed **basilica** (2); to the left, around the area of the forum (3) are public (4) and religious buildings, among which can be made out the presumed *curia*. To the south, on a man-made platform, the foundation remains of two perfectly equal **twin temples** (5); next to the access stairway to the temple, a small "quadrifrons" or *four-faceted arch* (6) of which only one side has been raised. A stairway behind the temples leads to the Flaminia up to the so-called **Arco di San Damiano** (7), a monumental arched gateway with three openings, of which the central one is preserved. Immediately outside this area begins the steep incline of the **monumental sepulchers**, two of which have been partially restored: one, circular and dome shaped (8), and resting upon a quadrangular basement; the other presenting a more vertical structure. On the opposite side of the lawn lies the **spectacle area**: the *amphitheater* (9) was built in a natural depression of the terrain; in line with the latter the *theater* (10), of which are visible the *orchestra* and the first two tiers of bleachers, the substructure of the *cavea*, and the stage foundations.

Upon the summit (elev. 781 m), which from the east overlooks the Carsulae ruins, rises the **Convento dell'Eremita**, founded on Roman remains by St. Francis in 1213.

## San Gemini

The borough (elev. 337 m, pop. 4,332) is perched upon a rise where already in Roman times stood a settlement linked to the Flaminia roadway, traces of which remain in a tomb known as the "Grotta degli Zingari" (The Gypsies' Tomb), a large villa with floor mosaics and wall structures located in the vicinity of the main square. The medieval perimeter occupies the highest part of the town, and abounds in environmental features. Via Casventino leads to the small Palazzo Vecchio square, and, beyond Piazza Garibaldi, to the parish church of San Giovanni, situated next to the gate of the same name. Piazza San Francesco constitutes a

## Archaeological site at Carsulae

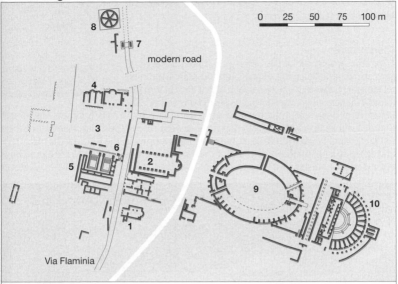

**1** San Damiano (11th C., over Roman building)
**2** Basilica
**3** Forum
**4** Public buildings
**5** Twin temples
**6** Quadrifrons arch
**7** Arched gateway of San Damiano
**8** Monumental sepulcher
**9** Amphitheater
**10** Theater

natural link with a Renaissance addition, along Via Roma and ending at Porta Romana. Turning to the left, shortly before reaching the gateway, Via Marconi leads to the Duomo. Outside the gate, at the end of Via Roma, the street to the right takes you in a few minutes to the church of San Nicolò.

**Piazza di Palazzo Vecchio.** This is the center of the elliptical medieval town, dominated by the 13th-century **Palazzo Pubblico**, with its toppled tower restored in the 18th century and internal staircase protected by an arcade. Inside are featured fresco fragments from the 14th to the 16th century. Also facing the square is the *Oratorio di San Carlo*, with frescoes from the 15th century.

**San Giovanni Battista.** The parish church, erected in the 12th century, has a fine Romanesque portal with mosaics laid by Latium craftsmen and various inscriptions in the upper part indicating the date of foundation (1199), together with the names of three architects: Nicola, Simone, and Bernardo. Awaiting restoration are the frescoes adorning the walls and octagonal pillars (14th-17th cent.).

**San Francesco.** Built between the 13th and 14th centuries, the church has a Gothic portal with rows of small columns and a coffered wood portal. Its aisleless interior resting on seven pointed arches, with a polygonal Gothic apse, is enhanced by a series of somewhat fragmentary wall fresco scenes (14th-16th cent.).

**Duomo and San Nicolò.** Slightly decentered, the Cathedral stands in the southern extremity of the town. The apse and part of its facade date from the 14th century, whereas its interior was remodeled in classical forms in the 19th century, probably during the time of Antonio Canova's sojourn. Outside the gate (1723) you come to the church of *San Nicolò* (private property), with its nave and aisles divided by columns and pillars. In the apse is conserved a *Madonna* dating from 1295, the only known work by Master Rogerino da Todi.

Slightly outside the town, in the direction of Narni, stands the church of **Santa Maria delle Grazie**, which from 1578 belonged to the Third Regular Order of St. Francis. On the altar, a *Madonna del Latte*, a fresco from the second half of the 14th century, crowned by *Angels and St. Lucy* (17th cent.).

# 6 Between Terni and the Tiber

## Area profile

"The Tiber would not be the Tiber were it not for the Nera" goes an old popular saying, expressing in a nutshell the close relationship between these two rivers, which have in turn profoundly influenced the way in which Umbria was settled. The broad Terni depression, the town of Narni, and the ridge of hills between Amelia and Guardea whose beech woods run down the eastern side of the Tiber Valley, describe a roughly triangular area full of deep, narrow gorges formed by the Nera and its many tributaries. Such a plentiful supply of water did though also result in a large number of bogs and marshy woodland, and the earliest inhabitants were forced to lay claim to whatever

*The spectacular show of the Marmore Falls seen from the lower road*

arable land they could, settling originally in the area at the very edge of the depression, as the huge Neolithic necropolis in Terni demonstrates (10th-9th cent. BC, in use until the 4th cent. BC, and with some 2,000 tombs), one of the most important protohistorical remains in the whole of central Italy.

In the Middle Ages the land was systematically drained by means of a dense network of canals to irrigate the fertile land around Terni extolled by Pliny and Tacitus in Roman times. The most spectacular manifestation of the region's water is unquestionably the Marmore Falls, which an awe-struck Lord Byron described as a "huge cloudy mass foaming forth, raging and roaring and plunging into the chasm", such was his reaction on beholding the breathtaking sight, an intriguing combination of human engineering and the forces of nature.

However, the area developed not only through its abundant supply of water but also through the many small towns that successfully exploited the resource for commerce, transport and irrigation. The area to the north of Amelia as far as the Tiber, is one of gentle rolling hills on which small feudal estates and settlements grew up around a lord's palace or castle (Giove, Alviano, Lugnano, Guardea and Baschi). The *condottiere* Bartolomeo d'Alviano controlled the routes to Orvieto and Rome from those same fortified residences which today offer visitors views over whole expanses of variously-colored fields that are a great source of wealth today, and which make the Terni depression such a unique feature of the Umbrian landscape.

## 6.1 Terni

**Tours of the historic town and the industrial estate** *(map on page 152)*
**Excursions to the Marmore Falls and in the territory around Terni** *(map on page 158)*

The historic town of Terni (elev. 130 m, pop. 108,435) began to develop into the industrial town it is today in the last two decades of the 19th century, when the arrival of the large manufacturing firms and hydro-electric power production of national importance earned it the nickname "the Manchester of Italy." The small town on the right bank of the Nera river was soon dwarfed by the sprawling working-class districts on the left bank, which eventually spread even further into the surrounding hills toward Rieti and across the plain to Narni, where new chemical plants were created in the 1930s. The de-industrialization process of recent years has halted the urban sprawl and focused attention on the historic quarters, on the older industrial areas, and on the area's smaller towns and villages.

The earliest traces of mankind in the

*The Sunday market in Terni*

Terni basin, dating back to the 10th century BC, were found on the Pentima hill, where a vast Umbrian necropolis in use up to the 6th century BC was discovered in 1884, during construction of the steelworks. With the arrival of the Romans (in the first half of the 3rd century BC), the settlement was enclosed by walls, and the neighboring areas rendered usable by the creation of a system of drainage canals. In the early days of the Roman Empire the walls were some 1,500 meters in length and the Via Flaminia crossed the town as its cardo maximus, intersecting with the decumanus maximus (today's Via Cavour and Via Garibaldi) at what is now Piazza della Repubblica. After the town was devastated by Totila and Narses (6th-8th centuries) and destroyed by Christian of Mainz under the orders of Frederick Barbarossa (in 1174), Terni recovered to some degree in the 13th and 14th centuries: the walls were enlarged and the canal system reorganized. Changes to the town's layout came about in the 18th and 19th centuries with the arrival of manufacturing activities, which culminated in the creation in the 19th century of the large industrial complexes on the left bank of

the Nera. But the real transformation of the area came with the arrival of the steel, chemical, and hydroelectric industries: manufacturing plants, pipelines and dams left their mark not just on the city but on the entire area between Terni and the lower Valnerina, and working-class housing districts appeared. An initial attempt to reorganize the city came between the wars. A competition was launched for a new development plan, which was not enacted until after World War II, through Wolfgang Frankl and Mario Ridolfi By the 1970s industrial activities in Terni were being scaled down, with the closure of the Centurini jute factory (1970) and of the electrochemical plant in Papigno (1973). Today only half as many people are employed in industrial activities as 15 years ago.

The route through the historic town along the ancient thoroughfares begins in Piazza Briccialdi, where the Roman gateway (Porta Romana) marked the point where the Flaminian Way (now Via Roma) entered the town. The narrow Via dell'Arringo leads to Piazza del Duomo, once the seat of the Assembly of the General Council, and continues along Via XI Febbraio. A lane off to the left leads to the Romanesque church of Sant'Alò, which forms a harmonious ensemble with the adjacent medieval building, the fountain and the 19th-century houses. Across Via Cavour, the street continues as Via Fratini, in which Palazzo Fabrizi, home of the municipal art gallery, stands. At the junction with Via Nobili a short detour to the left leads to the church of San Francesco. Via Fratini continues into Via Goldoni, widening out into Largo Villa Glori at the point where the two streets meet. The tour continues across Corso Tacito and along Via Angeloni, to Largo dei Banderari with the church of San Cristoforo. The street arrives at Piazza Bruno Buozzi, and turns back along Corso Vecchio, which begins at Piazza Corona. The Romanesque church of San Lorenzo is set slightly back from Corso Vecchio, which ends in a sequence of three squares that form the town

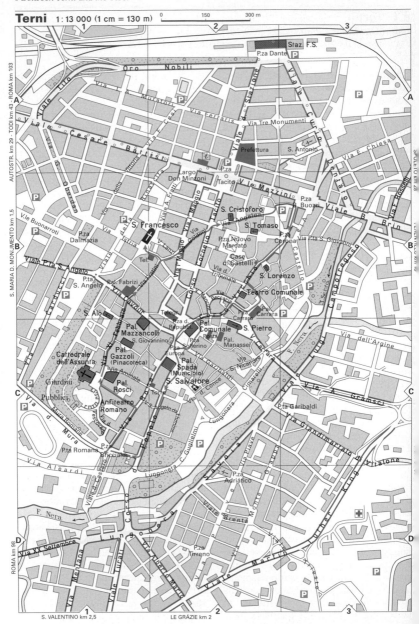

**Terni** 1:13 000 (1 cm = 130 m)

center: Piazza Solferino, Piazza della Repubblica and Piazza Europa, an area containing the City Hall (formerly Palazzo del Podestà), Palazzo Spada and the church of San Salvatore. From Palazzo Spada, Corso del Popolo leads back to Piazza Briccialdi.

**Cattedrale dell'Assunta** (C1). The somewhat secluded Piazza del Duomo was redeveloped in the 1930s in an effort to draw attention to the Cathedral, or Duomo, which was itself given a "facelift" in the same pe-

riod by the architect Piacentini. The church, remodeled in the 15th century, enlarged in the 16th century, and extensively renovated before being reconsecrated in 1653, occupies the site of remains dating back to the 6th and 11th centuries, which can be seen in the oratorium-type crypt. The facade, completed by a balustrade and statues designed by Marcello Piacentini, has a fine late 12th-century portal, with acanthus ornaments coiling round animals. The interior, in the shape of a Latin cross with

Terni Cathedral, dedicated to Our Lady of the Assumption

Flaminia, this palace was built for the future cardinal Luigi Gazzoli in 1795 to a design by Andrea Vici, who created a unified whole out of a number of existing buildings. Two rooms on the *piano nobile* have decorations with grotesques and *Scenes of Aurora* and *the Sun Chariot*, in the style of Liborio Coccetti. An apsed bathing pool found in the courtyard is believed to have been part of a Roman bathhouse. A side entrance to the theater was discovered in the stables.

nave and two side aisles, still has traces of the 17th-century decoration and works by Francesco Cincinnato, Livio Agresti, and Marten Stella. The main chapel has a polychrome altar by Antonio Minelli (1762), with a grand tabernacle. The aisled and apsed *crypt*, restored in 1904, is the burial place of St. Anastasius, bishop of Terni. The *treasury* includes a 13th-century astylar cross in gilt embossed silver, remodeled by Giovanni di Cristofano in 1333, and the early 17th-century *Reliquary of St. Proculus* in gilt copper.

**Palazzo Rosci** (C1). This 16th-century, Roman-style palace opposite the Cathedral has a rusticated doorway, a beautiful band of Angevin lilies, high windows on the *piano nobile* and a fine cornice. The decorations in the remarkable ground-floor hall, whose cloister vault is frescoed with grotesques, medallions and fine stucco cornices, depict *Allegories of the Arts and Sciences* and *Mythological Scenes* (second half of the 16th century, partly repainted). The fountain with travertine statues (representing the *Velino* and *Nera* rivers) by Corrado Vigni was added in 1935. The remains of a Roman theater discovered near the palace suggest that, ancient times, the entire district was given over to entertainments.

**Roman Amphitheater** (C1). Built in 32 AD by Faustus Titius Liberal, the presence of this theater can be seen both in the curve of Via del Vescovado and in the remains of two-zone *opus reticulatum* wall facing, which survived the construction of the *Bishop's Palace* over the amphitheater (enlarged in the 15th century).

**Palazzo Gazzoli** (C1). Located just off *Via XI Febbraio*, the former Via delle Carrozze and second main thoroughfare in Terni after the streets along the original Via

The rooms of the palace have recently been devoted to the **Pinacoteca Comunale** (open 10am-1pm and 4pm-7pm; closed Mon), whose collection of artworks, mainly from abolished religious institutes, span the period from the late 14th to the 19th centuries and have close connections with the town and the surrounding area. The finely decorated rooms display in chronological order such works as the **Crucifixion with Sts. Francis and Bernardine of Siena\*** by Alunno (1497); a carved *Crucifix with Mourners* by Spagna; the *Altarpiece of the Franciscans\**, by Pier Matteo Lauro and his workshop; and a **Mystic Marriage of St. Catherine\*** by Benozzo Gozzoli (1466). Art in the 17th and 18th centuries is documented by the works of Girolamo Troppa, Giuseppe Bastiani and artists in Antonio Gherardi and Benedetto Luti's circle. One room has works by Orneore Metelli, a naïf painter from Terni, who worked between 1922 and 1938. The collection also includes works of contemporary art, European graphic art, and sculptures by Aurelio De Felice and works by Picasso, Severini, Chagall, Mirò and others.

**Sant'Alò\*** (B1). The name of this church (probably built in the 11th century) is a corruption of the name Aloysius, the patron saint of goldsmiths and blacksmiths. It was owned in the 18th century by the Knights of Malta, who were based in the fine house built next to the Romanesque facade in the 14th century. Pillars and columns with interesting capitals divide the interior into a nave and two aisles; the aisles and the arch preceding the apse have an unusual barrel vaulting. The walls and apse were frescoed between the 12th century (fragment of a *Crucifixion*) and the 15th and 16th centuries. The last part of Via XI Febbraio is embellished by the fine 15th-century courtyard and loggia of *Palazzo Alberici*.

**Palazzo Mazzancolli** (B-C1). This fine surviving example of medieval architecture in Terni stands at the point where Via Cavour widens out into a small square. Built by Bishop Ludovico Mazzancolli in the 15th century over existing towers, it was restored in 1878 and again in 1927. The nearby church of **Santa Croce** contains an *Invention of the True Cross*, an altarpiece attributed to the Giacinto Brandi circle, as well as paintings by Ludovico Carosi (1629) and Liborio Coccetti.

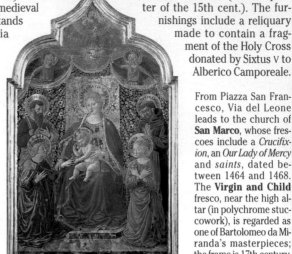

Mystic Marriage of St. Catherine,
*by Benozzo Gozzoli, at the Pinacoteca Comunale in Terni*

**Palazzo Fabrizi** (B1). This palace, whose 16th-century structures (including the elegant inner courtyard) were remodeled in the 18th century, stands on the corner of Via Cavour and Via Fratini. The 18th-century doorway in the fine front facing onto Via Fratini was altered by recent cement plaster work. The decorations on the *piano nobile* date back to the second half of the 18th century.

**San Francesco*** (B1-2). This church (1265) originally had a nave and transept in the Franciscan basilican style. Two aisles were added in 1437 together with the chapel of St. Bernardine (destroyed during World War II air raids). Remodeling in the 17th century, repairs following the 1703 earthquake and wide-ranging restoration in the 19th and 20th centuries, especially after wartime destruction, can be seen quite clearly on the facade, the central section of which has a Gothic portal with an oculus above. The side walls, added in the 15th century, have portals from that period and Gothic windows; the elegant campanile with two-and four-light Gothic windows is by Angelo da Orvieto. Inside there is a rare painting of the *Blessed Simone Camporeali* (early 14th century), one of the original founders of the Franciscan community in Terni. The **Paradisi Chapel*** built by Paolo and Angelo Paradisi, grandsons of Giovanni Paradisi and Captain of the People in Florence from 1333 to 1335, has walls frescoed with scenes based on Dante's *Divine Comedy* by Bar-tolomeo di Tommaso (second quarter of the 15th cent.). The furnishings include a reliquary made to contain a fragment of the Holy Cross donated by Sixtus V to Alberico Camporeale.

From Piazza San Francesco, Via del Leone leads to the church of **San Marco**, whose frescoes include a *Crucifixion*, an *Our Lady of Mercy* and *saints*, dated between 1464 and 1468. The **Virgin and Child** fresco, near the high altar (in polychrome stuccowork), is regarded as one of Bartolomeo da Miranda's masterpieces; the frame is 17th century.

**Largo Villa Glori** (B2). Created as part of the 1945 redevelopment plan (by Mario Ridolfi) at the end of Via Goldoni, this little square is bordered on the south by the *Casa Chitarrini*, designed by Ridolfi and Wolfgang Frankl in 1951 and noted for its characteristic triangular balconies.

**Palazzo Paglia** (B2). This 16th-century palace, on the corner with Via Goldoni, has an interesting Renaissance courtyard with loggias, and 17th-century grotesques. The doors leading off from the entrance way are late 15th century; the portico is later and has three tiers on the entrance side of the small courtyard (the top level, made of wood, dates back to the 19th century).

**San Cristoforo** (B2). This 13th-century church, built with spoil material and restored after being badly damaged in the last war, is divided into an ancient church and a modern one. Inside are Roman stone fragments from a cemetery found in the area. In the old church, where St. Francis is said to have preached, are some fragmentary and badly preserved votive frescoes (14th-15th cent.).

**Piazza Bruno Buozzi** (B3). Known locally as "Piazza Valnerina" or "Porta Valnerina," this square is the point where the old par of Terni meets the new industrial tow centered around Viale Brin (p. 156). Thre large lime trees, now dwarfed by the s rounding buildings, are all that is left of greenery that filled the square before the construction of the *Fratelli Fontana Complex*, by Mario Ridolfi and Wolfgang Frankl (1960-64).

**Corso Vecchio** (B2-3). "Gratitude Before All Else" was the title of an official bulletin issued by the town council in 1860 when it decided to name this long winding street after Italy's King Victor Emmanuel. The present name recalls not the fact that this was originally the Roman *cardo maximus*, but rather its demotion to a minor thoroughfare after the creation in the 19th century of Corso Tacito, a road much better suited to the traffic of the new industrial Terni.

**San Lorenzo** (B2). Built over a supposed Roman edifice in the 11th-12th centuries, and enlarged in the 17th century, this church was restored and isolated after being damaged in World War II. The facade has two triforate windows and a blind portal dated 1492. Inside are two naves on different levels.

**Case dei Castelli** (B2). Between the 14th and 15th centuries, the powerful Castelli family lived in the palaces it owned to the west of Corso Vecchio, accessible through the *San Lorenzo Arch*, almost opposite the church. Much of the medieval character of the area was lost during World War II.

A little further along Corso Vecchio is the **Teatro Comunale "Giuseppe Verdi,"** on the site of the ancient Palazzo dei Priori. Designed by Luigi Poletti and finished in 1849, it has a neoclassical pronaos; the interior was completely rebuilt after being destroyed in the last war. In Via del Tribunale (right) stands **Palazzo Giocosi**, later Palazzo Mariani (16th-17th cent.), now the home of the Briccialdi music school, which contains a hall decorated by Marten Stella and Gillis Congnet with fanciful compositions inspired by the name of the owner family ("jocose").

**Piazza Carrara** (B-C2). The most noteworthy building in this square, which underwent extensive demolition and redevelopment work in the 20th century, is **Palazzo dei Carrara**, an amalgamation of the medieval houses (14th century and later) belonging to the Carrara family. It was radically altered in the 1600s and was converted in the following century into the town hall (1712). The rooms on the *piano nobile*, most notably the *Room of Apollo and Daphne*, frescoed by Giro-

lamo Troppa, were decorated in the second half of the 17th century. Today the palace houses the **Biblioteca Civica**, whose holdings include incunabula, manuscripts and a collection of parchments.

**San Pietro** (C2). Rebuilt on the Corso in the 14th century by the Augustinians, to whom it belonged from 1287, the church underwent various restorations after the 1703 earthquake and World War II air raids. The Gothic portal is decorated with a 15th-century relief (*Christ Blessing*); the aisleless nave has fragments of late 14th- and early 15th-century frescoes which came to light during postwar restoration. There is also an interesting **Dormitio Virginis** and **Coronation of the Virgin**.

**Palazzo Manassei** (C2). Built in the 17th century in the street of the same name over medieval houses belonging to the noble Manassei family, this palace is designed in the typical style of noble buildings of Terni, based on the best-known Roman models: a broad entranceway for carriages, an inner courtyard and a fountain positioned so as to be visible from the main doorway.

**Main squares** (C2). The center of Terni is a complex, disjointed system of squares and open spaces that form a large area whose unity lies more in its function than in its spatial organization. Known as Piazza Maggiore in medieval times, today's **Piazza della Repubblica** remains the hub of town life. This square, which lost some of its unity with the creation of Corso Tacito, is closed off on the left by the elegant *Palazzo Manni* (restored in 1835), while on the southeast side stands the old City Hall, or *Palazzo Comunale Vecchio*, rebuilt in Renaissance style in 1878 by Benedetto Faustini. The ground floor still has remnants of the

*A view of the Terni countryside*

earlier 14th-century building that came to light after bombing in the last war. A 17th-century niche with an unusual fresco (*two cherubs*, one holding a lance, the other a sponge, beside a cross with the nails of martyrdom) has been reopened to the left of the main entrance. The work has been interpreted as a *signum pietatis*, or sign of piety, placed on the site where executions took place. Today the palace is a cultural center, housing among other things a multimedia library. On the left, before the adjacent Piazza Europa, on the south side of **Piazza Solferino** stands the fine *Palazzo Montani*. It has rooms decorated by Girolamo Troppa with mythological, biblical, and literary scenes, and a loggia frescoed with the *Four Corners of the Earth* by Cosimo Dandini (1624). The large, rectangular **Piazza Europa** was created after the war when a whole block that once stood between Palazzo Montani (home of the Spada family, see below), and *Palazzo Morandi-Rossi* was demolished. The ceilings of two rooms of this palace have a large canvas by Francesco Granieri (1793) and a tempera decoration with early 19th-century oriental-style ornamentation.

**Palazzo Spada\*** (C2). Begun by Michelangelo Spada in the mid-16th century, this palace was completed in 1576 to a design by Sallustio Peruzzi, son of the better-known Baldassarre, the architect of the Camera Apostolica. The building, now the town hall, was remodeled in the 18th century.

On the *piano nobile*, the so-called *Phaeton Room* is decorated with a cycle of frescoes by Karel van Mander and his assistants (1575-76). The decorations in the three adjacent rooms are attributed to Sebastiano Flori, pupil of Vasari, and his assistants (1575-80). Remains of a mosaic floor belonging to a Roman "domus" have been found in the vicinity of the palace.

**San Salvatore\*** (C2). Tradition has it (though the event is undocumented) that Longobard King Liutprand and Pope Zacharias met in this church, which now dominates the disjointed collection of spaces ending in the eastern facade of Palazzo Spada. This interesting building has a circular body with a rectangular apse and a rectangular front section. Underneath the apsed rotunda (possibly classical or early Christian, but no earlier than the 11th century) have been found the remains of a Roman peristyle-type "domus" dating back to the end of the Republic and the beginning of the Empire. Opening off from

the 12th-century two-bay nave (a typical feature of the Umbrian Romanesque style) is the *Manassei Chapel*, a 14th-century addition decorated with an interesting cycle of frescoes, probably from the middle of that century. The present-day sacristy was formerly the 17th-century Filerna Chapel, decorated with frescoes by Andrea Polinori and Ludovico Carosi.

**Lancia di Luce** (D1). This obelisk – 30 m high and in cast iron – stands on the crossroads between Viale Guglielmi and Corso del Popolo. It has been executed by Arnarlo Pomodoro to celebrate the centenary of the Steelworks, and has immediately become the symbol of industrial Terni.

## The industrial city

**Piazza Tacito** (A-B2). In the center of this regular rectangular space stands a *fountain* by Mario Ridolfi (1936) and Mario Fagiolo, who also designed the square (1932). A road leads up to the *Train Station*, which was opened in 1866.

**Viale Brin** (B3). This was the main thoroughfare of the industrial city in the late 1800s, and contains significant examples of early 20th-century factories and houses. Across the Serra river are two works of Italian Rationalist architecture from the 1930s: the *Palazzo Rosa* (or *"Pink Building"*) and the *Grattacielo* (*"Skyscraper"*), built to house workers of the Terni Company. Further on is the late-19th-century *Palazzone* and the long front of the neo-Renaissance **Fabbrica d'Armi** (Weapon Factory, 1875-81), now a military building with a small collection of weapons from 1870 to the present day (closed to the public). On the opposite side of the road are the turn-of-the-century *Office Workers' Buildings*.

**Steelworks** (B3, off map). Built between 1884 and 1887 and described as "the world's most beautiful steel-making plant," these buildings are now a mere collection of unprepossessing metal sheds. Time, war and demolition have destroyed much of the original structures.

### The Marmore Falls\*
This awe-inspiring "natural" spectacle was already described in Roman times and celebrated by travelers on the Grand Tour in the 18th and 19th centuries. The falls can be reached by either of two roads from Terni (both signposted): the upper road (or

## His Majesty's Rifles

The Royal Weapon Factory,
*in a turn-of-the-century photograph*

Up until the 1950s, anyone venturing into the industrialized outskirts of Terni would have been guided by the octagonal dome over the great forge hammer, a landmark described in 19th-century guidebooks as "Vulcan's new forge." Few of the factories and buildings that once composed the industrial estate are still standing, but the rusty relics that do survive are to industrial archaeologists what Umbria's palaces and churches are to art historians. They are a reminder of a period of intense activity that began with the Unification of Italy, when cast-iron and steel were in great demand for civil and – more importantly – military purposes. After the State decided against setting up a plant here, the task fell to the Fonderia di Terni, a highly reputable industrial group that had firmly established itself in an area far from regional borders and with an abundant supply of water. The plant grew to a size matched only by the large French and German steelworks, but was all the more remarkable in what was still very much an agricultural setting, one without the raw materials (coal in particular) found in countries north of the Alps. 1882 saw the opening of the Regia Fabbrica d'Armi (Royal Weapon Factory), the first part of a large complex, still in operation, whose impressive achievements included the excavation of one of Italy's first industrial canals, three kilometers in length. During World War I this factory had a workforce of 7,300 and turned out as many as 2,500 rifles a day, as well as manufacturing daggers, sabers, and bayonets.

But its economic fortunes were checkered: lucrative orders such as the casting of colossal statues would be followed by periods of deep recession, and although the world wars were prosperous times, when the "City of Steel" produced weapons of every description by the thousand, Terni was unable to adapt to the new industrial scene in the postwar years, and its fame as "the Manchester of Italy" began to wane.

*The Terni ironworks today*

"*Superiore*", 8 km), and the lower road (or "*Inferiore*", 7 km), which gives a spectacular view of the entire falls. The leap made by the Velino river here as it cascades down a precipice from the Marmore plateau into the Nera river is, however, largely the work of man. In 271 BC Roman consul Manius Curius Dentatus had a channel dug as part of his land reclamation scheme for the marshland around the Velino. The *Cavus Curianus*, as the channel was known, drained stagnant water from the river on the site of what is now the main waterfall. Today the foamy white mass of water makes three leaps, in a descent of some 165 meters, and although the spectacle is now rather less stunning than it would have been for visitors in centuries gone by (the water has now been harnessed by the nearby hydroelectric power station, building work on which has also affected the surrounding vegetation), the roar of the water and the prismatic effects created by the mist of tiny water droplets on certain days is an amazing sight.

### Around Terni

The three excursions in this area are to: Cesi to the northwest (8.7 km), Collescipoli to the southwest (4.5 km) and Stroncone to the south (8.5 km). This hilly area is still given over to traditional farming methods, with olives being one of the main crops.

## Cesi

This typical fortified hill town (elev. 437 m) on the slopes of Mt. Torre Maggiore, was an Umbrian settlement, as the remains of polygonal walls from the 6th century BC testify. The remains of the fortress, renovated in the 15th-16th century with the walls, survive. At the entrance to the village stands the former church of **Sant'Angelo**, a Romanesque building (documented as early as 1093), which was completely renovated in the early 16th. The brick portal was added in 1531. Further on is the 17th-century **Palazzo Contelori**, characterized by two wings with symmetrical doorways at either side of the main palace building. The parish church of **Santa Maria Assunta** (to the left of Sant'Angelo), built between 1515 and 1525 and enlarged in the mid-18th century, has side chapels occupied by elegant stucco altars with 17th- and 18th-century canvases. An adjoining building houses a collection of artworks and religious items from local churches. The street ending in Porta Tuderte leads to Piazza Cesi, site of the former church of *Sant'Andrea* (1160), now a community center, with fragments of Roman tombs. Also in the square, **Palazzo Cittadini-Cesi**, begun by Gian Giacomo Cesi in the first half of the 16th century, beside the 14th-century walls occupied a whole section of street. At the eastern end of the town is the *Monastery of Sant'Agnese*, an ancient Benedictine foundation, renovated in 1546-59 and again in 1611-13. A path leads from the upper part of Cesi, out into the woods and to the church *of Sant'Onofrio*, which commands a fine view and has the remains of a polygonal wall. On the plateau near the summit of *Mt. Erasmo*, surrounded by polygonal walls (6th cent. BC), stands the small 12th-century church of *Sant'Erasmo*, once part of an ancient Benedictine abbey.

## Collescipoli

This small town, built in an isolated spot high up over the Terni depression (elev. 238 m) is reached by the Collescipolana road (a left turn off the SS3 *Via Flaminia* to Narni), after passing the small Romanesque church of *Santo Stefano*, decorated with a long marble transcription of two legal documents dated 1094. The outer side of the Porta Ternana gateway into the town has an 18th-century bust of *Scipio Africanus* inside a clipeus (the name of the town is thought to derive from "Colle Scipione," or Scipio's Hill); while the inner side has an incomplete *Pietà* from the same period. Close to the gateway stands the early 18th-century *Palazzo Ungari*, whose unified facade conceals the fact that the palace is a combination of various buildings. In the main square stand the *Palazzo del Comune* (restored in 1718) and **Palazzo Catucci** (second half of the 16th cent.), a building with a central courtyard in the style of architect Giacomo Vignola. The collegiate church of **San Nicolò** (11th century), which was completely restored in the early 16th century under the orders of Pope Julius II,

## 6.1 Around Terni  6.2 Around Narni and Amelia

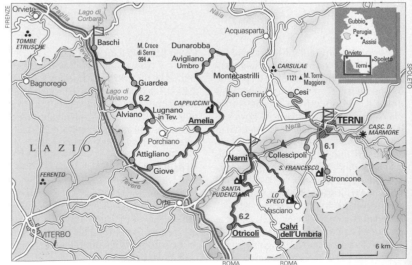

contains works by Evangelista Aquili, Sebastiano Flori and Bartolomeo Barbiani and a rare linen tablecloth that has been dated 1600-20. At the far end of the town, near Porta Sabina, stands the Romanesque church of **Santa Maria Maggiore**, restored between the 15th and 16th centuries, having a single-nave interior with stuccoes by Michele Chiesa and local craftsmen in the early 18th century.

*View of Stroncone surrounded by olive groves*

### Stroncone

This town (elev. 450 m, pop. 4,311), on a hill covered in olive groves, has preserved its ancient appearance and part of the 10th-century medieval walls are still standing. Just outside the town stands the church of **San Francesco**, traditionally believed to have been founded together with the adjoining convent by St. Francis himself in 1213. Beneath the portico before the church, in a chapel to the left, is a fresco by Tiberio d'Assisi (1509). Stroncone itself begins with a 17th-century *fountain* and the ancient gateway to the fortified town, leading to a charming little square dominated by the church *of San Giovanni Decollato*, an enlargement (from 1604) of an earlier building of 1435. The church of **San Nicolò**, from which there is a fine view, has a Romanesque portal (1171) decorated with a Byzantine-style bas-relief. Steps lead up to the 13th-century **Palazzo Comunale**, which has *nine parchment hymnbooks* from the churches of San Michele and San Nicolò, six of which have exquisitely illuminated capital letters.

## 6.2 Around Narni and Amelia

**A walk through the town of Narni** *(map on page 161)*
**An excursion from Amelia to Baschi, 30 km** *(map on page 158)*

The area around Amelia, known as "Amerina," is bordered to the north by the Martani mountains, to the east by the Terni depression and to the south by the Nera and Tiber rivers, which meet just past Orte at the southernmost tip. It is a predominantly hilly, even mountainous area, the higher ground to the east sloping down westward to the Tiber valley, and flattening out into the lower Nera valley plain in the south.

The area between Terni and Narni is densely populated as a result of industrialization, whereas the area between Narni and Amelia has been only marginally affected by modern development. In the last decade the demise of tenant farming and its replacement by specialized crop farming (although some traditional ways still survive) have brought changes to the countryside. The hilly area between Amelia and Baschi, known as "Teverina," has been settled and farmed since ancient times, thanks to its fertile soil, numerous roads and the river itself. It is dotted with fortified hilltop towns, most of them dating back to the Middle Ages to defend the area's chief town, Amelia.

## Narni

The ancient town of Narni (elev. 240 m, pop. 20,408) was built on a rocky spur overlooking the Nera gorge and the Terni basin for purposes of defense, and the town's development was largely dictated by the morphology of the site. Known as *Nequinum* in Roman times, Narni occupied a position of crucial importance for the control of routes between Rome and the Adriatic. This long, narrow town still has traces of the earliest Umbrian and Roman settlements in the north (the regular grid pattern of streets), and the medieval layout (11th-14th cent.) of the Fraporta and Mezule districts. The fortress, a symbol of papal power built by Cardinal Albornoz, dominates the whole town. As a result of its territorial importance, Narni was besieged and ravaged at various times in its history. One attack in particular (by German mercenary soldiers in 1527) resulted in wholesale death and destruction that left an indelible mark on the town. The extensive reconstruction work was rather more restrained, a sign of the much more peripheral role Narni played, both politically and culturally, under papal rule in the 17th and 18th centuries.

The construction of a rail line and freight yard encouraged the development of manufacturing and residential development in the valley in a way that was not possible on the rocky land above. This new settlement (Narni Scalo) was, however, too distant for the old upper town to benefit from the vitality of the new suburb.

Entry to the town is through Porta Ternana. Via Roma, which affords fine views over the Terni catchment basin, leads up to Piazza Garibaldi, the town's main square dominated by the Cathedral. The steep Via del Monte leads (along Via Nerva off to the left) to the church of Santa Margherita, and (straight ahead) up to the mighty Rocca, or fortress, on the hilltop. Piazza Cavour, opposite the Cathedral, leads into the main street through the town, which begins as Via Garibaldi and continues as Via Mazzini after Piazza dei Priori, the site of the ancient forum in which Narni's two main civil buildings, Palazzo dei Priori and Palazzo del Podestà, stand. Roughly halfway down Via Mazzini is Piazza XIII Giugno, the parvis of the church of San Domenico. Piazza Marzi leads to Via Marcellina and then Via Gattamelata, where the church of Sant'Agostino stands. Via Ferrucci, which has two imposing medieval tower houses, leads back to Piazza del Duomo.

**Porta Ternana.** Formerly known as Arvolta, this was the gateway into the medieval walled town along the Via Flaminia. The rusticated sides and arch are flanked by sturdy turrets.

**Piazza Garibaldi** (C2). This square was once called Piazza del Lago af-

ter the large medieval cistern, or *lacus*, built there over a previous Roman cistern. Today it boasts a large *fountain*, rebuilt after 1527, with a 16th-century polygonal brick basin, and a 14th-century bronze pool decorated with zoomorphic protomes. The square's irregular shape is the result of many transformations. A narrow passageway (widened in 1832, between the Cathedral and the Bishop's Palace) leads to the slightly higher *Piazza Cavour*, the square onto which the Cathedral opens at the end of the Roman city.

From Piazza Garibaldi the road leads up to the Mezule district, on the higher part of the rocky spur that ends at the castle. The panoramic route passes along Via del Monte and Via Cocceio Nerva, and takes in the church of **Santa Margherita** (C2), built in the early 17th century together with the Benedictine monastery, reserved for the nobility. The single-nave interior has a plastered ceiling and walls frescoed by Antonio Circignani.

Via del Monte leads to the **Rocca**\*or fortress (D3), 332 m. Recently restored (open Sat, 1pm-5pm; holidays, 10am-5pm; summer, always until 7pm), it was built in the second half of the 14th century by Cardinal Albornoz, possibly to a design by Ugolino di Montemarte. Two elegant doorways lead to the theatrical courtyard, which features an external staircase. Just below the castle is the *Feronia Fountain*, the site of a pre-Roman place of worship dedicated to the goddess Feronia, of which only an underground passageway to the natural spring survives.

**Duomo**\* (C2). The Cathedral stands on an early medieval necropolis – tombs dug out of the rock have been found under Piazza Cavour – from the time of the first bishop of the town, St. Juvenal, to whom the Cathedral is dedicated. Work on the building began in 1047 and continued for almost a century before finally being consecrated in 1145 by Pope Eugene III. In front of the simple, rectangular facade (transformed in the 14th century) is an elegant portico with arches raised on columns. The main portal is 12th century. The large blocks of stone to the right of the portico are the remains of the Roman town walls.

*The Rocca at Narni*

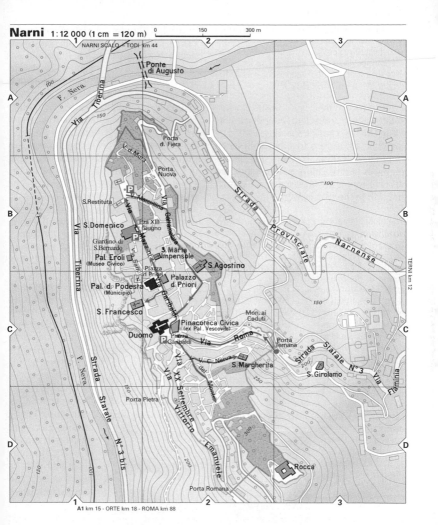

NARNI SCALO – TODI km 44

Ponte di Augusto

F. Nera

Via Tiberina

Porta d. Fiera

Porta Nuova

S.Restituta

S.Domenico

P.za XIII Giugno

Giardino di S.Bernardo

Pal. Eroli (Museo Civico)

S.Maria Impensole

Pal. d. Podestà (Municipio)

Piazza d.Priori

Palazzo d. Priori

S.Agostino

S.Francesco

Pinacoteca Civica (ex Pal. Vescovile)

Duomo

Piazza Garibaldi

Via Roma

Mon. ai Caduti

Porta Ternana

S.Margherita

S.Girolamo

Strada Statale N° 3

Via Flaminia

Strada Provinciale Narnense

Porta Pietra

Via XX Settembre

V. C. Nera

Via del Monte

Via V. Emanuele

Rocca

Porta Romana

TERNI km 12

A1 km 15 - ORTE km 18 - ROMA km 88

The basilica-style interior has a nave divided from the two aisles by 16 columns with capitals in a variety of shapes and with lowered arches. The north aisle was added between the 14th and 15th century to accommodate the **tomb of Sts. Juvenal and Cassius**\*, more correctly referred to as the *tomb of the Bishops of Narni*, whose front is divided into four orders of decorated pillars; above the portal is the *Burial Slab of Cassius and his Wife Fausta* (558 AD). The inner walls of the sanctuary, originally underground and thus hidden from view, are clad in slabs of marble, except for the wall on the left where several bishops are buried; on the back wall is a marble triptych from the above church (now destroyed), in which St. Juvenal was worshipped. The cave behind the altar contains the 8th-9th century *sarcophagus* which contained the body of St. Juvenal until 1642,

when the new confession was introduced below the altar. Above the entrance to the sacellum is a **Christ Blessing**\* in a late-9th century glory, flanked by frescoes of *saints*. In the south aisle are frescoes originally from the Romanesque church (12th-13th cent.) and a wooden **Statue of St. Anthony Abbot** \* by Lorenzo Vecchietta (1474).

The Cathedral **bell tower** can be seen from Via del Campanile, behind the church. This sturdy bell tower was built over Roman fortifications: the lower limestone part is Romanesque (12th cent.); the upper part is Renaissance (15th cent.) and built of brick, with decorative majolica inserts.

Between April and May, the **Corsa all'Anello** is held in the streets of the old town, a kind of jousting contest dating back to the 14th century. A historic procession winds its way through the town's old streets and out through Porta Ternana to the playing field next to the church of *San Girolamo*, where mounted teams representing the three districts (Fraporta, Mezule, and Santa Maria) tilt at a small silver ring 8 cm in diameter with their 2.8-meter lances, until one of them succeeds in spearing it. The winning team keeps the prize for a year (for more information contact the organizers: tel. 0744726233).

**Pinacoteca Civica\***. The town's new art gallery is to be housed in the 17th-century former bishop's palace. Paintings owned by the civic authorities together with items from the Cathedral Treasury will be displayed as part of a more general exhibition of the history of the town and Narni art from the 15th to the 19th century.

The highlights of the collection will be an **Annunciation\*** by Benozzo Gozzoli (1451-52) and a large work by Domenico Ghirlandaio and his workshop, painted in 1486 at the behest of Cardinal Eroli for the church of *San Girolamo* (*Coronation of the Virgin with Angels and Saints\**). The section on 16th- and 17th-century art will include works by Marcantonio Aquili, Livio Agresti, and Antonio Gherardi; the 18th century will be illustrated through works by Giacinto Boccanera. The Cathedral's treasures include six sculpted bronze candlesticks attributed to Andrea Briosco; and a monumental silver ostensory (18th cent.).

*Bas-relief on the facade of Palazzo del Podestà, Narni*

**San Francesco** (C1). This church was built on the site where St. Francis of Assisi is believed to have stayed in 1213, when he was called to Narni by Bishop Ugolino. The facade has an ornate Gothic portal that was altered several times (most extensively in the 17th century). The church has been closed since it was damaged by fire in August 1998. Inside, a series of votive paintings attributed to the Maestro del 1409 and the Maestro della Dormitio are the most important in the town.

*A moment of the Corsa all'Anello in Narni*

**Piazza dei Priori** (B-C 1-2). The forum of the Roman city and later the *Platea Maior* of medieval Narni, became a long, narrow square in the late 13th and early 14th centuries with the construction of two public build-ings opposite one another. **Palazzo dei Priori**, built in the mid-14th century, is dominated by the fine *Civic Tower* and embellished with a fine **loggia\*** attributed to Gattapone; to the right of the simple doorway is the pulpit from which public proclamations were made. In 1618 the Scolopi Fathers turned the building into a school which, under the ownership of the civic authorities, is now being restored for civic purposes. **Palazzo del Podestà\*** was built in the second half of the 13th century by joining together three tower-houses. The part to the right of the rusticated Renaissance doorway was originally the chapel, whose entry arch was later lowered with an unusual bas-relief composition (13th cent.). The interior, now the tourist information office, has a fresco attributed to Torresani, from the first half of the 16th century. The grand atrium, built into the central tower, houses a collection of archaeological material from Roman and medieval times, including a sarcophagus with *hunting scenes*. The upper floor (being restored) has a female Egyptian mummy in a wooden sarcophagus decorated with funerary scenes and hieroglyphics, which belonged to an Egyptian priest (Ramoses, 4th cent. BC); these exhibits will form the archaeological section of the museum being set up in Palazzo Eroli (p. 163). At the far end of the square, below the 16th-century *Palazzo Calderini*, stands the **fountain**, once fed by the ancient Formina aqueduct. It has a bronze bowl decorated with six zoomorphic protomes alternating with crests of the town. The dedicatory inscription reveals that it was built in 1303.

**Via Mazzini** (B1-2). This street, which is the continuation of Via Garibaldi, is lined with elegant ancient palaces, including the 17th-century *Palazzo Mosca* and *Palazzo Bocciarelli*, the latter standing opposite one of the oldest churches in Narni, **Santa Maria Impensole\*** (1175). The portico surrounds

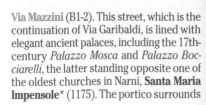

three sculptured portals* with sculpted acanthus scrolls in classical style; the interior has a nave separated from the side aisles by Romanesque columns. Traces of late 14th-century frescoes can be seen on the wall; the high altar is clad in 15th-century marble. The subterranean area (open to visitors, tel. 0744722292, 0744715362) consists of three rooms, one of which contains a 6th-century arcosolium-type tomb. Further along the street is **Palazzo Scotti** (mid-16th cent.): note the portal, windows

*Frescoes from the underground rooms of San Domenico*

and inner loggia, which have been variously attributed to Sangallo and Ippolito Scalza. The two lofty **Torri dei Marzi** on the right are a reminder of the illustrious Narnese family from which the 15th-century writer, astronomer and anatomist Galeotto Marzio came.

**San Domenico** (B1). Tradition has it that this religious complex was built as the town's first cathedral in the 12th century, on the site of an ancient temple to Minerva. Much transformed over the centuries, the church is currently used as municipal offices; it contains fragments of frescoes by artists from the workshop of the Maestro del 1409. The large Chapel of the Rosary, whose cross vault is frescoed with *Scenes from the Book of Genesis* by Flemish artists in the second half of the 15th century, houses a collection of paleontological material from the Upper Pleistocene period, along with other local archaeological finds (to be transferred to Palazzo Eroli).

The small square to the left of San Domenico leads to *St. Bernard's Garden*, once the herb garden of the convent (of which only the bell tower survives), and with a splendid view over the Nera valley. Here is the entrance to the **underground rooms of San Domenico** (open Sun and holidays only, June-September, 10am-1pm and 3pm-6pm; October-May, 11am-1pm and 3pm-5pm; by prior arrangement, tel. 0744722292, 0774715362). Of particular interest is the *Hypogean Church*, a single-nave, barrel-vaulted chamber, some of whose walls are excavated straight out of the rock, plastered and frescoed, although limestone concretions in some points have made the paintwork underneath irretriev-

able (the oldest date back to the 12th century). Beyond a room with a circular Roman well is another chamber in white and pink stone, originally the seat of the Inquisition; the graffiti scratched into the plasterwork of the adjoining cell is either devotional or connected to legal matters, and is mostly of obscure meaning.

One notable building in the medieval Via Saffi, which leads off from the square, is **Palazzo Eroli**, a 17th- and 18th-century remodeling of 14th- and 15th-century buildings. The building is now being restored and is to become the "E. Eroli" Municipal Library and *Civic Museum*, housing the collection of archaeological finds from the church of *San Domenico* and Palazzo dei Priori, and will include an industrial archaeology section.

**Via Gattamelata** (B2). This street runs through a characteristically medieval district, which also features much Renaissance restoration work. Here stands the supposed *birthplace* of Erasmo da Narni, called Gattamelata, captain of the Republic of Venice (b. 1370 ca.). Further on is the 16th-century *Palazzo Capocaccia*, which incorporates part of the *Oratory of San Valentino*, traditionally held to have been founded by St. Juvenal. The church of **Sant'Agostino**, which stands on a site above the walls, dates back to the 14th century. It was rebuilt in the 15th century, and remodeled and reconsecrated in 1728. The large interior, with its predominantly 18th-century decoration, contains a shrine painted in 1482 by Pier Matteo d'Amelia (behind the facade); the tribune in the apse is an important document of late 14th-century Umbrian painting, thanks to fragments still visible under the 18th-century of frescoes by various artists working under the Maestro della Dormitio. The *Chapel of San Sebastiano* (at the beginning of the nave), was decorated by Lorenzo Torresani, whose brother Bartolomeo took over after 1538. The sacristy has a *Crucifixion* attributed to the Maestro della Tomba di Cesi (1500).

**Bridge of Augustus***
The modern bridge over the Nera to the north of the old town near Narni Scalo is a good vantage point from which to observe the remains of the Roman bridge named after the Roman Emperor in power when work to modernize the Via Flaminia was being carried out. Some 160 m long and almost 30 m above water level, it was once completely clad in travertine. It had already fallen into disuse by the 12th century and

today only one of the original four (or three) arches survives.

Near the bridge is the sanctuary of the **Madonna del Ponte**, consecrated in 1728, destroyed in the last war and completely rebuilt. This church incorporates a cave used as a chapel, which includes Roman structures presumably connected with the Via Flaminia. Above is the Benedictine *Abbey of San Cassiano* (12th-13th cent.), with a fine portal on pillars and a later cusped campanile; the complex is surrounded by a wall with Guelph-type merlons (possibly 15th century).

### Speco di San Francesco

The *Convent of the Holy Grotto* (sacro speco) stands at 568 m in a beautiful wood of holm oaks and chestnut trees. It was founded by St. Francis in 1213 and later enlarged by St. Bernardine, and is named after the cave to which St. Francis retired to pray; the oratory of *San Silvestro* is decorated with a 14th-century fresco, while the wooden sculptures (*Crucifixion with Mourners*) in the convent church are 17th or 18th century.

Near the little village of Santa Lucia, at the end of the Strada dei Pini, is the **Formina Aqueduct** (1st cent. BC), which carried water along its brick-built structure and through channels hewn out of the rock from just north of the village of Sant'Urbano to Narni, collecting water from six springs along the way.

### Toward Otricoli

The SS3/ter road from Sangemini to Narni continues south out of the town to the church of **Sant'Angelo in Massa**, which adjoins an abbey founded in 996-999 AD by friars Pietro and Adriano over the remains of a Roman villa. The two monks are believed to have been of German origin because of the many similarities between this building and the Königshalle of the abbey in Lorsch in Germany. The *Chapel of the Madonna* inside the abbey was decorated by Michelangelo Braidi (1595). A turn-off to the right of the main road leads to the hamlet of **Visciano** (elev. 206 m), near which stands the church of **Santa Pudenziana**\* (12th-13th cent.), built using spoil from Roman buildings (capitals, good quality marble, roof tiles and fragments of floor mosaic). Frescoes of considerable interest have been found on the walls, some of them (behind the facade) painted at the time of the building's construction. The main road leads on to **Otricoli** (elev. 209 m, pop. 1,827), which grew up over the remains of the ancient *Ocriculum* (from the old Umbrian word

"ocre," meaning a hill), a town with an interesting layout, enclosed between arcaded rows of buildings which still display their ancient use as a place where coaches stopped to change horses. In the main square stands the ancient church of **Santa Maria Assunta** (7th or 9th cent.), which was drastically remodeled in the 18th century. Inside the church is a *Maestà*, a 13th-century painting similar in style to works by Simeone and Machilone. 1.5 km outside the town is ancient **Ocriculum**, an archaeological site with the remains of a large *theater*, adjoining a monumental arcaded substructure. On the flatter part of the site stand the remains of part of the ancient *Baths* (2nd cent. AD), including an octagonal room whose large mosaic floor depicting sea creatures is now in the Vatican Museums; to the south is the *amphitheater*, partly constructed and partly hewn out of the rock.

12 km to the southeast of Otricoli is **Calvi dell'Umbria** (elev. 401 m, pop. 1,804), a charming old village overlooking the Tiber valley, noted above all for its rare **Nativity Scene**\*, created in 1546 by Giovanni and Raffaele da Montereale and displayed in the church of *Sant'Antonio*: more than thirty large glazed terracotta figures were arranged on two levels in the 18th century to make room for the Ursuline Choir behind.

### Amelia

Attractively situated atop a limestone knoll between the Tiber and Nera valleys, the town of Amelia (elev. 406 m, pop. 11,342) has been inhabited since ancient Umbrian times. The historic center, with its array of fine architecture from Romanesque times to the 18th century, is one of the most interesting in the whole of southern Umbria. The atmosphere of the town is enhanced by the splendid surrounding countryside, which was once celebrated for the medicinal properties of its apples, as well as for its pears and willow trees. Founded in 1134 BC, the town was enclosed by an imposing wall in the 3rd century BC, and became a Roman *municipium* at the center of a highly fertile area dotted with farmhouses. Destroyed by the Goths under Totila, it later became a free town, and in 1307 came under church control. The only entrance to the town (because of the morphology of the site) is through the *Porta Romana*, and up along Via della Repubblica to the center. To the right is Piazza Augusto Vera, where stands the church of *San Francesco*. A brief detour to the left of Via della Repubblica leads to the imposing Palazzo Farrattini. Via della Repubblica continues up to the higher part of the town, where Via Cavour follows what would have been the path of the second walls, tracing a contour line around the hill. The *Arco di Piazza*, an archway reconstructed in the Middle Ages using older material, leads into Piazza Marconi, which has elegant 15th- and 16th-century buildings. The itinerary continues along the straight – and level – Via Garibaldi, to Piazza Matteotti, where the Palazzo Comunale (the Town Hall) stands. The church of *Sant'Agostino* is in nearby Via Cavour. Via Geraldini leads up to the Cathedral (dedicated to San Firmina, the patron saint of Amelia) on the site where the ancient acropolis lay.

**Porta Romana.** Remodeled in the 17th century in late Mannerist style, this gate, dating back to Roman Times, has always been the entrance to the walled town.

ti-Paladini collection (temporarily in Palazzo Petrignani), which includes works by Carlo Levi and Corrado Cagli.

**Palazzo Farrattini.** This is the finest noble palace in Amelia and was built by Antonio da Sangallo the Younger in the mid-16th century for the Farrattini family. Sangallo's design was only partly realized, thus sparing the large cistern from the Roman baths (it was transformed into a *viridarium*). Inside the building are two 2nd-century Roman bath mosaics (not accessible to visitors), still in their original position.

**Piazza Marconi.** This square stands on the top of the hill, once occupied by the ancient acropolis, access to which was through the present-day *Arco di Piazza*, a medieval archway made from the fornices of an ancient construction over which was built the **Loggia del Banditore** (where the town crier made his

*A view of Amelia with the Cathedral on the top of the hill*

To the sides, long stretches of the limestone **polygonal walls*** (3rd cent. BC) can be seen.

**Santi Filippo e Giacomo.** Also known as the church of *San Francesco*, this building dates back to 1287. In 1664 the nave was shortened and two side portions were added; Late Baroque modernization was completed in 1767. On the wall that was formerly the back of the facade are fragments of popular votive frescoes from the 15th century. The *Chapel of Sant'Antonio* contains six *tombs* of the Geraldini family: the tomb of *Matteo* and *Elisabetta* ends with a niche containing a bas relief (*St. Anthony of Padua with Two Angels*), by Agostino di Duccio and his workshop (1477).

The adjacent Collegio Boccarini is to house the **Museo Archeologico Comunale**, whose exhibits will mostly be stone sculptures and Roman remains, in particular a fine neo-Attic marble altar from the 1st century BC. The civic collections will also include an **art gallery** of works currently kept in the town hall and in Palazzo Petrignani, together with the Con-

proclamations), with a sail-vaulted campanile and an 18th-century clock. On the right-hand side of the square stands **Palazzo Petrignani**, begun in 1571 by Bartolomeo Petrignani, left unfinished in 1601 upon the death of the head of the family (Monsignor Fantino Petrignani), and bought in 1603 from the Monte di Pietà pawnbrokers (it is now municipal property). The frescoes decorating the rooms on the piano nobile are by local craftsmen working under Livio Agresti; those in the antechamber and the first three rooms are traditionally attributed to the Zuccari school. The square ends with the 15th-century **Palazzo Nacci**, which has a fine doorway and courtyard with an elegant *loggetta*.

**Piazza Matteotti.** The square was built over a huge **Roman Cistern** from the 1st century BC (open Sat, 3pm-6pm; Sun, 10.30am-12.30pm and 3pm-6pm), divided into ten vaulted, communicating chambers and serving as a substructure for the forum above. Here stands the **Palazzo Comunale**, or Town Hall, renovated in the 18th century, in whose courtyard archaeological materials are temporarily arranged, awaiting the opening of the new museum in the former Boccarini college. The simple exterior belies the rich ornamentation of the interior, which includes a notable painted frieze (17th cent.) in the Council Chamber, inspired by works by Raphael, Giulio Romano, and Giulio Campagnola.

**Sant'Agostino.** Also known as *San Pancrazio*, this church was built in the 14th century. The facade was redesigned in 1477, and the large ogival portal is elaborately decorated. The interior, remodeled in 1747, has a single nave, with frescoes by Francesco Appiani (ceiling vault and dome) and, in the side altars, 16th-17th century paintings, including a *Trinity and Saints* by Giacinto Gemignani. The large scenes in the apse are by Francesco Appiani.

**Duomo.** Erected at the top of the ancient acropolis in the 11th-12th century, the Cathedral was destroyed by fire in 1629 and completely rebuilt in 1640-80. Of the original structure only the massive twelve-sided campanile (1050) remains. The facade was remodeled in 1887. To the right of the entrance is a Romanesque pillar, to which St. Firmina, the patron saint of Amelia, is said to have been tied and martyred. The two banners on either side of the entrance to the 2nd chapel on the right, which are of Turkish origin, were taken at the Battle of Candia; inside the chapel are the tombs of Baldo and Bartolomeo Farrattini by Ippolito Scalza. The Oratory of the Sacrament contains two canvases by Niccolò Cercignani and a *Last Supper* by Giovan Francesco d'Amelia (1538); in the presbytery are frescoes of saints by Luigi Fontana dedicated to the town's protectors, whose relics are kept below the 1648 altar. On the first Saturday of each month, in May and on 15 August, a painting by Maestro dell'Assunta (*Assumption of the Blessed Virgin*) is displayed in the transept on the left. This area leads to the chapel of the winter choir, which has a 16th-century wooden *Crucifix*. The *Tomb of Bishop Giovanni Geraldini* (1476) was reassembled in the first chapel on the left after the loss of some of its architectural elements and bas reliefs.

The road to Orvieto leads out of Amelia and across the deep *Fosso Grande*, a deep gorge that separates two quite distinct landscapes: to the right of the river (facing downstream) are holm-oak woods that form a backdrop to small fortified towns, such as Collicello, Frattuccia and Toscolano; the scenery on the other side of the river meanwhile is dominated by farmland, pas-

ture and chestnut and oak woods. Along the old Amerina road, which followed a slightly different course from today's state road of the same name, are the villages of Sambucetole, Castel dell'Aquila and **Avigliano Umbro** (elev. 441 m), where the *Dunarobba Forest Visitors Center* (see below, visits by request, tel. 0744933701) has information panels and fossilized exhibits. In a brick quarry near the village of **Dunarobba** (elev. 448 m), are the remains of a **petrified forest**\* dating back to the Pliocene period (p. 167). The most interesting of this phenomenon from a scientific point of view is that the large tree trunks, which have preserved their ligneous structure, still stand in their original position. Recent studies have established that the forest was situated on the edge of Lake Tiberino, along a river that flowed from Todi to the Terni depression. The site is open to visitors (guided tours only) at different times throughout the year (tel. 0744940348). The main town in this area is **Montecastrilli** (elev. 391 m, pop. 4,500; 19 km north-east di Amelia), a fortified town with characteristic battlements. The church *of San Nicolò* has paintings by Bartolomeo Barbiani and Andrea Polinori; in the historic center is the *Convent of the Poor Clares*, with a large altarpiece by Girolamo Troppa (1678).

## Giove

A small town (elev. 292 m, pop. 1,717) surrounded by the remains of its fortifications and dominated by the imposing *Palazzo Ducale* (17th cent.), which belonged to the dukes of Acquarone and with an unusual spiral ramp designed to be used by horse-drawn carriages. The nearby *parish church of Santa Maria Assunta* (1775) has a late 15th-century painting. A few kilometers from Giove, in a panoramic position on a terrace overlooking the Tiber is **Attigliano** (elev. 95 m, pop. 1,755), a late medieval stronghold owned by the Orsini and Colonna families.

## Lugnano in Teverina

This small town (elev. 419 m, pop. 1,594), a 10.6 km drive from Amelia, began life as a stronghold atop a high, isolated hill that was contested by Todi, Orvieto, and Amelia. Rising majestically above the elegant noble homes (including the 16th-century *Palazzo Ridolfi-Farnese*, now the municipal hall) is the collegiate church of **Santa Maria Assunta**\*, regarded as one of the most important Romanesque buildings in Umbria. A 12th-century portico on twisted and smooth columns precedes the facade, which has double gables and a central rose window formed by a double ring of radial tracery. The tall, narrow nave and side aisles are divided by columns with variously-shaped capitals; the raised apse has a tabernacle by Alunno (after 1482). The

## The Petrified Forest

Millions of years ago the area around Avigliano Umbro was crossed by a large river that ran from Todi to the plain around Terni, and which geologists consider to be the western branch of Lake Tiberino. This lake is believed to have been around 120 km long and 30 km across at its widest point, and to have stretched from Sansepolcro to the Terni plain, widening out at Perugia into a deep gulf that extended all the way to Spoleto.

The plain was periodically flooded by this unpredictable stretch of water, causing silt deposits that gradually engulfed the riverside vegetation.

Thanks to this, today's visitors can now see an entire forest several million years old, made of fossilized tree trunks standing exactly where they were and almost as they were, near the town of Dunarobba.

These huge sequoia-like trees, which could reach over a meter and a half in diameter, were buried by the silt and were severed between 5 and 10 meters above ground.

In the early 1980s demolition work on an old brick factory led to the discovery of a number of tree trunks, which dendrological and typological studies showed to be from the Pliocene age, a period of tremendous atmospheric upheaval, as the inclined position of the trunks suggests.

*The open fossil museum at Dunarobba*

hills cut through with gullies. From the 15th century it belonged to the d'Alviano family, who made it the capital of a small state. The head of the family, Bartolomeo, captain of the Republic of Venice, rebuilt the grand **Castle**, now the Town Hall, in the shape of a square with corner towers around a Renaissance courtyard. The most interesting part of the castle is the chapel, frescoed throughout by Giuseppe Bastiani (among others) at the end of the 18th century as a replacement for the previous 16th-century decoration. Three rooms with decorations and friezes attributed to Pordenone open off from the courtyard at ground-floor level. The building houses Roman remains and a small ethnographic collection documenting peasant life in the Tiber Valley.

### Oasi d'Alviano

Created in 1978 in an area of 800 hectares as part of the Parco Fluviale del Tevere, this wildlife reserve (run since 1990 by the international WWF) is set in a context of riverside and marshland vegetation. It encompasses the Lake Alviano reservoir, which was formed by building a dam across the Tiber in 1964. The rare migratory birds that visit the area make it particularly popular with bird-watchers.

### Guardea

This small town (elev. 387 m, pop. 1,789) was rebuilt at the foot of the hill. It is noted for its 17th-century *Palazzo dei Marsciano* (now the Town Hall), and the parish church of *Santi Pietro e Cesareo*, which has a work by Pietro Paolo Sensini (*Virgin of the Rosary*). Up on the hill above is the *Castello del Poggio*, with large 15th-century windows and an elegant courtyard.

### Baschi

Perched charmingly on a rocky spur, this town (elev. 165 m, pop. 2,726), is dominated by the 16th-century parish church of *San Nicolò*, rebuilt by Ippolito Scalza between 1575 and 1586. Inside is a fine **polyptych\*** by Giovanni di Paolo thought to have been painted in 1440, and paintings by Andrea Polinori and Pietro Paolo Sensini.

crypt under the church has a ceiling with beams and stone slabs held up on ten columns; on the altar is a venerated alabaster *Crucifix*. The Town Hall contains an **Antiquarium**, with a variety of archaeological material (1st century BC-5th century AD) found in a Roman country villa at Poggio Gramignano.

### Alviano

This characteristic village (elev. 251 m, pop. 1,427) nestles picturesquely between

# 7 The Valnerina and the territories of Norcia and Cascia

## Area profile

It is no coincidence that the preferred symbol in sacred and profane figurative art in this area is the humble bee: an industrious creature, mystical even, like the white bees that reputedly "flew in and out of the mouth" of St. Rita: a creature so emblematic of the natural, hard-working spirit of the inhabitants of Valnerina.

The best way to acquaint oneself with the area and become familiar with the Nera and its hinterland, and get to know the people, is to follow the winding river along the course it has carved out of the countryside, with its impenetrable ravines, sudden clearings and unspoiled corners, where bridges, mills, and churches look out onto the river. Untamed landscapes and awkward mountains have endowed the area with an air of mys-

*Thick woods and undulating meadows near Cascia*

ticism, whence emerged the spiritual ventures of Sts. Benedict, Rita, and Scolastica.

Castles and other towers peer out from on high at the slow-flowing Nera river and its affluents: the castles of Cerreto di Spoleto and of Ponte stand opposite each other, dominating the valleys of the Vigi and the Tessino, which in turn were created over chasms of rust-colored limestone. The steep slopes are cloaked in the typical Mediter-

ranean *macchia* or scrub, whereas the more gently sloping faces are occupied by oaks (Tazzo forest), maples, and beach, followed by the wide, open highland pastures of the Avendita, Castelluccio, and Santa Scolastica.

But the original countryside was profoundly altered by the hand of the local inhabitants, who, by felling the woods managed to carve out clearings for to graze their sheep; they also reclaimed land at the foot of the hills to sow *farro*, or spelt (a variety of cereal), lentils (for which those of Castelluccio are renowned), corn, and *cicerchie*, or grass-peas. Since times of yore, the Valnerina provided a well-trod thoroughfare linking the Tyrrhenian with the Adriatic, and the many archaeological finds indicate that the gorges of Ancarano, and the passes of Canapine and Civita, were inhabited in prehistoric times.

The main political and economic hub, however, remained Norcia and its environs, given its position as a boundary point, and the ample opportunities of integration between the two economies of plain and mountain.

The general pattern of the territory is fundamentally inherited from the communes, and is delineated by a dense network of routes along which rise castles and farmsteads (*ville*). The strip of terrain that leads southward to Monteleone di Spoleto and the border with Lazio, and in a northern direction toward the towns of central Valnerina, orbits on Cascia, the fulcrum of an early road system that splays out in all directions, protected by a dense pattern of castles and look-out towers that vary from 750 to 1000 meters above sea level.

A single element common to the entire area, which has deeply affected the local history, is the presence of earthquakes. The last came in 1997, and shook a vast area of the Apennines in Umbria and the Marche region.

# From Spoleto to Norcia and to Cascia

**Excursions to Norcia, Cascia and Terni, 132.6 km**

**A walk through Norcia** *(map on page 173)*

Our explorations take us from Spoleto along the 19th-century road (now state road 395 "Passo di Cerro") which comes to a head at the Cerro pass before dipping rapidly into the valley at Piedipaterno. Moving upriver along the Valnerina we come to Triponzo, and then Pontechiusita, where we turn off the state road and toward Preci in the hollow carved by the Castoriana (or Campiano) river, amid gorges of rust-colored limestone, where the backdrop on either side is punctuated by cas-

then proceeds along the Corno valley as far as Monteleone di Spoleto, whence, by means of the hilltop road of Coscerno-Aspra for Gavelli and Caso, we make our way down to the Nera valley at Sant'Anatolia di Narco (121 km from Spoleto). From here, we follow signs for the castles of Scheggino and Ferentillo until the river's confluence with the Velino, with the rowdy Marmore Falls (p. 156), where the sight of industrial complexes announce our arrival in Terni.

## 7 From Spoleto to Norcia - From Cascia to Terni

*[Map showing the route from Spoleto to Norcia and from Cascia to Terni, with locations including Foligno, Montefalco, Trevi, Pissignano, Fonti del Clitunno, Castèl Ritaldi, San Brizio, Spoleto, San Giovanni di Baiano, Monteluco, Scheggino, Ceselli, San Pietro in Valle, Ferentillo, Parco Fluviale del Nera, Arrone, Terni, Casc. d. Marmore, Piediluco, L. di Piediluco, Sellano, Pontechiusita, Cerreto di Spoleto, Borgo Cerreto, Ponte, San Làzzaro, Triponzo, Vallo di Nera, Castel San Felice, Sant'Anatolia di Narco, Caso, Gavelli, Roccaporena, Monteleone di Spoleto, Ruscio, Leonessa, Posta, Preci, Campi Vecchio, Abb. di S. Eutizio, Norcia, Serravalle, Agriano, Avendita, Cascia, Madonna della Neve, Castelluccio, Forca Canapine, M. Serano 1429, Castelsantangelo sul Nera, Parco Nazionale dei Monti Sibillini, MARCHE, LAZIO, and inset map with Gubbio, Perugia, Assisi, Orvieto, Spoleto, Terni)]*

tles and abbeys: such as the complex of Campi Vecchio, the abbey of Sant'Eutizio, and the church of San Salvatore. From the pass (elev. 1,008 m) we descend into the plain of Santa Scolastica, where the town of Norcia is nestled, the main point of attraction for the entire valley.

Taking a hillside route for 22 km from Norcia, we traverse Agriano and Avendita, to Cascia (which is also linked to Norcia via state roads).

Cascia is an important site for pilgrims coming to worship St. Rita. Our itinerary

## The Nera River

Amid tilled fields and lines of poplar trees, the Nera (the Tiber's largest tributary) flows clear and rapid for 116 km. The river issues from sources 747 m above sea level on the northern slopes of Mt. Patino, and gathers up water from the Sibillini mountains and from the mountain

*Descent by canoe on the Nera river*

chain of Mt. Velino (the catchment area is 1,454 sq.m). The lower stretch that emerges with the confluence of the Velino (the main tributary) at the Marmore Falls, is the home of the **Parco Fluviale del Nera**, under regional management. The park's very rich flora stems from the valley's humidity, and from the dense woods on the slopes. Species of oak, hornbeam, and ash are among the most diffuse trees. Many species have made this particular corner of the world for their habitat, particularly the migratory aquatic birds and the fish.

## Vallo di Nera

The village (elev. 470 m, pop. 449), an offshoot of the scattered municipality of the same name, is perched on the summit of a hill, and has conserved the annular layout of the fortifications established in the early 13th century. Pinewoods accompany the curving roadway, linked by steep transverse streets and enclosed within the ancient walls enhanced by defensive towers dating from the days of Corrado di Spoleto, a feudal lord of the 12th century. The city center is strictly pedestrian, not so much for restrictions on circulation as for the uncommonly narrow alleys over which bridges give access from house to house, making vehicle traffic impracticable. Through the wide opening made in the old walls we reach the church of **Santa Maria** (formerly San Francesco, 13th century) with a Gothic portal surmounted by a rose window and, inside, a large fresco cycle of a votive nature painted by 15th-century Umbrian artists from the Spoleto area (including the Maestro di Eggi and his school), and Marchigian painters, including Cola di Pietro da Camerino; together with Francesco di Antonio, the latter also frescoed the church's apse (1383) with *Scenes from the Life of Christ, the Virgin, Saints, and Prophets*. The geometrical and floral patterns of the sacristy are from the 15th century. The highest part of the hillside is occupied with the parish church of **San Giovanni Battista**, built in the 13th and 14th cent. (apse), enlarged and partially rebuilt in the 1500s (portal and rose window). The apse is embellished by frescoes (1536) by Jacopo Siculo, and inspired by the apse decorations for Spoleto Cathedral.

In the 18th-century *borgo* of the so-called *casali*, now largely used for farming purposes, stands

*A fortified town in the Valnerina*

the little church of **San Rocco**, which is preceded by a portico of 1681; the interiors are graced with frescoes, the *Madonna del Latte* (15th cent.), stuccoes, and other fresco decorations (16th-17th cent.). Along the well-worn road for Castel San Felice rises the altar dedicated to the **Madonna delle Forche**, embellished with frescoes attributed mainly to Jacopo Zabolino (1494).

## Borgo Cerreto

Nestled at the confluence of the Vigi and the Nera (elev. 357 m) rivers, Borgo Cerreto was drastically altered upon the building of the Nursina highway in the 1800s. After crossing the river we come to the church of **San Lorenzo**, raised between late 13th century and early 14th. The church's facade is notable for its plain design, pointed portal, and small 14th-century rose window; the interiors boast numerous votive frescoes datable to between the 14th and 16th centuries.

## Ponte

In Lombard times, Ponte was a *gastaldato* or fortified manor, of which remains are visible on the rugged spur (elev. 441 m); in the early Middle Ages the manor exercised its military and economic power over a vast area reaching Nursino and Casciano. Until the 14th century the territory was controlled by the **Pieve di Santa Maria**, a 12th-century Romanesque building with a rectangular facade adorned with an elaborate rose window, framed by mosaics and symbols of the Evangelists. The aisleless interior is adorned with frescoes by the Umbrian school (14th-15th cent.); the baptistery's font is composed of a huge, single slab of Roman origin. The design on the right-hand wall as you enter is a replica of the rose window. Continuing along the street which unfolds in a somewhat solitary fashion, we pass the *Rocchetta* (elev. 793 m), passing close to the sanctuary of the **Madonna della Stella**, founded in 1308 as a hermitage for Santa Croce at the behest of the Augustinians; it was abandoned in 1630, but rebuilt in 1833. The church was partly dug out of the hillside, and is surrounded by two dozen monk's cells, also carved out of the rock; the frescoes in the sanctuary are 14th century.

## Cerreto di Spoleto

Poised like a sentinel over the Valnerina, occupying one of the most arduous sections of the valley, Cerreto di Spoleto (elev. 557 m, pop. 1,153) once boasted a castle, of which one can still see remains of the fortified walls from the 13th century, together with a tall tower. The name itself spells out the town's checkered history, disputed by the Duchy of Spoleto for its strategic position and for the lush, productive surroundings. In the parish church are frescoes by Felice Damiani (*Virgin of the Rosary*, 1583) and by the so-called Pittore di Poreta (*Adoration of the Magi*). In the town hall one can admire the *Virgin and Child with Sts. Anthony Abbot and Lucy* again by Damiani, and a *Visitation* by Camillo Angelucci. In the lower part of town stands the fortified monastic complex of **San Giacomo** (14th cent.), renovated at the end of the Cinquecento; the 15th-century frescoes decorating the walls were salvaged. In a nearby room, perhaps once the presbytery of the original church, are several paintings attributed to an artist from the Foligno sphere (15th cent.).

Proceeding along the right bank of the river, we come to the tunnel excavated through Mt. Lo Stiglio, which gives access to the Cascia state road (320) that replaced the old section of the Triponzo road. Before reaching Triponzo itself we pass through another stretch of tunnel carved out of the cliff, bored by the Romans in the Republican age, as confirmed by the inscription on the rock (naming the quaestors), and still used by the 19th-century roadway.

## Triponzo

The town stands at 420 m above sea level, and takes its name from the three bridges over the Nera, the Corno, and their tributary. Of the medieval castle which dominated the surrounding plain remain the girdle of defense walls with their square towers, and a single tall 14th century watchtower. Worth seeing is the painted wood statue of the Madonna kept in the church of the *Carmine* (15th

cent.). A mere 2 km from the town we come to **Bagni di Triponzo** (elev. 453 m), with sulfurous spa waters that were appreciated by the Romans. The main facility was erected in 1887 by the bishop of Norcia, but later abandoned; now property of the local council, restoration on the facility is under way.

## The Castoriana Valley

At Pontechiusita we branch out of the Nera valley into the so-called Campiano valley, which marks the western border of the Parco Nazionale dei Monti Sibillini (p. 175). Inhabited from prehistoric times, in the 5th century it was chosen by Syrian monks as a hermitage, from which would later emerge a Benedictine complex, and with this the conversion into farmland of the territory, and the formation of a network of habitation that would be controlled by the powerful abbey of Sant'Eutizio. The landscape consists of a series of gentle eminences modeled by the Campiano river through the limestone structure of the red scales of the land, which has been intensively farmed.

## Preci

A short distance from the main road, Preci (elev. 596, pop. 939) rose emerged in the 13th century as a fortification, but was devastated by an earthquake in 1328, and destroyed by the inhabitants of Nursia twice in the course of the 16th century. It was completely renovated in the second half of the 1500s. Between the 16th and 18th centuries, the town's school of surgery gained fame all across Europe, which specialized in complaints of the eyes and in the removal of kidney stones; the institute was sustained by the abbey of Sant'Eutizio, with its hospital and exhaustive library. In the upper section of

town stands the parish church of **Santa Maria** (damaged by the 1997 earthquake). The temple boasts a 14th-century portal in the facade, and a second lateral portal in the left flank, from the following century, composed, however, of elements of earlier date. The interior boasts fresco fragments (14th-15th cent.); the movable articles such as the fine reliquary cabinets painted by Angelucci da Mevale in 1545, have been transferred elsewhere.

Taking a 4-km detour toward the southwest we come to **Roccanolfi** (elev. 775 m), a medieval castle notable for its decorative work of traditional elements, and its original defensive systems. The local parish church of *Sant'Andrea* (also damaged by the 1997 quake) harbors several panels of a 15th-century polyptych, stolen in 1970 and only partially retraced. Continuing up the same road for 8 km, we come to **Poggio di Croce** (elev. 938 m): the portal of the enchanting parish church of *Sant'Egidio* bears 15th-century decorations. In the church of the *Annunziata* is a work by Giovanni del Biondo (*Annunciation*, 1385).

## Abbazia di Sant'Eutizio*

According to tradition, the grottoes near the abbey were used as cells by the hermit monks, who at the close of the 6th century were under the spiritual guidance of Spes first, then of Eutizio. In the 10th century the abbey was the principal political and economic fulcrum of the area; until the 12th century, the Benedictine monastery steadily expanded its control and influence over its surroundings. However, decline was inevitable, and the abbey's land was gradually ceded to the commune of Norcia, the last in 1259. It was from Sant'Eutizio that stemmed one of the earliest manuscripts in the vulgar tongue, dated to the end of the 11th century. The entrance courtyard (open 9.30am-11.30am, 3.30 pm-6pm) is enclosed in buildings belonging to a small Benedictine community, leading to the **church** built in 1190 by a certain Maestro Pietro, as noted on an inscription on the lunette. The portal boasts a double lintel and rose window with a double round of colonnettes (1236); the campanile was erected in the 17th century over a preceding medieval structure. The aisleless interior is roofed with timber beams, the presbytery is raised; until the 1950s the church housed altar paintings of the 1600s; today the walls are frescoed by G.B. Crescenzi (1596), the so-called Pittore di Piedivalle (early17th cent.), and Cristoforo Roncalli (1602); over the main altar

hangs a *Crucifixion* by Nicola da Siena, preluding the elegant *sepulcher of Sant'Eutitius*, attributed to Rocco di Tommaso (1519). The carved and inlaid choir stalls were completed in the Seneca workshop in 1519. The sacristy contains a lectern by Antonio Seneca (1519); a 15th-century cabinet; various reliquaries, silverwork, and liturgical accouterments from the early 1600s. From the second court, graced with a fountain (a recycled pluteus) there leads off a small road to the hermits' grottoes. Currently the abbey is organizing a small gallery that will tell the story of the Preci school for surgery (p. 171).

## Toward the Ancarano Pass

The extensive plain that characterizes the Castoriana valley fostered the emergence of numerous settlements along the hill slopes, such as **Piedivalle** (elev. 611 m), surrounded by rich water sources and notable for the little church of *San Giovanni Battista* with frescoes from the 16th and 17th centuries in the first bay, and 15th-16th century votive frescoes in the second. Proceeding along the main road, at the rather isolated cemetery of Campi rises the church of **San Salvatore***, formerly the parish of Santa Maria; the building has a memorable gabled facade with two portals, one from the 14th century (left), the other the result of alterations made in the late 15th century. The interior boasts an *iconostasis* painted by Giovanni and Antonio Sparapane in 1464; a large *Crucifixion* in fresco by an Umbrian painter of the 1300s; and a *Descent into Limb* by Nicola da Siena. From here we continue to the close-knit village of **Campi Vecchio** (elev. 870 m), perched on the hill slopes with tight rows of houses on three levels. Once past the 14th-century gate giving access to the town, we come to **Sant'Andrea** (14th cent.), enlarged and enhanced by a handsome loggia in the 1500s. In a fine polychrome wooden screen is mounted an altar; on the left wall stands a fine intarsiated pulpit from Seneca workshop (16th cent.). Not far from this site rises the church of *Santa Maria di Piazza*, whose nave conserves frescoes attributed to Giovanni Sparapane, and fragments of various paintings of the 15th century. Next we reach the highest point of the valley, the **Forca d'Ancarano**, a pass at 1,008 m above sea level, where remains testifying to a sanctuary in the 5th century BC have come to light, and a small settlement datable to the 1st century BC.

# Norcia

The ancient town of *Nursia* grew on the edge of the broad, fertile catchment of Santa Scolastica, bordered by a circle of mountains and irrigated by the Sordo and Torbidone rivers, and the springs of San Martino, creating a basin which, together with its open countryside, fostered the emergence of the town (elev. 604, pop. 4,911). The original settlement is thought to have been founded in the 5th-4th century BC, and became the northern capital of the Sabini, but was overrun and endowed with its defense wall by the Romans in 209 BC. The early accessibility of the town made it a fundamental crossroads for travelers along the Via Flaminia and the Adriatic; this leading territorial role was maintained through until the 16th century. After a spell as a diocese in the 5th

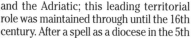

*Specialties from Norcia*

century, despoiled by the Goths and invaded by the Longobards and Saracens, Norcia became a thriving, free commune, equipped in the 13th century with a new defensive curtain that largely repeated the original Roman one. The area was shaken by terrible quakes in the centuries that followed: in 1328 the medieval town was razed to the ground, leaving only the defensive walls standing (still visible); further devastation followed in 1567, 1703, and 1730, such that the local authorities prohibited constructions of over two stories. But Norcia and its environs are not known for this destruction alone: its fame rests on a centuries-long perfection of local craft and farming. In the Middle Ages and the Renaissance, local wools and jewelry were most sought-after; today, as in the past, very popular are the meats (pork) produced by the

**Norcia** 1: 7 500 (1 cm = 75 m)

MADONNA D. NEVE km 15 - VIA SALARIA S.S.4 km 37

*Norcini* (butchers), and the black truffles, whose ripening is celebrated with a festival in February.

Our itinerary takes its cue from Porta Romana, which leads out into Corso Sertorio and off to the main town square, entitled to St. Benedict, born 480 and founder of the monastic orders in the west (feast day 21 March). We continue up Via Anicia, which climbs to the eastern sector of town, leading into the square graced by Sant'Agostino Minore (or Sant'Agostinuccio). Once past Santa Maria della Pace we come to Porta San Giovanni, with the church of the same name, near which an unusual little building stands, the so-called Edicola (shrine). Along Via Gioberti we return to Via Sertorio, and thence back to Porta Romana. On the west of the town the land has been turned into water-meadows, the only one of its kind in peninsular Italy, with fields irrigated permanently by underground springs at a constant temperature.

**Piazza San Benedetto\*** (B2). The square is arranged around the historical buildings along its borders, a collection point for the town's history and a fulcrum of the urban layout. At the center of the piazza stands the *monument to St. Benedict* by Giuseppe Prinzi (1880). The northeast flank is closed off by the **Palazzo Comunale**, whose medieval prospect and loggia were reconstructed (1876) after the quake of 1859, and decorated with two lions at the foot of the steps (by Domenico Mollaioli). Conserved in the *Sala del Consiglio* are the superb wooden stalls of the Prior and of the Consul (16th cent.), together with the pews for the councilors; the council coats of arms on the walls are from the 1400s. After the earthquake of 1979, the simulated tapestries from the *Sala dei Quaranta* were removed; these were created using plant

essences and decorated with allegorical figures of the four corners of the world (awaiting restoration). The neighboring *Priori Chapel* conserves the highly elaborate gilded silver reliquary of St. Benedict (1450) in Gothic-Renaissance style.

**San Benedetto\*** (B2). Tradition has it that the church was erected in the early Middle Ages over the house of the saint's family home. Though remodeled several times, the church has kept its 14th-century facade; it was reconstructed after 1859, but only in the upper part, with a fine Gothic portal complete with relief designs and wooden imposts in 1578. Along the right flank stands the 16th-century **Porticato delle Misure**, an arcade in which a stone slab carries a set of nine measurements for local cereal crops. The church's interior is graced with frescoes of the *Madonna and Norcia Saints* by Vincenzo Manenti, and an imposing 16th-century choir in engraved wood; two steps on the apse lead down to the crypt, a small chamber with a nave and two aisles, which tradition suggests was the place Benedict and his twin sister Scolastica were born; the crypt contains a *St. Benedict and Totila* by Filippo Napoletano (1621), and a *Raising of Lazarus* by Michelangelo Carducci (1560).

**Duomo** (B-C2). Set slightly back from the piazza, the Cathedral is entitled to Santa Maria Argentea, like the early medieval parish church demolished in 1554 to make way for the rocca, or fortress (see below). The church is notable for its thick, sloping walls, an anti-quake device invented in the 18th century, adopted after the terrible earthquakes of 1703 and 1730; restored after the 1859 quake, it was damaged again in 1997. The interiors keeps works by Giuseppe Paladini (1756), and Cristoforo Roncalli; noteworthy marbles carved by François Duquesnoy; and a detached fresco from the Sparapane workshop (1528).

On 9 December Norcia is lit up with the so-called **"Fire of the Faoni"**. The path of the miraculous translation of the Holy House of Loreto is illuminated by immense pyres, one for each of the town's neighborhoods; the winning pyre is the first-lit, the largest, and the one with the most powerful flames.

*Piazza San Benedetto, with the Palazzo Comunale and San Benedetto*

**Castellina\*** (B2). This grandiose fortified building was commissioned by Pope Julius III as the seat of the apostolic governors to designs by Vignola (1554). The interiors bear witness to the substructures of the parish church of Santa Maria Argentea and the Palazzo del Po-

*The lunette over the entrance of the church of San Benedetto, at Norcia*

destà, demolished to make way for the fortress. Only partially impaired by the earthquakes of the 1700s, the building has conserved its square plan, reinforced at each corner by a tower with a sloping escarpment. The togaed Roman statue was mistakenly identified as Vespaia Polla, the mother of Emperor Vespasiano and a native of Norcia. The Castellina now hosts the **Museo Civico-Diocesano**, with paintings and sculptures from Norcia and environs; the museum was closed after the earthquake of 1979 and is currently being completely reorganized. The collections include a *Painted Crucifix* from the early 13th century, and a *Risen Christ* by Nicola da Siena (ca. 1450); together with stone sculptures by Giovanni Dalmata, and a glazed terracotta *Annunciation* by Luca della Robbia.

**Sant'Agostino** (B2). Built in the 1300s, the church was renovated in the 17th century in the Baroque style, though without creating clashes with the earlier frescoes (14th-16th cent.), of which largish sections have survived. In addition to the votive frescoes executed from the 1300s to the 1500s, are works by Gaspare Angelucci da Mevale (1541), and G.B. di Giovannofrio (1497

**Via Anicia**. This street leads to the northeast sector of the town, wedged between the products of the building programs of the 17th and 18th century. Worthy of note are *Palazzo Bucchi* (17th cent.) and *Palazzo Colizzi* (17th-18th cent.).
A little further on we encounter the 16th-century *Oratorio della Confraternita dei Cinturati di Sant'Agostino Minore* (an oratory called fondly by the locals **Sant'Agostinuccio**). The church has an elaborate gilded wooden ceiling; finely-crafted sculptures line the walls, together with

the stalls for the order's members (both ceiling and stalls from the 1600s); over the Baroque altar hangs a 15th-century *Crucifix*.

**Edicola\*** (A2). Known also as the *Tempietto*, this little shrine was created in 1354 by a certain Vanni Tuzi, and is a discreet monument in limestone, built on a square plan, as a votive stopping-place. A keen eye will pick out the curious admixture of classical architectural elements and the series of sculpted geometric, zoomorphic, and anthropomorphic designs of the decoration.

At 12 km from the town, going south, we proceed steeply down to the Renaissance church of the **Madonna della Neve** (1565-71), which the quake of 1979 reduced to just the four arms, somehow sparing the fresco decorations of the niches, executed between 1570 and 1584 by the brothers Camillo and Fabio Angelucci.

## Parco Nazionale dei Sibillini

From the road that winds its way up to the Civita pass, a picturesque route passes into the national park, which still resounds with the mythical past of the Apennine Sybil, and the popular legends of Guerin Meschino, names that are reflected in the localities, such as the so-called grotto of Meschino, and Mt. Sibilla. The park was set up in 1993, and extends through some 70,000 hectares of protected land in Umbria and the Marche, reaching heights that vary between 500 m to 2,476 m (Mt. Vettore). Here we can witness a typical limestone landscape; the peaks are not high, the slopes are sheer, with steep cliffs; oaks, pines, hornbeam, and beach trees dominating the higher reaches. Equally abundant is the water table, with copious springs and courses cutting through the valley in with deep gashes, the spectacle they offer is enhanced by the glacial residue they contain. But what offers a truly splendid sight is the huge carsic catchment of the **Piano Grande\*** (elev. 1,270 m), reached after the Santa Croce pass (elev. 813 m) with its splendid view over Norcia and the valley basin. This impressive natural "amphitheater," dominated at the east by the tall chain of the Sibillini is, forms, with the three smaller basins of Piano Perduto, Piano dei Pantani, and Piano Piccolo, the system of the **Castelluccio Plateau**, considered the largest single closed carsic catchment in Italy (a full 18 km across).

The outstanding quality of the environment, with its rare and varied flora, comprises numerous geographical features specific to the area. The lentil crops prelude our entry into **Castelluccio** (elev. 1,452 m), which dominates the Piano Grande and the Piano Perduto from a point of outstanding beauty. Of the old castle in the political orbit of Norcia, which once provided protection for the east side of town and the pastures, remains the church of *Santa Maria Assunta*, built in the first half of the 1500s and having a central plan with an octagonal dome.

Before reaching Cascia, it is worth visiting several villages scattered over the hills and mountains: in particular **Agriano** (elev. 912 m) with the church of *San Vito* with its Baroque interiors; **Avendita** (elev. 873 m),

where many vestiges of the Roman presence have been brought to light; and **Fogliano** (elev. 827 m), over which the vestiges of the *Castello di Frenfano* continue to keep guard.

## Cascia

Founded in the Middle Ages as a hillside castle in a dominant position overlooking the thoroughfares between the Nursia range and the Roman Campagna, over the centuries Cascia (elev. 653 m, pop. 3,264) was regularly overrun by the Longobards and Saracens; was contested by Spoleto; the Church, the Kingdom of Naples, by Norcia and above all by the cruel force of the earthquakes, which determined urban renewal patterns. This also explains why today Cascia's historic center is so bland and characterless, impaired by all the modern transformation effected to accommodate the influx of devotees to St. Rita, who was born in the nearby town of Roccaporena. Several monuments replete with art works are a reminder that Cascia served as the political and cultural pole for its environs.

## Lentils and hang-gliding: the rebirth of the Castelluccio highlands

Fry a little garlic, together with some *puntarelle* (a kind of vegetable) and when they are nicely browned, add the tomato and sausage meat to complete the

*Hang-gliding acrobatics*

Norcia dish known as "lentils, *puntarelle*, and sausage," a dish that the inhabitants of the Castelluccio highland invented to do honor to their famous local lentils.

The fields of lentils lie some 1,400 meters above sea level, a very tasty small, green variety, much appreciated for its flavor and its brief cooking time, and the compact form of the seed, which withstands the winter cold in this broad plateau on the Sibillini mountain chain. At one end of the Piano Grande the town of Castelluccio (elev. 1,452 m) overlooks the plain of abundant water sources, and is covered by a thick blanket

of flowers, so magnificent that it has earned the name "Fioritura dei Piani." It is an explosion of colors – from poppy red to narcissus white, with fior-de-lys and the yellow of the lentil flowers themselves, transforming the entire plain into a bed of many colors. Many will tell you that the best position to admire this stretch of almost 1,300 hectares of land is from the air, in a hang-glider. The experts take advantage of tall peaks of Castelluccio, using them as a kind of trampoline for their antics. Assisted by upcurrents and galvanized by the breathtaking views, the hang-gliders soar over the plain in panoramic leaps, gliding over the peaks and rivulets, which brim with rainwater – especially when the snow is melting.

*Local peas, lentils, and chick-peas*

At the entrance to the town is the church of **San Francesco**, rebuilt in 1339, and again in 1424, graced by a facade with a fine rose window (1424); the interior, transformed in the 1600s and then in 1738, presents an elaborate program of Baroque stuccowork and works by Nicola da Siena, Bartolomeo di Tommaso, and Antonio Carocci; of particular note are the wooden *choir stalls\** of Gothic manufacture (apse), and the *Ascension* (1596, left transept), the last known work of Niccolò Pomarancio. Emerging from the east portal we come to the former church of **Sant'Antonio Abate** (14th-15th cent.), now the municipal museum, with altarpieces and furnishings from the 17th to 18th centuries, plus to important cycles of the 15th century: the sixteen panels with the *Scenes from the Life of St. Antony Abbot*, attributed to the Maestro della Dormitio di Terni (apse), a *Tales of the Passion* by Nicolò da Siena (1461, choir of the former monastery). Back within the old walls, near the Porta di Santa Maria (or Leonina), we come to the collegiate church of **Santa Maria**, an ancient parish church erected in the 12th century, and enlarged in the 15th, and then rebuilt in 1532; the church contains frescoes datable to between the 15th and 17th century, including a panel 1547) by Gaspare and Camillo Angelucci, and the *Mysteries of the Rosary* by Niccolò Frangipani; a small chapel has been furnished with the font at which St. Rita was purportedly baptized in 1381. Passing down the right of the church we take a brief detour to the church of *Santa Margherita*, whose convent accommodates a small museum, the *Raccolta Etnografica*, that illustrates the cycle of domestic cloth production. Again at Santa Maria, we continue to the basilica of Santa Rita, in a succession of town houses, each one restyled to some extent: **Palazzo Carli** (16th cent.), seat of the municipal library and archives; **Palazzo Frenfanelli** (16th cent.), now housing the municipal council; and **Palazzo Santi**, which has recently welcomed the *Museo Civico*, comprising an archaeological section and picture gallery. Dis-

*Sainta Rita Chapel, in the basilica at Cascia*

played in the first are finds that hark back to the 8th century BC; in the second, paintings of local provenance (16th-18th cent.), and wood sculptures (13th cent.), including a statue of *St. Sebastian* attributed to the workshop of Antonio Rizzo.

Thus we come to the religious hub of the town, dominated by the impressive basilica of **Santa Rita** (1937-47) on the former site of the early Augustinian church annexed to the convent in which the saint died (1457). The building, which is slightly outsize with respect to the surrounding fabric, mixing imitation Byzantine and Romanesque styles, was built to designs by the Vatican engineer Mons. Spirito Maria Chiapetta; the interiors are replete with marble and fresco decorations, and conserve on the high altar the relic of the Corpus Christi; in Santa Rita Chapel, the mummified body of the saint is laid out in a crystal urn set in silver; the furnishings of the presbytery are by Giacomo Manzù. The monastery conserves remembrances of the saint such as the grape vine she planted, the hive of the bees, and the cell in which she passed away.

On 17 January the shepherds of Cascia and the "Santesi" assemble to celebrate St. Anthony, protector of animals: horses, mules, cows, cats and dogs, all blessed and done up for the parade through the town with all the dignity of their owners.

Some 5.5 km from Cascia we come to **Roccaporena** (elev. 707 m), the birthplace of St. Rita. The house in which she came into the world was converted to a church in 1630; near the church in which the saint was married in 1946 a *sanctuary* was erected in 1946 with a house for pilgrims. The town is dominated by a pointed hill, known as Rita's cliff (*scoglio*), because it was her preferred retreat for prayer.

## Monteleone di Spoleto

The vantage point for control over the roadways gave Monteleone (elev. 978 m, pop. 668) its strategic importance; the town's spatial organization pivots on two contrasting nuclei: one fans out from the fortress that was destroyed and walled up in the early Middle Ages, whereas the

## The farmer saint

When Rita Lotti was born in 1381 at Roccaporena, an unassuming group of houses in the Cascia neighborhood, no one could have predicted her imminent path to sainthood. After the first miracle of the swarm of bees that buzzed about her infant head without stinging her, Rita led a simple life with a brutal, cruel man, chosen by her family, and from whom she had twin sons. After the death of her parents and husband, Rita prayed that the sons might die innocent, before they could vindicate their father, and pleaded with God to let her enter a convent so that she could be helped by her patron saints John the Baptist, Augustine, and Nicola da Tolentino, who transferred her miraculously to the Augustinian monastery, where she remained until her death. The prodigious events tied to the life and death of Rita – suffering that might have assailed any woman or family –

*Santa Rita receives her wounds*

made her a "saint of the people," or a "saint of the impossible." Apart from the wound on her forehead caused by the spines of Christ's crown of thorns – a physical sign of suffering – it was the farming community that remained the prime movers of Rita's miracles: the white bees of birth, the black bees of death that disappear into the walls of the monastery (where they are reputed to dwell still); the withered grapevine, watered once a year as a vote of obedience and which finally put out shoots; or the white rose that flowered in winter amid the snow in the kitchen garden of the old house in Roccaporena. These were the kind of episodes that caught the imagination of the common folk, simple sensations and impressions that continue to draw worshipers to evoke the saint on 22 May each year by means of a procession through Cascia, concluding with the blessing of the roses she held so dear.

other nucleus has developed on an orthogonal, 15th-century plan. From the clearing dominated by *Palazzo Bernabò* (15th cent.), a set of steps climb to the *Torre dell'Orologio*, erected in place of the ancient gateway into the castle, of which scant vestiges remain. Serving as a visual bridge between the two nuclei is the church of **San Francesco**, built toward the end of the 1200s through the enlargement of an existing Benedictine building, and remodeled expensively at the end of the next century. The church presents a magnificent Gothic portal* that gives onto the two naves of unequal width. The main nave is decorated with fresco fragments datable to the 14th-16th century; the lower church has choirstalls decorated with figures of saints and geometrical patterns by a painter from southern Umbria (early 15th cent.). In the early 1900s, in the vicinity of the church an important necropolis was discovered, the **Colle del Capitano**, which was in use from the late Bronze Age. The most interesting object found so far comes from a tomb dating from the

mid-6th century BC: a wooden *biga* (two-horse chariot) clad in bronze plates with relief designs representing scenes from the life of Achilles; the piece is now in the Metropolitan Museum of Art, New York.

### Gavelli

Standing at 1,153 meters above sea level, Gavelli began its life as a medieval castle alongside the church of **San Michele Arcangelo**, which conserves various works by Spagna (from 1518 and 1523), and Bernardino di Nanni (1492). Visitors may be less attracted to the town itself than to the beauty of the *Piana di Gavelli*, a valley considered one of the finest natural scenery of the upcoming Coscerno-Aspra natural park, with centuries-old trees and the flora of the so-called Laghetto. After Gavelli we cross through an enchanting Apennine landscape dominated by Mt. Civitella (elev. 1,565), to **Caso** (elev. 667 m) with the church of *Santa Maria delle Grazie*, which still contains the shrine around which the present church was built; the walls are almost completely hidden by votive frescoes, including an eye-catching *Virgin on Horseback* (15th cent.), and an *Annunciation* by Spagna (1516-22).

## Sant'Anatolia di Narco

This small town (elev. 328 m, pop. 566) developed in medieval times around the castle (1198), and is enclosed by an elliptical circuit of walls (13th-14th cent.) reinforced by two 15th-century towers. Immediately outside the Porta della Madonna stands the **Oratorio di Santa Maria delle Grazie** (1572-75), which was damaged by the 1997 earthquake; a fresco by the Maestro di Eggi is kept at the high altar.

Briefly returning up the Valnerina road, we come to **Castel San Felice** (elev. 334), whose original nucleus grew at the foot of the hillside around the church of *San Felice di Narco*\*, built in 1194. The temple is held to be one of the finest examples of the Spoleto Romanesque style, typified by the double lintel; in the corbel table and rose window appear symbols of the Evangelists, and jambs are carved with geometrical motifs. The high-relief marble frieze below the rose window tells the legend of Sts. Felix and Maurus, a metaphor for the reclamation efforts – both physical and spiritual – of the inhabitants.

## Scheggino

This place (elev. 282 m, pop. 487) lives in close symbiosis with the Nera river: the flowing waters lap against the riverfront houses, and a small canal cuts the town in half. Around the triangular castle with its tall tower, a few vestiges of the original solid defense walls remain (13th-14th cent.), put to the test by the memorable offensive mounted by the Spoletini, and made famous particularly by the steadfast efforts of the town's womenfolk. The 13th-century church of **San Nicola**, completely rebuilt at the end of the 1500s, boasts some frescoes by Giovanni di Girolamo (1526, regrettably very worn), concluded by Piermarino di Giacomo (1553).

## San Pietro in Valle\*

The hillock of Mt. Solenne, on which the abbey in question rises, was chosen as the seat of a hermits' retreat when in 720 Faroaldo II, the duke of Spoleto, retired to this place, and here founded a nucleus of the Benedictine order. After the destruction wrought by the Saracens (end 9th cent.), Otto III launched a restoration campaign (996), which was taken to its conclusion by his successor, Enrico III; the present building is the upshot of renovations carried out in the 1930s, and comprises a single hall with

trussed ceiling, very wide, rather reminiscent of vessels such as Cluny II and St. Michael's at Hildesheim. The imposing *bell tower*, dated to the second half of the 11th century (the same period as the sculptures of *Sts. Peter and Paul* that grace the southern door) harks back to Roman models, with Lombard interferences. In 1995 work was completed on the general restoration of the **cycle of frescoes**\* that decorated the nave, which is considered one of the most magnificent testaments to Romanesque art in Italy (late 12th-early 13th cent.). The cycle is arranged on four registers: the first three with scenes from the New and Old Testaments; the last, badly damaged, was probably taken up with ornamental elements and votive imagery; each scene is set in a simulated frame with salamonic columns, and commented by a *titulus*. The central apse is occupied by a huge fresco on three registers, attributed to the Maestro di Eggi (ca. 1445); of particular note is the **high altar**\*, a rare exemplar of Longobard mastery. In the right transept lies the so-called **sarcophagus of Faroaldo II**\*, a Roman urn (mid-3rd cent. BC), in which the church's founder was supposedly buried. At the back of the transept other sarcophagi are visible, these too from the 3rd century BC. The ex convent, now private property, will be turned into a conference center, with congress facilities.

## Ferentillo

In a wooded enclosure of great beauty at the mouth of the chasm known as Salto del Cieco (on the Nera), stands Ferentillo (elev. 260 m, pop. 1,977), divided into two sections named Matterella and Precetto, of

*The fortress that protected the valley of Ferentillo*

medieval origin and closely bound to the abbey of San Pietro in Valle. This ancient-looking town grew up in the valley bottom, but one can distinguish the two original settlements that climb the defense works on the mountain. Close to Matterella stands the 13th-century parish church of **Santa Maria**, rebuilt in the 1500s and altered in the 1900s, with interior decorations by Pierino Cesarei, Jacopo Siculo, and Piermatteo Piergili. The church of *Santo Stefano* dominates from above the quarter of Precetto, on two stories: the lower one datable to the 13th-14th century, the upper to the 1500s (enlarged in the 1700s). The crypt, which runs the full length of the vessel, after the construction of the upper story was used as a burial ground; today the mummies, which have brought a certain notoriety to the town, have been recomposed to create a cemetery-museum (visits: 10am-12.30pm, 2.30pm-5pm; in winter the opening time is earlier, and the closing later).

The hill that rises behind Matterella is crowned by an impressive **Rocca** or fortress, with bailey and cylindrical towers and a tall keep; forming a counterbalance to the fort is another fort, erected on the crag that overlooks Precetto.

### Toward Terni

As the valley opens out, becoming broader and more cultivated, once past Ferentillo we come to **Arrone** (elev. 243, pop. 2,810), a castle resting on the left bank of the Nera, which covered a role of primary importance in the Middle Ages for keeping watch over traffic headed for the town of Rieti. The newer part of the town spreads outside the castle perimeter, and pivots on the church of **Santa Maria Assunta**, whose 15th-century portal gives onto an aisled nave with frescoes by Francesco Cozza, Jacopo Siculo (1544), Vincenzo Tamagni, and Giovanni da Spoleto (1516); among the furnishings are fine sculptures in glazed terracotta dating from the 16th century (left apse).

The castle road climbs to the so-called **Terra**, the oldest section of the settlement, where rises the Gothic church of **San Giovanni Battista**, built in the 14th-15th century, and graced with a lively fresco cycle that embellishes the tribune (2nd half 15th cent.)

## The Mummies of Ferentillo

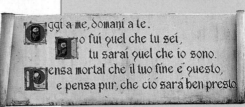

*The inscription at the entrance to the Museo delle Mummie*

"Giacomo had his workshop at the beginning of the old houses. He was a lad of twenty years old, with curly black hair, and in love with the pretty Agne- se..." This was only one of the countless stories people told about the various personalities that populate the Museo delle Mummie in Ferentillo.

At 18 km from Terni, the little town ensconced in a woody clearing was the stage of an extraordinary natural phenomenon: in the crypt of the church of Santo Stefano, 30 m above the valley below, are preserved almost intact the bodies of many local folks, foreigners, humble locals, nobles, who found their burial place here, where the unusual climatic conditions mummified their dead bodies. Around twenty cadavers lie in large cabinets around the walls and against the piers; the bodies lie there with their clothes, hair, nails, and facial hair intact.

Each mummy has a story behind it: one lost his life during a surgical operation (signs are visible); another was stabbed to death (the wounds are still evident); sister Aurelia is still proudly dressed in her habit, to the envy of her fellow sisters; meanwhile the gluttonous *messere,* who was never quite sated by his meals and indulged in every possible culinary excess was struck by an incurable illness that deformed his mouth and left him unable to eat, so that he now looks out with a fixed, anguished expression. And who could forget the story of the two Chinese newlyweds who sought relief from the curative waters against the cholera contracted in Rome, where they had perhaps traveled for the Holy Year. They too came in Ferentillo to die.

# 8 Orvieto and the western hills

## Area profile

The gentle undulating horizon, the local dialect and its historical roots, the red of the tufa stone contrasting with the surrounding rock and the river cobbles, make the landscape resemble Etruria of Pitigliano and Sovana and the culture of Viterbo and Rome rather than the region to which this district official belongs (since 1860). This is a corner of Umbria which extends from the cultivated reaches of the volcanic highlands around Lake Bolsena as far as the Tiber valley; from whatever direction one reaches the place, be it along the modern highway, or from the banks of Lake Bolsena along the antique causeways, the traveler is greeted by an extraordinary sight: there rises the town of Orvieto on its tall spur, defended by the sheer reddish face of the rock that plunges down into the vineyards of the Paglia valley. The natural environment is full of curious features, such as the tufaceous formations of Rocca Ripesena in the northwest, and Rocca Sberna in the southeast, all characterizing the *contado* of Orvieto, whose

*View across Orvieto, with the tall Torre Civica, and the Palazzo del Popolo to its left*

livelihood has always depended almost exclusively on farming. The two large necropolises, of the Crocifisso del Tufo and of Cannicella, testify to the Etruscan presence on this soil; on the southwest slopes one can admire the excavations of two decorated burial chambers (Settecamini and Castel Rubello). Scattered hamlets, churches, and fortified towers denote the intense inhabitation process on the farmland in the Middle Ages. The vast Orvieto catchment was split up into 34 *pivieri* and castles, as can be seen from the land register of 1292; and at the end of the 13th century the inhabitants were some 20,000 souls, "controlled" by a system of extraurban convents which developed toward the south at the same height as the town itself; among these, of monumental interest is the abbey complex of Santi Severo e Martirio. The territory from Orvieto to Città della Pieve saw the growth of numerous clusters on the surrounding hills, not far from the rubbly bed of the Chiani, constituting a fairly uniform settlement pattern based on sharecropping of corn, grape vines, and olives; but also on grazing and fishing, an activity on which they also earned on the tolls for transition over the fords and the felling of the woods. Today the towns and hamlets on the hillside have been converted into holiday resorts, though a taste of the farmer and crafts tradition has lingered. All the other local activities have migrated to the valley, boosted by the construction of the Autostrada del Sole, the motorway from Milan to Naples. Orvieto itself has spread out at the foot of the spur on which it stands, a fact that has ensured the integrity of the upper, historic part of the town. It is here that the many traditional events continue to be held, such as the Palombella festival, devoted to the dove symbolizing the Holy Spirit, which takes place on the Pentecost; since 1337, for the day of Corpus Domini, the townsfolk evoke the miracle of Santo Corporale of Bolsena with a procession and a historical pageant, in which 400 people take part.

# 8.1 Orvieto

**A circular itinerary from Piazza Cahen** *(map on pages 184-185)*

"The town of Urbiveto [*sic*] is very high and most strange," wrote in the mid-1300s Fazio degli Uberti, evoking the atmosphere of this ancient and mysterious place, bolstering the myths surrounding Orvieto (elev. 325 m, pop. 20,863). The town's main feature is the harmonious way it interrelates with the soaring tufa cliff, creating a continuum between the natural platform and the built-up fabric. The Etruscan settlement is illustrated in finds made over a period of 120 years of excavation, enabling researchers to identify the ancient Etruscan town of *Velzna*. Called *Volsinii* by the Romans it was the focus of the federal sanctuary of *Fanum Voltumnae*, which was almost surely sited in the Campo della Fiera. Thanks to its favorable position at the junction of the main arteries toward the Tyrrhenian and to the Po valley, in the 8th-7th century BC Orvieto flourished economically. In 264 BC the Romans sent in the army, theoretically to help the highborn subjects in their attempts to suppress the rising dissent among the subordinate population, but in reality to raze the city and deport its inhabitants. Those who managed to escape set up home on the banks of the Bolsena, and founded *Volsinii Novi*. However, the barbarian invasions of the 5th-6th century forced the population to return to the original hilltop site, where they founded the early-medieval citadel of *Ourbibentos* which, after few centuries became *Urbs Vetus* (meaning old city). During the 13th century Italy saw the formation of a network of city-states, or free communes, in which the towns were self-governing. Orvieto found itself with jurisdiction over a larger and larger area, from which it drew both human and economic resources. The pattern of the town also grew unchecked, leading to the so-called tripartite city of the 14th century: the Palazzo Comunale, the Cathedral flanked by the Palazzo Papale,

*The mosaic of the Assumption over the main entrance of Orvieto Cathedral*

and the new Palazzo del Popolo became the three functional poles of the town, whose center was the Palazzo dei Sette in which the seven magistrates of the art guilds (1292) met and expounded their ideas of good government. The arrival of the lords system marked the start of a political and economic crisis, aggravated by the arrival of the Black Death in 1348, which was not over until Orvieto had passed under the Papal States. This was the moment (1364) for the fortress commissioned by Cardinal Albornoz, to which was added the famous well, the Pozzo di San Patrizio, though not until 1527. From the 16th century urban renovation was begun, and changed the face of the town, transforming the medieval housing stock to designs by such master architects as Sangallo the Younger, Mosca, Raffaello di Montelupo, and above all Ippolito Scalza. This constant renewal continued right through the 1800s. Porta Cassia was demolished upon the construction of the water-powered funicular (1888) which (now run by electricity) makes it possible to swiftly climb to the top of town from the rail station below. In the late 20th century the town expanded rapidly in the plain, especially beyond the Paglia river, thereby consenting the safeguard of the historic center. This was helped by the creation of funiculars, elevators, and escalators for direct access to the town above. Besides improving the quality of life for the inhabitants, they enabled visitors to enjoy the history of the town, documented in the monuments and museums and through the tradition of wood craftsmanship, wrought iron, lacework, and above all pottery. Orvieto's past resounds with the handicraft of the medieval *vascillari*, masters of the production of majolica, and thanks to the colored *tesserae* of mosaics on the facade of the Cathedral this work continues to dazzle us even today.

Our itinerary begins in Piazzale Cahen (with the castle and well), and the three roads that lead out of the opposite side, we take Via Postierla (which continues into Via Soliana), which leads straight to the main piazza. After a brief diversion in Via Duomo (lined with shops), we proceed along Via Maitani as far as the church of San Francesco. Once in Via Ippolito Scalza we follow the contours of the hillside to take a look at the valley from Via Ripa Medici, then down Via Garibaldi we come to the small Piazza della Repubblica, commanded by the Palazzo Comunale or Loggia dei Mercanti and the church of Sant'Andrea. Leaving through Via Loggia dei Mercanti as far as Piazza de' Ranieri, we reach San Giovanni, and from here we descend along the banks of Ripe di Porta Maggiore, and then up to the church of San Giovenale. Via Malabranca runs on the flat until the inclined Via Filippeschi; this leads us back to Piazza della Repubblica. From here starts Corso Cavour and, level with the Torre del Moro on the left, Via della Costituente takes us to Piazza del Popolo, the third of the town's poles – where stands the superb palace in a dominating central position – and now used as a market square. Going round the Palazzo del Popolo as far as the Piazza Vivaria behind, and following the twisting Via della Pace, we come to Piazza XXIX Marzo to visit the remains of San Domenico, and below the nearby church, the Etruscan well, a superb feat of engineering.

**Rocca dell'Albornoz** (B4). Raised by order of Cardinal Albornoz in 1364 to designs by the military architects Ugolino di Montemarte and Giovanni Orsini, this fortress has been turned into a public garden. Destroyed in 1390, the fort was rebuilt on the behest of Pope Nicholas V in 1450-57 and a tower was added. In the decades that followed the complex fell into disrepair, and in 1888 the moats were filled in for the work on the funicular. Thanks to the repairs made to the chemin-de-ronde, visitors can proceed on foot to the late-13th-century *Porta Postierla* (or della Rocca), on an ogival plan with double archway, set into the 14th-century enclosure wall. Further up, in an alcove, stands the *statue of Boniface VIII*, datable to the end of the 13th century.

**Pozzo di San Patrizio\*** (A-B4). During the times of the Sack of Rome, Pope Clement VII decided to take refuge in Orvieto. To guarantee the supply of water during a siege, he had the famous castle well built. The task was entrusted to Antonio da Sangallo the Younger, who dreamed up a unique system in a double helix, thereby creating two separate, non-communicating routes up and down the well (visits 10am-6pm; in summer until 7pm). The part of the well that emerges above ground is a low cylindrical construction with two doors on opposite sides. The well is 62 meters deep and 13 wide, and its stairways wind down a central well in two spirals of 248 steps each, and wide enough to accommodate pack animals to bring up the water. Seventy-two windows give air and light to the stairways, while a small bridge crosses from one side to the other, just above the water line. The name "St. Patrick's" commonly used for this ingenious well (according to the Servite friars) refers to the medieval legend that suggested – in compliance with the Irish saint's practices – of spending a moment at the bottom of the well in order to purge one's sins, as if it were a kind of Purgatory, the third station of the afterlife. For others the name comes from the vague resemblance to the chasm in Ireland that the saint used to retire to for prayer.

**Tempio del Belvedere** (A3). On a panoramic clearing stand the ruins of this temple; the deity to which it is dedicated remains unknown, and the place was discovered only in 1828 and explored in 1920-23. The temple is Etruscan, tetrastyle, perhaps divided into three cells, and datable to the early 5th century BC. It appears to have been frequented up until the early decades of the 3rd century BC. Some of the statues of the entrance were exca-

*The spiral staircase in the Pozzo di San Patrizio, in Orvieto*

**Orvieto** 1:14 000 (1 cm = 140 m)

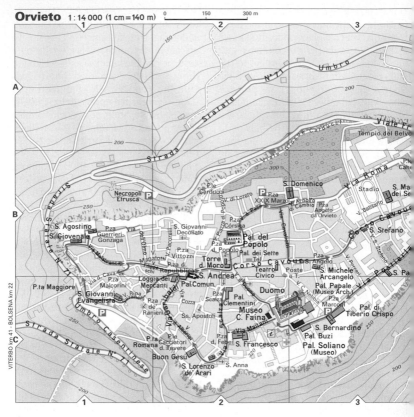

vated (now in the Museo Faina), together with decorative furnishings for the votive cell.

**Via Postierla** (B-C3). Accompanied by doorways and windows of medieval manufacture, that enliven the ancient borough of San Martino, we continue up this time-worn thoroughfare linking the religious center and Porta Postierla. The building work that took place in the 13th century in this corner of the town is documented by the complex of **San Paolo** (B3), a church and convent founded in 1221 by the Benedictine order, when groups of monks began to transfer their facilities to the top of the cliff. Restructured in the 16th and 17th centuries, the church boasts a ceiling and walls decorated by an artist in the circle of Pietro da Cortona (first half 17th cent.). Continuing up the same side we come to the **Palazzo di Tiberio Crispo**, nephew of Pope Paul III Farnese; the building was raised around the mid-1500s on an earlier design by Antonio da Sangallo the Younger, and is now converted to the council financial offices. Alongside stands the church of **San Bernardino** (C3), founded

1666, which contains a holy water stoup thought to be by Ippolito Scalza (1588), and a panel by Sinibaldo Ibi. Pierced by handsome two-light windows is the neighboring building, **Palazzo Buzi** (ca. 1580), the work of Scalza, which lost its portal and two windows to make it match the Palazzo Gualtiero next door.

**Duomo**\*\* (C2-3). Piazza Duomo was enlarged to give more room to the Cathedral, where seven steps of alternative white and red slabs lead up to one of the most impressive architectural creations of medieval Italy. The foundation stone was blessed by Pope Nicholas IV and set in place on 13 November 1290. Four centuries later the church was ready, and dedicated to Santa Maria della Stella, a name that was altered to *Santa Maria Assunta in Cielo* in 1800. In the first phase of building work local records document the presence of Fra Bevignate as director of works, or perhaps as chief administrator; the arrival on site of Lorenzo Maitani (1308) brought several radical innovations to the building's design, first the buttresses, and then the six huge rampant

Duomo, p. 188), together with the destruction of the stuccoes and frescoes commissioned from Scalza over the 16th and 17th centuries. From the piazza the visitor is confronted with a huge, three-part design in which the relief elements are both structural and decorative, lending uniformity, and the mosaic inserts accentuate the overall geometry of the architecture. The facade is an extraordinary synthesis of architecture and decorative detail; the building's skeleton is composed of four composite pillars that rise out of solid piers and terminate in a crown of spires. Three richly ornate portals punctuate the base; each cusped tympanum meets with a delicate loggia of trilobed arches that divides the facade horizontally. The upper section is set with a splendid rose window, and terminates in a repetition of the three-pointed scheme below. In 1320-30 the **bas-reliefs\*** that adorn the four pilasters between the portals were added, giving the facade a singular wealth of decorative detail.

Starting with the left pier, we can admire *Stories from the Old and New Testaments* and *Scenes from the Novissimi*: six series of stories from the Creation to Jubal unfold among twined ivy strands; acanthus leaves enclose two vertical series, and represent the outcome of the Biblical scenes, particularly Messianic prophesies; also amid acanthus leaves arranged vertically are *Stories of the Evangelists*; and finally, once again in a crown of ivy the *Last Judgment* is related. The bronze panels of the **central door** carry reliefs by Emilio Greco featuring the *Works of Mercy* (1964-70); the *Maestà* group (1325) in bronze nd marble in the lunette of the central doorway, has been removed for restoration. Above the piers the *Symbols of the Evangelists*, bronze statues by Maitani. The **rose window\*** with its double circle of column with interlaced arches is the work of Andrea Orcagna; at its center is the *Head of the Redeemer*. The figures of the *Four Doctors of the Church* decorate the corners of the panel into which the window is inserted; along the border are 52 relief heads of the 14th century. At either side, the 14th-century marble

arches, giving the building a new Gothic outlook, with extended transepts and a large four-sided tribune. Maitani was also responsible for the tripart facade (1310), clear reference to Siena Cathedral; soon after rose the Chapel of the Corporale 1350-55), and the San Brizio Chapel 1408), and the transept was completed. Maitani was not the only illustrious *capomaestro* at work on the Cathedral; there were also Andrea Pisano from 1347 to 1348, Andrea Orcagna (1359), Antonio Federighi (1415-56), who inserted the twelve Renaissance aedicules in the facade, and Antonio da Sangallo the Younger, who redid the door. In around 1890 conservative restoration was effected in a bid to restore the purity of the original design: the side altars and statues were removed (on exhibition soon at the Museo dell'Opera del

*The main portal of Orvieto Cathedral*

185

statues of the *Twelve Prophets*, surmounted by travertine statues of the *Apostles*, the work of Moschino, Ippolito Scalza, and Vico Scalza, Raffaello da Montelupo, Fabiano Toti and others (1556). The entire facade is embellished with fine **mosaics** that pick out the architectural elements and outline the various representations, the larger fields recounting the *Life of the Virgin*, this last almost entirely reworked over the centuries. Before entering the temple we recommend looking at the flanks in banded black and white stone: the one on the right opens with the **Porta di Postierla\***, a stunning ogival entrance in the Pisan style, perhaps once part of the demolished church of Santa Maria de Episcopatu, over which the new cathedral was founded; the left flank is ornamented with the marble statue by Antonio Federighi, the *Erythraean Sibyl*, one of this Tuscan artist's greatest accomplishments.

The **interior\*** (open Nov-Feb, 7.30am-12.45pm, 2.30pm-5.15pm; Mar and Oct, 7.30am-12.45pm, 2.30pm-6.15pm; Apr-Set, 7.30am-12.45pm, 2.30pm-7.45pm) follows a basilican plan, with a nave and aisles resting on ten columns and two piers capped with elaborate *capitals\**, some of which were carved by Fra Guglielmo da Pisa, and Ramo di Paganello. One is struck immediately by the boldness of the original Romanesque forms; the light effects are created by the light filtering through alabaster panels, and large four-light window in the apse, and further exalted by the soaring nave. The floor is in red Prodo limestone with a gradient from the facade to the apse, makes the vessel appear longer (88.33 m). After the holy water stoup (1485) by Antonio Federighi (nave) and the five semicircular chapels of the right-hand aisle, with some interesting remains of frescoes (14th-15th cent.), we come to the right transept, which gives access to the **Cappella Nova** (or **San Brizio Chapel**), one of the greatest examples of Italian painting. The **cycle of frescoes\*\*** that decorates the chapel, executed in part by Fra Angelico (1447-49) and Luca Signorelli (1499-1504), together with the space's unusual spatial concept, have made this chapel a totally unique expression of Italian art. In fact, Signorelli did not conceive it as a square chamber, but as a sphere in which all points have the same optical value focused on the viewer (open Nov-Feb, 10am-12.45pm, 2.30pm-5.15pm; Mar and Oct, 10am-12.45pm, 2.30pm-6.15pm; Apr-Set, 10am-12.45pm, 2.30pm-7.15pm). Between the two spandrels painted by Fra

## Orvieto Cathedral

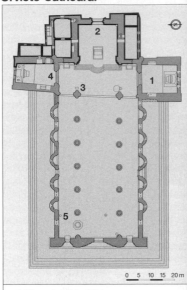

1 Chapel of San Brizio
2 Wooden choir by Giovanni Ammannati, Crucifix by Niccolò Nuti, frescoes by Ugolino di Prete Ilario
3 Pietà by Ippolito Scalza
4 Chapel of the Corporal
5 Maestà by Gentile da Fabriano

Angelico (with the assistance of Benozzo Gozzoli, Giovanni d'Antonio da Firenze and Giacomo da Poli), and the six spandrel by Signorelli reveal a huge technical gap due largely to the absolute care and prec sion of the former, and the pictorial syn thesis applied by Signorelli to create sense of unity. The theme is the *Last Jud ment (Finimondo)* framed in a fictive arch tectural framework, such as the colonnad in the lower part and the windows out which various illustrious personage loo down on the scene, carrying books o codices resting on the banister in an ill sionistic play of perspective which gives th viewer the feeling of having stepped int the painted scene. The center of the pre bytery (currently being restored) is ove shadowed by a large wooden **Crucifix\*** b the school of Maitani; along the walls ar placed **wood choirstalls\*** in Gothic styl carved and engraved by Giovanni Amma nati da Siena (1331-40 ca.). With many a sistants, Ugolino di Prete Ilario decorate the tribune walls with *Scenes from the Life Mary* (1370-80). In the left transept opens th **Chapel of the Corporale\*** (1350-55), chapel that takes its name from the **re quary** of the Corporale, which containe

Resurrection of the Flesh, *by Luca Signorelli (details), from the San Brizio Chapel in Orvieto Cathedral*

the sacred material of the miracle of Bolsena. A masterpiece of Italian craftsmanship, the reliquary is decorated with the translucent enamel technique, which involves incision with a burin of each scene on silver, and a further coat of enamel to accentuate the sense of depth. Today the sacred cloth is hung in the marble tabernacle of the Corporale (1358). The cycle that decorates the chapel is by Ugolino di Prete Ilario and assistants, though they were overpainted in 1855, and detached in the second half of the 1900 to retrieve the *sinopia*, or colored drawings beneath, which will be put on exhibit at the Museo dell'Opera; recent restoration work has reinstated the colors of an excellent panel by Lippo Memmi, the **Madonna dei Raccomandati\*** (1320). Finally, worth seeing at the start of the left aisle is an important fresco by Gentile da Fabriano (1425), a **Maestà\*** (recently restored).

**Palazzo Faina** (C2). On the opposite side from the Cathedral stands the **Museo "Claudio Faina"**, whose collection is the fruit of years of archaeological research made by Mauro Faina and his nephew Eugenio, who began in 1864. The collection vaunts a prolific aggregation of bucchero ware, bronzes, coinage, and masterpieces of antique goldwork and vase-painting, both Greek and Etruscan, mostly coming from the Orvieto area, covering a span of time from the Archaic to the Hellenistic periods. The ground story presents exhibits from the **Museo Civico Archeologico**, with the so-called *Venus of Cannicella\** (530-520 BC), a striking nude figure; and the *Etruscan sarcophagus\** (end 4th cent. BC), with remains of polychrome decoration and bas-reliefs. On the first story is the **Mostra Permanente "Gli Ori dei Faina,"** with jewelry datable from the 6th century BC to the early period of Roman rule. In 1868 the coin collection comprised some 3,000 pieces (origin unknown). The collection of painted vases includes certain examples of outstanding value, such as the black- and red-figure **Attic vases\*** (6th-5th cent. BC). The vases of Etruscan production are documented by the works of the Pittore di Micali (6th cent. BC), and those of the **Gruppo di Vanth\*** (320-300 BC). Completing the collection are prehistorical and protohistorical finds, datable from the Aeneolitic to the Iron Age.

**Palazzi Papali\***. After a radical restoration (still under way), the former papal palaces have been united, as it were, forming a single complex from the three distinct buildings, a design that the common use of tufa does not entirely cancel out. Alongside the apse of the Cathedral rises the **Palazzo di Urbano IV** (1262-64), the first to be

constructed, a facade of which is punctuated by a series of three-light windows which attenuate the checkerboard pattern typical of the town. Next to this stands **Palazzo di Gregorio** X (1272-73), a building with greater articulation that the previous one, but with similarities in the barrel-vaulted ceiling with timber trusses such as the large hall on the first story, and the three-light windows in the facade. Standing on its own on the south side is the **Palazzo di Martino** IV (1281-84), having a ground story open with an arcade and the facade orchestrated with two-light apertures. In 1983 the ground story was fitted out with the **Museo Archeologico Nazionale** which, according to a topographic schema, exhibits the material belonging to the archaeological sector of the Cathedral museum, together with finds from the Cannicella and Settecamini necropolises and other archaeological sites (visits: 8.30am-7.30pm). Worth noting are the two *stamnoi* bearing Dionysiac scenes; a *kantharos* with the head of Silenus and head of a Maenad; and the detached paintings from two tombs in Settecamini (2nd half 4th-early 3rd cent. BC).

*A vase of the so-called Gruppo di Vanth, Museo Claudio Faina, Orvieto*

**Palazzo Soliano\*** (C3). An austere and forbidding mass of tufa stone whose construction began in 1297 at the behest of Pope Boniface VIII and left unfinished upon his death, the ground story hosts the **Museo Emilio Greco**, set up in 1991 with works donated to the Sicilian artist's native town. The collection comprises 32 sculptures, 60 among lithographies, etchings, drawings dating from the early forties (*Il Lottatore*), to the 1980s.

**Museo dell'Opera del Duomo\*\***. Soon to be set up in the Palazzi Papali and in Palazzo Soliano is a broad exhibition of the city's collections, a move that will allow visitors also to admire the halls and rooms of these historic buildings. The collection in question (paintings, sculptures, and sacred furnishings from the Cathedral and various private bequests, has been arranged chronologically into two main groups: the medieval and early Renaissance works will be installed in the Palazzi Papali; those from the Renaissance, Mannerism, and 18th-century in Palazzo Soliano; the buildings will be connected. Among the most signal work to be put on display in the **Palazzo Papali** will be the *Virgin enthroned with Child and Angels\**, attributed to Coppo di Marcovaldo (ca. 1270); two small statues representing acolytes, headless, by Arnolfo di Cambio; a reliquary of the skull of St. Savinus\* in copper with gilded enamel, the handiwork of Ugolino di Vieri and Viva di Lando (1340); some *works\** of Simone Martini, the *polyptychs of Saints Dominic and Francis* (14th cent.). Other important works include the *Coronation of the Virgin\** (ca. 1340) attributed to Andrea Pisano, and a *Virgin with Child and four Saints*, recently reassigned to Lippo Vanni. Lastly, on exhibition will be the exceptional *strip of linen\**, designed and embroidered, datable to no later than 1290. **Palazzo Soliano** will accommodate the large *statues of the Apostles and Saints\** sculpted for the interior of the Cathedral, and removed at the end of the 1800s; the large *altarpieces* from the Cathedral and art works from the 1500s to 1700s. Other works of note are the *drawings* by Ippolito Scalza, which reproduce the various projects for the transformation of the interior of the Cathedral, datable to 1571-95.

The southern border of the square opens out on the so-called Giardino delle Grotte, where one can visit the **hypogeum of Santa Chiara**, one of the countless galleries dug out from the cliff over the centuries (around 1,200 have been discovered so far). The visit (with guide at 11am, 12.15pm, 4pm, 5.15pm) takes one through various chambers, some of which have their own well; these were used until the 1800s as a *frantoio* or oil mill, and then as a quarry for pozzolana.

**Casette dei Canonici** (C2-3). In stark contrast with the imposing Palazzi Papali, on the north side of the square stand a set of unpretentious houses erected in the 15th century for the canons. The curtain of houses is closed (northwest corner) by the

**Torre del Maurizio**, a tower on which is an automata cast in 1348 in the metal used for bell-making, which marked out the time for the Cathedral building site. The name of the tower supposedly stems from a corruption of "ariologium de muriccio," i.e., the site clock.

Taking **Via del Duomo** (C2), a street traced out in the 1200s to link the new urban fulcrum with the religious center, we come to *Piazza Gualtiero*, where stands a palace of the same name, whose facade has been embellished with a portal by Ippolito Scalza (transferred from Palazzo Buzi). Abutting the square is the 17th-century church of *San Giuseppe*, raised by the Società dei Falegnami, a guild; whereas on the left along Via de' Gualtieri we come to *Palazzo Mangrossi*, an example of Mannerist restraint.

**San Francesco** (C2). Begun in 1240, the church was enlarged at the bidding of St. Bonaventure, and consecrated in 1266; in this church Pope Boniface VIII proclaimed the canonization of Louis IX king of France (1297). The gabled frontage, with three pointed portals, is part of the original design; the interior, with a single nave and intercommunicating chapels, was originally a single vessel with five tall Gothic arches. On the high altar hangs a wood *Crucifix* of the school of Maitani (14th cent.); in the apse, a set of wood choirstalls carved and inlaid by Alessandro Tosi (1794).

In the first stretch of Via Scalza (C2) we come to **Palazzo Clementini**, one of Scalza's finest bequests to his native Orvieto, the architect to whom the city owes much of its renovation in the 1500s. Also called *Palazzo del Cornelio*, the building is currently the seat of a Liceo-Ginnasio (school), and of the *Biblioteca Comunale*, which conserves some exquisite incunabula and autograph documents. Also on the square rises the **Palazzo Monaldeschi della Cervara**, the abode of one of Orvieto's most distinguished families, and allies of the papacy (1570-75). Worth seeing in the interiors is the *Salone della Caminata* on the first floor, decorated with a cycle of frescoes painted by various hands from the workshop of Cesare Nebbia; the coffered ceiling is divided into 15 parts, and the panels are painted with astrological and mythological scenes.

**Via Scalza, Via Alberici** (C2). Following the curve of Via Scalza, we come to the church of **San Lorenzo de' Arari**, re-

built in 1291 in the Romanesque style; the interiors are hung with interesting paintings of the 14th-15th century; the main chapel houses the Etruscan altar from which the church takes its name, and supports the slab of today's altar. Annexed to the successive Clarissan monastery (15th-16th cent.) is the **Chiesa del Buon Gesù**, built in 1618 and decorated throughout with Baroque stuccoes and frescoes by Salvi Castellucci (1647). A line of old houses marks off the successive Via Alberici, onto which faces the **Palazzo Saracinelli**, the work of Scalza again, with a plain late-Renaissance facade that remained unfinished.

Descending beyond the city walls we reach Piazzale Cacciatori del Tevere, which is breached by **Porta Romana** (1882), built over the remains of an Etruscan gate. The parapet affords a splendid view of the valley, crossed in a straight line by the **medieval aqueduct** (13th cent.), a masterpiece of hydraulic engineering that started at the springs of the Alfina hills, traversing Settecamini, from where the water was channeled to the town via conduits made of lead.

**Palazzo del Comune** (B-C2). The palace was built in 1216-19 in *Piazza della Repubblica*, which is presumed to be the original gathering point and the site of the *Platea Comunis* of medieval times. Completely remodeled in 1573-81 to designs by Ippolito Scalza, the palazzo has a series of arches supporting a broad terrace with giant-order windows.

**Sant'Andrea**\* (C-C2). The site upon which the collegiate church was built was chosen back in Etruscan times for the construction of a temple, as testified by the walls of massive blocks of tufa brought to light, over which an original place of worship was founded in late Roman times (see fragments of geometric mosaics), followed by the early Christian church. The facade is the work of Vito di Marco da Siena, and next to it rises the ponderous **twelve-sided tower**\*, whose walls are covered with coats of arms applied during restoration work in 1926-28; the tower culminates in an embattled crown. The tower gave hospitality to Pope Innocent III, who proclaimed the Fourth Crusade (1281) in the presence of Charles II of Anjou; it is di-

*A sculpture from the Museo Emilio Greco in Orvieto*

189

vided into three naves by single-piece columns of oriental stone (2nd cent.) and boasts frescoes by the school of Signorelli (14th-15th cent.); a wooden altar attributed to Scalza; works by Piero di Puccio, Cesare Nebbia, and Angelo Righi.

In the neighboring Piazza dell'Erba stands **Palazzo Mancini**, one of the few 15th-century palaces left, and can be recognized by its four cross-mullioned windows.

**Via Loggia dei Mercanti** (B-C 1-2). Here we have come to the medieval quarter of Serancia, which bristles with noble family towers (the only intact ones are the *Torre Polidori*, and the *Torre Ranieri*), relics of the key social role played by this corner of the town. On the street stand the remains of the former Gothic church of **San Giovanni**, which belonged to the Order of Malta, with its memorable Gothic portal. At the end of the street, the church of the **Carmine** (since converted to a cultural venue of mixed functions), the outcome of remodeling (1308) by the Carmelites of the 13th-century Loggia dei Mercanti: the archways were filled in and a pointed basalt doorway was added.

**San Giovanni Evangelista** (C1). The church stands in the old square in one of the more characteristic medieval neighborhoods of the city. Founded in the year 916, the temple was rebuilt (1704) on a smaller scale and was reoriented after the demolition of 1687; the single, octagonal, nave develops round a marble stoup from the 1400s, supported by a 4th-century column.

**Porta Maggiore** (C1). Before reaching the main access point to the Etruscan part of the city, visitors should stop to look at the merloned wall that follows the western border of the cliff, a point from which one can admire on the opposite slopes several religious buildings belonging within the Orvieto diocese. We then leave via the city gate, which bears a marble statue of Pope Boniface VIII, dated 1294.

**San Giovenale\*** (B1). The sturdy tower that occupies the facade of San Giovenale reflects a past in which the church was fortified to justify its strategic position at the edge of the precipice. Rebuilt in

*Orvieto's church of Sant'Andrea, with its twelve-sided tower*

the year 1004 on an earlier religious building, the church has a nave and two aisles, supported on columns of tufa and covered in fine frescoes (13th-16th cent.); at either side of the high altar stand two lecterns with bases sculpted with human figures and symbolic animals (12th cent.). From the little piazza in front, one can see out to Cetona and the Paglia valley.

**Sant'Agostino** (B1). The Augustinians had in mind to build a building larger than the existing church of Santa Lucia, but the project was interrupted after the construction of the apse and parts of the nave (now a restaurant).
In 1487 the monks decided to renovate and reinforce the old building, adding a fine Gothic portal in limestone. The altars in gilded stucco and the organ belong to the 18th-century renovations. The former Augustinian convent behind the building, with its 16th-century cloister has been attributed by many to Antonio da Sangallo the Younger; today it houses an army barracks.

**Via Malabranca** (B1). Also known as **Palazzo Caravajal**, remodeled in the 1500s by Ippolito Scalza, the building overlooking the precipice is decorated with Latin mottoes in the lintels of the windows and in the fascia running below them, with an inscription by Scalza himself. At no. 22 rises the 15th-century **Palazzo Filippeschi-Simoncelli**, with its elegant little courtyard of Renaissance columns.

Sloping down sharply toward Porta Maggiore, **Via della Cava** (B-C1) was said by Procopius to be the most accessible street in the town, excavated as it was directly from the tufa cliff. On the way down, in one of the shops one can visit a *forno a reverbero* that was active from the end of the 14th to mid-way through the 16th century; frequent finds include wells and hypogeums. Where the road divides its way,

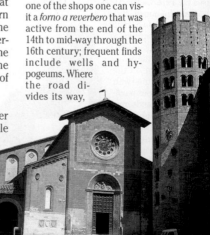

on the left stands the small church of the *Madonna della Cava*; on the right is the entrance to the *Pozzo della Cava*, dug out from the tufa by the Etruscans, and adapted for use in the 15th century.

**Palazzo dei Sette** (B2). At the end of the Dugento the palazzo was designated as the seat of the magistracy of the Signori Sette, the councilors representing the guilds: the building consequently became the cardinal point for all further urban renewal. From here spread out the "new" streets for the Cathedral and the Palazzo del Popolo. In the second half of the 1500s the L-shaped palazzo was completely reworked, with the addition of the rusticated portal and stairway. Since 1996 the building has once again been renovated and turned into an exhibition and conference center; excavation in the cellars has revealed a series of cisterns and galleries dating back to Etruscan times.

In the corner rises a **Torre Civica**, once belonging to the Della Terza counts; it was known as Torre del Papa, and from the 1500s as the Torre del Moro, perhaps owing to the coat of arms of the Pucci family of bankers (on a doorway alongside the tower).

At the top hangs a bell bearing the symbols of the 24 guilds, originally made for the Palazzo del Popolo (1316) and transferred here in 1876.

**Piazza del Popolo** (B2). The square was conceived as the fulcrum of the 13th-century town; in addition to the public palace of the same name (see below), the square contains the church of **San Rocco**, which boasts an apse decorated with frescoes by Cristoforo da Marsciano and Eusebio da Montefiascone; the other major building in the square s the *Palazzo Bracci-Testasecca*, designed by Virginio Vespignani, and now transformed in to a hotel, the Grand Hotel Reale.

**Palazzo del Popolo\*** (B2). In 1281 the palazzo makes its first appearance in the annals of the commune (Palatium Populi); the building was in basalt and tufa, intended to symbolize the new independent power of the communes. The initial project envisioned an arcade along the street, and a large hall on the first story; during work, however, the plans were enlarged to contain the residence of the head of the council, and by 1308 a bell tower had been

added. Having lost its original function, the palazzo underwent numerous alterations – some radical – until the restoration program of 1990, in which it was reassigned as a venue for cultural events and conventions. The mighty stairway on the first-story hall, known as the *Sala dei Quattrocento*, presents remnants of frescoes that

*The three-light windows on the facade of Palazzo del Popolo in Orvieto*

illustrate the feats of the various Capitani del Popolo, or mayors, and pontiffs from the 14th to the 17th century. During restoration work, the ground floor revealed remains of antique walls of Etruscan origin, a medieval aqueduct, and a large cistern of the same period.

**San Domenico** (B2-3). Between 1230 and 1233 the friars settled in the town and took over an existing chapel. In 1260-80 they had a new seat built, originally designed as an oblong block with nave and aisles. At the end of the 17th century the church was given a Baroque facelift, and in 1934 the nave was completely demolished. Among the main features inside is the **monument to Cardinal Guglielmo de Braye\*** by Arnolfo da Cambio (1285); beneath the tribune is the **Petrucci Chapel\*** by Michele Sanmicheli (1516-18).

**Corso Cavour** (B2-3). This was the medieval Via della Marcanzia, the town's most elegant street streets now lined with shops and which crosses right through the town, confirming its role as a long-standing axis giving order to the built-up area. Reaching the corso from Via Cavallotti, level with *Palazzo Guidoni* (which some attribute to Scalza), we find the **Teatro Civico** (1866), a theater entitled to the Orvietan musician

Luigi Mancinelli, and decorated inside by Annibale Angelini with grotesques, putti, and festoons in the Roman style. Opposite, the unfinished *Palazzo Petrucci*, commissioned by a Sienese family from Michele Sammicheli; flanking this is the vast *Palazzo della Greca-Alberi* the so-called *Palazzaccio* (the ugly palace), which is

chamber tombs carved from the blocks of tufa, containing benches and ceiling in rough, jutting masses; on the lintel over the doorway is carved the name of the deceased. The excavations, carried out rather haphazardly, were shared between the Louvre, the British Museum, and other collections abroad.

In the southern side of the rock we find the burials of the

*The Crocifisso del Tufo necropolis, near Orvieto*

the fruit of various periods, most noticeably elements dating from the 13th and 15th centuries. Continuing our descent we come to **San Michele Arcangelo**, a modern-looking church but actually of early origin, as proved by the remains of the 12th-14th century recently come to light in the sacristy.

Once past the little church of **Santo Stefano**, which contains fragments of 15th-century frescoes, our path takes us to **Santa Maria dei Servi**, founded in 1259 and completely transformed in neoclassical style by Virginio Vespignani; the single nave boasts a 14th-century wood *Crucifix*, and frescoes by Pietro di Nicola Baroni. Here we are at the end of the corso, which branches off from medieval walls to become the tree-lined street leading to Piazza Cahen.

The valley surrounding the peak is dotted with interesting archaeological and natural sites to visit. At 1.6 km from Orvieto proper one reaches one of the famous necropolises, known as **Crocifisso del Tufo** * (6th-3rd cent. BC), which is of special interest for its regular, carefully planned layout. The burial alleys are lined with

chamber type, this is the **necropolis of the Cannicella**, which was in use from the 7th to the 3rd century BC.

Still on the state road (no. 71), and hence on the right, after 3km we come to the monastic complex of the abbey of **Santi Severo e Martirio** *, founded in the early Middle Ages. Three separate construction phases can be detected: the church and tower belong to the Romanesque-Lombard phase (2nd half 12th cent.); the abbey building and the atrium of the church date from around 1240; the west wing from 1260. Today the abbey is a hotel, but this does not prevent visitors from seeing the *Oratorio del Crocifisso*, an ancient refectory with 13th-century frescoes, and the ruins of the *Aula Capitolare*, which afford a superb view of the rock and the Cathedral. The old *Casa Abbaziale*, in Cistercian style, is now a restaurant; remaining intact, however, is the *church* * (12th cent.), clad in reinforcement walling and a handsome Cosmatesque floor. In the intercommunicating chapels, which nowadays serve as the sacristy, one can admire a set of 14th-15th-century frescoes.

Two kilometers further on from the abbey we come to the so-called Etruscan tombs of the **Settecamini** (2nd half of the 14th to early 3rd cent. BC) discovered in the later 1800s; many of the wall paintings were detached and conserved in the Museo Archeologico Nazionale.

## 8.2 From Orvieto to Città della Pieve

**A tour from Orvieto to Città della Pieve, 42 km** *(map on page 193)*
**A walk through Città della Pieve** *(map on page 195)*

Once beyond the Paglia, we leave the Orvieto area at Ciconia, and climb through wooded hills close to Bagni, and, to our left, the Castello della Sala, toward Mt. Nibbio. Once beyond the pass over Mt. Nibbio (elev. 544 m) the road begins to descend toward Ficulle; at Fabro Scalo it meets the Chiani once again, and contin-

ues beyond it for a brief stretch on flat land before ascending once more to Monteleone d'Orvieto and Città della Pieve, the birthplace of Pietro Perugino.

**From Orvieto to Ficulle**

Once we leave the town proper, we come to *Ciconia* a suburban borough (elev. 120 m) that takes its name from **Villa Ciconia**, a building of modern design erected for the Buzi to designs by Ippolito Scalza, with a little park that now offers amenable surroundings for the restaurant and hotel installed in the villa. Continuing our climb, we pass close to the houses of **Bagni** (elev. 311 m), a *villa* in the late medieval sense, which subsequently evolved into the castle of the vicariate of Ficulle. Just near the state road rises the **Castello della Sala**, which emerges from the gently sloping vineyards with its polygonal design and imposing cylindrical tower. Today the castle is the center of a wine-producing company, Antinori; in the past it was part of the fortified circuit protecting the north of Orvieto.

### Ficulle

The town (elev. 437 m, pop. 1,708) has antique origins: founded in a dominant position of the Chiani valley, the Romans chose it as an observation point along the Via Cassia, and in the Middle Ages is was heavily contested. The ancient defensive walls enclose a network of alleyways and little squares, among which of note are the parish church of *Santa Vittoria*, built to designs by Scalza, and the 13th-century church of *Santa Maria Vecchia*, with a fine Gothic portal and fragments of frescoes from the 15th century. Along the way, the numerous workshops attest to the ancient tradition for the production of glazed terracotta and household articles made in earthenware.

### Castello di Carnaiola

The original *castrum* was built around the year 1000 by the Orvietans to guard the ford over the Chiani, where in Roman times a *muro grosso* (fortress) was built, and was later transformed into a formidable castle with corner bastions in the 16th century. Initially the property of the Filippeschi, and then the Marsciani counts, the castle gave rise to a full-fledged *borgo* (elev. 350 m) arranged in a linear pattern.

### Monteleone d'Orvieto

Leaving the fertile plain of the Chiani, we resume the climb along the hilltop to reach the town of Monteleone (elev. 500, pop. 1,615), which maintains a strategic dominance over the valley below. As early as the 11th century, Monteleone was chosen as a key point along the Perugia road, and from a simple *castrum* developed into a *borgo* along the rocky ridge, arranged along three parallel streets. Of the original set-

## 8.2 From Orvieto to Città della Pieve

tlement, nothing remains but the old *Torre Mozza*, a now topless tower that once oversaw the entrance to the town. Along the main street stand the collegiate church of **Santi Pietro e Paolo** (which conserves two works by the school of Perugino), and the *Teatro Comunale dei Rustici*, which until 1732 was the seat of the town council. Each year on 16 August, the town reenacts the *Rimpatriata*, a historical pageant in which the houses of Montemarte and Marsciano challenge each other.

## Città della Pieve

Not far from the border with Tuscany, the town rises on a panoramic outcrop of the local hill system, at 59 meters above sea level (pop. 6,828). A fortified outpost for the Longobard Tuscia, in the course of the centuries Città della Pieve has played a marginal political and territorial role, a role that allowed it a certain self-sufficiency which shows up in the town layout, the monuments, and the artistic development (the town is the birthplace of the great Pietro Vannucci, known as Perugino). The countryside around the town was dotted with rural villages originating in Etruscan and Hellenistic times, whereas in the town proper there is no evidence of occupation before the early Middle Ages. Due to the ongoing threat of swamping in the Chiana val-

*The countryside around Orvieto*

oratorio of Santa Maria dei Bianchi, which contains a fine fresco by Perugino. Emerging from the Porta del Casalino, which was demolished in 1800 to be rebuilt to a more ample design (but still unfinished), after the vast complex of Sant'Agostino, Via G. Marconi brings us back to Largo della Vittoria.

ley, the settlement established itself further up the hillside. Two farm lanes reached the Pieve castle, and along these during the late 12th century out-of-town housing gradually came into being. By the end of the 1200s the urban matrix was configured to the standard medieval hillside pattern, and in the ensuing centuries the processes of modification and expansion did nothing to alter this aspect. Even today the town's noticeable feature is the intense red of its *cotto*, echoing the local specialization of brick production.

The road accessing the town, outside the defensive walls and the gate of the Vecciano, is announced by the church of Santa Maria dei Servi. Following the walls we climb up to Largo della Vittoria, where once there stood the medieval gateway of Porta Prato (or Porta San Francesco), demolished in 1914. Opposite rises the church of San Francesco, and, alongside, the Benedictine oratory of San Bartolomeo. The entrance to town at this point is dominated by the Rocca, opposite which rises the Chiesa del Gesù. Following Via Vittorio Veneto we come to Piazza del Plebiscito which, together with Piazza Gramsci, provides a hub of the street network from which the other neighborhoods take their cue (Borgo Dentro, Casalino, and Castello). From here we continue along Via Garibaldi to Piazza XIX Giugno, with the elegant front prospect of the Palazzo della Fargna; the opposite side of the square is taken up by the Teatro degli Avvaloranti. Continuing down Via Garibaldi (on the left, Palazzo Baglioni), we reach the antique church of Sant'Antonio (now San Pietro) set into the wall where once the Porta Castello stood. Once again in Piazza del Plebiscito we take Via Vannucci toward Porta del Casalino. Here we pass by the front prospect of the

**Santa Maria dei Servi** (C2). Built in 1343 over 13th-century church of Madonna della Stella (now a chapel), has a Gothic interior scheme with 17th-18th-cebntury reworkings which largely canceled the devotional frescoes commissioned from Perugino; all that is left is a mutilated **Deposition from the Cross\*** (1517), considered the most significant work by the hand of the aging master. The convent was converted to a municipal hospital.

**San Francesco** (B2-3). Erected in the 13th century outside the defense walls, the church was completely rebuilt in the second half of the 1700s, and was transformed as a sanctuary honoring the *Madonna di Fatima* after World War II. The six large stucco altars belong to the 18th-century renovations; note the panels by Domenico Alfani and Antonio Pomarancio.

Next to the church stands the Benedictine oratorio of **San Bartolomeo**, anterior to the Franciscan church and successively reascribed by the Friars Minor as a capitular hall and refectory. There remains an interesting *Crucifixion* from the mid-1300s, a large-scale fresco known as the *Weeping of the Angels* owing to the plethora of mourning figures; the work is almost certainly attributable to Jacopo di Mino del Pelliciao.

**Rocca** (B2). Built by the inhabitants of Perugia in 1326 in the highest point still free within the walls, the *rocca*, or fortress, has five square towers, and was commissioned by the dominating town as a symbol of Castel della Pieve's subjugation. The original plan was perhaps the work of Lorenzo Maitani who, together with his brother Ambrogio, oversaw the ongoing fortifications of the territory; the building continues to perform military functions and therefore remains inaccessible to visitors. Opposite the fort stands the *Chiesa del Gesù*, erected in 1798 to designs by Andrea Vici.

**Via Vittorio Veneto** (B2). This is the thoroughfare of the Borgo Dentro neighborhood, onto which abut the *Palazzo Orca*, begun in 1703 as a college for the Piarist Fathers, and was reassigned as the council offices in 1875 (today the town hall is in Palazzo Fargna), and the former church of *Sant'Anna* (1737-54), developed vertically to the point that in 1932 it was made to accommodate the civic aqueduct.

**Palazzo Bandini\*** (B2). Belonging to the lords of the castle from the 15th to the16th century, the palazzo looks out over Via Roma with a brick facade, the fruit of merging the 14th-century structures to designs probably by Baldassarre Peruzzi; the palazzo has a fine Renaissance portal of smooth rustication.

**Piazza del Plebiscito** (B2). The square is right in the center of town, bordered by the Cathedral and by a series of buildings of varying architectural quality, such as the neoclassical *Palazzo Cartoni* by Giovanni Santini (1845). On the piazza itself the **Palazzo della Corgna**, created by Galeazzo Alessi for Ascanio della Corgna, develops in three sections around a harmonious courtyard; since 1975 it has been the property of the municipality and it now hosts a university research center and the municipal library, as well as offering a temporary exhibition space. The interiors were decorated by Niccolò Circignani and Salvio Savini.

**Cathedral** (B-C2). Dedicated to Sts. Gervase and Protase, the Cathedral was built over a 14th century parish church, and was variously reworked until the year 1600, when it was raised to the status of cathedral. The aisleless interior on a Latin cross plan contains works by Annibale Ubertis (1895), Giovanni Tedesco (wood *Crucifix*, 16th cent.), Domenico Alfani (1521), Giannicola di Paolo, and Salvio Savini. The largest of the chapels (3rd right) has frescoes by Giacinto Boccanera (1714) with *Scenes from the Old Testament*; on the back wall of the

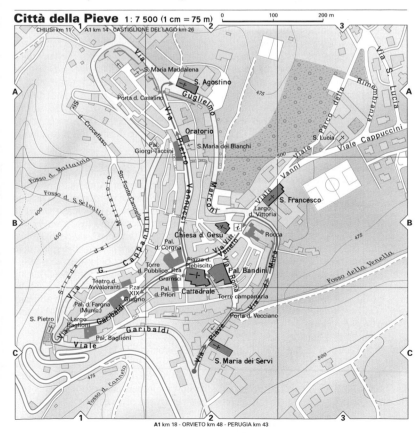

**Città della Pieve** 1: 7 500 (1 cm = 75 m)

CHIUSI km 11 - A1 km 14 - CASTIGLIONE DEL LAGO km 26

A1 km 18 - ORVIETO km 48 - PERUGIA km 43

## Città della Pieve: the crèche tradition

A land of saints and religious movements, Umbria could hardly overlook such a primal religious event as Christmas without staging special ceremonies. Religious choirs, and concerts of sacred music are performed in all the region's places of worship; the hillsides behind Gubbio suddenly light up with the colored lights of the huge Christmas tree. But among the most significant celebrations that take place in this particularly special religious moment of the year are those concerning the *presepe* (nativity scenes) or model crèches (works of great craftsmanship) and of course the "living" tableaux in which the cast is played by real people. Such celebrations are set up in main towns throughout the region: Giove, Lugnano,

*Craftmen preparing the crèches*

Calvi, Perugia, Orvieto – particularly picturesque are the mangers set up in the grottoes along Via delle Cava – and Città della Pieve. In the latter, not far from Tuscany, constructed in a panoramic setting overlooking the valley below, from Christmas to the Epiphany, the historical Palazzo della Corgna hosts a magnificent "Monumental Crèche." In homage to the *Adoration of the Magi* by Perugino, a native of the town, local artists and craftsmen bring to life sacred representations devoted to some particular biblical event. Characters sculpted in wood, carved to human scale, animate the spacious rooms in the 16th-century palazzo, which for the occasion are dressed up with straw and artless wooden furniture.

apse hangs a *panel*\* by Perugino, signed and dated 1514. The semidome of the apse was frescoed by Antonio Circignani, while the *Baptism of Christ* (1510) is another work by Perugino (1st chapel). Through the right transept one can visit the *Raccolta d'Arte* belonging to the Curia, an art collection comprising decorative material relative to the various phases of the church's construction, together with other works from the town and environs.

Hard by the facade of the Cathedral rises the **Torre Civica,** in Romanesque travertine at the base (12th cent.) and in brick (14th cent.) above. Opposite the Cathedral stands the **Palazzo dei Priori**, seat of local government until 1875.

**Piazza XIX Giugno** (B-C1). The square was created midway along the descent of Via Garibaldi, and is commanded by **Palazzo della Fargna** (now the town hall), erected around mid-18th century, with a fictive perspective background in the courtyard and, inside, stucco decorations throughout. Also overlooking the piazza is the **Teatro degli Avvaloranti**, built on the site of previous timber construction (1720) to designs by Giovanni Santini (1834), with an auditorium of four tiers of seats.

**Via Garibaldi** (C1). Almost at the end of the street, which runs through the Castel-

lo neighborhood, we come to **Palazzo Baglioni** (2nd half 18th cent.), designed and built by Andrea Vici for the girls' orphanage. At the edge of this sector of town stands the church of **San Pietro**, which was built in the 1200s under the defensive walls and frequently remodeled in the course of the centuries; inside one can admire a fresco (transferred to canvas) attributed to Perugino; the work is hard to assess, owing to the multiple retouchings.

**Santa Maria dei Bianchi** (A2). Once again from Piazza del Plebiscito, along the rows of 18th-19th-century town houses of Via Vannucci, the thoroughfare of the Casalino borough, we come to the *oratory* where in 1504 Perugino painted his fresco of the **Adoration of the Magi**\*, one of his finest works. The Compagnia dei Disciplinati, to whom the oratory belonged, also sponsored the restoration of the neighboring church, finished at the end of the 1700s by Andrea Vici, containing frescoes and canvases by Giovanni Miselli (1743-44), and coeval stuccoes by Stefano Cremoni.

**Sant'Agostino** (A2). Raised outside the defensive walls in the 1200s, and remodeled at the end of the 1700s, Sant'Agostino is now a congress and entertainments center run by the town hall.

# Itineraries

## In the footsteps of St. Francis

"In the city of Assisi, in the Spoleto valley area, there once lived a man by the name of Francis, whose bad upbringing by his parents had since his very first days taught him the vain ways of worldly life […]". These are the opening words of the earliest account of the life of St. Francis of Assisi, written between 1227 and 1229 almost in the style of a fairy tale, by Tommaso da Celano on the orders of Pope Gregory IX. Francis had died in 1226, been revered as a holy relic, his praises sung by rich and poor alike, buried in a solemn ceremony and just two years later canonized amid great ceremony. The story of St. Francis is one of a human life run through with an extraordinary mysticism. He embodied simplicity and peace in a way that revolutionized Christian thinking, his life and

*St. Francis preaching to the Birds, one of Giotto's frescoes in the basilica of San Francesco in Assisi*

works bearing witness to the drama of human existence in an age ravaged by war and marked by profound social and cultural changes. But the saint of joy and happiness was in reality racked by profound, lacerating spiritual crises, such as the one he experienced on the way to the La Verna sanctuary. It was here that he received the stigmata, an extremely private matter for Francis, who replied to an inquisitive fellow's questions about the wounds on his feet: "Concern yourself with your own affairs," writes Tommaso da Celano (XCVIII, 135). The trail of St. Francis in Umbria begins of course in Assisi, in the very heart of the city at the site of the house of his merchant father Pietro di Bernardone. Philip III of Spain ordered the remains of

### St. Francis in Assisi

Basilica of St. Francis
(Relic and tomb of St. Francis)

Giotto fresco
(St. Francis gives his cloak to a poor horseman)

Sacro Convento

Via S. Francesco

Rocca Maggiore

Crypt of San Nicolò
(The saint's vocation is confirmed)

Via Bernardo da Quintavalle
(House of the Blessed Bernard)

St. Francis as a child
(Legend of the birth)

Rocca Minore

P. za d. Comune

Chiesa Nuova
(Birthplace of St. Francis)

Cathedral of San Rufino
(Baptism of St. Francis)

Leper hospital of San Salvatore
(St. Francis kisses a leper)

Vescovado
(St. Francis renounces worldly goods)

Basilica of Santa Chiara
(The crucifix speaks to St. Francis)

S. MARIA D. ANGELI

EREMO D. CARCERI

0    200m

CONVENTO DI S. DAMIANO

197

## St. Francis in Umbria

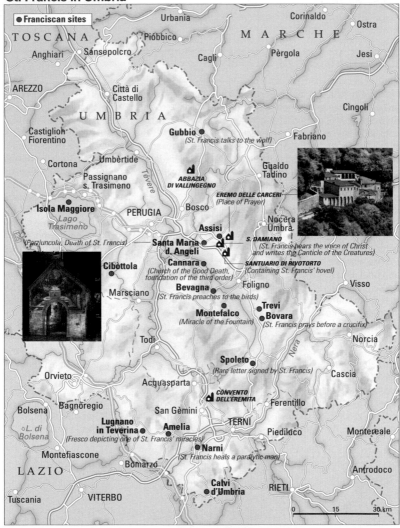

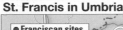

● Franciscan sites

the house to be incorporated into the Chiesa Nuova, which some say is also the place where the young rebel was "imprisoned" by his family to curb his scandalous contacts with the needy and with lepers. According to accounts by his best friends Angelo, Rufino, and Leone, Francis (who was baptized at the font of *San Rufino*), went to a school in Piazza Santa Chiara that adjoined the hospital of San Giorgio; the remains can be seen in the crypt of the basilica named after the saint. Inside is displayed the crucifix which spoke to him as he prayed in the church of *San Damiano*, and bade him to: "Go out and rebuild my Church, which, as you see, stands in ruins." And out Francis went, traveling through Italy and abroad

like few men of his day, spreading his revolutionary message of peace: the young, cultured and ambitious man arrived as far as Damietta in Egypt. While the crusaders besieging the town had no time for him, he was courteously received by the Muslim sultan. After renouncing worldly goods in the Bishop's Palace in Assisi, he took refuge in Gubbio with his friends the Spadalonga. Here, Francis soothed the ferocious wolf he had encountered in the out-of-town church of the Vittorina (the beast had often been found taking refuge in the church of *San Francesco della Pace*, where the stone on which the saint placed his feet to pray can still be seen). On his many travels St. Francis stopped in various places, including

Cannara (the church of the Buona Morte, where he is said to have founded the Third Order), in Bevagna (the stone from which he preached to the birds in Pian d'Arca is now in the local church of *San Francesco*), in Vecciano near Montefalco (where he is believed to have caused water to gush forth from the rock), in San Francesco di Bovara near Trevi (with the crucifix St. Francis prayed at), in Lugnano in Teverina, in Narni (where he healed the paralytic Pietro), on the main island in Lake Trasimeno and at the sanctuary of Monteluco near Spoleto: an extremely rare letter signed by St. Francis and sent to his friend Leone who accompanied him to La Verna is displayed in Spoleto Cathedral. The trail continues in Assisi to three sites. the place where he wished to die "a happy man," namely the little Porziuncola Chapel ("this place," said Francis to his friends as he lay dying, "is truly sacred, the House of God; [...] whosoever prays here with devotion will have his prayers answered"); the Transito Chapel in the basilica of Santa Maria degli Angeli where he eventually died; and the Basilica of San Francesco, where he is buried. The superb cycle of frescoes in the upper church is the main iconography of the saint, the basis for stories about his life and teachings that have been handed down from generation to generation. The earliest "official" biography of St. Francis in written form is the *Legenda Maior* compiled in 1263 by the minister general of the Franciscan order, the so-called "Seraphic Doctor," Bonaventura da Bagnoregio. It was surely not in deference to the saint himself that the terrible order was given out, to hunt out and destroy every previous biography and all other documents relating to the life of St. Francis of Assisi.

## Clear, fresh, sweet waters

With just under half its surface area cloaked in spontaneous plant life, woods, meadows, pasture and farmland, Umbria is indeed "the green heart of Italy." The lushness of the vegetation is a natural consequence of the extraordinary abundance of water, a reminder that in prehistoric times the region was completely covered by the Tiber Sea, while today's dry land is watered by a comprehensive network of rivers, lakes, and streams. It seems something of paradox that this is the only region in central Italy that does not actually border

*View of Lake Trasimeno with the two islands, Maggiore and Minore*

on the sea. Water makes its presence felt most dramatically at the Marmore Falls, whose deafening roar and dazzling white cloud of spray entranced 19th-century poets, writers and painters, and today attract millions of tourists. But the falls, which mark the point where the Velino river plunges into the Nera, are the work not of nature but of man – one among many examples of human intervention in the management of Umbria's water resources. For while the region may be rich in rivers, lakes and springs, the geography has not always made the resource easy to exploit, often leading to the formation of insalubrious marshy valleys and destructive forces of nature such as Lake Trasimeno, whose waters have proved to be capable of destroying anything and everything made by man.

The Romans had had to find ways of holding back the flood water from central Italy's largest lake (named after "Transimeno son of Turreno who drowned there ..."), which they did by creating an artificial underground outlet.

More radical steps were taken in the 15th century when two of the lake's tributaries were diverted into the Tiber, and other restraining work was done to reduce the level of the lake.

Substantial changes were also made to Lake Piediluco, the region's second largest lake charmingly located amid woodland: water from the Nera and Corno rivers was channeled into the lake to turn it into a reservoir, which is now used to create hydroelectric power. One natural phenomenon not affected by all these changes was the perfect echo of sounds made from the lakeside toward Mt. Caperno, from which they are returned a good four seconds later. Various natural or artificial lakes and tarns are to be found in the more mountainous parts of the region: the most noteworthy is arguably the one between Mt. Coscerno and Mt. Aspra, whose banks are noted for their crown imperial – a rare bluebell-like plant with purple flowers.

But the region's main waterway, historically and geographically, is of course the Tiber, which cuts across the region from north to south before reaching Rome, and is fed by a whole system of tributaries. The Chiascio, which is in turn fed by the Topino, the Paglia and of course the Nera, Umbria's second largest river, are the driving forces behind this great water system, themselves generating complex basins.

The source of the Clitunno river, in a charming, peaceful site near Trevi gushes forth from clefts in the rocks to form small pools before pouring into a larger collecting pool no more than four meters deep, from whose white sandy bottom the water bubbles up.

Mineral waters renowned for their therapeutic properties also abound, and the region has a large number of spas. "Sangemini" is widely used as a pediatric cure, while "Fontecchio" waters are used in mudbath and hydromassage treatment.

## Cooking the natural way

Not surprisingly for a region with such a deep-rooted peasant and farming tradition, Umbria has over the centuries developed a style of cooking based on simple, hearty dishes, made from the wholesome local produce that comes with each season of the farming year, and prepared with such imagination that no two areas produce the same version of any particular recipe.

The region's culinary traditions offer a wealth of tantalizing dishes whose origins go way back to a time when the same meal could be breakfast, lunch or supper, when farmhouse life revolved around the huge earthenware cooking pot hanging over the fire, filled with the legumes that formed the basis of the local soups, usually followed by any of a range of main meat courses.

As well as beef, mutton, farmyard animals and game (including wood pigeon, thrush, quail, and hare), pork played an important part in the diet. In Norcia, where this meat is a specialty, the local pork butchers have over the centuries turned their work into an art form, and indeed the word *norcino* has entered the Italian language as a synonym for a pork butcher.

Truffles play an important part in the regional cuisine: black truffles, eaten between Christmas Eve and March, grow in the Spoleto and Norcia area; white truffles are found mainly in the upper Tiber valley.

One of the secrets of enjoying their flavor to the full is never to slice or grate them when using them in a recipe: once they have been washed and dried they should be crushed with a pestle and mortar.

Lentils, grown at an altitude of 1,400 me-

*Fish from Lake Trasimeno cooked on the grill*

ters on the Castelluccio plateau, are a firm favorite not least of all because of the speed with which they can be cooked. The local variety is ready in 20-25 minutes without being left to soak beforehand,

## Traditional produce

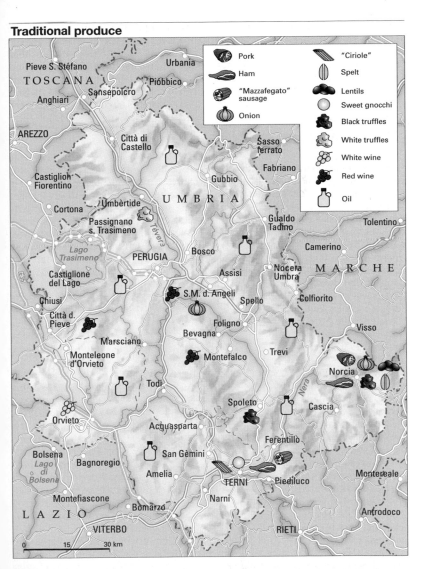

| | |
|---|---|
| Pork | "Ciriole" |
| Ham | Spelt |
| "Mazzafegato" sausage | Lentils |
| Onion | Sweet gnocchi |
| | Black truffles |
| | White truffles |
| | White wine |
| | Red wine |
| | Oil |

and there is no danger of them containing pesticide residues, since weevils do not feed on the tiny seeds when they are planted.

Onions are also widely used, as is spelt, one of the so-called "dressed wheats," which families centuries ago would prepare using a special machine to grind the corn together with the husks before cooking it with legumes and saffron. Such savory recipes are dressed with olive oil, an extremely fine, easy-to-digest and wholesome version of which is widely produced in the region. While Norcia has become synonymous with pork, the whole Valnerina area in which it lies is known for its high-quality ham, which is still prepared by hand.

The skill that goes into its preparation, together with the special environment and climate in which it is cured (clean, fresh air rich in oxygen is essential) give this ham its unmistakable aroma. Another cured meat from this area is the so-called *mazzafegato*, made of pig's liver, pine-nuts, raisins, orange peel and sugar.

Needless to say, pasta (homemade and industrial) features just as prominently here as anywhere else in Italy, appearing in savory dishes, as well as in vegetable soups. "Ciriole," from Terni, are a shorter kind of "bucatini" (thick, hollow spaghetti), served with hot oil and fried garlic. Sweet "gnocchi" are squares of pasta covered in a walnut and chocolate sauce. Meals are ideally washed down with wines of guaranteed, controlled origin (the abbreviation DOCG on the label vouches for the quality), such as Sagrantino, a dry wine made with the purest sagrantino grapes, which Pliny the Elder referred to as "Itriola."

Orvieto white wine, noted for its delicate bouquet and hint of bitterness; Torgiano from the sun-drenched Torgiano hills; and the dry, ruby-red Montefalco wine, are just three more of the delights awaiting visitors who want to get more than just a "taste" of all the region has to offer.

## St. Clare and other saintly maidens

Umbria's charm lies not only in the beauty of its landscape, but also in that special blend of history, spirituality and art that invites visitors to look inward and explore the human realm of religious devotion, to discover how the region's saints were inspired by their surroundings to turn to mysticism.

Who better to turn to as examples, than Umbria's women saints in the three centuries from the late Middle Ages to the early Renaissance? These saints usually go unsung, but the remarkable stories of Clare of Assisi, Margaret of Cortona, Angela of Foligno, Giovanna of Orvieto, Clare of Montefalco, Margaret of Città di Castello, Angelina of Montegiove, Rita of Cascia, Colomba of Rieti, and others, can give visitors from outside some understanding of what gives the region its mystical quality.

*St. Clare*

Although they lived cloistered convent lives, these women were involved in social, economic and political matters of which married women in the outside world – whose roles were limited to housekeeping and childbirth – would have been totally oblivious. It is impossible here to describe the spiritual journeys made by Umbria's many mystics, but certain anecdotes can help to give an idea of the devotional stresses and strains under which these devout women lived. "Clare was of noble extraction, born of an honest mother and father [...]", began Sister Pacifica di Guelfuccio in her testimony during the canonization of St. Clare in 1253, in which she went on to trace the remarkable life of the saint. Like other female saints, she had to overcome

tremendous obstacles in her everyday existence in order to follow the dictates of her spiritual conscience. Many families were prepared to go to any lengths to settle disputes with other families, even if it meant using their daughters as pawns: Clare of Assisi was given away as a bride for such a reason. Some families looked on what they considered to be the abnormal behavior brought on by mystical rapture as shameful: Angela of Foligno was ostracized for her "detachment" in the church of St. Francis and left ever more alone in her dialog with God. Others were even more brutally cast out: Margaret of Città di Castello, who was blind from birth, was abandoned by her parents at the age of six when their prayers that she receive the gift of sight went unanswered. Angelina of Montegiove's biography recounts how she developed her mystic beliefs when she was little more than a child: at the tender age of twelve she took a vow of chastity which she maintained even when she was forced by her family to marry. These women also showed outward signs of saintliness: Rita of Cascia carried the visible signs of the stigmata for fifteen years; the lifeless body of St. Margaret was found to contain three stones of equal size, a symbol of her devotion to the Holy Family, while Clare of Montefalco's heart carried the symbols of the Christ's Passion. The "living saint" Colomba of Rieti and her visions linked to the political and civil fate of Perugia offer an insight into the political role played by some of these saints, guardians of the towns, comforters of the weak, but above all women.

# Information for Travelers

## Where to eat, where to stay other tourist attractions

# Other places: hotels, restaurants, curiosities. Timetables and addresses

Town by town, this list includes recommended hotels, campsites and holiday camps (as well as hostels) indicating the official star classification as provided for by Italian low of 17th May 1983. For the restaurants mentioned, we give the following general indications of price level: ¶ under 23 €; ¶¶ between 24 and 34 €; ¶¶¶ between 35 and 44 €; ¶¶¶¶ between 45 and 54 €; ¶¶¶¶¶ over 54 €.
The telephone numbers include both local code and subscriber's number. Those calling from abroad must dial Italy's international code (0039), followed by the local code and subscriber's number. The symbols ⒜ American Express, ⒟ Diner's, ⒱ Visa, and ⒨ Master Card indicate which credit cards are accepted. Several of the hotels, restaurants, holiday farms and museums in this section of the guide offer discounts and reductions to members of the TCI (Italian Touring Club). A complete list can be found in the two illustrated brochures included in the Members' Pack. The guide book *Hotels and restaurants*, distributed in bookshops and updated annually, also includes the complete list of places of accommodation and restaurants offering special prices to TCI members. They can be distinguished by a special symbol.

The information given in the following pages has been carefully checked before going to press. Nevertheless, since the data presented is subject to variations, we advise readers to make a further check before departure. All suggestions and observations are welcome.

## Acquasparta ⊠ 05021
*Page 148*

 *IAT of Terni*. T. 0744423040-0744401147.

 **Hotels, restaurants, campsites and holiday camps**

★★★ **Holiday Hill.** Locality Selvarelle Alte, t. 0744941061, fax 0744941101; info@holiday hill.it; www.holidayhill.it. 28 rooms. Facilities for disabled. Air conditioning; parking, garden, open-air pool. ⒜ ⒟ ⒱ ⒨

★★★ **Villa Stella.** Via Marconi 37, t. 0744930758, fax 0744930063. Seasonal. 10 rooms. Meublé. Parking, garden. ⒜ ⒟ ⒱ ⒨

¶ **L'Agapé.** Via Marconi 26, t. 0744943696; ama martini@libero.it; www.digilander.iol.it/ama martini. Closed Tuesday, from October to May. Air conditioning; parking, garden. Local and classic cuisine - grilled meat, mushrooms and truffles. ⒜ ⒟ ⒱

 **Spas Resorts**

**Terme dell'Amerino.** Via S. Francesco 1, t. 0744943128, fax 0744943921. *Open: May-October.*

 **Shows and other festivities**

**Course of chamber singing «The German Lied»** (July).
**Commemoration of the Marriage of Federico Cesi** (September).

## Alviano ⊠ 05020
*Page 167*
**Hertz car renting**, Via Carpineto 4/C, t. 0744904646, fax 0763390506.

 **Museums and cultural institutions**

**Exhibition of Peasant Civilisation.** Castello di Alviano, t. 0744904421, fax 0744904678. *Open: morning office time.*

**Audiovisual Documentation Centre of the Fauna Oasis of Alviano.** Castello di Alviano, t. 0744904421, fax 0744904678. *Open: morning office time.*

 **Shows and other festivities**

**Stations of the Cross** (March or April).

**Alvianese August** (August). Festivities in honour of Our Lady's Assumption, sports tournaments and cultural exchanges with the twinned town of Vajnory.

**Real-life Nativity** (24 December). Historic representation of the Birth of Jesus with figures in period costume.

**Local guides and excursions**
*at Guardea, 5.5 kms* ⊠ 05025

**Comunità Montana «Amerino e Croce di Serra».** Via V. Emanuele 107, t. 074493222, fax 0744903223.

**Natural areas, parks and reserves**

**Oasi di Alviano.** Information c/o Guardia Oasi, t. 0744903715. Itineraries: nature studies, walks, observations.

## Amelia ⊠ 05022
*Page 164*

 *IAT* (Territorial Tourist Service). Via Orvieto 1, t. 0744981453, fax 0744981566.

 **Hotels, restaurants campsites and holiday camps**

★★★ **Anita.** Via Roma 31, t. 0744982146, fax 0744

983079. 31 rooms. Air conditioning; parking. AE VISA MC

★★★ **Scoglio dell'Aquilone.** Via Orvieto 23, t. 0744982445, fax 0744983025; nazzarenoho tel@tiscali.it. 38 rooms. Air conditioning; parking, garden. AE ⓪ VISA MC

ŤŤ **Il Carleni.** Via Carleni 21, t. 0744983925. Closed Tuesday, period between January and February. Garden. Local cuisine. AE ⓪ VISA MC

 **Museums and cultural institutions**

**Archeological Museum and Municipal Art Gallery.** Palazzo Boccarini, t. 0744 976220. *Closed for restoration.*

**Cisterne romane.** Via Garibaldi, t. 0744 978436; www.ameliasotterranea.it. *Open: Saturday, 3-6; Sunday and holidays, 10:30-12:30 and 3-6; in summer, Saturday, 4:30-7:30; Sunday and holidays, 10:30-12:30 and 4:30-7:30.*

**Teatro sociale.** Via del Teatro.

 **Shows and other festivities**

**Stations of the Cross** (March or April).

**Infiorata del Corpus Domini (Procession with flowers)** (2nd Sunday after Pentecost).

**Amerino Organistic May** (May-June). Organ concerts performed by well-known Italian and foreign artistes.

**Musical Summer** (August). Classical music and jazz concerts.

**Historical Festivities in commemoration of the Municipal Statues of 1346** (August).

▨▨ **Shops, arts and crafts**

**Azienda Girotti.** Via della Repubblica 116, t. 0744982354. Production and sales of dried figs for all tastes.

---

## Arrone ▨ 05031
*Page 180*

 **Hotels, restaurants, campsites and holiday camps**

### at Casteldilago, 2 kms

Ÿ **Grottino del Nera.** Colleporto 21, t. 0744389104. Closed Wednesday. Air conditioning; parking. Local cuisine. AE ⓪ VISA MC

"Ÿ" **Sports**

**A.S. Jump Marmore.** T. 07444228105; www. comtel.it/bungee. Bungee jumping from the bridge of the Canale di Rosciano.

---

## Assisi ▨ 06081
*Page 97*

ℹ *IAT* (Territorial Tourism Service). Piazza del Comune 1, t. 075812450, fax 075813727.

*Tourist Information.* Piazza del Comune 12, t. 075812534.

 **Hotels, restaurants, campsites and holiday camps**

★★★ **Subasio.** Via Frate Elia 2, t. 075812206, fax 075

816691. 61 rooms. Air conditioning. AE ⓪ VISA; (A1).

★★★ **Dei Priori.** Corso Mazzini 15, t. 075812237, fax 075816804; hpriori@tiscali.it; www.assisiho tels.net. Closed mid-January-February. 34 rooms. Facilities for disabled. Air conditioning; special terms for parking garage. AE ⓪ VISA MC; (B4).

★★★ **Fontebella.** Via Fontebella 25, t. 075 812883, fax 075812941. 40 rooms. Facilities for disabled. Air conditioning; parking, garden. AE ⓪ VISA MC; (A2).

★★★ **Il Castello.** Viale Marconi 1/B, t. 075 812384, fax 075812567. Seasonal. 46 rooms. Facilities for disabled. Air conditioning; special terms for parking garage, garden. AE ⓪ VISA MC; (B2).

★★★ **San Francesco.** Via S. Francesco 48, t. 075 812281, fax 075816237; info@hotelsanfran cescoassisi.it; www.hotelsanfrancescoassisi.it. 44 rooms. Air conditioning. AE ⓪ VISA MC; (A2).

★★★ **San Pietro.** Piazza S. Pietro 5, t. 075812452, fax 075816332. 37 rooms. Facilities for disabled. Air conditioning; parking, special terms for parking garage. AE VISA MC; (B2).

★★★ **Umbra.** Via degli Archi 6, t. 075812240, fax 075813653. Closed mid-January-mid-March. 25 rooms. Air conditioning; special terms for parking garage, garden. AE ⓪ VISA MC; (B3).

★★★ **Windsor Savoja.** Viale Marconi 1, t. 075 812210, fax 075813659; hotelwindsor@ediso ns.it. 34 rooms. Facilities for disabled. Air conditioning; special terms for parking garage, garden. AE ⓪ VISA MC; (B1-2).

★★ **Berti.** Piazza S. Pietro 29, t. 075813466, fax 075816870; albergoberti@tiscali.it; web.ti scali.it/hotelberti. 10 rooms. Meublé. Air conditioning; garden. AE ⓪ VISA MC; (A-B2).

★★ **Minerva.** Piazzetta Bonghi 7, t. 075812416, fax 075813770. Seasonal. 28 rooms. AE ⓪ VISA MC; (A2).

★★ **San Giacomo.** Via S. Giacomo 6, t. 075816778, fax 075816779. 25 rooms. Facilities for disabled. AE VISA; (A2).

★★ **Sole.** Corso Mazzini 35, t. 075812373, fax 075813706; soleassisi@hotmail.com; www. italyhotels.it. 37 rooms, 34 with bath or shower. Special terms for parking garage. AE ⓪ VISA MC; (B4).

ŤŤ **Buca di San Francesco.** Via E. Brizi 1, t. 075 812204; www.assisi.com/bucasfrancesco. Closed Monday. July. Garden. Local cuisine. AE ⓪ VISA MC; (B3).

ŤŤ **Frantoio.** Vicolo Illuminati, t. 075812883; in fo@fontebella.com; www.fontebella.com. Also hotel. Air conditioning; parking, garden. Local cuisine. AE ⓪ VISA MC; (A-B2).

ŤŤ **San Francesco.** Via S. Francesco 52, t. 075 812329. Closed Wednesday, period in July. Air conditioning. Specialised local cuisine. AE ⓪ VISA MC; (B3).

Ÿ **La Fortezza.** Vicolo della Fortezza B/2, t. 075812418; lafortezza@lafortezzahotel.com;

www.lafortezzahotel.com.Also hotel.Closed Thursday,February,period in July.Air conditioning.Local cuisine.`AE` `DC` `VISA` `MC`;(B4).

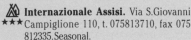 **Viaggiatore.** Via S.Antonio 14,t.075 812424. Also hotel.Closed Tuesday.Air conditioning. Local cuisine.`DC` `VISA` `MC`;(B4).

 **Internazionale Assisi.** Via S.Giovanni
★★★ Campiglione 110, t. 075813710, fax 075 812335.Seasonal.

### at Armenzano,10 kms     ✉ 06083

★☆★ **Le Silve.** T. 0758019000, fax 0758019005; hotellesilve@tin.it;www.lesilve.it.Seasonal.15 rooms.Parking,garden,open-air pool,tennis courts.`AE` `DC` `VISA` `MC`.

### at Petrignano, 9 kms

 **Ai Cavalieri.** Via Matteotti 47,t.0758030011; info@aicavalieri.it; www.aicavalieri.it. Also hotel. Closed Monday, variable holiday closure. Air conditioning; parking, garden. Specialised local cuisine.`AE` `DC` `VISA` `MC`.

🌲 **Farm Holidays**

**Villa Gabbiano.** Locality Capodacqua, t. 0758065278. An 18th century villa with several modernized farmhouses buried in the naturalistic area of Subasio Park.Open-air pool.No dogs allowed.

🏛 **Museums and cultural institutions**

**Galleria d'Arte contemporanea.**Via degli Ancajani 3,t.075813231,fax 075812445.*Closed for restoration.*

**Mostra etnografica dell'Amazzonia.** Via S. Francesco,t.075812280.

**Museo Antichi mestieri (Ancient Crafts Museum).** Via Fortini,c/o Teatro Metastasio, t.075812534. *Open: on request.*

**Museo della Cattedrale.** Piazza S.Rufino,t. 075812283.*Open:April-October,10-1 and 2-5.*

**Museo civico e Foro romano.** Via Portica, t. 075813053. *Open: 16 March-15 October, 10-1 and 3-7; 16 October-15 March,10-1 and 2-5.*

**Museo-Tesoro e Collezione Perkins.** Basilica di S.Francesco,piazza S.Francesco 1,t.075 812238.*Closed Sunday.Open:April-October,9-12 and 2-5:30.*

**Pinacoteca comunale. (Municipal Art Gallery).** PalazzoVallemani,Via S. Francesco 10, t. 075812033-075815292. *Closed Sunday. Open: 16 March-15 October, 10-1 and 3-7; 16 October-15 March,10-1 and 2-5.*

**Rocca Maggiore.** T. 075815292. *Open: 10-sunset.*

### at Santa Maria degli Angeli, 4 kms     ✉ 06088

**Museo d'Arte moderna «Padre Felice Rossetti».** Hotel Domus Pacis,t.0758043530. *Presently closed.*

**Museo Etnografico universale.** Piazza della Porziuncola 1,t.and fax 0758043769.*Closed at present.*

**Museo della Porziuncola.** Basilica di S. Maria degli Angeli, t. 07580511, fax 075 8051418. Closed from 1 November to 30 March.*Open: 9-12 and 3:30-6:30.*

 **Churches and monuments**

**Basilica of San Francesco.** T.075819001;roma giubileo.it/assisi.*Open: Easter-November, 6:30-7; Sunday and holidays, 6:30-7:30; other months, 6:30-6, except Sunday morning and holidays.*

**Eremo delle Carceri (Carceri Hermit-age).** Colle di S.Rufino,t.075812301.*Open: Easter-November,6:30-7:15; other months,6:30-5:30.*

**Monastero di S. Damiano.** T. 075812273. *Open: summer 10-12:30 and 2-6; winter 10-12:30 and 2-4.*

 **Shows and other festivities**

**Procession of the Dead Christ** (Holy Week). Moving commemoration of the Deposition.

**Ascension Day** (Sunday) Religious celebrations and games in costum in procession up Monte Subasio.

**Beflowering of Corpus Domini.** At S.Maria degli Angeli on the day of Corpus Domini,at Assisi the following Sunday.

**Assisi Antique** (April-May). National Antique Market and Show.

**Festa del Calendimaggio (May Day Fetes)** (May).Processions,theatre shows,music and sing-ing,dances,archery and crossbow shows, flag-waving displays in contests between «Parte de Sopra» and «Parte de Sotto».

**Feast of the Vow** (22 June). A procession from piazza del Comune to S.Domenico in remembrance of St.Clare chasing out the Saracens.

**Feast of the Pardon** (1-2 August).At S.Maria degli Angeli solemn celebrations of the Pardon.

**Palio di S. Rufino** (30 August).Ancient crossbow contest by the Assisi crossbow team, with historic procession with flag waving.

**National celebrations in honour of St. Francis** (3-4 October).

**March for World Peace.** Since 1986 every year an immense procession in the name of the brotherhood of nations.

**Film Festival** (November).A festival of Italian films with well-known guests.

**Christmas in Assisi** (24 December-6 January).Solemn Lithurgies in church,concerts of Christmas music and Nativity Scenes.

 **Shops, arts and crafts**

**Ditta Roberti Rita.** Corso Mazzini 17,t.075 812201. Embroidery Assisi stitch, Umbrian arts and crafts,weaving,school of embroidery.

**Ditta Rossi.** Via Frate Elia 1,t.075812555.Ceramicas, copper, lace, Assisi stitch embroidery,school of embroidery.

**F.lli Rinaldi.** Via Giovanni XXIII t.075812232. Copper and wrought iron works, also made to order.

**Il Fra Goloso.** Via Portica 24/a, t.075815264. Ices, cakes, typical regional cakes and pastries.

**Prosperi Francesco.** Via S. Francesco 11, t. 075812663. In his shop Professor Francesco realises modern wood-engravings, paint-ings and sculptures.

 **Sports**

Le Silve di Armenzano. Locality Armenzano, t.0758019003. Riding school.

 **Local guides and excursions**

**Associazione Guide turistiche dell'Umbria.** Via Antonio Cristofani 2/d, t. 075815228, fax 075815229.

**Comunità montana «Monte Subasio».** Via Flaminia, t.074275191, fax 0742751937.

 **Natural areas, parks and reserves**

**Parco regionale del Monte Subasio.** T.075 815181, fax 075815307; www.parks.it. Other towns included in the park: Nocera Umbra, Spello.

---

## Avigliano Umbro     ✉ 05020

*Page 166*

 **Museums and cultural institutions**

**Centro di paleontologia vegetale - Foresta fossile di Dunarobba.** Viale Matteotti 9, t.0744940348; www.caribusiness.it/forestafossile. *Open: April-September, 9:30-11:30 and 3-5 (Sunday and holidays); July-September, 3-5 (Saturday); October, 9:30-11:30 and 2:30-4:30 (Sunday).*

---

## Baschi     ✉ 05023

*Page167*

**Hotels, restaurants, campsites and holiday camps**

★★★ **Villa Bellago.** Corbara Lake, 4 kms, t. 0744 950521, fax 0744950524; villabellago@tiscali.it; www.argoweb.it/hotel_villabellago. it. 14 rooms. Parking, garden, open-air pool, tennis courts. ⒶⒺ ⓄⒹ 🆅🅸🆂🅰 🅼🅲

 **Scacco Matto.** SS 448 at 3.7 kms, t. 0744 950163, fax 0744950373. Seasonal.
★

*at Civitella del Lago, 12 kms*     ✉ 05020

 **Vissani.** SS 448, t.0744950396, fax 0744950186; info@vissani.net; www.nissani. net. Closed Sunday evenings, Thursday lunchtime and Wednesday, mid-August-mid-September. Air conditioning; parking. Specialised cuisine. ⒶⒺ ⓄⒹ 🆅🅸🆂🅰 🅼🅲

 **Trippini.** Via Italia 14, t.0744950316. Closed Monday, variable winter holiday closure. Specialised cuisine. ⒶⒺ ⓄⒹ 🆅🅸🆂🅰

 **Natural areas, parks and reserves**

**Parco regionale fluviale del Tevere.** T.

---

0744950732; www.parks.it. Other towns included in the park: Alviano, Guardea, Monte Castello di Vibio, Montecchio, Orvieto, Todi.

---

## Bastìa Umbra     ✉ 06083

*Page 109*

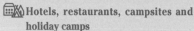 *Pro Loco*. Piazza Umberto I, t.0758004152.
*Pro Bastia. Association* Via Roma 44, t. 0758011493.

**Hotels, restaurants, campsites and holiday camps**

★★★ **La Villa.** At Bastiola, 1 km, SS 147 Assisana 124, t.0758010011, fax 0758010574; mail@lavi lla.it; www.lavilla.it. 23 rooms. Air conditioning; parking, garden, open-air pool. ⒶⒺ ⓄⒹ 🆅🅸🆂🅰 🅼🅲

★★ **Campiglione.** Via Campiglione 11, t. 075 8010767, fax 0758010768; hotel@hotel-campiglione.it; www.hotel-campiglione.it. 42 rooms. Facilities for disabled. Air conditioning; parking, parking garage, garden. ⒶⒺ ⓄⒹ 🆅🅸🆂🅰 🅼🅲

*at Ospedalicchio, 5 kms*     ✉ 06080

★★★ **Lo Spedalicchio.** Piazza Buozzi 3, t. 075 8010323, fax 0758010323; info@lospedalicchio.it; www.lospedalicchio.it. 25 rooms. Air conditioning; parking, garden. ⒶⒺ ⓄⒹ 🆅🅸🆂🅰 🅼🅲.

 **Shows and other festivities**

**Procession of the Rinchinata** (Easter). Representation of the Meeting between Christ and Our Lady.

---

## Bettona     ✉ 06080

*Page 111*

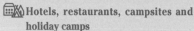 *Pro Loco*. Piazza Matteotti, t.0759869482.

🌲 **Farm Holidays**

**Torre Burchio.** Vocabolo Burchio, t. 075 9885017. Facilities for disabled. A 19th-century farmhouse in a 1,500 acre fauna reserve. Open-air pool. Horse riding. Organically grown produce. No dogs allowed except by agreement.

 **Museums and cultural institutions**

**Pinacoteca civica.** Piazza Cavour 3, t. and fax 075987306; www.sistemamuseo.it. *Open: November-February, 10:30-1 and 2.30-5; March-May and September-October, 10:30-1 and 2-6; June-July, 10:30-1 and 3-7; August, 10:30-1 and 3-7:30.*

 **Shows and other festivities**

**Commemoration of the Passion** (Holy Week). Procession with figures in costume presenting the canonical episodes of the Passion of Christ.

 **Sports**

**Il poggio degli olivi.** Via Monte Balacca, t. 0759869023. Riding school, tennis courts, open-air pool.

## Bevagna ✉ 06031

*Page 114*

ℹ️ *Pro Loco*. Piazza Silvestri 1, t. 0742361667.

### 🏨 Hotels, restaurants, campsites, and holiday camps

*★☆★* **L'Orto degli Angeli.** Via Dante Alighieri 1, t. 0742360130, fax 0742361756; ortoangeli@or toangeli.it; www.ortoangeli.it. 9 rooms. Air conditioning; garden. AE OD VISA MC

*★★★* **Palazzo Brunamonti.** Corso Matteotti 79, t. 0742361932, fax 0742361948; hotel@bruna monti.com; www.brunamonti.com. 16 rooms. Meublé. Facilities for disabled. Air conditioning. AE OD VISA MC

🍴 **El Rancho.** Via Flaminia 55, t. 0742360105. Closed Monday, period in August. Air conditioning; parking, garden. Regional cuisine. AE VISA MC

*★★★* **Pian di Boccio.** Locality Pian di Boccio t. 0742360391, fax 0742360391. Seasonal.

### 🌲 Farm Holidays

**Il Poggio dei Pettirossi.** Madonna delle Grazie, vocabolo Pilone 301, t. 0742361744. Facilities for disabled. Vast panoramic view of Assisi, Spello, Montefalco and Trevi from the complex of buildings that make up this holiday farm. In the swimming pool, courses in deep-sea diving to become internationally qualified.

### 🏛 Museums and cultural institutions

**Museo civico.** Corso Matteotti 70, t. and fax 0742360031; www.sistemamuseo.it. Closed Monday, except in August. *Open: October-March, 10:30-1 and 2:30-5 (Friday, Saturday and Sunday); April, May, and September, 10:30-1 and 2:30-6; June-July, 10:30-1 and 3:30-7; August, 10:30-1 and 3-7:30.*

**Mosaico romano.** Via Porta Guelfa 4, t. 0742 361667. *Open: on request.*

**Raccolta materiale archeologico.** Corso Matteotti - c/o Town Hall, t. 0742360123. *Closed at present.*

### 🎭 Shows and other festivities

**The Race of Christ Resurrected** (Easter). Commemoration of the Resurrection of Christ.

**Gaite Market** (June). Sale of products manufactured following traditional techniques.

### ⚖️ Shops, arts and crafts

**Cartiera S. Giovanni.** Via dell'Anfiteatro, t. 0742361189 (Francesco Proietti). Production of paper from rags using Medieval processes.

---

## Campello sul Clitunno ✉ 06042

*Page 125*

ℹ️ *Pro Campello Association.* Via Manzoni 6, t. 0743520825.
*Tourist Office.* S. Cipriano complex (Seasonal), t. 0743275558.

### 🏨 Hotels, restaurants, campsites and holiday camps

*★★★* **Benedetti.** Locality Settecamini, via G. Verdi 32, t. 0743520078, fax 0743275466; benedetti@ mail.caribusiness.it; www.hotelbenedetti.it. 22 rooms. Air conditioning; parking, garden. AE OD VISA MC

🍴 **Le Casaline.** T. 0743520811; casaline@libe ro.it. Closed Monday. Also hotel. Parking, garden. Regional cuisine - mushrooms and truffles. AE OD VISA MC

*at Pettino, 13 kms*

🍴 **Trattoria Pettino.** T. 0743276021; fhnqqc@ tin.it. Closed Tuesday. Also hotel. Parking, garden. Regional cuisine. AE OD

### 🏛 Museums and cultural institutions

**Fonti del Clitunno.** T. 0743521141. *Open: January-15 March, 10-1 and 2-6; 16 March-April, 9-7; May-August, 8:30-8; September, 9-1 and 2-7:30; October-3 November, 9-1 and 2-6:30; 4 November-December, 10-1 and 2-5.*

**Tempietto del Clitunno.** T. 0743275085. Closed Monday. *Open: April-October, 9-8; November-March, 9-2.*

### ⚖️ Shops, arts and crafts

**Cooperativa Agricentro.** Fonti del Clitunno 116, t. 0743275057. Typical regional products and wines.

---

## Cannara ✉ 06033

*Page 111*

### 🏨 Hotels, restaurants, campsites and holiday camps

🍴 **Perbacco.** Via Umberto I 14, t. 0742720492; er parzi@tin.it. Open only evenings. Closed Monday, period from July to August. Regional cuisine. OD VISA MC

### 🎭 Shows and other festivities

**Procession of the Rinchinata (Bowing)** (Easter). Representation of the Meeting between Christ and Our Lady.

**Infiorata (strewing with flowers) of the Corpus Domini** (2nd Sunday after Pentecost).

---

## Cascia ✉ 06043

*Page 176*

ℹ️ *IAT* (Territorial Tourist Service). Via G. Da Chiavano 2, t. 074371401, fax 074376630; info@cas cia.pg.it.
*Tourist Information.* T. 074371147.

### 🏨 Hotels, restaurants, campsites and holiday camps

*★★★* **Cursula.** Viale Cavour 3, t. 074376206, fax 074376262; hotelcursula@inwind.it; www.um briatravel.com. Closed January-February. 31 rooms. Facilities for disabled. Parking, parking garage, garden. AE OD VISA MC

★★★ **Monte Meraviglia.** Via Roma 15, t. 0743 76142, fax 074371127; www.montemeraviglia.com. 165 rooms. Parking, open-air pool, tennis courts.  VISA MC.

*at Roccaporena, 5 kms*

★★★ **Roccaporena.** T. 07437549, fax 0743 754800; hotelroccaporena@tin.it; www.roccaporena.com. Seasonal. 71 rooms Facilities for disabled. Parking, garden. AE ⊙ VISA MC

 Farm Holidays

**Casale S. Antonio.** Locality Casale Sant'Antonio, t. 074376819. A small collection of agricultural instruments and many excursions in the Park of the Sibillini Mts.: all this and more offered in this modernized farmhouse.

 Museums and cultural institutions

**Museo chiesa di S. Antonio Abate.** Via Porta Leonina, t. 0743753055. *Open: October-April, 10:30-1 and 3-5 (Saturday and Sunday); May-June, 10:30-1 and 4-6:30 (Tuesday-Sunday); August, 10:30-1 and 4-7.*

**Museo civico di Palazzo Santi.** Via Palombi, t. and fax 0743751010. *Open: October-April, 10:30-1 and 3:5 (Saturday and Sunday); May-June, 10:30-1 and 4-6:30 (Friday, Saturday and Sunday); July and September, 10:30-1 and 4-6:30 (Tuesday-Sunday); August 10:30-1 and 4-7.*

Shows and other festivities

**Procession of the Dead Christ** (Good Friday).

**St. Rita Celebrations** (21-22 May). Religious celebrations in honour of St. Rita, with the traditional «Luminaria».

---

## Castiglione del Lago    ✉ 06061

*Page 67*

ⓘ *IAT* (Territorial Tourist Service). Piazza Mazzini 10, t. 0759652484-0759652738, fax 075 9652763; info@iat.castiglione-del-lago.pg.it; www.umbria2000.it.

Hotels, restaurants, campsites and holiday camps

★★★ **La Torre.** Via Vittorio Emanuele 50, t. 075951666, fax 075951666; latorre@trasinet. com; www.trasinet.com/latorre. 8 rooms. Meublé. Air conditioning. AE ⊙ VISA MC

★★★ **Miralago.** Piazza Mazzini 6, t. 075951157, fax 075951924; hotelmiralago@tin.it; www.hotelmiralago.com. Closed Epiphany-mid-March. 19 rooms. Air conditioning. AE ⊙ VISA

★★ **Fazzuoli.** Piazza Marconi 11, t. 075951119, fax 075951112. Closed mid-December-February. 27 rooms. Meublé. Parking, garden. VISA MC

🍴 **Acquario.** Via Vittorio Emanuele 69, t. 075 9652432; ristorante.acquario@inwind.it; www.castiglionedellago.it/acquario. Closed Wednesday (and Tues-day in winter), period between January and February. Regional cuisine - fish from the lake. AE VISA

🍴 **Cantina.** Via Vittorio Emanuele 93, t. 0759652463; aurorascrl@bcc.tin.it; www.castiglionedellago.it/cantina. Closed Monday except summer. Garden. Regional cuisine and of Tuscania - fish from the lake, grilled meat. AE ⊙ VISA MC

 **Badiaccia.** Locality Badiaccia, Via Trasimeno
★★★ I 91, t. 0759659097, fax 0759659019. Seasonal.

 Farm Holidays

*at Petrignano, 12 kms*    ✉ 06086

**I Cucchi.** Vocabolo I Cucchi, t. 0759528116-0337653583, fax 0755171244. The rural buildings of this vineyard are built around the swimming pool. Nature weeks for children. No dogs allowed.

 Museums and cultural institutions

**Palazzo della Corgna-Castello del Leone.** Piazza Gramsci 1, t. 0759658210. *Open: January-mid-March and November-December, 10-4 (Saturday and holidays); mid-March-October, 10-1 and 3:30-7:30; Christmas holidays, 10-4.*

 Shows and other festivities

**Colouring the sky** (30 April-3 May). Biennial festivity with kite-flying on the banks of Lake Trasimeno.

**International Festival of Choir Singing** (July).

**International Folklore Festival** (August).

 Sports

**Circolo Sci nautico.** Locality Lacaioli, t. 0759652836.

**Club Velico Castiglionese.** Via Brigata Garibaldi, t. 075953035. Boathouse, sailing school, water-skiing.

**La Merangola.** Via Lido Arezzo, t. 075 9652445. School of windsurf; windsurfs, canoes, bicycles, mountain bikes and rickshaws to hire.

---

## Città della Pieve    ✉ 06062

*Page 193*

ⓘ *Pievese Tourist Association.* Piazza Matteotti 4, t. 0578298031.

*Tourist Information.* C/o Municipio, t. 0578 299375.

 Farm Holidays

**Madonna delle Grazie.** Vocabolo Madonna delle Grazie 6, t. and fax 0578 299822. An old farmhouse in a panoramic position offers Aiab certified organ-ically grown produce and the possibility to go horse riding.

Museums and cultural institutions

**Palazzo della Corgna - Oratorio di S. Maria dei Bianchi - Chiesa di S. Agostino.** Circuit «open museum», t. 0578 299375. *Open: June-September, 10-12:30 and 3:30-6; other months, only from Friday to Sunday.*

**Raccolta d'Arte diocesana della Catte-**

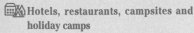

**drale.** Piazza Gramsci, t. 0578299375-0578 291219 (Municipio). *Open: on request.*

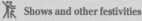 **Shows and other festivities**

**Living Pictures** (Holy Week). Representation of scenes from the Passion to the Resurrection, in the vaults of Palazzo Orca (terziere Borgo Dentro).

**Scenes from the Passion of Christ** (Easter).

**Palio of the Terzieri** (August). Antique Renaissance Festival with procession of figures inspired by the works of Perugino.

**Monumental Nativity.** From Christmas to the Epiphany in the vaults of Palazzo della Corgna.

**Sports**

**Tenuta Le Coste.** Locality Moiano 12, t. 0578 294525. Archery.

---

## Città di Castello                    ✉ 06012

*Page 75*

*IAT* (Territorial Tourist Service). Via S. Antonio 1, t. 0758554817, fax 0758552100.

*Tourist Information.* Palazzo del Podestà, piazza Fanti, t. 0758554922.

**Hertz car renting**, Via E. Kant 29/G, Zona Industriale Cerbara, t. 0758511766, fax 0758511486.

 **Hotels, restaurants, campsites and holiday camps**

★☆★ **Tiferno.** Piazza R. Sanzio 13, t. 0758550331, fax 0758521196; info@hoteltiferno.it; www.hotel tiferno.it. 38 rooms. Air conditioning; parking, parking garage. ⯐ ⯐ ⯐ ⯐

★★★ **Garden.** Via A. Bologni, t. 0758550587, fax 0758521367; info@hotelgarden.com; www.ho telgarden.com. 56 rooms. Air conditioning; parking, parking garage, garden, open-air pool. ⯐ ⯐ ⯐ ⯐; (A3, *f.p.*).

¶¶¶ **Il Postale di Marco e Barbara.** Via Raffaele de Cesare 8, t. 0758521356; il.postale@libero.it. Closed Monday and Saturday at midday), variable holiday closure. Air conditioning; parking. Specialised cuisine. ⯐ ⯐ ⯐ ⯐; (A3).

¶¶ **Bersaglio.** Via Vittorio Emanuele Orlando 14, t. 0758555534. Closed Wednesday, period in January and July. Parking, garden. Regional cuisine and of Tuscania - mushrooms and truffles. ⯐ ⯐ ⯐ ⯐; (C3, *f.p.*).

⛺ **Montesca.** Locality Montesca, t. 0758558566, fax 0758520786. Seasonal.

### at Terme di Fontecchio, 3 kms

★★★ **Terme di Fontecchio.** T. 0758520614, fax 0758557236; hotel@termedifontecchio.it; www.termedifontecchio.it. 101 rooms. Facilities for disabled. Parking, garden, indoor and open-air pool, tennis courts. ⯐ ⯐ ⯐

### at San Donnino, 6 kms

★★★ **Villa San Donnino.** T. 0758578108, fax 0758520765; gitasrl@gita.it; www.gita.it. Seasonal. 38 rooms. Air conditioning; parking, garden, open-air pool, tennis courts. ⯐ ⯐ ⯐ ⯐

 **Farm Holidays**

### at Cerbara, 6 kms                    ✉ 06011

**Villa Bice.** Villa Zampini 43/45, t. and fax 078511430. Two attractive farmhouses adjacent to the 18th-century villa with a large park offering the possibility of romantic walks.

 **Museums and cultural institutions**

**Collezione Burri.** Palazzo Albizzini, via Albizzini 1, t. 0758554649-0758559848, fax 0758554649; www.cdnet.net/museo_burri. Closed Monday. *Open: 9-12:30 and 2:30-6; holidays, 10:30-12:30 and 3-5.*

**Collezione Burri.** Ex Tobacco driers, via Pierucci, t. 0758554649-0758559848, fax 0758554649. Closed Monday and from 1 November to 18 March. *Open: 9-12:30 and 2:30-6; holidays, 10:30-12:30 and 3-5.*

**Collezione Tessile di Tela Umbra.** Via S. Antonio 3, t. 0758554337; www.sistema museo.it. Closed Monday. *Open: 10-12 and 3:30-5:30.*

**Mostra permanente del Mobile in stile.** Northern Industrial Area, t. 0758550966. Closed Sunday (July and August). *Open: 9-12:30 and 3-7; holidays, 3-7.*

**Museo delle Arti grafiche.** Printing House Grifani Donati, corso Cavour 4, t. 0758554349. Closed Sunday. *Open: 9-12:30 and 2:30-6:30.*

**Museo del Duomo.** Piazza Gabriotti 3, t. and fax 0758554705; www.museoduomocdc.it. *Open: October-March, 10-1 and 2:30-6:30; April-September, 9:30-1 and 2:30-7.*

**Pinacoteca comunale.** Palazzo Vitelli alla Cannoniera, via della Cannoniera 22/a, t. 0758520656. Closed Monday. *Open: November-March, 10-12:30 and 3-5:30; April-October, 10-1 and 2:30-6:30.*

**Raccolta civica.** Municipal Library, via delle Giulianelle, t. 0758555687. Closed Wednesday, Saturday afternoons, Sunday. *Open: 9-1 and 3-7.*

**Torre civica.** Piazza Gabriotti. Closed Monday. *Open: 10-12:30 and 3:30-6:30.*

### at Garavelle, 2 kms

**Centro di Documentazione delle Tradizioni popolari.** Villa Cappelletti, t. 075 8552119. Closed Monday. *Open: 9-12 and 2-5.*

 **Churches and monuments**

### at Morra, 20 kms                    ✉ 06010

**Oratorio di S. Crescentino.** *Open: 9-12:30 and 3-6:30.*

**Shows and other festivities**

**Procession of the Dead Christ** (Good Friday).

**Festival of the Nations di Musica da camera** (August-September). T. 0758527399. Founded as a festival of chamber music, for some years now open to other kinds.

### at San Leo Bastia, 29 kms

**Mascherata (Masquerade)** (last but one Carnival Sunday). A parade of personages in grotesque masks performing a farcical, allegorical streetshow.

 **Spas Resorts**

### at Terme di Fontecchio, 3 kms

**Terme di Fontecchio.** T. 075862851. *Open: all year.*

 **Shops, arts and crafts**

**Mastriforti Renato.** Via Rignaldello, t. 075 8558642. Copper and wrought iron works.

**S.M.A.I.** Via Morandi, t. 0758550966. Restoration and reconstruction of period furniture using old and new materials.

**Tela Umbra.** Via S. Antonio 2, t. 0758554337. Hand-woven products using antique Umbrian cloth. Courses in weaving.

 **Local guides and excursions**

**Comunità montana «Alto Tevere Umbro».** Via S. Girolamo Pomerio, t. 0758550033-075862901, fax 0758550697.

---

## Corciano  06073

*Page 62*

 *Pro Loco.* Via della Corgna 6, t. 0756979109.

**Hotels, restaurants, campsites and holiday camps**

★★★ **Conca del Sole.** At Ellera Umbra, 3 kms, Via Pascarella 13, t. 0755171149; info@concadelsole.it; www.concadelsole.it. 43 rooms. Parking, garden, open-air pool, tennis courts. AE VISA MC

★★★ **El Patio.** At Taverne di Corciano, 1 km, via dell'Osteria 5, t. 0756978464, fax 0756978580; info@hotelpatio.com; www.hotelpatio.com. 44 rooms. Facilities for disabled. Air conditioning; parking, garden. AE VISA MC

 **Museums and cultural institutions**

**Museo della Casa contadina.** Via Tarragone 12, t. 0755188253-4-5, fax 0755188237. *Open: on request.*

**Museo paleontologico.** Town Hall, corso Cardinale Rotelli, t. 0755188253-4-5. *Open: on request.*

**Museo di Arte sacra o della Pievania.** Chiesa di S. Cristoforo, t. 0755188253-4-5. *Open: on request.*

 **Churches and monuments**

**Chiesa Museo di S. Francesco.** T. 075 5188254-5 (Municipality). *Open: on request.*

 **Shows and other festivities**

**National Poetry Contest Città di Corciano** (June).

**Corciano Festival** (August). Including a visual arts festival, theatre performances, concerts, conventions and the national contest of original compositions for brass bands.

 **Sports**

**Colle Verde.** Near Colle Corno, t. 075605858. Indoor riding, riding school, club house,

restaurant, tennis courts, open-air pool, mini football ground.

### at Ellera Umbra, 3 kms

**Circolo del Golf di Perugia.** Locality Santa Sabina, Via delle Cave 5, t. 0755172204; www.golfclubperugia.it. 18-hole course, driving range, club house, bar, restaurant, pro-shop.

---

## Costacciaro  06021

*Page 91*

 **Museums and cultural institutions**

**Vecchio Frantoio.** Via Massarelli, t. 075 9170124-228, fax 0759170647. *Open: 8-7:30.*

 **Sports**

**CENS.** Via G. Galeazzi 1, t. 0759170236; www.cens.it. National Speleology Centre Monte Cucco.

---

## Deruta  06053

*Page 140*

 *Pro Deruta Association.* Piazza dei Consoli 4, t. 0759711559.

**Hotels, restaurants, campsites and holiday camps**

★★★ **Melody.** SS E45 at 55.800 kms, t. 0759711022, fax 0759711018; info@hotelmelody.it; www.melodyhotel.it. 55 rooms. Facilities for disabled. Air conditioning; parking, parking garage, garden. AE VISA MC

**Museums and cultural institutions**

**Museo regionale della Ceramica.** Largo S. Francesco, t. 0759711000, fax 0759711037. Closed Tuesday (October-March). *Open: October-March, 10:30-1 and 2:30-5; April-June, 10:30-1 and 3-6; July-September, 10:30-1 and 3:30-7.*

**Pinacoteca civica.** Piazza dei Consoli, t. 0759711143, fax 0759711037. *Open: same hours as Museo regionale della Ceramica.*

**Churches and monuments**

**Santuario della Madonna dei Bagni.** T. 075973455. *Open: contact the Sanctuary.*

**Shows and other festivities**

**End of summer fete** (September). Cultural celebrations, theatrical performances and sports events.

**Ceramics Festival** (25th November). Dedicated to the veteran ceramic artists.

**Shops, arts and crafts**

**Bottega d'Arte di Ficola Augusto.** Via Ziporovic 14, t. 0759710222. Artistic ceramics (production and sales).

**L'Antica di Moretti Alviero.** SS E 45, t. 075 9711270. Quality Deruta Majolica ware.

**Maioliche Artistiche Grazia.** Via Tiberina 181, t. 0759710201. The oldest and most traditional factory of local Deruta ceramics.

**Sambuco.** Via della Tecnica, t. 0759711625. Artistic Deruta Majolica and products in first quality gold.

## Fabro  05015

*Page 192*

 **Shops, arts and crafts**

**Cortellini Renato.** Contrada della Stazione, t.07581007.Manufacturing and decorating of ceramics.

 **Sports**

**Maneggio El Gaucho.** Locality Colonnetta, t.076382170.

## Ferentillo  05034

*Page 179*

 *Pro Loco.*Via della Vittoria 61,t.0744780990.

Hotels, restaurants, campsites and holiday camps

 **Piermarini.** Via F. Ancaiano 23, t. 0744 780714; ristorantepiermarini@libero.it.Closed Sunday evenings and Monday,period in September.Air conditioning;parking,garden.Regional cuisine - mushrooms and truffles. AE ⓪ VISA MC

 **Museums and cultural institutions**

**Cimitero - Museo delle Mummie.** Via della Rocca, t. and fax 0744780204. *Open: 9-12 and 2-7.*

 **Churches and monuments**

**Abbazia di S. Pietro in Valle.** T.0744780316. *Open: 10:30-1 and 2:30-5.*

## Ficulle  05016

*Page 193*

 **Sports**

**Centro ippico La Casella.** Locality La Casella,t.076386684.Country rides,trekking,training of colts,club house,bar,restaurant,tennis courts, open-air pool.

**Shops, arts and crafts**

**Del Croce Costantino.** Via Cassia 53,t.075 86044.Manufacturing and decorating of ceramics.

## Foligno 06034

*Page 116*

*IAT* (Territorial Tourist Service).Corso Cavour 126, t. 0742354459-0742354165, fax 0742 340545; info@foligno.pg.it; www.comune.foli gno-pg.it.

Hotels, restaurants, campsites and holiday camps

★★★ **Italia.** Piazza Matteotti 12,t.0742350412,fax 0742352258; hotel.italia@libero.it; www.ho telitaliafoligno.com. 35 rooms. Air conditioning; special terms for parking garage. AE ⓪ VISA MC; (B2).

★★★ **Le Mura.** Via Bolletta 27, t. 0742357344, fax 0742353327; albmur@bcsnet.it; www.alber

golemura.com.29 rooms.Meublé.Facilities for disabled. Air conditioning; parking, parking garage. AE ⓪ VISA MC; (A2).

★★★ **Poledrini.** Viale Mezzetti 2,t.0742341041,fax 0742352973;hotelpoledrini@tin.it;www.folig nohotel.com. 42 rooms. Air conditioning; parking,parking garage. AE ⓪ VISA MC; (C3).

★★★ **Villa Roncalli.** Viale Roma 25,t.074 2391091, fax 0742671001.Closed for a period in August. 10 rooms.Air conditioning; parking, garden, open-air pool. AE ⓪ VISA; (C3).

★★ **Valentina.** Via F.Ottaviani 19,t.074 2353990, fax 0742356243. 20 rooms. Meublé. Air conditioning; parking, parking garage. AE ⓪ VISA MC; (B3).

 **Villa Roncalli.** Viale Roma 25, t. 074 2391091,fax 0742391001.Closed Monday,period in August and January. Air conditioning,parking,garden.Specialised regional cuisine. AE ⓪ VISA MC; (C3).

*at Colfiorito, 25 kms* 06030

★★★ **Villa Fiorita.** Via del Lago 9,t.0742681326,fax 0742681327; villafiorita@cline.it; www.hotelvil lafiorita.com.40 rooms.Facilities for disabled. Air conditioning; parking, garden, open-air pool. AE ⓪ VISA MC

 **Farm Holidays**

*At Pontecentesimo, 10 kms* 06030

**Pontecentesimo.** Via Casa Ricci, t. 06 6570415.A long,tree-lined avenue leads to the 17th century villa converted into a holiday farm.Excursions by bicycle or on horseback. Swimming pool.

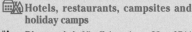 **Museums and cultural institutions**

**Centro di documentazione del Teatro Piermarini.** Corso Cavour, t. 0742350487. *Closed for restoration.*

**Museo dell'Istituzione comunale.** Piazza della Repubblica, t. 0742330226. *Closed at present.*

**Pinacoteca comunale e Museo Archeologico di Palazzo Trinci.** Piazza della Repubblica,t.0742357697;www.comune.foligno pg.it/cultura/paltrinci.html. Closed Monday *Open: 10-7.*

**Raccolta d'Arte sacra.** Palazzo delle Canoniche, piazza della Repubblica, t. 0742350734 (cultural office).*Closed at present.*

 **Shows and other festivities**

**Quintain Merry-Go-Round** (June and September).Representation of a Medieval horse riding contest.

**Baroque Signs** (September).Theatre, film and musical shows and exhibitions in perfec Baroque style.

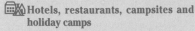 **Shops, arts and crafts**

**Centro Agro Alimentare dell'Umbria** Via N. Sauro 4/c, t. 0742344214, fax 0742 341001; www.umbriadoc.com.The Cente promotes several initiatives for typical re gional productions, with possibility to pur chase on-line.

**Cooperativa Cuore verde.** Via Agostini 5. Cereals, grapes and wines and typical dried pulses such as the Colfiorito lentils, produced organically.

**Editoriale Umbra.** Via Pignattara 34, t. 0742 357541. Antiques bookshop.

**Fabbrica artigiana di organi Pinchi.** Via Fedeli 24, t. 074224164. A visit (on request) to the laboratory is worth-while for understanding the extraordinary, elaborate work necessary for realising the solemn Pinchi organs.

*at Colfiorito, 25 kms*  06030

**The Red Potatoes of Colfiorito.** Every day, along the main road between Foligno and Macerata, close to Colfiorito, peddlars sell these characteristic long, oval-shaped potatoes with their light yellow pulp. Imported from Holland ten years ago, they have become the symbol of the district. Also on sale are cereals and vegetables, like the rare «cicerchie» (flat peas).

 Sports

**Aeroclub Foligno.** Airport, t. 0742670201. Hang-gliding.

**Centro ippico Verchiano.** Locality Verchiano, t. 0742315273.

**Cooperativa Umbria Trekking.** Via Monti Martani 2, t. 074224677. Trekking along the central Appennine plateau, in Valnerina, on Martani Mount, in Santa Valley and in Valdiserra, white water, bird watching, environment learning.

**Sibillini Rafting Center.** Via Monte Cervino 6, t. 074223146; www.folmedia.com/gaia.torrentismo.

 Local guides and excursions

**CAI.** Via Giuseppe Piermarini 3, t. 0742 358804.

 Natural areas, parks and reserves

*at Colfiorito, 25 kms* 06030

**Parco regionale di Colfiorito.** Foligno, piazzetta del Reclusorio 1, 0742 349714; www.parks.it.

---

**Fossato di Vico** 06022
*Page 90*

 Museums and cultural institutions

**Mostra della Civiltà contadina.** Via Venturi 1, t. 075914951.

---

**Giano dell'Umbria** 06030
*Page 141*

 Hotels, restaurants, campsites and holiday camps

**Pineta di Giano.** Locality Montecerreto, t. 0742930040, fax 0742930040. Seasonal.

---

**Gualdo Cattaneo** 06035
*Page 141*

 Hotels, restaurants, campsites and holiday camps

*at San Terenziano, 14 kms* 06058

**★★★ Dei Pini.** Via Roma 9, t. 074298122, fax 0742 98378; info@deipini.it; www.deipini.it. 50 rooms. Parking, garden, open-air pool, tennis courts. AE OD VISA MC

---

**Gualdo Tadino** 06023
*Page 92*

 *Pro Tadino Association.* Via Calai 39, t. 075 912172.

 Hotels, restaurants, campsites and holiday camps

 **Valsorda.** At Valsorda, t. 075913261. Seasonal.

 Farm Holidays

*At San Pellegrino, 6 kms*

**Bonomi Fabrizia.** Locality Monte Camera, t. 075918145. 20 kms from the naturalistic area of Colfiorito – the birdwatchers' paradise – two late 18th-century farmhouses surrounded by oak forest.

 Museums and cultural institutions

**Museo della Ceramica.** T. 075912172. *To be prepared.*

**Rocca Flea - Pinacoteca and Antiquarium.** T. 0759150248; www.sistemamuseo.it. Closed Monday; Monday-Wednesday from October to June. *Open: 10:30-1 and 3-6.*

Shows and other festivities

**Representation of the Passion** (Good Friday).

**International Ceramics Exhibition - Contest** (July-August).

**Games of the Doors** (last Sunday in September). Historical procession in costume, catapult and archery contests, donkey-cart and running races.

Shops, arts and crafts

**Ceramiche Artistiche di Garofoli Dante.** Via Marcinelli, t. 0759108113.

**Ceramiche La Sovrana di Danti Dante.** Via Flaminia 191, t. 0759108172.

**Nedo da Gualdo.** Largo Porta Romana, t. 075 910210. Precious creations in majolica by Mastro Nedo who prefers interiors of farm cottages, pastoral scenes, popular figures of saints and nude women.

---

**Gubbio** 06024
*Page 80*

 *IAT* (Territorial Tourist Service). Via Ansidei 32, t. 0759220790, fax 0759273409; info@iat.gubbiopg.it.

*Tourist Information.* Piazza Oderisi 6, t. 075 9220693.

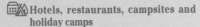 **Hotels, restaurants, campsites and holiday camps**

★☆★ **Park Hotel ai Cappuccini.** Via Tifernate, t. 0759234, fax 0759220323; inf@parkhotelai cap puccini.it; www.parkhotelaicappuccini.it. 95 rooms. Facilities for disabled. Air conditioning; parking, parking garage, garden, indoor pool, tennis courts. AE ⓪ VISA MC; (A1, f.p.).

★☆★ **Sporting.** Via del Botagnone, t. 0759220753, fax 0759220555; info@urbaniweb.com; www.urbaniweb.com. 52 rooms. Air conditioning; parking, parking garage, garden. AE ⓪ VISA MC; (B1, f.p.).

★★★ **Bosone Palace.** Via XX Settembre 22, t. 075 9220688, fax 0759220552; hotel.bosone@li bero.it; www.mencarelligroup.com. Closed February. 30 rooms. Meublé. AE ⓪ VISA MC; (B2).

★★★ **Gattapone.** Via Ansidei 6, t. 0759272489, fax 0759272417; hotel.gattapone@libero.it; www. mencarelligroup.com. Closed mid-January-mid-February. 18 rooms. Meublé. Facilities for disabled. Garage. AE ⓪ VISA; (B2).

★★★ **San Marco.** Via Perugina 5, t. 0759220234, fax 0759273716; info@hotelsanmarcogubbio. com; www.hotelsanmarcogubbio.com. 63 rooms. Facilities for disabled. Air conditioning; garage, garden. AE ⓪ VISA MC; (B1-2).

★★ **Oderisi-Balestrieri.** Via Mazzatinti 2-12, t. 0759220662, fax 0759220663. 40 rooms. Meublé. Special terms for parking garage. AE ⓪ VISA MC; (B1-2).

🍴 **Taverna del Lupo.** Via Ansidei 6, t. 075 9274368, fax 0759271269; mencarelli@menca relligroup.com; www.mencarelligro up.com. Closed Monday. Also hotel. Air conditioning. Regional cuisine. AE ⓪ VISA MC; (B2).

🍴 **Villa Montegranelli.** Locality Monteluiano, t. 0759220185, fax 0759273372; villa.monte granelli@tin.it; www.villamontegranellihotel. it. Air conditioning; parking, garden. Regional and Apulian cuisine - mushrooms and truffles, fish. AE ⓪ VISA MC; (C1, f.p.).

🍴 **Federico da Montefeltro.** Via della Repubblica 35, t. 0759273949. Closed Thursday (except August and September), February. Garden. Regional and classical cuisine - mushrooms and truffles. AE ⓪ VISA MC; (B2).

🍴 **La Fornace di Mastro Giorgio.** Via Mastro Giorgio 2, t. 0759221836; info@rosa tihotels.it; www.rosatihotels.com. Closed Tuesday and Wednesday at midday; period in January. Regional cuisine. AE ⓪ VISA MC; (B2).

⛺ **Villa Orto Guidone.** Locality Orto Guidone, ★★★★ t. 0759272037, fax 0759276620. Seasonal.

⛺ **Città di Gubbio.** Locality Orto Guidone, t. ★★★ 0759272037, fax 0759276620. Seasonal.

🌲 **Farm Holidays**

**Abbazia di Vallingegno.** Locality Vallingegno, t. 075920158, fax 0759221578. Facilities for disabled. Adjacent to the charming

monastery, several farmhouses converted into rustic holiday homes. Nature weeks for children in Spring. Open-air pool.

 **Museums and cultural institutions**

**Museo diocesano.** Palazzo del Capitolo dei Canonici, via Federico da Montefeltro, t. 0759220904-0759273980; www.museogub bio.org. Closed Monday and from 8 January to 15 March. *Open: winter, 10-1 and 3-6; summer, 9-1 and 3-6; Saturday and holidays, 10-6.*

**Museo della Ceramica a lustro e Torre medievale di Porta Romana.** Via Dante 24, t. 0759221199. *Open: 9-1 and 3-7:30.*

**Museo civico e Pinacoteca comunale.** Piazza Grande, t. and fax 0759274298. *Open: winter, 10-1 and 2-5; summer, 10-1 and 3-6.*

**Museo di Palazzo Ducale.** Via Ducale, t. 075 9275872. Closed Monday. *Open: 8:30-7.*

**Raccolta d'Arte di S. Francesco.** Piazza Quaranta Martiri, t. 0759273460. *Open on request.*

**Teatro romano e Antiquarium.** Via Teatro Romano, t. 0759220992. *Open: 8-2.*

 **Shows and other festivities**

**Procession of the Dead Christ** (Holy Week).

**Race with the Ceri** (15 May). Race through the town with giant candle-shaped wooden structures as far as Mount Ingino, where the Basilica of the Holy Patron stands.

**Palio of the Balestra** (last Sunday in May). Medieval crossbow contest followed by historic procession.

**Biennale di scultura** (June-September). Exhibition of contemporary art.

**Classical Performances** (July-August). Classical performances held inside the monumental Roman theatre.

**Gubbio Festival** (July-August). T. 0759220230. Chamber and symphonic music festival, performed in the town's most highly valued artistic buildings.

 **Shops, arts and crafts**

**Antichità Lunani.** Via dei Consoli 70, t. 075 9274765. Antique, modern and curious works of art.

**Antichità Marcelli di Minelli.** Via del Popolo 23, t. 0759273687. English silverware and period ceramics.

**Anna Maria Radicchi.** Via B. Telesio, t. 075 9276427. Gastronomic products for the pleasure of all palates.

**Ceramiche Fumanti Aldo.** Locality Zap pacenere, t. 0759276413. Artistic ceramics.

**Laboratorio F.lli Minelli & C.** Via B. Croce 12 t. 0759276734. Products in wood, reproduction of period furniture, gilding and painting.

**Le ghiottonerie eugubine.** Via Mastro Gior gio, t. 0759277579. From bitters to truffles, tc preserves.

**Pompeo.** Via Cavour 6, t. 0759273850. Ap petising hams and many other local gastro nomical delights.

**Scavizzi.** Via Baldassini 22, t. 0759273079. Copper and wrought iron works.

**Volpotti Maria.** Via Vantaggi, t. 0759273879. Woven cloth, lace and all kinds of refineries.

 **Local guides and excursions**

**Comunità Montana Alto Chiascio.** Via Giacomo Matteotti 17, t. 0759222629.

**CAI - Sezione di Gubbio.** C/o Informagiovani, piazza S. Pietro, t. 0759273618.

 **Natural areas, parks and reserves**

**Gola del Bottaccione.** SS Eugubina from Porta Castello. Information c/o *IAT*, Gubbio, piazza Oderisi 6, t. 0759220693, fax 075 9273409.

---

## Lugnano in Teverina    ✉ 05020

*Page 166*

 **Museums and cultural institutions**

**Antiquarium.** Via Umberto I, t. 0744902321 (Town Hall). *Open: on request.*

---

## Magione    ✉ 06063

*Page 64*

 *Pro Loco.* Corso Marchesi 14, t. 075843859.

 **Hotels, restaurants, campsites and holiday camps**

*at San Feliciano, 7 kms*    ✉ 06060

★★★ **Le Tre Isole.** Locality Riva del Sole, t. 075 8400127, fax 0758400600; letreisole@tin.it; www.letreisole.com. Closed for a period between November and December and mid-January-mid-March. 39 rooms. Meublé. Facilities for disabled. Air conditioning; parking, parking garage, garden, open-air pool, tennis courts, private beach. 💳 💳 💳

**Settimio.** Lungolago Alicata 1, t. 075 8476000. Also hotel. Closed Thursday off season, November. Air conditioning; parking, garden. Regional cuisine - fish from the lake.

*at Sant'Arcangelo, 10 kms*    ✉ 06060

★★★ **Villaggio Italgest.** Via Martiri di Cefalonia, t. 075848238, fax 075584725. Seasonal.

★★★ **Polvese.** Via Montivalle, t. 075848200, fax 075848050. Seasonal.

*at Caligiana, 10 kms*

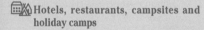 **Farm Holidays**

**Podere I Sette.** Via Case Sparse, t. and fax 0758409364; www.isette.it. A large olive grove with trees hundreds of years old and 300 acres of meadows and woods surround this farm.

 **Museums and cultural institutions**

**Castello dei Cavalieri di Malta.** Viale Cavalieri di Malta, t. 0755009681. *Open: on request.*

---

*at San Feliciano, 7 kms*    ✉ 06060

**Museo della Pesca del lago Trasimeno.** Lungolago della Pace e del Lavoro, t. and fax 0758479261; www.sistemamuseo.it. *Open: February-March and October, 10:30-12:30 and 2:30-5:30 (Thursday-Sunday); April-June and September, 10-12:30 and 3-6 (Tuesday-Sunday); July-August, 10:30-1 and 4-7; November-January, 10:30-1 and 2:30-5 (Saturday and Sunday).*

 **Shops, arts and crafts**

**Fer Lavori.** SS Magione-Chiusi, t. 075840363. Copper and wrought iron works.

 **Sports**

**Fitness Sport Club.** Via dell'Università (Monte del Lago), t. 0758400030. School and hire of windsurf and canoes; water bikes and mountain bikes to hire.

 **Natural areas, parks and reserves**

**Oasi naturalistica «La Valle».** Locality San Savino, t. 0758476007. Four-hour guided visits with a naturalist, to be booked in advance.

---

## Marsciano    ✉ 06055

*Page 63*

 **Farm Holidays**

**Teveraccio.** Locality Cerro, t. 0758743787, fax 0758744049. Facilities for disabled. A 75 acre farm surrounds the farmhouse dating back to 1620 restored to its original condition.

 **Shops, arts and crafts**

**Ditta C. Sposini.** San Valentino della Collina, t. 0758784134. Characteristic Umbrian cloth.

 **Local guides and excursions**

*At San Venanzo, 11 kms*    ✉ 05010

**Comunità montana «Monte Peglia e Selva di Meana».** Piazza Roma 1, t. 075875322, fax 075875120.

---

## Massa Martana    ✉ 06056

*Page 142*

 *IAT* (Territorial Tourist Service) *del Tuderte*, t. 0758943395.

 **Hotels, restaurants, campsites and holiday camps**

★★★ **Delle Terme San Faustino.** At Terme di San Faustino, SS E45 at 19 kms, t. and fax 075 8856421; hotel@sanfaustino.it; www.sanfaustino.it. 27 rooms. Air conditioning; parking, special terms for parking garage, garden, open-air pool. 💳 💳 💳

 **Museums and cultural institutions**

*at Villa San Faustino, 5 kms*

**Catacombe di Villa San Faustino.** Vocabolo Viagetti 84, t. 0758856248. *Open: on request.*

## Spas Resorts

### at Terme di San Faustino, 7 kms

**Terme di S. Faustino.** T.0758856421.*Open: May-October.*

---

## Montefalco     ✉ 06036

*Page 120*

ℹ️ *Town Hall.*T.0742378673.

*Tourist Information.* c/o Museo Civico di S. Francesco,t. 0742379598.

🏨 **Hotels, restaurants, campsites and holiday camps**

★☆★ **Villa Pambuffetti.** Viale della Vittoria 20, t. 0742378823, fax 0742379245; villabianca@interbusiness.it; www.umbria.org.15.rooms.Facilities for disabled. Air conditioning; parking, garden, open-air pool.⒜⒟⒱⒨;(A1,*f.p.*).

🌲 **Farm Holidays**

**Camiano Piccolo.** Via Camiano Piccolo 5, t.074379492.This complex,of 16th-century origin,is buried in an olive grove in a magnificent position overlooking the Spoleto Valley.Open-air pool.No dogs allowed.

🏛 **Museums and cultural institutions**

**Museo civico di S. Francesco.** Via Ringhiera Umbra, t. 0742379598; www.sistema museo.it.Closed Monday (November-February). *Open: November-February, 10:30-1 and 2:30-5; March-May, September-October, 10:30-1 and 2-6; June-July, 10:30-1 and 3-7; August, 10:30-1 and 3-7:30.*

⛪ **Churches and monuments**

**Abbazia dei Ss. Fidenzio e Terenzio.** *Open: Sunday, 10-12.*

🎭 **Shows and other festivities**

**Agosto Montefalchese.** (August). Music and culture, performances for children, flag bearers shows; the most representative moment of the event is the "Fuga del Bove" (The Ox Escape), historical representation of a Medieval merry-go-round.

**Enological Week** (Easter period).Exhibition and sales of the Montefalco D.O.C. wines, the wines of Umbria and the Italian raisin wines.

**Resurrection of Christ** (Saturday of Holy Week).Religious representation in a framework of fireworks and music.

⚖️ **Shops, arts and crafts**

**Tessitura Montefalco (Ditta Pardi).** Via G. Pascoli, t. 074279383.Artisan Umbrian cloth woven on the loom.

🏟 **Sports**

**Campo comunale.** Via A. Franchi, t. 0742 378673.Tennis courts.

---

## Montone     ✉ 06014

*Page 74*

ℹ️ *IAT dell'Alta Valle del Tevere.*T.0758554817.

🏛 **Museums and cultural institutions**

**Museo comunale.** Ex convento di S. Francesco,via S.Francesco,t.0759306535;www.sistemamuseo.it. *Open: winter, 10:30-1 and 3-5:30 (Saturday and Sunday); summer 10:30-1 and 3:30-6 (Friday, Saturday and Sunday).*

🚶 **Local guides and excursions**

**CO.S.T. Cooperativa Servizi Turistici.** Via S.Francesco 4,t.0759306415.

---

## Narni     ✉ 05035

*Page 159*

ℹ️ *Pro Narni Tourist Association.*Piazza dei Priori 3,t.0744715362;www.comune.narni.tr.it.

🏨 **Hotels, restaurants, campsites and holiday camps**

★★★ **Dei Priori.** Vicolo del Comune 4, t. 0744 726843, fax 0744726844; info@loggiadeipriori.it; www.loggiadeipriori.it. 19 rooms. Air conditioning.⒜⒟⒱⒨;(B-C1).

★★★ **Il Minareto.** Via dei Cappuccini Nuovi 32,t. 0744726343, fax 0744726284; hotelminareto @libero.it;www.hotelminareto.com.8 rooms. Air conditioning; parking, garden.⒜⒟⒱⒨;(C3,*f.p.*).

★★★ **La Rocca.** Via Flaminia at 91 kms, t. 0744 744423, fax 0744744424; info@laroccahotel.it; www.laroccahotel.it. 34 rooms. Meublé. Facilities for disabled.Air conditioning; parking, garden.⒜⒟⒱⒨; (C3,*f.p.*).

🍴 **Cavallino.** Via Flaminia Romana 220,t.0744 761020. Closed Tuesday, July and Christmas period.Parking,garden.Regional cuisine.⒜⒟⒱; (C3,*f.p.*).

🏕 **Monti del Sole.** At Borgheria,t.0744796336, ★★ fax 0744796336.Seasonal.

🏛 **Museums and cultural institutions**

**Circuito Narni Sotterranea.** Associazione culturale Subterranea, via S. Bernardo 12, t. 0744722292;www.narnisotterranea.it.

**Sala consiliare e Raccolta archeologica.** Palazzo comunale, piazza dei Priori, t. 0744 7471.*Open: winter, 3-6 (Saturday), 10-1 and 3-6 (holidays); summer, 4-7 (Saturday), 10-1 and 4-7 (holidays).*

**Raccolta paleontologica e preistorica.** Ex chiesa di S.Domenico,via Mazzini,t.0744 747216 (Municipal Library).

**Rocca Albornoziana.** T.0744747216.*Open: winter, 1-5 (Saturday), 10-5 (holidays); summer, 1-7 (Saturday), 10-7 (holidays).*

**Strutture ipogee di S. Domenico.** T.0744 722292.*Open: only holidays, June-September, 10-1 and 3-6; October-May, 11-1 and 3-5; to be booked in advance.*

**Shows and other festivities**

**Corsa all'Anello (Ring Race)** (2nd Sunday in May). Contest in costume followed by a procession through the town.

 **Shops, arts and crafts**

**Norcineria di Cecchetti.** Via Roma 5, t. 0744722659. Pork-butcher.

**Pasticceria Evangelisti & C.** Piazza Garibaldi 25, t. 0744715256. Production of «panpepato», typical cake of Ternano.

 **Sports**

**Centro ippico Narnese.** Strada di Borgaria 6, t. 0744715224.

**La Mongolfiera.** Via del Parco 27, t. 0336 607781. Trekking, white water, excursions, potholing, cross-country skiing, bird watching.

---

## Nocera Umbra  ☒ 06025

*Page 93*

☒ *IAT del Folignate - Nocera Umbra.* T. 0742 354165 - 0742354459, fax 0742340545.

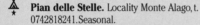 **Hotels, restaurants, campsites and holiday camps**

 **Pian delle Stelle.** Locality Monte Alago, t. 0742818241. Seasonal.

 **Farm Holidays**

**La Lupa.** Locality Colpertana, t. and fax 0742 813539. Facilities for disabled. This beautiful stone building situated on a hill dominates the cultivated fields and surrounding woods. No dogs allowed.

 **Museums and cultural institutions**

**Museo civico S. Francesco.** Piazza Caprera, t. 0742812058. *Closed at present.*

**Shows and other festivities**

**Festa delle Acque** (August). Concerts, cultural events exhibitions.

**Palio of the Quartieri** (from the 1st Thursday in August to the following Sunday). Representation of two different historical periods of ancient Nocera, 1400 and 1800.

---

## Norcia  ☒ 06046

*Page 173*

☒ *Tourist Information.* Via Solferino 22, t. and fax 0743828173.

**Hotels, restaurants, campsites and holiday camps**

★★★ **Grotta Azzurra.** Via Alfieri 12, t. 0743816513, fax 0743817342; info-booking@bianconi.com; www.bianconi.com. 46 rooms. Facilities for disabled. Air conditioning; special terms for parking garage. ⒶⒺ ⓪ 𝕍𝕀𝕊𝔸 𝕄𝕔; (B2).

★★★ **Salicone.** Strada Montedoro, t. 0743828076, fax 0743828081; info-booking@bianconi.com; www.bianconi.com. 71 rooms. Meublé. Facilities for disabled. Air conditioning; parking,

parking garage, garden, tennis courts. ⒶⒺ ⓪ 𝕍𝕀𝕊𝔸 𝕄𝕔; (A1).

 **Granaro del Monte.** Via Alfieri 12, t. 0743 816513; info-booking@bianconi.com; www.bianconi.com. Closed Tuesday. Air conditioning. Regional cuisine - mushrooms and truffles. ⒶⒺ ⓪ 𝕍𝕀𝕊𝔸 𝕄𝕔; (B2).

**Trattoria dal Francese.** Via Riguardati 16, t. 0743816290. Closed Friday except summer, period in January. Air conditioning. Regional cuisine - truffles and wild boar. ⒶⒺ 𝕍𝕀𝕊𝔸 𝕄𝕔; (B2).

 **Museums and cultural institutions**

**Museo civico diocesano La Castellina.** Piazza S. Benedetto, t. 0743817209, fax 0743 817030. Closed Monday (October-March). *Open: October-March, 10-1 and 3-5; April-July and September, 10-1 and 4-7; August, 10-1, 4-7:30 and 9:30-11.*

 **Shows and other festivities**

**Feast of the black truffle and the typical products of Valnerina** (last weekend in February). An occasion to taste local produce.

**Procession of the Dead Christ** (Good Friday).

 **Shops, arts and crafts**

**Prodotto del Cavatore.** Via Cairoli 1/b, t. 0743816689. Typical Umbrian gastronomical produce (olive oil, caciotta cheese, grappa, truffles).

**Sports**

**Soc. Nordica Impianti Scioviari.** Locality Forca Canapine, t. 074336808217-0330279063. Ski-lifts.

 **Local guides and excursions**

**Comunità montana Valnerina».** Via Manzoni, t. 0743816938, fax 0743817566.

**Natural areas, parks and reserves**

**Parco nazionale dei Monti Sibillini.** Casa del Parco, via Solferino 22, t. 0743817090; www.parks.it.

---

## Orvieto  ☒ 05018

*Page 182*

☒ *IAT (Territorial Tourist Service).* Piazza del Duomo 24, t. 0763341911-0763343658, fax 0763344433; info@iat.orvieto.tr.it.

*Tourist Information.* Piazza del Duomo 24, t. 0763341772, fax 0763344433.

**Hertz car renting**, at Railway Station, via 7 Martiri 32/F, t. 0763301303, fax 0763390506.

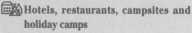 **Hotels, restaurants, campsites and holiday camps**

★★★ **La Badia.** At La Badia, 3 kms, t. 0763301959, fax 0763305396; labadia.hotel@tiscali.it; www.la badiahotel.it. Closed January-February. 28 rooms. Facilities for disabled. Air conditioning; parking, parking garage, garden, open-air pool, tennis courts. ⒶⒺ 𝕍𝕀𝕊𝔸 𝕄𝕔; (C2, f.p.).

**\*☆\* Maitani.** Via Maitani 5, t. and fax 0763342011; infoargo@argoweb.it; www.argoweb.it/hotel _maitani. Closed for a period in January. 40 rooms. Meublé. Air conditioning; parking garage, open-air pool, tennis courts.  **(C2)**.

**\*☆\* Palazzo Piccolomini.** Piazza Ranieri 36, t. 0763341743, fax 0763391046; piccolomini.hotel@orvienet.it; www.hotelpiccolomini.it. Closed mid-January-February. 32 rooms. Meublé. Facilities for disabled. Air conditioning; parking, parking garage.  (C1-2).

**\*\*\* Corso.** Corso Cavour 343, t. and fax 0763 342020; hotelcorso@libero.it. 16 rooms. Meublé. Facilities for disabled. Air conditioning; special terms for parking garage.  (B3).

**\*\*\* Filippeschi.** Via Filippeschi 19, t. and fax 0763343275; albergofilippeschi@tiscali.it. Closed Christmas period. 15 rooms. Meublé. Air conditioning.  (B1).

**\*\*\* G.H. Italia.** Via di Piazza del Popolo 13, t. 0763342065, fax 0763342902; htitalia@tin.it. Closed mid-January-mid-February. 45 rooms. Meublé. Garage.  (B2).

**\*\*\* Valentino.** Via Angelo da Orvieto 32, t. and fax 0763342464; hotelvalentino@libero.it; www.argoweb.it/hotelvalentino. Closed for a period between January and February. 19 rooms. Meublé. Facilities for disabled. Air conditioning; garage.  (B3).

**\*\*\* Virgilio.** Piazza Duomo 5/6, t. 0763341882, fax 0763343797. Closed for a period between January and February. 13 rooms. Meublé. Special terms for parking garage.  (C2).

**¶¶ Giglio d'Oro.** Piazza Duomo 8, t. 0763341903. Closed Wednesday, variable holiday closure. Air conditioning. Specialised regional and classic cuisine.  (C2).

**¶¶ Grotte del Funaro.** Via Ripa di Serancia 41, t. 0763343276; funaromercanti@libero.it; www.ristoranti-orvieto.it. Closed Monday (except August), period in July. Air conditioning. Regional cuisine.  (C1).

**¶¶ I Sette Consoli.** Piazza S. Angelo 1/A, t. 0763 343911; mstopp@tin.it. Closed Wednesday (from November to March also Sunday evenings), period in February. Garden. Specialised regional cuisine.  (B3).

**¶¶ Maurizio.** Via Duomo 78, t. 0763341114. Closed Tuesday, variable holiday closure. Regional cuisine.  (C2).

**¶ Dell'Ancora.** Via di Piazza del Popolo 5, t. 0763342766. Closed Thursday, period between January and February. Garden. Regional cuisine.  (B2).

**¶ Pozzo Etrusco.** Piazza Ranieri 1/A, t. 0763 344456. Closed Tuesday, period in June and Christmas. Garden. Regional cuisine.  (C1).

**¶ Trattoria la Grotta.** Via Luca Signorelli 5, t. 0763341348. Closed Tuesday, period in January. Air conditioning. Regional cuisine.  (C2).

---

*at Orvieto Scalo, 5 kms*  05019

**\*\*\* Villa Ciconia.** Locality Ciconia, SS 71 to Arezzo, at 35.2 kms, t. 0763305582, fax 0763 302077; villaciconia@libero.it; www.bellaumbria.net/Hotel-Villaciconia/home. Closed for a period in January or February. 12 rooms. Air conditioning; parking, garden, open-air pool.  (B5, f.p.).

**\*\*\* Europa.** Via Gramsci 5, t. 0763302171, fax 0763305227; hoteleuropa@libero.it; www.argoweb.it/hotel_europa. Closed mid-January-February. 52 rooms. Air conditioning; parking, parking garage.  (A5).

**\*\*\* Gialletti.** Via Costanzi 71, t. 0763301981, fax 0763305064; hgialletti@libero.it; www.hotelgialletti.it. 51 rooms. Air conditioning; parking, parking garage.  (B5, f.p.).

**\*\*\* Kristall.** Via Costanzi 69, t. 0763302103, fax 0763302765; kristall@orvienet.it; www.argoweb.it/hotelkristall. 37 rooms. Meublé. Facilities for disabled. Air conditioning; parking, special terms for parking garage.  (B5, f.p.).

---

*at Rocca Ripesena, 6 kms*  05010

🌲 **Farm Holidays**

**Sassosogna.** T. and fax 0763343141. Midst oak, chestnut and walnut trees, the rustic stone house. Open-air and games in the nearby natural spring.

🏛 **Museums and cultural institutions**

**Complesso ipogeo del Mulino di S. Chiara.** T. 0763344891. *Guided visits (11, 12:15, 4, 5:15) with departure from Piazza del Duomo.*

**Museo Archeologico nazionale.** Palazzo Papale, piazza del Duomo, t. and fax 0763 341039. *Open: 8:30-7:30.*

**Museo Claudio Faina e Museo civico Archeologico.** Palazzo Faina, piazza del Duomo 29, t. 0763341511, fax 0763341250. Closed Monday (September-March). *Open: 31 March-28 September, 10-1 and 2-6; 29 September-30 March, 10-1 and 2:30-5.*

**Museo Emilio Greco.** Palazzo Soliano, piazza del Duomo, t. 0763344605, fax 0763344664. Closed Monday. *Open: October-March, 10-6; April-September, 10-7.*

**Museo dell'Opera del Duomo.** Piazza del Duomo, t. 0763342477, fax 0763340336. *Closed at present.*

**Orvieto Underground-Parco delle Grotte.** Potholes run by the Speleotechnical Association, t. 0763344891-03397332764.

**Pozzo della Cava.** Via della Cava 28, t. 0763 342373. Closed Monday. *Open: 8-8.*

**Pozzo di S. Patrizio.** Viale Sangallo, t. 0763 343768. *Open: 10-6; summer, 10-7.*

**Torre del Moro.** Corso Cavour, t. 0763344567. *Open: March-April and September-October, 10-7; May-August, 10-8; November-February, 10:30-1 and 2:30-5.*

*at 1.6 kms from Orvieto, SS 71*

**Necropoli di Crocifisso del Tufo.** T. 0763 343611. *Open: April-September, 8:30-7:30; October-March, 8:30-5:30.*

 **Churches and monuments**

**Cappella di S. Brizio (Duomo).** Piazza del Duomo 26, t. 0763342477, fax 0763340336. *Open: working days November-February, 10-12:45 and 2:30-5:15; March and October, 10-12:45 and 2:30-6:15; April-September, 10-12:45 and 2:30-7:15; holidays, 2:30-5:45; holidays July-September, 2:30-6:45.*

**Chiesa di S. Angelo (tempio di S. Michele Arcangelo).** Via S. Angelo, t. 0755722624 (chiesa di S. Agostino). *Open: 9:30-12 and 3:30-6:30.*

**Duomo.** Piazza del Duomo, t. 0763341167. *Open: November-February, 7:30-12:45 and 2:30-5:15; March and October, 7:30-12:45 and 2:30-6:15; April-September, 7:30-12:45 and 2:30-7:15.*

 **Shows and other festivities**

**«G. Rodari» Literary Contest** (September). Biennal National Award for Children's Literature.

**Feast of the Woodpigeon** (Pentecost). An event not to be missed, bringing good luck for the year.

**Corpus Domini** (2nd Sunday after Pentecost). Spectacular event, after a parade in period costume of 1300 with court ladies, music and flag waving.

**Umbria Winter Jazz Festival** (late December-early January). Winter concert festival.

*at Allerona, 13 kms*

**Processione dei Pugnaloni** (3rd Sunday of May). Religious procession of the «Pugnaloni», processional veichles depicting scenes of rural life and a miracle by Saint Isidoro.

 **Shops, arts and crafts**

**Consorzio tutela vino Orvieto DOC.** Corso Cavour, t. 0763343790; consvino@tin.it. Cooperative for the supervision of Orvieto wines.

**Bottega del Michelangeli.** Via Albani 1, t. 0763342660. Gualverio Michelangeli, considered by all the most original carpenter of the region, creates fanciful, highly refined objects in wood and other materials. His dolls and model aeroplanes are well-known throughout Europe.

**C.A.E.M. Ceramiche Artistiche Etrusche di Maricchiolo.** Via Postierla 12, t. 076341645. Laboratory of Etruscan ceramics.

**Cantina Foresi.** Via del Duomo 2, t. 0763 341611. Wines and gastronomical products.

**Ditta Moretti Merletti.** Via del Duomo 84, t. 0763341714. Typical Orvieto lace.

**Fratelli Batalocco.** Via del Duomo 11, t. 0763 343965. Home-made bread, liver sausages, strong cheese, truffle paste - just some of the

Orvieto specialities on sale.

**L'arte del Vasaio di Tiberi Umberto.** Via Pedota 3, t. 0763342022. In the shop of Umberto Tiberi, the best faker in town during the fifties, his grandsons carry on the tradition - Precious Etruscan vases.

**Luigi Patrizia.** Via dei Gerani 3-5, t. 0763 91829. Decoration of ceramics and other materials.

**Mastro Paolo di Cosenza Paolo Emilio.** Via Felice Cavallotti 43, t. 076342892. Earthenware and ceramics.

**Propana Sandro.** Via dei Tigli, t. 076391458. Pottery manufacturing and decorating.

**Valentini Livio Orazio.** Via Lorenzo Maitani 8, t. 0763344085. Decorative majolica, metals and graphics laboratory.

 **Sports**

**Club ippico orvietano.** Locality La Cacciata, t. 0763301346.

---

## Paciano  06060

*Page 68*

**Hotels, restaurants, campsites and holiday camps**

**Locanda della Rocca.** Viale Roma 4, t. 075 830236; l.buitoni@flashnet.it; www.umbria travel/locandadellarocca/rocca.htm. Also hotel. Closed Tuesday, from mid-January to mid-February. Parking, garden. Specialised regional cuisine.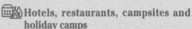

 **Museums and cultural institutions**

**Raccolta d'Arte S. Giuseppe.** Via della Pitalessa, t. 075830120. *Open: on request.*

 **Shops, arts and crafts**

**Belardinelli Alessandro.** Via Sensini 6, t. 075 830458. Copper and wrought iron works.

---

## Panicale  06064

*Page 68*

*Pro Loco.* Via Ceppari 5, t. 075837581.

**Hotels, restaurants, campsites and holiday camps**

★★★ **Le Grotte di Boldrino.** Via V. Ceppari 43, t. 075837161, fax 075837166. 9 rooms. Garden.

**Museums and cultural institutions**

**Chiesa di S. Sebastiano - Teatro Cesare Caporali.** Circuit «open museum», t. 075 837183-075953654. *Open: May-September, 10:30-12:30 and 4-7; October-April, 10-12 and 3-5 (Saturday and holidays; tutti i giorni in Christmas and Easter periods).*

**Pinacoteca Mariottini.** Town Hall, t. 075 837581. *Open: 9-1.*

**Shows and other festivities**

**Festa della Fraschetta (Branch)** (Easter

Monday). Religious commemoration of ancient tradition.

⚖️ **Shops, arts and crafts**

**Baldoni Mario.** Via Castiglionese 9, t. 075 837231. Copper and wrought iron works.

**Ditta Fratini Quartini.** Piazza Umberto I 11, t. 075837269 (Pro Loco). Weaving and embroidery. Panicale tulle.

🏇 **Sports**

**Golf Club Lamborghini.** Locality Soderi 1, t. 075837582. 9-hole course (doublestarting points), practice field, illuminated putting and pitching, pro-shop, club house.

**Skydive Trasimeno.** Locality Soderi, t. 0758350026. Skydiving.

---

## Passignano sul Trasimeno ✉ 06065
*Page 66*

ℹ️ *Pro Loco*. Via Roma 36, t. 075827635.

**Hotels, restaurants, campsites and holiday camps**

★★★ **Lido.** Via Roma 1, t. 075827219, fax 075827251; hlido@libero.it; www.umbriahotels.com. Seasonal. 52 rooms. Air conditioning; parking, garden, open-air pool. 📧 ⑩ 💳 MC

★★★ **Villa Paradiso.** Via Fratelli Rosselli 5, t. 075 829191, fax 075828118; info@bluhotels.it; www.bluhotels.it. Closed mid-January-mid-March. 110 rooms. Parking, garden, open-air pool. 📧 ⑩ 💳

### *at Castel Rigone, 10 kms* ✉ 06060

★☆★ **Relais la Fattoria.** Via Rigone 1, t. 075845322, fax 075845197; info@relaislafattoria.com; www.relaislafattoria.com. 30 rooms. Parking, garden, open-air pool. 📧 ⑩ 💳 MC

🍴 **La Corte.** Via Rigone 1, t. 075845322; info@re laislafattoria.com; www.relaislafattoria.com. Closed for a period between January and February. Parking. Regional and classical cuisine. 📧 ⑩ 💳 MC

### *at San Donato, 3 kms*

 **Kursaal.** Viale Europa 24, t. 075828085, fax 075827182. Seasonal.

🏃 **Shows and other festivities**

**Palio delle Barche** (last Sunday of July). Boat contest between the four quarters of the town.

🏇 **Sports**

**Club Velico Trasimeno.** Locality Darsena, t. 0758296021. Boathouse, beaching and launching of boats, sailing school, windsurf school and hire, courses in catamaran.

**Poggio del Belveduto.** Vocabolo Campori di Sopra, t. 075829076. Riding school, training school and boarding for horses, around the lake trekking lasting several days, archery.

 **Natural areas, parks and reserves**

**Parco regionale del Lago Trasimeno.** Via le Europa, t. 075828059, fax 0755044695; www. parks.it. Other towns included in the park: Castiglione del Lago, Magione, Panicale, Tuoro sul Trasimeno.

---

## Perugia ✉ 06100
*Page 40*

ℹ️ *Umbria Region*, ente@regione.umbria.it; www.regione.umbria.it.

*Tourist Promotion Association.* Via Mazzini 21, t. 075575951, fax 0755736828; call centre 848883355; info@apt.umbria.it; www.umbria 2000.it; www.umbria-turismo.it.

*IAT* (Territorial Tourist Service). Via Mazzini 6, t. 0755728937-0755729842, fax 0755739386; info@ iat.perugia.it.

*Tourist Information.* Sala S. Severo, palazzo dei Priori, piazza IV Novembre 3, t. 075 5736458.

**Hertz car renting**, c/o S. Egidio Airport, terminal building, t. 0755002439, fax 0755926266; piazzale Vittorio Veneto 4, t. and fax 0755002439.

**Hotels, restaurants, campsites and holiday camps**

★★★★ **Brufani.** Piazza Italia 12, t. 0755732541, fax 0755720210; brufani@tin.it; www.brufani palace.com. 94 rooms. Facilities for disabled. Air conditioning; parking, parking garage, indoor pool. 📧 ⑩ 💳 MC; (II, C2).

★☆★ **Giò Arte e Vini.** Via R. D'Andreotto 19, t. and fax 0755731100; hotelgio@interbusiness.it; www.emmeti.it/gio.it.html. 130 rooms. Facilities for disabled. Air conditioning; parking. 📧 ⑩ 💳 MC; (I, C1).

★☆★ **La Rosetta.** Piazza Italia 19, t. and fax 075 5720841; larosetta@perugiaonline.com. 94 rooms. Special terms for parking garage, garden. 📧 ⑩ 💳 MC; (II, C2).

★☆★ **Locanda della Posta.** Corso Vannucci 97, t. 0755728925, fax 0755732562; www.umbria travel.com/locandadellaposta. 40 rooms. Meublé. Air conditioning; special terms for parking garage. 📧 ⑩ 💳 MC; (II, C2).

★☆★ **Perugia Plaza Hotel.** Via Palermo 88, t. 075 34643, fax 07530863; perugiaplaza@umbria hotels.com; www.umbriahotels.com. 108 rooms. Air conditioning; parking, parking garage, garden, open-air pool. 📧 ⑩ 💳 MC; (I, F2, f.p.).

★☆★ **Sangallo Palace Hotel.** Via Masi 9, t. 075 5730202, fax 0755730068; hotel@sangallo.it; www.sangallo.it. 93 rooms. Facilities for disabled. Air conditioning; parking, parking garage, indoor pool. 📧 ⑩ 💳 MC; (II, D2).

★★★ **Fortuna.** Via Bonazzi 19, t. 0755722845, fax 0755735040; fortuna@umbria@hotels.com; www.umbriahotels.com. 33 rooms, 32 with bath or shower. Meublé. Air conditioning; parking, special terms for parking garage. 📧 ⑩ 💳 MC; (I, C2).

★★★ **Grifone.** Via Pellico 1, t. 0755837616, fax 075 5837619; info@grifone.com; www.grifoneho tel.com. 50 rooms. Air conditioning; parking,

parking garage.AE OD VISA MC; (I, F3, *f.p.*).

*** **Ilgo.** Via A. Di Duccio 1, t. 0755736641, fax 0755720720; hotelilgo.prenotazioni@tin.it; www.hotelilgo.com. 80 rooms. Air conditioning; parking, parking garage, garden, tennis courts.AE OD VISA MC; (I, B5, *f.p.*).

** **Ideal.** Via Tuderte 1/G, t. and fax 07530869; hotel.ideal@tiscali.it; www.wel.it/Hideal.it.htlm. 20 rooms. Meublé. Parking, parking garage, garden.AE OD VISA MC; (I, F5, *f.p.*).

** **Signa.** Via del Grillo 9 off corso Cavour, t. and fax 0755724180; hotelsigna@tin.it; www.hotelsigna.com. 23 rooms. Meublé. Parking garage, garden.VISA MC; (I, E4).

¶¶ **Da Giancarlo.** Via dei Priori 36, t. 075 5724314. Closed Friday, period in August. Air conditioning. Regional cuisine.AE OD VISA MC; (II, B1).

¶¶ **Enoteca Gio.** Via R. D'Andreotto 19, t. 075 5731100; hotelgio@interbusiness.it; www.hotelgio.it. Also hotel. Closed Sunday evenings and Monday lunchtime. Air conditioning, parking. Regional cuisine.AE OD VISA MC; (I, C1).

¶¶ **Fortebraccio.** Via Palermo 88, t. 07534643; perugiaplaza@umbriahotels.com; www.umbriahotels.com. Closed Monday. Air conditioning, parking, garden. Regional cuisine.AE OD VISA MC; (I, F2, *f.p.*).

¶¶ **Grifone.** Via Pellico 1, t. 0755837616. Closed Sunday. Air conditioning; parking. Regional cuisine.AE OD VISA MC; (I, F3, *f.p.*).

¶¶ **Il Falchetto.** Via Bartolo 20, t. 0755731775. Closed Monday, period between January and February. Air conditioning. Regional cuisine - truffles.AE OD VISA MC; (II, A2).

¶¶ **La Bocca Mia.** Via Rocchi 36, t. 0755723873. Closed Sunday, Monday lunchtime, Christmas period and August. Air conditioning. Regional cuisine.AE VISA MC; (II, A2).

¶ **Osteria del Gambero.** Via Baldeschi 17, t. 0755735461; www.osteriadelgambero.it. Open only evenings. Closed Monday, period in January and June. Specialised cuisine.AE OD VISA MC; (II, A-B2).

⚠ **Il Rocolo.** Locality L'Olmo, strada Fontana 1/N, t. 0755178550, fax 0755178550. Seasonal.
**

*at Bosco, 10 kms*      ✉ 06080

*★* **Relais San Clemente.** T. 0755915100, fax 0755915001; info@relais.it; www.relais.it. 64 rooms. Air conditioning; parking, garden, open-air pool, tennis courts.AE OD VISA MC

*at Cenerente, 8 kms*      ✉ 06070

*★* **Castello dell'Oscano.** Via della Forcella 37, t. 075584371, fax 075690666; info@oscano.com; www.oscano.com. 20 rooms. Air conditioning; parking, garden, open-air pool. AE OD VISA MC

*at Ponte San Giovanni, 8 kms*    ✉ 06087

*★* **Deco Hotel.** Via del Pastificio 8, t. 0755990950, fax 0755990970. 35 rooms. Facilities for disabled. Air conditioning; parking, parking garage, garden.AE OD VISA MC

*★* **Park Hotel.** Via A. Volta 1, t. 0755990444, fax 0755990455; info@perugiaparkhotel.com; www.perugiaparkhotel.com. 140 rooms. Facilities for disabled. Air conditioning; parking, parking garage, garden, indoor pool.AE OD VISA MC

*** **Tevere.** Via Manzoni 421/E, t. 075394341, fax 075394342; mail@tevere.it; www.tevere.it. 50 rooms. Facilities for disabled. Air conditioning; parking, parking garage, garden.AE OD VISA MC

*** **Volumni.** SS Southern Tiberina 5/A, t. 075 397141, fax 075397819; info@volumni.it; www.volumni.it. Closed Christmas period. 36 rooms. Facilities for disabled. Air conditioning; parking, special terms for parking garage, garden, open-air pool.AE OD VISA MC

*at San Martino in Campo, 12 kms*   ✉ 06079

*** **Le Querce.** SS. E45, 81 kms, t. 075609722, fax 075609725. 60 rooms. Meublé. Air conditioning; parking.AE OD VISA MC

*at Ponte Vallecèppi, 7 kms*      ✉ 06078

*** **Vega.** Strada di Montalcino 2/A, t. 0756929534, fax 0756929507; vegahot@tin.it; www.hotel-vega.com. 42 rooms. Facilities for disabled. Air conditioning; parking, garden, open-air pool.AE OD VISA MC

*at Ferro di Cavallo, 6 kms*      ✉ 06074

*★* **Golf Hotel Quattrotorri.** Centro direz. Quattrotorri, t. 0755171722, fax 0755171707; golfhotel@tecnonet.it. 118 rooms. Facilities for disabled. Air conditioning; parking, parking garage.AE OD VISA

*★* **Hit Hotel.** Strada Trasimeno Ovest 159/Z/10, t. 0755179247, fax 0755178947; info@hit-hotel.com; www.hit-hotel.com. 82 rooms. Air conditioning; parking, parking garage.AE VISA MC

*at Ramazzano, 13 kms*      ✉ 06080

🌲 Farm Holidays

**La Breccia de' I Tigli.** T. 0755734357, fax 075 5722632. The guests can choose between the lovely, well-kept 17th-century manor house with swimming pool inside the park or the old rustic farmhouse set apart in the solitude of the fields, with, of course, a verandah and large, open fireplace. No dogs allowed.

🏛 Museums and cultural institutions

**Accademia di Belle Arti «P. Vannucci».** Piazza S. Francesco al Prato 5, t. 0755730631-0755733864. *Closed at present.*

**Area archeologica.** Piazza Cavallotti. *Open: on request to the Umbria Archeological Superintendent*, piazza G. Bruno, t. 0755727141.

**Cappella di S. Severo.** Piazza Raffaello, t. 075 5733864; www.sistemamuseo.it. *Open: November-February, 10:30-1:30 and 2:30-4:30 (Saturday and Sunday until 5:30); March-October, 10-1:30 and 2:30-6:30.*

**Città della Domenica.** T. 0755054941. *Open: from April to mid-September, 10-6; from mid-September to mid-November, only Saturday* *and holidays.*

**Collegio del Cambio.** Palazzo dei Priori, corso Vannucci 25, t. 0755728599. Closed Monday (November-February). *Open: March-October and 20 December-6 January, 9-12:30 and 2:30-5:30 (working days), 9-12:30 (holidays); 1 November-19 December and 7 January-28 February, 8-2 (working days), 9-12:30 (holidays).*

**Collegio della Mercanzia.** Palazzo dei Priori, corso Vannucci 15, t. 0755730366. Closed Monday (November-February). *Open: March-October and 20 December-6th January, 9-1 and 2:30-5:30 (working days), 9-1 (holidays); 1 November-19 December and 7 January-28 February, 8-2 (Tuesday, Thursday, Friday), 8-4:30 (Wednesday and Saturday), 9-1 (holidays).*

**Collezione Dottori-Beuys.** Palazzo della Penna, piazza Podiani 11, t. 0755772444, fax 0755723206. Closed Monday. *Open: 10-1 and 3-7.*

**Galleria nazionale dell'Umbria.** Palazzo dei Priori, corso Vannucci 19, t. 0755741247, fax 0755720316. Closed first Monday of every month. *Open: 8:30-7:30.*

**Gipsoteca greco-romana.** Via dell'Aquilone 7, t. 0755853807, fax 0755853838. *Open: on request.*

**Mosaico romano.** Chemistry Institute, via Pascoli, t. 0755855604. Closed Saturday and holidays. *Open: 8-7.*

**Museo Archeologico nazionale dell'Umbria.** Piazza Giordano Bruno 10, t. 075 5727141, fax 0755728200; www.archeopg.arti.beniculturali.it. Closed Monday. *Open: 8:30-7:30.*

**Museo capitolare di S. Lorenzo.** Chiesa di San Lorenzo, piazza IV Novembre, t. 075 5723832. *Open: 11-1 (Monday-Friday); 11-1 and 4-6 (Saturday and Sunday).*

**Museo di Storia naturale «G. Cicioni».** Piazza IV Novembre, t. 0755771 (Town Hall), 0755736458 (APT). *Closed at present.*

**Orto botanico.** Via Roma 4/b, t. 07532643. Closed Sunday and holidays. *Open: winter, 9-5; summer, 9-6; Saturday, 9-1.*

**Orto botanico medievale.** Borgo XX Giugno 74, 0755856421 (Department of Vegetable Biology of Perugia University). Closed Sunday and holidays. *Open: summertime, 8-6:30; true solar time, 8-5; Saturday, 8-1:30.*

**Pozzo Etrusco.** Piazza Piccinino 1, t. 075 5733669, fax 0755723132; www.sistemamuseo.it. *Open: November-February, 10:30-1:30 and 2:30-4:30 (Saturday and Sunday until 5:30); March-October, 10-1:30 and 2:30-6:30.*

**Rocca Paolina.** Centro Servizi museali, t. 0755728440. Entrance from via Marzia, piazza Italia, via Masi.

**Sala dei Notari.** Palazzo dei Priori, piazza IV Novembre. Closed Monday (except Jun-September). *Open: 9-1 and 3-7.*

*at Ferro di Cavallo, 4 kms*

**Ipogeo di S. Manno.** Opera Agnus Dei, t.

0755736776. *Open: on request.*

*at Ponte San Giovanni, 8 kms*

**Ipogeo dei Volumni.** Via Assisana 53, t. 075 393329. *Open: September-June, 9-1 and 3:30-5; July-August, 9-1 and 4:30-7:30.*

*at San Sisto, 10 kms*

**Museo storico della Perugina.** Nestlé Italiana Plants, t. 07552761. Closed Saturday and holidays. *Open: 9-1 and 2-5:30.*

 **Churches and monuments**

**Complesso monumentale di S. Giuliana.** Via Baldassarre Orsini 3, t. 0755732745. *Open: holidays, 9-12:30.*

**Monastero della Beata Colomba.** *Open: 9-11 and 3:30-5 (ring the bell).*

 **Shows and other festivities**

**La Desolata** (Holy Week). Scared representation of the Passion accompanied by songs and the recitals of praises, poetry and prayers.

**Umbriafiction TV** (late March-early April). Festival of television films.

**Rockin'Umbria** (late June). Festival of rock music, graphics, photography, comics.

**Umbria Jazz** (July). T. 0755732432.

**Sagra musicale umbra** (September). Concerts of sacred and contemporary music with artists of international fame.

**Eurochocolat** (October) A major annual event which transforms Perugia into a huge pastry shop.

**Antiques Festival Città di Perugia** (October).

**Antiques Market** (last Sunday of every month and the previous Saturday). In the Carducci gaardens antique lovers can indulge their whims among all kinds of objects for all tastes.

**Ceramics Market** (every Tuesday and Saturday). In piazza Danti, in the courtyard of the Duomo, this display of local ceram-ics dates back to Medieval times.

⚖ **Shops, arts and crafts**

**Capitini Simonetta.** Via dell'Avvenire (Ponte Valleceppi), t. 0756929554. Glass-ware, artistic windows.

**Ditta Ceccucci - Bottega d'arte.** Corso Vannucci 38, t. 0755735143. Accurate reproductions of the famous Perugian «arazzetti» (little tapestries) and table linen of the XIV and XV centuries.

**Enoteca provinciale.** Via Ulisse Rocchi 18, t. 075572482. Selection of the best qual-ity Umbrian wines. Wine-tasting includes gastronomical tit-bits.

**La Bottega del Sagittario.** Via Ulisse Rocchi 8, t. 0755726154. Antiquities, prints, jewellery and silverware.

**Legart di M. L. e P. R.** Borgo XX Giugno 74, t. 07530991. Book-binding and restoration of books, frames and parchments.

**Libreria Natale Simonelli.** Corso Vannucci 82, t. 0755723744. The town's old-est bookshop. All kinds of books, in particular guidebooks and maps of the town.

**Il Telaio.** Via Bruschi 2/b, t. 0755726603. All the charm of the antique Umbrian cloth produced by the craftsmen of the laboratory of the Ditta Sposini di Marsciano.

**Studio Secchi.** Via Cartolari 20/a, t. 075 5734163. Creation of old-fashioned marionettes, miniature theatres, dolls and puppets toys.

**Talmone.** Via Maestà delle Volte 10, t. 075 5725744. In the ex-laboratory of a smithy, Umbrian gastronomical products including the typical local sweets and candies (hundreds of varieties of Perugian chocolate and the Colussi cakes and biscuits). A wide choice of liqueurs and grappas.

 Sports

**Antognolla Golf & Country Club.** Strada S. Giovanni del Pantano, t. 0756059563; www.antognolla.com. 9-hole course, available also for championships.

**Canoa Club Perugia.** At Ponte Felcino, via della Ghisa 23, t. 075691558; www.infinito.it/utenti/canoaclubperugia.

**FISE - Federazione Italiana Sport Equestri.** Via Martiri dei Lager 65, t. 0755054935; www.fise.it.

 Local guides and excursions

**CAI - Gruppo speleologico.** Via Santini 8, t. 0755847070; www.geocities.com/gspeleocaipg. Expeditions to the region's 700 or so potholes.

**Comunità montana «Monti del Trasimeno».** Via S. Bonaventura 10, t. 075582941, fax 0755829471.

**Legambiente Umbria.** Via della Viola 1, t. 0755721021, fax 0755722083; legambiente@tin.it. Information also on the fishing technique known as "no kill".

---

**Pietralunga** ✉ 06026

*Page 74*

 Museums and cultural institutions

**Raccolta Fauna umbra.** Locality Candeleto, t. 0759469707. *Open Friday, Saturday and Sunday; other days on request.*

---

**Preci** ✉ 06047

*Page 171*

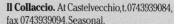Hotels, restaurants, campsites and holiday camps

 **Il Collaccio.** At Castelvecchio, t. 0743939084, fax 0743939094. Seasonal.

**San Gèmini** ✉ 05029

*Page 148*

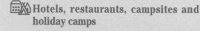 *Pro Loco.* Via Garibaldi 1, t. 0744630130 (Seasonal).
*Municipal Library.* T. 0744331438.

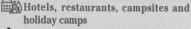Hotels, restaurants, campsites and holiday camps

★★★ **Antica Carsulae.** Locality S. Gemini Fonte, Via Tiberina 2, t. 0744630163, fax 0744333068; info@sangeminihotels.com; www.sangeminihotels.com. 9 rooms. Facilities for disabled. Parking, garden. 🆎 ⑩ 𝚅𝙸𝚂𝙰 𝙼𝙲

 Museums and cultural institutions

**Area archeologica di Carsulae.** Umbria Archeological Superintendent, t. 0755727141. *Open at all times.*

 Spas Resorts

**Terme di San Gèmini.** Via Fonte, t. 0744 333075, fax 0744333064. *Open: May-early October.*

 Shows and other festivities

**Giostra dell'Arme (Arms Merry-Go-Round)** (2nd Sunday of October). Contest between the quarters of Rocca and Piazza.

---

**Sigillo** ✉ 06028

*Page 90*

🦅 Natural areas, parks and reserves

**Parco regionale del Monte Cucco.** Villa Anita, t. 0759177326, fax 0759177071; www.parks.it. Other towns included in the park: Costacciaro, Fossato di Vico, Scheggia-Pascelupo.

---

**Spello** ✉ 06038

*Page 111*

ℹ️ *Pro Loco.* Piazza Matteotti 3, t. 0742301009.

🏨Hotels, restaurants, campsites and holiday camps

★★★ **Palazzo Bocci.** Via Cavour 17, t. 0742301021, fax 0742301464; bocci@bcsnet.it; www.emmeti.it/pbocci.it.html. 23 rooms. Meublé. Air conditioning; garden. 🆎 ⑩ 𝚅𝙸𝚂𝙰 𝙼𝙲; (C2).

★★★ **Del Teatro.** Via Giulia 24, t. 0742301140, fax 0742301612; hoteldelteatro@mclink.it; www.greenline.it/hoteldelteatro. 11 rooms. Meublé. Parking garage. 🆎 ⑩ 𝚅𝙸𝚂𝙰 𝙼𝙲; (B2).

🍴 **La Bastiglia.** Via dei Molini 17, t. 0742651277, fax 0742301159; faucelli@labastiglia.com; www.labastiglia.com. Also hotel. Closed Wednesday and Thursday lunchtime, period in January-February and July. Air conditioning; parking. Regional cuisine. 🆎 ⑩ 𝚅𝙸𝚂𝙰 𝙼𝙲; (A2).

🍴 **Il Molino.** Piazza Matteotti 6/7, t. 0742 651305; bocci@bcsnet.it. Closed Tuesday, period in January. Air conditioning; garden.

Regional cuisine.  AE ⓓ VISA MC; (C2).

 **Umbria.** Locality Chiona, via Spineto 27, t. 0742651772. Seasonal.

 **Farm Holidays**

**Le Due Torri.** Locality Limiti di Spello, t. and fax 0742651249. From the farmhouse built in the pink and white stone of Mount Subasio you can enjoy the enchanting view of Assisi. Stone mill for cereals and olive press.

 **Museums and cultural institutions**

**Collezione Straka-Coppa.** Villa Fidelia, via Flaminia 72, t. and fax 0742301866; www.sistemamuseo.it. *Open: April-June and September, 10:30-1 and 2:30-5:30 (Thursday-Sunday); July-August, 10:30-1 and 4-7; October-March, 10:30-1 and 2:30-5:30 (only Saturday and Sunday).*

**Pinacoteca civica.** Piazza Matteotti 10, t. 0742301497; www.sistemamuseo.it. *Closed Monday. Open: April-May, 10-1 and 3-6:30; June-August, 10-1 and 4-7; September, 10-1 and 3:30-6:30; October-March, 10-1 and 3-6.*

 **Shows and other festivities**

**Infiorate (Strewing with Flowers) of Corpus Domini** (2nd Sunday after Pentecost). Floral carpets along the streets and squares of the historic town centre.

**Shops, arts and crafts**

**Morstad Live.** T. 0742652800. Hand-woven fabrics, original designs on fabric and yarn, planning and realisation of fabrics. School of creative weaving.

**Peppoloni Luigi.** T. 0742301095. Copper and wrought iron works.

---

## Spoleto    ✉ 06049

*Page 125*

ℹ *IAT* (Territorial Tourist Service). Piazza della Libertà 7, t. 074349890, fax 074346241.
*Tourist Information.* Piazza della Libertà 7, t. 0743220311, fax 074346241.
*Tourist Information Centre.* Via Minervio 14, t. 074346484.

**Hertz car renting,** Via Cerquiglia 144, t. and fax 074347195.

**Hotels, restaurants, campsites and holiday camps**

★★★ **Albornoz Palace Hotel.** Viale Matteotti, t. 0743221221, fax 0743221600; info@albornozpalace.com; www.albornozpalace.com. 96 rooms. Facilities for disabled. Air conditioning; parking, parking garage, garden, open-air pool. AE VISA MC; (D1-2).

★★★ **Dei Duchi.** Viale Matteotti 4, t. 074344541, fax 074344543; hotel@hoteldeiduchi.com; www.hoteldeiduchi.com. 49 rooms. Air conditioning; parking, garden. AE ⓓ VISA MC; (C1-2).

★★★ **Gattapone.** Via del Ponte 6, t. 0743223447, fax 0743223448; hgattapone@tin.it; www.hotel

gattapone.it. 15 rooms. Meublé. Air conditioning; garden. AE ⓓ VISA MC; (C3).

★★★ **Il Barbarossa.** Via Licina 12, t. 074343644, fax 0743222060. 10 rooms. Facilities for disabled. Air conditioning, lift; parking facilities, garden (A3, f.p.).

★★★ **Palazzo Dragoni.** Via Duomo 13, t. 0743222220, fax 0743222225. 15 rooms. Meublé. Lift; garden (B2).

★★★ **San Luca.** Via Interna delle Mura 21, t. 0743 223399, fax 0743223800; sanluca@hotelsanluca.com; www.hotelsanluca.com. 35 rooms. Meublé. Facilities for disabled. Air conditioning; garage, garden. AE ⓓ VISA MC; (B1).

★★★ **Clarici.** Piazza della Vittoria 32, t. 0743223311, fax 0743222010; clarici@tiscali.it; www.qsa.it/hotelclarici. 24 rooms. Meublé. Air conditioning; parking. AE ⓓ VISA MC; (A2).

★★★ **Europa.** Viale Trento e Trieste 201, t. 0743 46949, fax 0743221654; europahotel@tin.it. 24 rooms. Meublé. Air conditioning. AE ⓓ MC; (A2, f.p.).

★★ **Aurora.** Via Apollinare 3, t. 0743220315, fax 0743221885; info@hotelauroraspoleto.it; www.hotelauroraspoleto.it. 15 rooms. Facilities for disabled. Parking. AE ⓓ VISA MC; (C1-2).

¶¶¶ **Apollinare.** Via S. Agata 14, t. 0743223256, fax 0743221885; hotelaurora@virgilio.it. Closed Tuesday except in summer and Festival period. Air conditioning; parking, garden. Specialised regional cuisine. AE ⓓ VISA MC; (C1-2).

¶¶¶ **Tartufo.** Piazza Garibaldi 24, t. 074340236; truffles@libero.it. Closed Sunday evenings and Monday; period in July. Air conditioning. Specialised regional cuisine - mushrooms and truffles. AE ⓓ VISA MC; (A2).

¶¶ **Pentagramma.** Via Martani 4, t. 0743223141; www.jazzitaly.com. Closed Monday, period in January and between July and August. Specialised regional cuisine - pasta dishes. ⓓ VISA MC; (C2).

¶¶ **Sabatini.** Corso Mazzini 52/54, t. 0743221831. Closed Monday, period in January and between July and August. Garden. Classical and regional cuisine. AE ⓓ VISA; (B-C2).

¶ **Trattoria del Festival.** Via Brignone 8, t. 0743 220993. Closed Friday, February. Air conditioning. Local cuisine. AE ⓓ VISA MC; (C2).

 **Monteluco.** Locality San Pietro, t. and fax 0743220358. Seasonal.

*at Monteluco, 8 kms*

★★★ **Paradiso.** T. 0743223082, fax 0743223427; paradiso@libero.it. 24 rooms. Parking, garden. AE ⓓ VISA MC

*at Poreta, 11 kms*

¶¶ **Casaline.** T. 0743521113. Closed Monday. Also hotel. Parking, garden. Regional cuisine - mushrooms and truffles. AE ⓓ VISA

*at San Giacomo, 7 kms*

¶ **Palazzaccio.** SS 3 at 134 kms, t. 0743520168. Closed Monday. Parking, garden. Classical and local cuisine - truffles and grilled meat. VISA MC

*at Torrecola, 8 kms*

 **Il Capanno.** T. 074354119; ilcapannoristo rante@tin.it. Closed Monday, variable holiday closure. Parking, garden. Regional cuisine - mushrooms and truffles.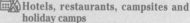

 **Farm Holidays**

**Cirimpiccolo.** Locality Madonna di Lugo 42, t. and fax 0743223780. Facilities for disabled.Inside an English-style park with swimming pool,a peaceful farmhouse offers every comfort for a holiday buried in nature.Large dogs not allowed.

 **Museums and cultural institutions**

**Casa romana.** Via Visiale, t. 0743437707. Closed Tuesday (from 15th October to 15 March).*Open: 10-1 and 3-6.*

**Festival dei Due Mondi.** Headquarters and Administration,via del Teatro,t.074344325;relazioni pubbliche, piazza del Duomo 8, t. 0743220321.

**Galleria civica di Arte contemporanea.** Palazzo Collicola, piazza Collicola, t. 0743 46434-074343707; www.sistemamuseo.it. Closed Tuesday (from 15 October to 15 March).*Open: mid-October-mid-March,10:30-1 and 2:30-5; mid-March-mid-October,10:30-1 and 3-6:30.*

**Museo archeologico nazionale e Teatro romano.** Via S.Agata,t.0743223277.*Open: 9-7.*

**Museo diocesano di Spoleto-Norcia.** Palazzo arcivescovile, via Saffi 13, t. 0743231021. Closed Tuesday.*Open: May-September,10-12:30 and 3:30-7; October-April,10-12:30 and 3-6.*

**Museo del Teatro.** Teatro Nuovo, via Filitteria 1, t.0743223419. *Open: on request.*

**Pinacoteca comunale.** Piazza del Municipio 1,t.0743218301.Closed Monday.*Open: 10-1 and 3-6.*

**Rocca Albornoziana.** Piazza Campello, t. 074343707-0743223055.*Visits for groups with entrance at each hour: November-14 March,3 and 4 (Monday-Friday), 10-4 (Saturday and Sunday);15 March-10 June and 16 September-October,10-12 and 3-6 (Monday-Friday),10-6 (Saturday and Sunday);11 June-15 September, 10-7.*

 **Churches and monuments**

**Basilica di S. Salvatore.** Via della Basilica, t. 074349606. *Open: November-February, 7-5; March,April and October,7-6; May-September, 7-7.*

**Cattedrale di S. Maria Assunta (Duomo).** Piazza del Duomo, t. 074344307. *Open: November-February, 7:30-12:30 and 3-5; March-October,7:30-12:30 and 3-6.*

**Chiesa di S. Ansano e cripta di S. Isacco.** Via Brignone,t.074340305. *Open: November-March,7:30-12 and 3-6:30;April-October,7:30-12 and 3-5:30.*

 **Shows and other festivities**

**Spoleto Festival** (June-July). Piazza Duo-mo 8, t. 0743220321. Performances of prose and dance, concerts, exhibitions and film festivals.

**A. Belli Experimental Opera Theatre** (September-October).

 **Shops, arts and crafts**

**Desir.** Via Saffi 20, t. 074345776. Boutique Gift shop with articles of antique and modern design.

**Il Forno di Santini Alessandro.** Via dell'Arco di Druso 14, t. 074346669. Delicious breads and pasties, including the famous tasty cheese pizza shaped like a «panettone».

 **Sports**

**Centro ippico Clitunno di Ceccaroni Graziano. (Horse riding).** Locality Camporoppolo,t.074356176.

**Maneggio (Riding stables) La Somma.** Locality Aia Cucilli,t.074354370.

 **Local guides and excursions**

**CAI.** Vicolo Luigi Pianciani 4,t.and fax 0743 220433.

**Comunità montana «Monti Martani e del Serano».** Via dei Filosofi, 0743224596, fax 0743223757.

---

**Stroncone**  ✉ 05039

*Page 159*

📧 *Pro Loco.* Piazza S. Giovanni 6,t.0744607008.

**Hotels, restaurants, campsites and holiday camps**

**Taverna de Porta Nova.** Via Porta Nuova 1, t.074460496.Open only evenings except Sunday and holidays; closed Wednesday,period between January and February,August. Regional cuisine.

**Museums and cultural institutions**

**Museo di Storia naturale.** Via S.Angelo 8, t.0744607047 (Town Hall).*Open: on request.*

**Sacrario dei Caduti.** Via Contessa, t. 0744 607047.*Open: on request.*

---

**Terni**  ✉ 05100

*Page 151*

📧 *IAT* (Territorial Tourist Service).Palazzo Gazzoli,via del Teatro Romano 13,t. 0744423040-0744401147,fax 0744402132;info@iat.tern.it. *Tourist Information*.Viale C. Battisti 7/A, t. 0744423047,fax 0744427259.

**Hertz car renting**,Via Curio Dentato 42,t.and fax 0744403902.

**Hotels, restaurants, campsites and holiday camps**

**★★★ Garden Hotel.** Viale Bramante 6, t. 0744 300041,fax 0744300414;info@gardenhotelterni.it; www.gardenhotelterni.it. 94 rooms. Air conditioning; parking, parking garage, garden, open-air pool. AE OD VISA MC; (A1, *f.p.*).

★⋆★ **Valentino.** Via Plinio il Giovane 3/5, t. 0744
402550, fax 0744403335; htlvalentino@tin.it;
www.bellaumbria.net/hotelvalentino. 60
rooms. Air conditioning; parking, parking
garage. AE OD VISA MC; (B2-3).

★★★ **De Paris.** Viale della Stazione 52, t. 0744
58047, fax 074458047; info@hoteldeparis.it. 63
rooms. Facilities for disabled. Air conditioning;
parking, parking garage. AE OD VISA MC; (A2).

★★ **Brenta II.** Via Montegrappa 51, t. and fax
0744273957. 21 rooms. Meublé. VISA; (D2).

❦❦ **La Fontanella.** Via Plinio il Giovane 3, t.
0744402550; htlvalentino@tin.it; www.bella
umbria.net/hotelvalentino. Closed Sunday,
August. Air conditioning; parking. Classic and
regional cuisine. AE OD VISA MC; (B2-3).

❦❦ **Villa Graziani.** At Papigno, 4 kms, Villa Valle
11, t. 074467138. Closed Sunday evenings and
Monday, period in August. Parking. Regional
cuisine. AE OD VISA MC

❦ **Lu Somaru.** Viale Cesare Battisti 106, t. 0744
300288. Closed Mondat. Air conditioning;
parking, garden. Regional cuisine. AE OD VISA;
(A1, *f.p.*).

△ **Cascata delle Marmore.** At Màrmore, Lo-
★★ cality I Campacci, t. 074467198. Seasonal.

*at Piediluco, 13 kms* ✉ 05038

❦ **Tavoletta.** Vocabolo Forca 4, t. 0744368196.
Closed Monday, Tuesday and Wednesday, period in June, October and December. Garden. Classic and regional cuisine - fish.

🏛 **Museums and cultural institutions**

**Museo paleontologico.** Ex chiesa di S. Tommaso, t. 0744434202. Closed Sunday and holidays. *Open: 9:30-1 and 4-7.*

**Pinacoteca comunale.** Palazzo Gazzoli, via
del Teatro Romano, t. 0744434209. Closed
Monday. *Open: 10-1 and 4-7.*

**Raccolta archeologica.** Biblioteca comunale, piazza dei Carrara, t. 0744432234. *Open:
on request.*

*at Màrmore, 8 kms*

**Cascata delle Màrmore.** T. 07445491 (Town
Hall). *Open: November-15 March, 3-4 (holidays); 16 March-April, 11-1 and 4-9 (Saturday), 10-1 and 4-9 (holidays), 12-1 and 4-5
(working days); May 11-1 and 4-10 (Saturday),
10-1 and 3-10 (holidays), 12-1 and 4-5 (working days); June, 11-1 and 3-10 (Saturday), 10-
1 and 3-10 (holidays), 4-5 and 9-10 (working
days); July-August, 11-1 and 3-10 (Saturday),
10-1 and 3-10 (holidays), 12-1, 5-6 and 9-10
(working days); September, 11-1 and 4-9 (Saturday), 10-1 and 3-9 (holidays), 12-1, 4-5 and
9-10 (working days); October, 11-1 and 4-8
(Saturday), 10-1 and 3-8 (holidays).*

⚖ **Shops, arts and crafts**

**Galleria Mentana di Moscatelli Marcella.**
Corso Vecchio 117, t. 074458108. Artisan production of the Malvarosa laboratory (old
prints, dried flowers).

🏹 **Sports**

**Associazione Valserra.** Vocabolo Giunca-
no 10, t. 0744238259. Trekking, bird watching,
environment learning.

**CAI.** Via Flli Cervi 31, t. 0744286500. Excursions on foot.

**Centro Rafting Le Marmore.** At Collestat-
te, t. 0686212249; www.raftingmarmore. Rafting
on the Le Marmore Falls on the Nera River
(approx. 3 kms).

**Federazione Arrampicatori sportivi ita-
liana.** Via G.B. Vico 14, t. 0744427019-0744
282728.

🚶🚶 **Local guides and excursions**

**CAI.** Via Flli Cervi 31, t. 0744286500. Gruppi
roccia e grotte Pipistrelli.

**Comunità montana «Valle del Nera e
monte S. Pancrazio».** Via Cesi 14, t. 0744
400010, fax 0744400260.

**Cooperativa Velino.** Viale Noceto Piediluco,
t. 0744368555. Navigation on the Lake Piediluco and the Velino River.

🦅 **Natural areas, parks and reserves**

**Parco regionale fluviale del Nera.** Palazzo De Sanctis, via Plinio il Giovane 21, t. 0744
583565, fax 0755044695; www.parks.it. Other
towns included in the park: Arrone, Ferentillo, Montefranco.

---

**Todi** ✉ 06059

*Page 142*

ℹ *IAT* (Territorial Tourist Service). Piazza Umberto I 6, t. 0758943395, fax 0758942406; info@
ia.todi.pg.it.

*Ufficio Turistico comprensoriale.* Piazza Umberto I 5, t. 0758945416.

🏨🍴 **Hotels, restaurants, campsites and
holiday camps**

★⋆★ **Bramante.** Via Orvietana 48, t. 0758948381,
fax 0758948074; bramante@hotelbramante.it;
www.hotelbramante.it. 57 rooms. Facilities
for disabled. Air conditioning; parking, garden,
open-air pool, tennis courts. AE OD VISA; (C1).

★⋆★ **Fonte Cesia.** Via L. Leony 3, t. 0758943737, fax
0758944677; fontecesia@fontecesia.it; www.
fontecesia.it. 35 rooms. Facilities for disabled.
Air conditioning; parking, garden. AE OD VISA
MC; (C2).

★★★ **Villa Luisa.** Via Cortesi 147, t. 0758948571, fax
0758948472; villaluisa@villaluisa.it; www.vil
laluisa.it. 40 rooms. Facilities for disabled. Air
conditioning; parking, parking garage, garden, open-air pool. AE OD VISA; (C3, *f.p.*).

❦❦ **Umbria.** Via S. Bonaventura 13, t. 0758942737.
Closed Tuesday. Regional cuisine - truffles. AE
OD VISA; (B2).

❦ **Cavour.** Corso Cavour 21/23, t. 0758943730.
Closed Christmas period and between January and February. Garden, parking. Regional cuisine - grilled meat. AE OD VISA MC; (B2).

*at Pian di Porto, 6 kms*

 **Europalace.** Vocabolo Campette 144/1, t. 0758987474, fax 0758987476; info@europalacetodi.com; www.europalacetodi.com. 76 rooms. Facilities for disabled. Air conditioning; special terms for parking garage, garden. Ⓐ Ⓔ Ⓥ Ⓜ

 **Farm Holidays**

**La Palazzetta.** Locality Asproli 23, t. 075 8853219, fax 0758853358. The old houses of the rural hamlet surrounding the 16th-century villa have been converted into holiday homes. Open-air pool. Large dogs not allowed.

 **Museums and cultural institutions**

**Museo Pinacoteca.** Palazzo comunale, piazza del Popolo, t. 0758944148; www.sistemamuseo.it. Closed Monday (except April). *Open: October-February, 10:30-1 and 2-4:30; March and September 10:30-1 and 2-5; April-August 10:30-1 and 2:30-6.*

**Museo della Civiltà contadina.** Locality Badoglie, t. 0758989402-0330646366. *Open: on request.*

**Shows and other festivities**

**Italian Antiques Festival** (April). Palazzo delle Arti.

**Todi Arte Festival** (August-September). Plays, music, ballet, cinema and cultural events.

**National Arts and Crafts Exhibition and Market** (September-October). Palazzo delle Arti. This events includes artisans from all over Italy but, in particular, the furniture artisans of Umbria.

**Shops, arts and crafts**

**Lo Studiolo.** Corso Cavour 48, t. 0758944585. Antiquities and artbooks.

**Giornelli Giuseppe.** Via Borgonuovo 2, t. 075 8943306. Copper and wrought iron works.

**Pasticceria Mazzuoli & C.** Via Giuseppe Mazzini 12, t. 0758942551. Quality pastry-makers and local products.

**Sports**

**Circolo ippico Pian di Monte.** Asproli 47, Locality Pian di Monte, t. 0758853349. Country rides, riding lessons.

---

**Torgiano** ✉ 06089

*Page 139*

ⓘ *IAT* at Perugia. T. 0755728937.

**Hotels, restaurants, campsites and holiday camps**

★★★ **Le Tre Vaselle.** Via Garibaldi 48, t. 075 9880447, fax 0759880214; 3vaselle@3vaselle.it. 60 rooms. Air conditioning; parking, parking garage, garden, indoor and open-air pool. Ⓐ Ⓔ Ⓥ Ⓜ

---

**Le Tre Vaselle.** Via Garibaldi 48, t. 075 9880447, fax 0759880214; 3vaselle@3vaselle.it. Air conditioning; parking, garden. Classic and regional cuisine. Ⓐ Ⓔ Ⓥ Ⓜ

 **Museums and cultural institutions**

**Museo del Vino Fondazione Lungarotti.** Palazzo Graziani-Baglioni, corso Vittorio Emanuele II, t. and fax 0759880200; www.lungarotti.it. *Open: true solar time, 9-1 and 3-6; summertime, 9-1 and 3-7.*

 **Shows and other festivities**

**I Vinarelli** (August). Exhibition and market of paintings using the technique of wine in place of water for diluting the colours. All profits for the restoration of works of art.

**Italian Wine-Tasting** (November). Event with the most highly qualified Italian wine experts.

 **Shops, arts and crafts**

**L'Arte delle terrecotte.** Via S. Damiano 1, t. 075982031. Production of popular ceramics (earthenware), also sold abroad.

**Le Cantine Lungarotti.** Via Mario Angeloni 16, t. 0759880348-9. The wine-shops - cultural and gastronomical heart of the town - produce wine from their own vineyards. Courses in viticulture, oenology and wine-tasting.

**La Spola.** Via G. Garibaldi 68, t. 0759880447. In a XVI century cottage, hand-woven fabrics, embroidery, precious paper articles of the Maestri Cartai, articles in wood, wrought iron, copper, basketware, glassware, glazed chinaware.

**Osteria del Museo.** Corso Vittorio Emanuele, t. 0759880069. In the Palazzo Baglioni environment, the tavern which gets its name from the nearby Wine Museum, offers the opportunity to discover, taste and purchase the well-known Torgiano wines.

**Sports**

**Il Piccolo Ranch.** Vocabolo Renabianca di Sotto, t. 0759889048. Country rides.

---

**Trevi** ✉ 06039

*Page 123*

ⓘ *Pro Trevi Association.* Piazza Mazzini 5 (Seasonal), t. 0742781150.

**Hotels, restaurants, campsites and holiday camps**

★★★ **Trevi Hotel.** Via Fantosati 2, t. 0742780922, fax 0742780772; trevihotel@tiscali.it; web.tiscali.it/trevihotel. 12 rooms. Meublé. Facilities for disabled. Parking, garden. Ⓐ Ⓔ Ⓥ Ⓜ

*at Matigge, 3 kms*

**L'Ulivo.** Via Monte Bianco 23, t. 074278969. Closed Monday and Tuesday, period in July. Also hotel. Parking, garden. Regional cuisine - grilled meat, truffles. Ⓐ Ⓔ Ⓥ Ⓜ

*at Pigge, 4 kms*

**Taverna del Pescatore.** Via Chiesa Tonda

50, t. 0742780920; info@latavernadelpescatore. com; www.latavernadelpescatore.com. Closed Wednesday, period in January. Parking, garden. Updated regional cuisine.  ᴁ ⓐ 🆅🆂🅰 MC

## at Faustana-Bovara, 3 kms

 Farm Holidays

**I Mandorli.** Locality Fondaccio, t. and fax 074278669. Facilities for disabled. Three detached cottages and an old farmhouse buried in the countryside offer the opportunity for a relaxing holiday. Large dogs not allowed.

 Museums and cultural institutions

**Raccolta d'arte di S. Francesco.** Largo Don Bosco, t. and fax 0742381628; www.siste mamuseo.it. Closed Monday (from April to July and September). *Open: October-March, 10:30-1 and 2:30-5 (Friday-Sunday); April-May and September, 10:30-1 and 2:30-6; June-July, 10:30-1 and 3:30-7; August, 10:30-1 and 3-7:30.*

**Trevi Flash Art Museum.** Palazzo Lucarini, via Lucarini 1, t. 0742381818. Closed Monday and Tuesday. *Open: winter, 10:30-12:30 and 3-6 (Saturday and Sunday); 3-6 (Wednesday-Friday); summer 10:30-12:30 and 2-7 (Saturday and Sunday); 2-7 (Wednesday-Friday).*

 Shows and other festivities

**Procession of the Illuminata** (27 January). Procession of very old origin with a parade of the Arts and Corporations «candles».

**Autumn Events** (October). Historic commemorations and gastronomical festivals and meetings.

 Shops, arts and crafts

**Cooperativa Agricola di Trevi.** Via Flaminia km 141, t. 074238600; www.olioumbro.com. Production and sales of one of the best Umbrian olive oils.

**Elle Esse.** Via Faustana 24, t. 0742381678. Production of refined truffle and game paté.

---

## Tuoro sul Trasimeno ⌧ 06069

*Page 66*

 *IAT del Trasimeno.* T. 0759652484. *Pro Loco.* Via Ritorta 1, t. 075825220.

 Hotels, restaurants, campsites and holiday camps

⚠ **Punta Navaccia.** Locality Tuoro Lido, t. 075
★★★ 826357, fax 0758258147. Seasonal.

 Museums and cultural institutions

**Centro di documentazione permanente su Annibale e la battaglia del Trasimeno.** Via Ritorta 1, t. and fax 075825220. Closed Sunday. *Open: 9-12 and 3-6.*

**Museo all'Aperto Campo del Sole.** Locality Punta Navaccia-Lido di Tuoro, t. and fax 075825220 (Pro Loco). Open at all times.

 Sports

**Balneazione Tuoro.** Locality Punta Navaccia, t. 0330646281. Windsurf and rowing boats to hire.

**Scuola Federale Sci Nautico.** Camping Punta Navaccia, t. 075826357. Water-skiing.

---

## Umbèrtide ⌧ 06019

*Page 73*

 *Tourist Information.* Piazza Caduti del Lavoro, t. 0759417099.

 Hotels, restaurants, campsites and holiday camps

★★ **Moderno.** SS 3 bis, t. and fax 0759413759; hotelmoderno@hotmail.com. 21 rooms. Air conditioning; parking, parking garage, garden. 🆅🆂🅰 MC

 Farm Holidays

**Colle del Sole.** T. 0759414266, fax 075 9414390. Facilities for disabled. The 16th-century manor house has been converted into flats and rooms furnished in the period style. Organic production of olive oil and wine. Open-air pool.

Museums and cultural institutions

**Museo civico di Santa Croce.** Piazza S. Francesco, t. 0759420147. *Open: April-September, 10:30-1 and 3:30-6 (Friday-Sunday); October-March, 10:30-1 and 3-5:30 (Saturday and Sunday).*

**Rocca - Centro per l'Arte contemporanea.** Piazza Fortebraccio, t. 0759413691. Closed Monday. *Open: winter 10:30-12:30 and 4-7; summer 10:30-12:30 and 4:30-7:30.*

 Shows and other festivities

**Jazz Fest** (March-May). Festival of Jazz.

**Rockin'Umbria** (late June). Festival of rock music, graphics, photography and comics.

# Index of names

The following index comprises artists and historical figures mentioned in the guide, in order of surname, or – in cases where the surname is unfamiliar or unknown – of the name by which the figure is generally known (pseudonym, nickname or first name followed by patronym or place of origin). Each entry includes a brief biographical note and references to the pages where the name occurs.

*Abbreviations:*
*A.*, architect; *Arch.*, archaeologist; *act.*, active; *b.*, born; *Bshp.*, bishop; *Cab.*, cabinet maker; *Card.*, cardinal; *Carv.*, wood carver; *cent.*, century; *Cer.*, ceramicist; *Comp.*, composer; *Cond.*, condottiere., *Cons.*, consul., *Cr.*, Critic; *d.*, died; *Dec.*, decorator; *Dip.*, diplomat; *Des.*, designer; *Dir.*, film director; *doc.*, documented; *Emp.*, emperor/empress; *F.*, founder; *Fam.*, family; *G.*, goldsmith; *Gen.*, general; *Geo.*, geographer; *Gov.*, governor; *Hist.*, historian; *Ill.*, illuminator; *Ind.*, industrialist; *Intars.*, intarsia artist; *L.*, man-of-letters; *Med.*, medal designer; *Mgr.*, Monsignor; *Mld.*, moulder; *Mos.*, mosaicist; *not.*, noted; *Org.*, organ builder; *P.* painter; *p.* page; *Po.*, poet(-ess); *S.*, sculptor; *Stg. Des.*, stage designer; *Stucc.*, stucco artist; *Urb.*, urban planner; *Wr.* writer.

# Index of places

This index comprises place names mentioned in the itineraries and excursions; page numbers in *italics* refer to the «Other places, hotels, restaurants, curiosities» section in which the place is listed. Monuments, churches and other places of interest in the region's most important towns are grouped together in sub-indexes under the town's own heading.
All sights are listed by their Italian names.

# Italy: useful addresses

Citizens of Australia, Canada, New Zealand, and the United States can enter Italy with a valid passport, and stay for a period of not more than 90 days; citizens of Great Britain and Ireland, as members of the European Union, can travel either with valid passport or with a valid identification card. No vaccinations are necessary.

## Foreign Embassies in Italy

**Australia:**
Corso Trieste 25, Rome, tel. 06852721

**Canada:**
Via G.B. de Rossi 27, Rome, tel. 06445981

**New Zealand:**
Via Zara 28, Rome, tel. 064402928

**United States of America:**
Via Vittorio Veneto 119/A, Palazzo Margherita, Rome, tel. 0646741

**Great Britain:**
Via XX Settembre 80/A, Rome, tel. 06 42200001

**Ireland:**
Piazza Campitelli 3, Rome, tel. 066979121

## Foreign Consulates in Italy

**Australia:**
Via Borgogna 2, Milan, tel. 02777041/217

**Canada:**
Via Vittor Pisani 19, Milan, tel. 0267583420

**New Zealand:**
Via F. Sforza 48, Milan, tel. 0258314443

**United States of America:**
– Lungarno A.Vespucci 38, Florence, tel. 0552398276
– Via Principe Amedeo 2/10, Milan, tel. 02290351
– Piazza Repubblica, Naples, tel. 081 5838111
– Via Vaccarini 1, Palermo (consular agency), tel. 091305857

**Great Britain:**
– Via S. Paolo 7, Milan, tel. 02723001
– Via dei Mille 40, Naples, tel. 0814238911

**Ireland:**
Piazza San Pietro in Gessate 2, Milan, tel. 0255187641

## Italian Embassies and Consulates Around the World

**Australia:**
12 Grey Street - Deakin, Canberra, tel. (06) 273-4223
*Consulates at:* Adelaide, Brisbane, Melbourne, Perth, Sydney

**Canada:**
275 Slater Street, 21st floor, Ottawa (Ontario), tel. (613) 2322401
*Consulates at:* Edmonton, Montreal, Toronto, Vancouver

**New Zealand:**
34 Grant Road, Wellington, tel. (4) 4735339
*Consulates at:* Auckland, Christchurch, Dunedin

**United States of America:**
3000 Whitehaven Street, NW, Washington DC, tel. (202) 612-4400
*Consulates at:* Boston, Chicago, Detroit, Houston, Los Angeles, Miami, New York, Newark, Philadelphia, San Francisco

**Great Britain:**
14, Three Kings' Yard, London, tel. (020) 73122200
*Consulates at:* London, Bedford, Edinburgh, Manchester

**Ireland:**
63, Northumberland Road, Dublin, tel. (01) 6601744

## ENIT (Italian Tourist Board)

**Canada:**
Office National Italien du Tourisme / Italian Tourist Board, 175 Bloor Street, Suite 907 - South Tower, Toronto, Ontario M4W 3R8, tel. (416) 925-4882, fax (416) 925-4799

**United States of America:**
– Italian Tourist Board, 630 Fifth Avenue, Suite 1565, New York, N.Y. 10111, tel. (212) 245-4822, fax (212) 586-9249
– Italian Tourist Board, North Michigan Avenue, Suite 2240, Chicago, Illinois 60611, tel. (312) 644-0996, fax (312) 644-3019
– Italian Tourist Board, Wilshire Blvd., Suite 550, Los Angeles, CA 90025, 12400, tel. (310) 820-9807, fax (310) 820-6357

**Great Britain:**
Italian Tourist Board, 1 Princes Street, London W1B 2AY, tel. (020) 73993562

## Emergency numbers
112 Carabinieri
113 Police Help
115 Fire Department
116 Road Assistance
118 Medical Emergencies
176 International inquiries
12 Phone directory assistance

# Notes

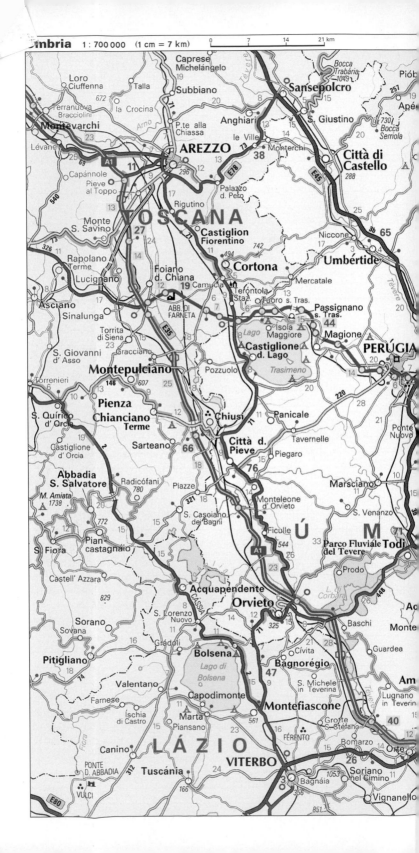

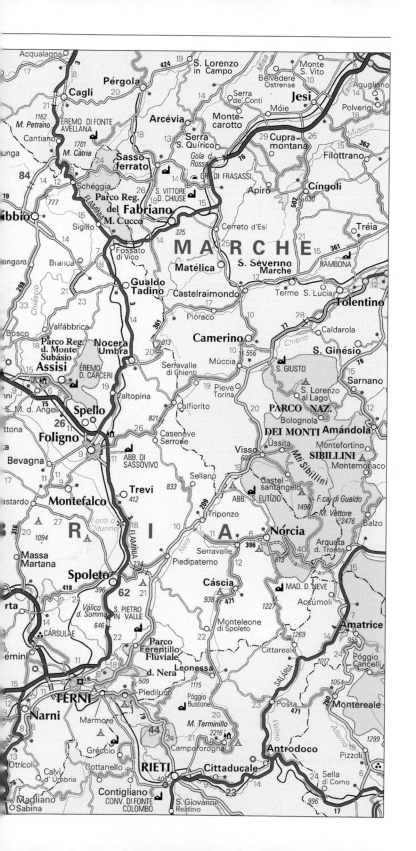

# Borgo San Faustino

**Orvieto**
Loc. S. Faustino, 11
05010 Morrano Orvieto (TR)
Ph. ++39 0763215303 - Fax ++39 0763215745
E-mail: borgosf@tin.it
www.agriturismoborgosanfaustino.it

# Casella del Piano

**Gubbio**
Loc. S. Marco
06024 Gubbio (PG)
Ph. & Fax ++39 0759229324 - ++39 0759229321
Mobile 3334314511
E-mail: casella@caselladelpiano.com
www.caselladelpiano.com

# Fattoria di Vibio

**Montecastello Vibio**
Loc. Buchella, 9
Montecastello Vibio (PG)
Ph. ++39 0758749607- Fax ++39 0758780014
E-mail: info@fattoria di vibio.com
www.fattoriavibio.com

# Il Casale nel Parco

**Norcia**
Loc. Fontevene, 8
Norcia (PG)
Ph. & Fax ++39 0743816481
E-mail: agriumbria@casalenelparco.com
www.casalenelparco.com

# Il Giardino delle Meraviglie

**Amelia**
Loc. Papile - Montecampano Amelia TR
Ph. ++39 0744998083 - Fax ++39 0744998149
E-mail: giardinomeraviglie@yahoo.it
www.umbriacountry.it

# L'Ulivo

**Spoleto**
Bazzano di Sotto, 63 - Spoleto (PG)
Ph & Fax ++39 074349031 - Fax ++39 0743222527
Mobile 3381818161
E-mail: agriulivo@tin.it
www.agriulivo.com

# Le Colombe

**Assisi**
Loc. Rocca S. Angelo 42/43 - 06086 Assisi (PG)
Ph. ++39 0758098101 - Fax ++39 0758099336
Mobile 3483863254 - E-mail: info@lecolombe.com
www.lecolombe.com

# Le Serre di Parrano

**Nocera Umbra**
Loc. Serre di Parrano - Nocera U. (PG)
Ph. ++39 0755054668 - Fax ++39 0755004537
Mobile 3356270955 - E-mail: bpilar@tin.it
www.serrediparrano.com

# Collelignani

**Spoleto**
Fraz. Eggi - 06049 Spoleto (PG) - Tel. ++39 074349676
Ph. & Fax ++39 0743229361 - 337593930
E-mail: collelignani@collelignani.com
www.collelignani.com

# Malvarina

**Assisi**
Località Malvarina - 06080 Assisi (PG)
Ph. & Fax ++39 0758064280
E-mail: info@malvarina.it
www.malvarina.it

# San Cristoforo

**Amelia**
Strada S. cristoforo, 16 - 05022 Amelia (TR)
Ph. ++39 0744988249 - Fax ++39 0744988459
E-mail: info@agriturismosancristoforo.com
www.agriturismosancristoforo.com

# Serena

**Assisi**
Loc. San Presto - 06081 Assisi (PG)
Ph. ++39 075802458 - Fax ++39 075813047
E-mail: info@residenceserena.it
www.residenceserena.it

# Valle Verde

**Gubbio**
Loc. Villamagna - 06024 Gubbio (PG)
Ph. & Fax ++39 0759273629 - 3683877769
E-mail: umbria@agriturvalle.com
        umbria@agriturverde.com
www.agriturvalle.com
www.agriturverde.com

# Villamagna Palazzo

**Gubbio**
Loc. Villamagna - 06024 Gubbio (PG)
Ph. & Fax ++39 0759221809 - 3355756329
E-mail: villam@agriturgubbio.com
www.agriturgubbio.com/villamagna

## AZIENDA AGRITURISTICA

# *Il Casale nel Parco*
## *dei Monti Sibillini*
# *Norcia*

Loc. Fontavena, 8/14 - 06046 NORCIA (PG)
Tel. e Fax 0743/816481

*Familiar hospitality in a recently restored old farmhouse, deep in the heart of Monti Sibillini National Park 1 km. from Norcia center, with parking area, telephone, fax, leisure rooms (TV-reading) barbecue. The building is made of three suite with five, single - double or three bedded rooms with toilets. The rooms propose different themes on the varied countryside. The farmhouse has been renewed in typical mountain style in the same stone, on the same foundation with original wooden forniture and forged iron-beds. The farm produces biological cultivation, spelt, vegetables, and the small lentills of Norcia. The picture here below represents its harvesting. Bed and breakfast terms: breakfast is served at any time in the morning. Half board terms: dinner only. Simple food freshly baked cakes, honey opf the valley, delicious jam rediscover the ancient flavour of these home-made products.*